Agricultural Input Subsidies

Agricultural Input Subsidies

The Recent Malawi Experience

Ephraim Chirwa and Andrew Dorward

OXFORD
UNIVERSITY PRESS

OXFORD
UNIVERSITY PRESS

Great Clarendon Street, Oxford, OX2 6DP,
United Kingdom

Oxford University Press is a department of the University of Oxford.
It furthers the University's objective of excellence in research, scholarship,
and education by publishing worldwide. Oxford is a registered trade mark of
Oxford University Press in the UK and in certain other countries

© Ephraim Chirwa and Andrew Dorward 2013

The moral rights of the authors have been asserted

First Edition published in 2013

Impression: 1

Published in the United States of America by Oxford University Press
198 Madison Avenue, New York, NY 10016, United States of America

British Library Cataloguing in Publication Data
Data Available

Library of Congress Cataloging in Publication Data
Data Available

ISBN 978-0-19-968352-9

Printed and bound in Great Britain by
CPI Group (UK) Ltd, Croydon, CR0 4YY

Acknowledgements

This book emerges from longstanding concerns we have had about the problems facing poor smallholder farmers in rural economies in Africa, and particularly in Malawi, as with great resourcefulness and resilience they battle with limited and unreliable resources and support to better their livelihoods and the options for their children. A critical focus of our different research activities has been on the roles of markets and governments in supporting poor smallholder farmers: to increase their production and incomes, to ensure affordable food security for themselves and others, and to expand opportunity and choice.

In 2006 we began working together on an evaluation of the Malawi Agricultural Input Subsidy Programme, as it was then known. The programme was attracting international attention, with the *New York Times* and *The Economist* publishing hopeful and sceptical articles, respectively. We needed to review past experience with such programmes, understand new thinking and practice, and study different facets of the implementation and impacts of a large, complex, and politically sensitive programme.

Six years later we are still engaged in this task: this book sets out much of what we have learnt so far. We hope it will be useful to policy makers, policy analysts, researchers, and students of agricultural and rural development who are concerned with the problems facing poor smallholder farmers in poor rural economies and considering, planning, or implementing agricultural input subsidies as a possible way of addressing some of these problems. We hope it will also be of value as a source of information on Malawian agriculture, rural livelihoods and agricultural policy.

Many organizations and people have contributed to the work in this book.

The Malawi Ministry of Agriculture and Food Security and the UK Department for International Development in Malawi have over the years given us the opportunity to undertake this work and, with others, engaged with us, asked us challenging questions, and provided both access to critical information about the programme and the resources to study it. We are particularly grateful to the AISP/FISP programme coordinators over the period (Alex Namoana, Idrissa Mwale, and Christine Mtambo), to Charlie Clark and colleagues in the Logistics Unit, to Teddie Nakhumwa and colleagues in DFID, and to David Rohrbach in the World Bank.

We have benefited greatly from working with different colleagues on the 2006/7, 2008/9, and 2010/11 evaluation teams: Duncan Boughton, Massy Chiocha, Valerie Kelly, Thom Jayne, Mirriam Matita, Peter Mvula, Jake Ricker-Gilbert, Rachel Slater, Maxwell Tsoka, and the National Statistical Office and Wadonda Consult field team members. We are also indebted to many farmers' and other respondents' sharing of their time and information.

The University of Malawi and SOAS, University of London, gave us time to write while on sabbatical, and our colleagues have then taken on extra responsibilities during our absences.

The Future Agricultures Consortium provided financial support for some specific parts of the work reported here: special thanks are due to Stephen Devereux, Rachel Sabates-Wheeler, Blessings Chinsinga, and John Thompson for their encouragement and insights.

Frank Ellis and Peter Hazell provided critical but encouraging comments on drafts on a very tight schedule—leading to some significant improvements in the text.

Adam Swallow, Aimee Wright, and Jenny Townshend at OUP have encouraged, guided, and helped us as novices through the task of publication.

Many others have in different ways enabled us to write and publish this work. The views expressed and any omissions or errors are, however, our responsibility.

We are grateful to Taylor and Francis for permission to include Figures 2.2, 4.1, 5.1, and 7.4 which are reproduced or adapted from Dorward and Chirwa (2011c).

Finally, Ireen and Sam Ling have patiently suffered our pre-occupation with writing (and with the Malawi FISP over a number of years) and encouraged and supported us in taking on this project and seeing it through. Theirs is a very special part of this work.

Ephraim Chirwa and Andrew Dorward
Zomba, Malawi
November 2012

Contents

Contents

Contents

List of Figures

List of Tables

List of Abbreviations

ADC	Area Development Committee
ADMARC	Agricultural Development and Marketing Corporation
AE	Analyst's estimates
AISAM	Agricultural Input Suppliers Association of Malawi
AISP	Agricultural Input Subsidy Programme
AISS	Agricultural Input Subsidy Survey
BCA	Benefit–cost analysis
BCR	Benefit–cost ratios
CNFA	Citizens Network for Foreign Affairs
CPI	Consumer Price Index
DDC	District Development Committee
DFID	Department for International Development
DPP	Democratic People's Party
Ed	Elasticity of demand
FAM	Fertiliser Association of Malawi
FAO	Food and Agriculture Organization of the United Nations
FE	Fiscal efficiency
FEWS NET	Famine Early Warning System Network
FGDs	Focus Group Discussions
FISP	Farm Input Subsidy Progra
FISS	Farm Input Subsidy Survey
Ganyu	Hired casual labour
GDP	Gross Domestic Product
IHS2	Integrated Household Survey 2 (2004/5)
IHS3	Integrated Household Survey 3 (2010/11)
IRR	Internal rate of return
IMF	International Monetary Fund
MCP	Malawi Congress Party
MK	Malawi Kwacha (approximately 140MK to the US$ from 2005 to 2010)
MOAFS	Ministry of Agriculture and Food Security
MVAC	Malawi Vulnerability Action Committee
NASFAM	National Smallholder Farmers Association of Malawi
NEPAD	New Economic Partnership for African Development

List of Abbreviations

NGO	Non-Governmental Organization
NPV	Net Present Value
NSO	National Statistical Office
OPV	Open pollinated varieties (of maize)
PLWHA	People Living With HIV/AIDS
SFFRFM	Smallholder Farmers' Fertilizer Revolving Fund of Malawi
STAM	Seed Traders Association of Malawi
TA	Traditional Authority
TIP	Targeted Inputs Program
UDF	United Democratic Front
VDC	Village Development Committee

1

Introduction

1.1. Background: challenges in African agricultural development

In the first decade of the twenty-first century sub-Saharan Africa moved, in the words of *The Economist*, from being 'hopeless Africa' to 'the hopeful continent'.[1] Economic growth indicators from 2000 to 2010 show an impressive recovery from the poor performance of previous decades, although growth rates vary considerably between regions and countries within Africa, with West and East African coastal countries growing faster than other regions (United Nations Economic Commission for Africa (UNECA) and African Union, 2012).

There are, however, concerns about the quality of economic growth in Africa. The United Nations Economic Commission for Africa (UNECA) and African Union (2012) note that Africa has witnessed jobless growth due partly to the fact that most of the growth has occurred in capital intensive extractive sectors with limited forward and backward linkages to the local economies. This is associated with high levels of unemployment and underemployment, particularly among the youth, with most of the youth trapped in less productive informal sectors. At the same time, not much structural transformation in African economies has taken place, implying that a large proportion of African people still depend on agriculture as a source of livelihood. These observations underlie concerns about growing inequity within African economies, and continuing high levels of poverty and particularly rural poverty (Africa Progress Panel, 2012). There are also major concerns about food insecurity in Africa, with adverse welfare and developmental effects of high national and international food prices on both the urban and rural poor,

---

[1] *The Economist* (13 May 2000). 'Hopeless Africa', <http://www.economist.com/node/333429> and *The Economist* (3 December 2011). 'The Hopeful continent: Africa Rising' <http://www.economist.com/node/21541015> (18 September 2012).

despite the offsetting effects of economic growth (Headey, 2011b; Dorward, 2012b, 2013; Verpoorten et al., 2012). These concerns link into a set of long-standing but resurgent debates and controversies about agricultural development in Africa regarding

- the importance and role of agriculture in development;
- the extent and causes of African agriculture's poor historic performance;
- the relative advantages and disadvantages of large and small farms in agricultural development; and
- the best means of promoting agricultural development in Africa.

Emphasis on agriculture as a critical sector for development has fluctuated over the last 50 years or so. At independence, most developing country governments saw agriculture as either a driver of growth in their economies or as a foreign exchange earner, with a large reserve of unutilized labour to be taxed to support industrial development for a modern economy. With a weak and/or mistrusted private sector, this led to large public investments in agricultural development. In many African countries these large investments were either ineffective or, where they were effective, very expensive and—in the context of over-extension of government budgets and activities—unsustainable without donor support. This was not forthcoming with both the emerging Washington Consensus (promoting structural adjustment and market liberalization) and disenchantment with agricultural investments—which were seen as ineffective and unnecessary in the context of increasing global food production and falling prices (although paradoxically these were partly the result of large and highly successful public investments in the Asian Green Revolution). Emphasis on agriculture was further undermined by empirical studies that revealed the widespread importance of non-farm incomes in the livelihoods of rural farming households (for example, Ellis, 2000; Haggblade et al., 2007b; Reardon, 1998).

With time, however, the pendulum began to swing back as a result of further empirical work showing the importance of the agricultural sector to poor rural economies and to the livelihoods of poor people within those economies (see, for example, Datt and Ravallion, 1996; Mellor, 2000; Thirtle et al., 2003; de Janvry and Sadoulet, 2010; Christiaensen et al., 2011). This coincided with growing concern among governments and donors about the lack of growth in African agriculture (particularly in staple crop production). In 2008 the World Development Report made a powerful case for the importance of agriculture in poverty reduction (World Bank, 2007b) and this was brought home by the 2008 global food price spike and recognition that the era of low and stable food prices was over, if it ever existed (Dorward, 2011, 2013).

Table 1.1. Annual changes in cereal production from 1961 and 2000

		East Asia & Pacific	Latin America & Caribbean	South Asia	Sub-Saharan Africa
Cereal prodn	1961–2009	2.80%	2.58%	2.27%	2.45%
Cereal land	1961–2009	0.39%	0.61%	0.31%	1.73%
Cereal yield	1961–2009	2.40%	1.95%	1.95%	0.95%
Cereal prodn	2000–09	1.93%	1.78%	1.01%	3.65%
Cereal land	2000–09	0.72%	0.41%	-0.01%	2.20%
Cereal yield	2000–09	1.20%	1.37%	1.01%	1.42%

Source: Author calculations from World Bank (2011).

As noted above, resurgent interest in agricultural development was in part stimulated by African agriculture's poor performance and associated problems of food insecurity, lack of rural growth, and persistent rural poverty. Cereal production faced particular difficulties in that, while production grew (just keeping pace with population growth), most of this growth was the result of expansion in cereal areas, with very limited increases in yields. Table 1.1 shows that in contrast to Latin America and Asia, annual average growth in land under cereals was higher than growth in yields in sub-Saharan Africa from 1961 to 2009, and this applied both before and after 2000, though with higher rates of growth in both cereal areas and yields after 2000.

Wiggins and Leturque (2010) provide a helpful summary of different explanations for sub-Saharan Africa's poor agricultural performance, while pointing to considerable variation in performance between regions within Africa. They identify core problems as limited production potential (due to geography, environmental degradation, and fertility decline which they link to lack of technical innovation), unfavourable external conditions (arising from OECD subsidies and trade rules and from limited demand for farm output), and government and market failures (the former involving a policy that deters investors and too little investment, the latter failing to deliver credit and input services and overcome poverty traps). These difficulties are of course interrelated. However, the lack of technical innovation is arguably the proximate cause of the lack of land and labour productivity growth in African agriculture and is the outcome of other difficulties—which reduce benefits, raise costs, or in other ways inhibit technical change—particularly on poor, small-scale farms.[2]

---

[2] We do not address here the longstanding debate on the relative merits of investment and support for large- and small-scale farms (see, for example, Collier and Dercon, 2009; Hazell et al., 2010; Hazell, 2012). We favour the complementary approach to large and small farms advocated by Hazell (2012), but our focus is on the potential multiple benefits of overcoming problems faced by poor, small-scale farmers.

Table 1.2. Fertilizer use, cereal yields, and value of cereal production, 2002–9

	Nitrogen application, kg/ha	Cereal yield, kg/ha	Value of cereal prodn as % agric. value added
Asia	106.0	3404	
Northern America	58.8	5723	
Europe	44.2	3563	
Central America	38.6	2967	
South America	36.6	3447	
Northern Africa	37.8	1852	
Sub Saharan Africa	*5.9*	*1274*	*23%*
Mauritius	96.3		0%
South Africa	27.2		41%
Malawi	22.8		55%
Zambia	17.6		18%
Zimbabwe	15.1		27%
Kenya	12.3		13%

Sources: Author calculations from FAO (2012), World Bank (2011), World Bank (2012).

A critical and widely recognized difference between agriculture in sub-Saharan Africa and in other regions is the low rate of fertilizer use in sub-Saharan Africa. The extent of this is illustrated in the upper part of Table 1.2, which shows FAO estimates of mean rates of inorganic fertilizer application (measured in kg nitrogen per ha arable and permanent crop land) from 2002–9 in different regions of the world. Even allowing for the difficulties of gathering and interpreting such data, the table shows a striking contrast between sub-Saharan Africa and other parts of the world. Although significant amounts of fertilizer use is for non-cereal crops (and the importance of this varies between countries), a similar contrast is evident for cereal yields.

The lower part of Table 1.2 shows estimated nitrogen application rates for the six sub-Saharan African countries with the highest fertilizer rates. It also provides an indicator of the importance of cereal production in the agricultural sector.[3] Mauritius has a very high rate of fertilizer use but negligible cereals production, so the high rates of fertilizer use are largely on other crops. Fertilizer use in South Africa is spread across both cereals and other crops but is affected by substantial maize production by the large-scale commercial sector.[4] Malawi then stands out for its relatively high rate of fertilizer use (by African but not global standards), large share of cereals in the agricultural

---

[3] Due to difficulties in sourcing better data the indicator used is value of cereal production at international grain prices (estimated with prices and grain index weights taken from World Bank, 2012) as a percentage of agricultural value added (World Bank, 2011) in current US$.

[4] The 2002–9 average rate of nitrogen application per ha arable and permanent crop land in sub-Saharan Africa, excluding Mauritius and Swaziland, is only 4.0 kg/ha.

sector, and (not shown in Table 1.2) the overwhelming importance of small-holder agriculture in cereal production.[5] Many would argue that a major factor in Malawi's high rate of fertilizer use in a poor and smallholder maize-based agricultural economy has been its longstanding use of agricultural fertilizer subsidies. In Table 1.2, data for Zambia, Zimbabwe, and Kenya are presented below data for Malawi. Smallholder cereal production accounts for a smaller share of agriculture in all three of these economies as compared with Malawi. Zambia has, however, also been implementing an agricultural input subsidy programme. The basis for the relatively high rates of fertilizer use reported for Zimbabwe is not clear, but contributors to higher fertilizer use in Kenya without subsidies have been explored by Minde et al. (2008) and Ariga and Jayne (2011) and these include: good transport links to and through Mombasa, high export volumes reducing back-load costs, and high fertilizer demand for use on smallholder cash crops alongside food crops (stimulating market development and lowering retail unit costs as well as supporting a variety of mechanisms for easing cash flow constraints on purchases of fertilizer for food crops).

In this book we examine the often controversial roles and impacts of agricultural input subsidies (generally dominated by fertilizer subsidies) in promoting technical change in agricultural development, with particular attention to lessons and insights from the large agricultural input subsidy programme which Malawi embarked on in 2005.

The topics addressed are important for many countries in sub-Saharan Africa, as well as for Malawi. As discussed above, agricultural production has been stagnant in many parts of sub-Saharan Africa, and associated with high incidence and severity of rural poverty and food insecurity. The challenges in 'getting agriculture moving' are exacerbated by local resource pressures from rapid population growth, the threat of climate change leading to increasingly uncertain rainfall in many parts of the region, high and volatile world food prices, and uncertainties about the global economy. As we shall discuss, the number of African countries implementing large-scale agricultural input subsidies has been growing, and these programmes are costly—in terms of fiscal costs, lost benefits from investments of these resources in alternative uses (such as in education, health, infrastructure, or agricultural research), and the long term distortions they can foster in political, financial, social, and economic structures. Failure will not only blight the lives of millions of poor rural people and their children, it may also prejudice policy makers against future investments in agriculture.

---

[5] Smallholder maize production is estimated to account for 97% of the maize and total cereal areas in Malawi in 2009/10 (Ministry of Agriculture and Food Security, 2010).

Malawi is, unfortunately, no exception to this. However, its post-2005 subsidy experience provides a good case study for examining the potential strengths and weaknesses of agricultural input subsidies in addressing these issues. The programme follows and builds on a long history of different forms of subsidy in Malawi, with fertilizer price subsidies to smallholder farmers from the 1960s to 1980s, which were then removed and reinstated in the 1990s, and then replaced by an initially universal Starter Pack but later Targeted Input Programme (TIP) of free distribution of small fertilizer and seed packs to smallholder farmers. This programme (thoroughly documented in Levy, 2005) adopted increasingly innovative systems involving private distributors of seed and fertilizer and was continued until the 2004/5 season. Following the 2004 elections and food shortages in 2005, however, the increasing political significance of fertilizer subsidies led to the introduction of a much larger programme providing approximately 50% of Malawian smallholder farmers with much larger packs of inputs at highly subsidized prices. This new programme, the Agricultural or Farm Input Subsidy Programme (AISP or FISP),[6] attracted immediate controversy, from both supporters (for example, Dugger, 2007; Denning et al., 2009) and detractors (for example, *The Economist*, 2008) but was very popular in Malawi and has since continued.[7] The programme has been held up as an example for other countries to follow, and large-scale input subsidies are now being implemented in a large number of African countries. Many of these are both drawing on Malawi's experience and introducing their own innovations to address perceived opportunities for improvement. There are, however, also significant concerns among many economists, development analysts, and policy makers both in Malawi and elsewhere about the effects and cost of Malawi's programme.

The FISP has also been the subject of a range of different studies, of varying scope and quality, and advocates and sceptics, supporters and detractors of the programme often draw on contradictory evidence to support their positions.[8] There is therefore a need to bring these different perspectives and studies together and to set these in the context of wider debates and experience

---

[6] The names Agricultural Input Subsidy Programme and Farm Inputs Subsidy Programme (AISP and FISP) are often used interchangeably. We generally use the former in discussion of the earlier years of the programme, when AISP was its official title, and the latter when discussing the later years of the programme or the programme as a whole.

[7] Chinsinga (2006) provides a detailed analysis of the political narratives of the farm input subsidy programmes including broad agreement across political parties on the need for farm subsidies in varying form, and the sceptical views of development partners. We discuss these issues in Chapter 4.

[8] Indeed Ricker-Gilbert and Jayne (2012) suggest that debates on agricultural input subsidies are addressing a 'wicked problem' that is difficult or impossible to resolve because of contested framings of the problem, incomplete and contested information, and absence of agreement on the core issues.

to draw robust conclusions where these are possible, to recognize areas of disagreement and ambiguity, and to identify outstanding questions for agricultural policy makers, programme implementers, and researchers not only in Malawi but across Africa. That is the purpose of this book.

1.2. Objectives and outline

In this book we aim to contribute to a greater understanding of the roles, contributions, and pitfalls of agricultural input subsidies as instruments for promoting food security, poverty reduction, social protection, and wider economic growth in poor agrarian economies. The specific objectives are

- to update and develop theoretical understanding of agricultural input subsidies' impacts, allowing for new delivery systems and instruments and specific constraints inhibiting the livelihoods of poor subsistence farmers and the economies of which they are a major part;

- to derive from Malawi's experience lessons about the implementation and impacts of a large-scale agricultural input subsidy programme, with specific focus on the contextual, design, and implementation determinants of economy-wide, beneficiary, and market impacts; and

- to promote debate about strategic policy decisions in the design of large-scale agricultural input subsidies in contemporary low income agrarian economies, including targeting and graduation, to foster their sustainable contribution to agricultural development and poverty reduction.

In order to achieve these objectives the book is divided into three parts following this introduction. The first part provides the theoretical and empirical context for the rest of the book. It is consists of three chapters. Chapter 2 sets out the longer standing empirical evidence and theories on the roles of agricultural input subsidies in poor agrarian economies. It then extends conventional theories to provide a richer account of the potential contributions of innovative delivery systems and instruments to microeconomic, mesoeconomic, and economy-wide processes promoting poverty reduction, food security, economic diversification, and wider economic growth. This provides the basis for a broad understanding of the potential roles and impacts, positive and negative, of a large-scale subsidy programme in poor agrarian economies with different characteristics. Chapter 3 follows with a review of the limited information available on twenty-first century agricultural input subsidy programmes in sub-Saharan Africa—but leaves to later chapters any discussion of Malawi's post-2005 programme. It identifies a number of commonalities across different programmes, against which the Malawi programme is compared in later chapters. Chapter 4 completes the first part of the book with a review of Malawi's political, livelihood, market, and agricultural policy history.

The second part of the book draws on panel household surveys, market surveys, monitoring and implementation reports, close engagement with a range of stakeholders, and the authors' detailed studies of the Malawi subsidy programme from 2006/7 to 2011/12. Chapter 5 describes in detail its evolving implementation. Chapters 6, 7, and 8 analyse various potential impacts— direct impacts on beneficiaries and on production, indirect impacts on the wider economy, and direct and indirect impacts on input markets. Returns to investment are considered in Chapter 9.

The final part of the book examines two major issues that emerge from Malawi's recent subsidy experience, focusing on targeting (in Chapter 10) and graduation (in Chapter 11). The concluding chapter summarizes the main arguments and evidence presented in Chapters 2 and 3, draws out the major lessons from the Malawi experience, and considers the question of agro-ecological, fiscal, and political sustainability. It concludes with a brief discussion of possible ways forward for agricultural input subsidies in sub-Saharan Africa.

Although parts of the book are written from an economist's perspective, most of the book should be of much wider interest, addressing general policy and implementation issues concerned both with agricultural input subsidies and wider problems of development in poor agrarian economies. There is also explicit consideration of the political influences on policy and its implementation: these considerations have wider relevance beyond policies concerned only with input subsidies.

1.3. Data and methods

We conclude this introductory chapter with a brief discussion on the main sources of information used in analysis of the Malawi subsidy programme. We draw on four main sources of information:

- implementation records on the subsidy programme;
- household and input supplier surveys conducted in 2006/7, 2008/9, and 2010/11 as part of the evaluation of the programme;
- official statistics;
- other studies on the subsidy programme.

We discuss each of these in turn.

1.3.1. Implementation records on the Malawi subsidy programme

Since 2006/7 the logistics of subsidized fertilizer distribution and payments to fertilizer suppliers, fertilizer transporters, and seed suppliers have been managed by the Logistics Unit, working in close cooperation with the Ministry of Agriculture and Food Security (MoAFS), donors, the two parastatals involved in subsidized fertilizer and seed distribution (Agricultural Marketing and Development Corporation and Smallholder Farmer Fertilizer Revolving Fund of Malawi, ADMARC and SFFRFM), and contracted transporters and seed and fertilizer suppliers. In Chapter 5 extensive use is made of information from the Logistics Unit's weekly and annual reports, supported by minutes of weekly task force meetings and information supplied directly by the MoAFS.

1.3.2. Programme evaluation studies

Much of the information and analysis on implementation is also contained in various reports of FISP evaluations led by the authors (for example, SOAS et al., 2008; Dorward et al., 2010; Dorward and Chirwa, 2011). Since 2006/7 the authors have led annual evaluations of the subsidy programme, with more intensive and 'light touch' evaluations in alternate years. More intensive evaluations of the 2006/7, 2008/9, and 2010/11 programmes involved household surveys with focus group discussions and a community survey and in 2006/7 and 2008/9 an input supplier survey. 'Light touch' evaluations of the 2007/8, 2009/10, and 2011/12 programme years have drawn mainly on implementation records as outlined above, together with information from other studies and official statistics, and analysis of data from more intensive evaluations.

The 2006/7 survey used a sub-sample of households sampled in the National Statistical Office (NSO) 2004/5 second Integrated Household Survey (IHS2) in order to provide panel data for analysis of programme impacts on beneficiaries. A total of 3298 households were sampled across all districts in Malawi. After data cleaning this gave 2431 balanced matched panel households also sampled in the IHS2. Agro-economic livelihood zones defined by the Malawi Vulnerability Assessment Committee (MVAC) were used to stratify the sample (Malawi National Vulnerability Assessment Committee, 2005). Urban, peri-urban, and protected areas (national parks and reserves) were omitted from the sample. Data collection and entry were conducted by the National Statistical Office. The survey provided very valuable information on household access to subsidized and unsubsidized inputs and on many aspects of programme implementation. Unfortunately it was less successful as regards plot areas and production reported by farmers: these were not found to give reliable and consistent results, and this prevented estimation of production impacts of the programme. The 2006/7 input supplier survey involved focus group discussions, key informant interviews, and a survey of 271 retail outlets in 6 districts. This was supplemented by information from fertilizer and seed importers and sellers. The findings were reported in School of Oriental and African Studies et al. (2008).

The household survey in 2008/9 was conducted by the evaluation team with a sample of 1982 households across 14 districts and represented almost all livelihood zones. The sample was a sub-set of the 2006/7 sample and therefore provided a panel data set across three surveys going back to the IHS2. The input supply retailer survey sampled 230 retailers in 6 districts. Both surveys were again supplemented by focus group discussions, key informant interviews, and a community survey, but detailed fertilizer import information was not available. Findings were presented in a portfolio of reports focusing on different aspects of the programme (for example, Dorward et al., 2010a, b; Kelly et al., 2010). The survey again provided valuable information on programme implementation and outputs. However, the introduction of innovative approaches to production and yield measurement (such as yield sub-plots with enumerator and farmer harvests), plot areas, and production data did not give reliable and consistent results. This not only precluded estimation of production impacts of the programme, it also raised questions about the reliability and consistency of area, production, and yield estimates from other studies which rely mainly on farmer estimates and recall of production (see Dorward and Chirwa, 2010b).

The 2010/11 study did not include an input supplier survey, and the sample size of the household survey was reduced further to 760 households across 8 districts in the 3 regions. The sample represented 8 major maize growing livelihood zones covering 77% of all rural households and was again a subset of the previous survey (this time the 2008/9 survey). The 2010/11 survey replaced attrition households with younger and newly formed households. The IHS2 and three FISP evaluation surveys generated a matched panel of 461 households. As for 2008/9, findings were reported in a portfolio of topic-specific reports (for example, Chirwa et al., 2011d; Dorward and Chirwa, 2011a; Mvula et al., 2011).

A number of specific studies were conducted and reported within the programme evaluation—for example, on programme impacts, benefit–cost analysis, targeting, and graduation. These are explained and cited where appropriate. It is, however, necessary to provide a little more information here on the development and use of the partial equilibrium Informal Rural Economy or IRE model to explore some of the economy-wide impacts of the programme. This model is fully described in Dorward and Chirwa (2012b). It is based on detailed programming models of different farm household types in the two most populous livelihood zones in Malawi. These models allow for seasonal constraints affecting farm household activities and the direct impacts of the subsidy are investigated by simulating the livelihood effects of specific households' access to subsidized inputs. These effects are then aggregated in order to estimate impacts on supply and demand of seasonal labour and maize. Wage rates and maize prices are then adjusted iteratively to find new equilibrium wages and prices and to derive estimates of economy-wide impacts on both subsidy recipients and non-recipients. The nature of the data available and of the models means that results should be interpreted as indicative of possible effects rather than predictive of actual effects. Nevertheless, when taken together with other information they provide useful insights into possible economy-wide impacts.

A full set of evaluation reports from 2006/7 to 2011/12 can be found at <http://www.wadonda.com/>. These provide further documentation of analytical methods and references are provided whenever their findings are drawn upon.

1.3.3. *Official statistics*

Malawi has an extensive set of agricultural and other national statistics.

The Ministry of Agriculture publishes valuable monthly information on market prices for major crops, with data collected on a weekly basis from a large number of markets around the country. The Ministry also publishes annual estimates of crop areas, production, and yields, and reports annual estimates of the number of farm families. The annual production estimates, with large increases in estimated maize production following the introduction of the subsidy programme in 2005/6, have been widely cited as evidence of the impact of the subsidy programme. However, there are inconsistencies between the large estimated production increases from 2005/6 and the very high domestic maize prices experienced in some years, notably in 2008/9. These inconsistencies are discussed in Chapter 7. There are also inconsistencies between national maize areas, production, and yield estimates from the Ministry of Agriculture, and from different reports by the National Statistical Office (National Statistical Office, 2005a, 2010a). These discrepancies are discussed in more detail in Dorward and Chirwa (2010b) and summarized in Chapter 6. Another set of discrepancies between Ministry of Agriculture and NSO data concerns the number of farm families (reported annually by the Ministry of Agriculture) and the number of rural households enumerated in the 2008 census (National Statistical Office, 2008a). This discrepancy and the difficulties it raises are discussed in Chapter 5.

Apparent discrepancies also arise between maize prices reported by the Ministry of Agriculture and the consumer price index reported by the NSO.

No detailed analysis of this has been published, to our knowledge, but the high maize prices observed in 2008/9 and in 2011 do not appear to be consistent with consumer price index figures for the same period, given the high weighting of food and particularly maize in the consumer price index. We also note that the NSO itself refers to revised 'CPI data' with 'overall inflation between the IHS2 and IHS3 periods of 128.9 per cent' (National Statistical Office, 2012: p. 207), when official CPI estimates for the same period suggest a considerably lower rate of inflation. This also raises wider questions about the deflator used in recent years' GDP estimates, and hence about these GDP estimates themselves.

Integrated Household Surveys (IHS) conducted by the NSO in 2004/5 (IHS2) and 2010/11 (IHS3) provide national estimates on a wide range of variables. We refer to these in Chapters 4 and 7. However, we also note some apparent discrepancies between and within some of the results presented, and—with the publication of the first report on the 2010/11 survey (National Statistical Office, 2012) as the manuscript for this book was being finalized—it has not been possible to resolve these.

1.3.4. *Other studies on the subsidy programme*

A number of other studies have been made of different aspects of the subsidy programme. Due to their varied nature and focus we do not discuss these here but refer to them at relevant points in the following chapters. In broad terms the main focus of most other work has been to use survey data to compare observations on recipients and non-recipients in order to examine targeting of and direct outcomes and impacts of subsidy receipt—in terms of differences in wealth, gender, and other household characteristics affecting access to and use of subsidized and unsubsidized inputs, and subsequent differences in changes in wealth and other household characteristics. There has been much less examination of indirect and economy-wide impacts, of impacts on market development, of benefits relative to costs, and of the important question of graduation, though we discuss notable exceptions where appropriate.

Part I
Background

In this part of the book we provide essential theoretical and empirical context for the rest of the book. The three chapters

- set out and extend more conventional theories on agricultural input subsidies' strengths and shortcomings;
- review limited information available on twenty-first century agricultural input subsidy programmes in sub-Saharan Africa; and
- describe Malawi's specific political, economic, and agricultural features.

These chapters structure and underpin the description, analysis, and evaluation of the Malawi subsidy programme, and the wider application of that evaluation, in the remainder of the book.

2

Agricultural input subsidies: changing theory and practice

2.1. Introduction

This chapter sets the scene and identifies critical issues addressed in the rest of the book by setting out evolving understandings on agricultural input subsidies in low income countries. We begin with a summary of conventional economic theories regarding agricultural input subsidies' potential benefits and of the difficulties experienced in realizing these. This leads on to consideration of different theoretical and practical challenges to conventional criticisms of input subsidies. The chapter concludes with a conceptual framework that sets out key elements and processes linking input subsidies' design, implementation, and impacts—a framework that underpins the structure and content of the rest of the book.

2.2. 'Conventional' input subsidies in agricultural development—theory and practice

Large-scale (so called universal) agricultural input subsidies were a common and major feature of agricultural development policies in poor rural economies from the 1960s to the 1980s. They were generally implemented as 'across the board' price subsidies accessible to all producers, or to all producers of a particular category. If they were sold through a state monopsony then there were common attempts at price discrimination, with, for example, only smallholder farmers supposed to purchase subsidized fertilizer and forbidden from selling it on. Fertilizer subsidies were particularly expensive and made heavy and growing demands on government budgets as they stimulated increased fertilizer consumption (and hence increased volumes of fertilizer subsidy) while political pressures also led to pressures for the subsidy rate to increase, or at least not contract, in the face of rising fertilizer prices.

Conventional arguments for subsidies in agricultural development focused on promoting agricultural productivity by making adoption of new technologies more attractive to smallholder farmers (Ellis, 1992). The reduced costs of subsidized inputs increase their profitability and reduce the risks perceived by farmers with a limited knowledge of input benefits and of correct usage. With credit and extension services, input subsidies were supposed to help farmers implement, benefit from, and—with later subsidy withdrawal—buy and use inputs on their own: rapid learning about input use and benefits would mean that subsidies should be needed for only a short time and could be rapidly phased out. However, subsidies were often subsequently implemented more widely with pan territorial pricing to support agricultural development in more remote areas, and to counteract taxes on agriculture through export tariffs, managed exchange rates, and controls on domestic prices.

Standard economic analysis of price subsidies considers the costs and benefits of subsidies in shifting farmers' supply curves for agricultural produce (see Figure 2.1). If there are no market failures then a subsidy of $Z per unit output increases effective producer price above the market price by $Z. If the subsidy is addressing a market failure then a subsidy of $Z per unit output will increase effective producer price above the market price by more than $Z (say $Z'). The increase in effective producer price causes a downward shift in the market price supply curve (S to S' in Figure 2.1). This leads to an expansion in supply (from Q to Q') and a fall in market or consumer price of the

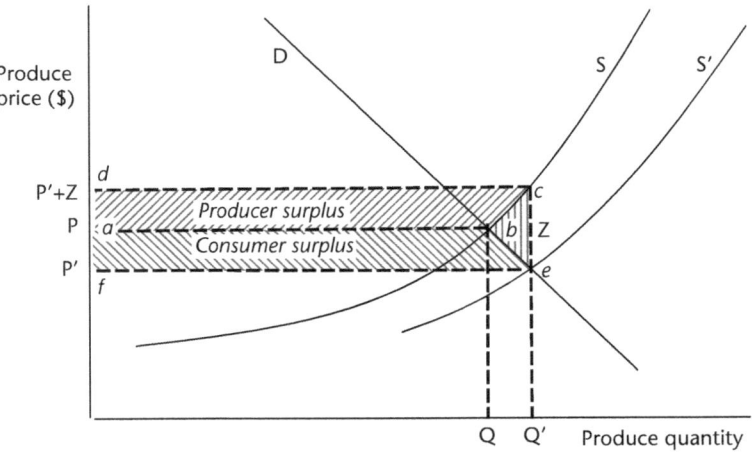

Figure 2.1. Input subsidy impacts on output supply, price, and stakeholder welfare

product (from P to P' in Figure 2.1, assuming that the good is a non-tradable with a downward sloping demand curve), with an increase in both producer surplus (shown in Figure 2.1 by the shaded area *abcd*) and consumer surplus (shown by the shaded area *abef*). The total cost of the subsidy is the total subsidy paid (new equilibrium quantity multiplied by the per unit subsidy, Q'.Z, shown by the shaded area *dcef*) plus administration costs (not shown in the graph). The total subsidy paid is greater than the sum of the increased consumer and producer welfare by a deadweight loss indicated in Figure 2.1 by the triangle *bce* (Siamwalla and Valdes, 1986). Under such circumstances, and even without allowing for administration costs, the subsidy leads to a net economic loss to the country and an income transfer from taxpayers to consumers and producers.

Three related points emerge from this analysis.

First, a subsidy only generates a positive overall net economic return if there is some market failure so that the downward shift in the supply curve is greater than the total cost of the subsidy (that is Z, the per unit cost of the subsidy to the government including administration costs, is less than Z', the effective increase in output price—or reduction in per unit costs—received by producers). This may occur where farmers' perceived private cost of inputs is higher than the true social or economic cost, and/or farmers' perceptions of private benefits from increased input use are lower than the actual social or economic benefits.[1] This may occur where

- farmers' lack of knowledge about input use means that their expectation of its benefits are less than the actual benefits;
- there are learning costs, so that initial farmer returns to input use are low but will increase with experience (see, for example, Ellis, 1992; Crawford et al., 2006; Morris et al., 2007);
- farmers' private costs of working capital for input purchase are greater than the social cost of capital; and
- farmers' risk assessment and aversion in investing in input purchase and use are higher than society's.

The first two divergences between farmers' and society's costs, benefits and perceptions of them, should decline with experience, knowledge, and efficiency in using inputs (and are effectively an infant industry argument), the latter two may decline with increasing farm productivity, wealth, and market integration.

Second, the size of the deadweight loss and the distribution of benefits between consumers and producers depend on elasticities of supply and

---

[1] Dorward (2009b) shows this using marginal value product and marginal factor cost analysis.

Table 2.1. Effects of demand and supply inelasticities on consumer and producer gains and on deadweights

	Perfectly elastic demand	Unitary demand	Perfectly inelastic demand
Perfectly elastic supply, shifts down	n/a	All gains to consumers, Large deadweight	All gains to consumers, No deadweight
Unitary supply, shifts down/to the right	All gains to suppliers, Large deadweight	Shared gains, Some deadweight	All gains to consumers, No deadweight
Perfectly inelastic supply (may shift to the right)	All gains to suppliers, No deadweight	Gains shared (depending on supply shift), No deadweight	n/a

demand, as shown in Table 2.1. This is important, as larger deadweight losses are associated with increasing inefficiencies, and the distribution of gains and costs between producers, consumers, and taxpayers has equity and poverty reduction impacts, depending on the relative wealth and incomes of the producers, consumers, and taxpayers concerned.

Elastic demand or supply tends to be associated with larger deadweight losses while producer and consumer shares of benefits are determined by relative supply and demand elasticities: inelastic demand is associated with larger shares of consumer surplus benefits, and inelastic supply (both price elasticity and in response to the subsidy) is associated with larger shares of producer surplus benefits. Supply and demand elasticities therefore affect both the efficiency of subsidy programmes and their equity and poverty reduction impacts (depending upon the relative wealth and incomes of affected producers and consumers). These observations are significant when linked with supply and demand characteristics of different crops in different contexts. Staple food markets in land-locked countries (with large import/export parity price differentials) tend to be associated with more inelastic demand (where prices lie between export and import parity prices). Demand tends to be more elastic for cash crops, particularly export cash crops, for traded staples and where subsidy implementation is not on a large enough scale to affect output prices (small-scale subsidies that do not significantly affect production and product prices are analytically equivalent to subsidies with highly elastic product demand: subsidy benefits are largely captured by suppliers/producers, and deadweight costs depend upon the elasticity of supply).

Third, transfers to producers can be analysed in terms of inefficiencies associated with *economic rents*. Rents arise in three ways. First, part of the cost of a general input subsidy goes to reducing the cost of production for produce that would be produced anyway (this is the producer surplus on produce that would be produced without the subsidy). This is an inefficient way of stimulating increased production and increased productivity, unless there is some social or economic benefit from transferring income to producers already using the subsidised input. Second, producer transfers often end up affecting the demand for agricultural land and labour, and bid up the demand for inputs. Apparent transfers to producers may then be passed back to the suppliers of these factors of production as pure economic rents. This is not a problem if the providers of this land and labour are poor, indeed as will be argued later this can be an important way for subsidies to promote pro-poor growth. Third, where subsidized inputs are rationed (officially or unofficially), then this leads to opportunities for those controlling subsidized inputs (politicians, government officials, fertilizer suppliers, farmer organization office bearers, etc.), to divert subsidized inputs from their intended beneficiaries for a side payment or to demand payments from beneficiaries in return for provision of subsidized inputs. Economic rents mean that even if there are net economic and social gains from a subsidy (as discussed above), much of the subsidy cost may be a straight transfer from the state (or taxpayers) to producers and suppliers of land, labour, and inputs without any economic gain, with the relative shares of transfers depending on the elasticities of supply and demand.

Another concern with input subsides relates to the extent of leakages and diversion of subsidized inputs away from their intended use. This can be considered in three ways:

a) Diversion between products: farmers are likely to apply inputs to the use with the greatest expected return. Fertilizers, for example, may be applied to a variety of crops. Even if subsidies are intended to expand production of the food staples consumed by poor people with inelastic demand (and benefit poor consumers with low deadweight losses), farmers may apply subsidized fertilizers to (cash) crops with more price elastic demand if these offer higher returns. Direct switching of inputs between crops or products may not be so easy for subsidized seeds, although some indirect switching may happen due to wider capital fungibility.

b) Diversion from intended beneficiaries: input subsidies in developing countries have commonly been intended for smallholder rather than commercial farmers. With a general subsidy it is difficult to channel subsidized inputs to smallholders unless there are a limited number of tightly controlled supply chains, clear ways of identifying intended beneficiaries, and control of private fertilizer transactions. Use of subsidized inputs by larger scale commercial farms is likely to increase the diversion from staple food to cash crops and to less-poor producers less constrained by market failures. Similar issues arise in subsidy access between richer and poorer smallholders.

19

c) Cross-border leakages: these arise when subsidized inputs are sold outside the country at a discount. The value of the discount represents a straight loss from the transfer of resources outside the country, with the loss of any chance of consumer benefit or economic gain from increased input use.

The final point to note from analysis of input subsidies' effects on product supply and demand is that the extent of supply shifts is critical in determining deadweight losses, the distribution of transfers between producers and consumers, and the extent of wider economic gains. The supply shift depends upon the technical efficiency of input use—determined by the quality and appropriateness of the inputs to the product they are used on, timing of their delivery to farmers, availability of complementary resources (for example, seed and fertilizer together, market access), and technical skills in input use.

This analysis of product supply and demand impacts of input subsidies helps to identify features of subsidies that are likely to yield more benefits and reduce the dangers of things going wrong, with additional insights into where subsidies are most likely to be useful, and into the ways that subsidies should be implemented. It suggests that inputs subsidies should be focused

- on producers who are not using inputs because of market failures;
- on inputs for products where they can induce a substantial supply shift (and this may also require complementary investments in, for example, other input supply, extension and output markets' infrastructure and services); and
- on inputs for products with inelastic demand and supply (particularly inelastic demand) among poor producers and consumers: staple grain production tends to have these characteristics in poor land-locked countries or large countries with suitable agro-ecological conditions.

Although input subsidies are directed at producers and at changing production methods and producer behaviour, this analysis emphasizes the importance of consumer benefits in addition to (or rather than) producer benefits for maximizing both economic and welfare gains from subsidies. Input subsidies should also be implemented in ways that (a) reduce deadweight losses and rents from straight transfers, (b) reduce leakages, and (c) have low administration costs. Subsidies may also be less efficient instruments if they are primarily aimed at delivering income transfers to producers and remote areas, because of high deadweight and administration costs, generation of rents, and the difficulties in developing/delivering complementary services needed for technically and economically efficient use of subsidized inputs. The distributional impacts and multipliers from expenditure on input subsidies also need to be considered against alternative (tax and subsidy or transfer) instruments for changing income distribution and for stimulating growth.

The conclusions from the theoretical analysis above matches (and influenced) the conventional wisdom among most economists and northern policy analysts on the difficulties with input subsidy programmes. This also emphasized difficulties with

- controlling costs, as there tend to be strong political pressures for the expansion of subsidies, and only weak pressures for their control;
- 'exits', as there is strong political resistance to scaling down or termination of subsidies;
- effectiveness of targeting of input subsidies to particular farmer types, with the problems of diversion and leakage noted above both expanding programme cost and reducing efficiency;
- over use of inputs, or adoption of input intensive production methods, as a result of artificially low input prices;
- regressive benefits favouring larger farmers who can afford subsidized inputs (the poorest farmers may not be able to afford inputs even where they are subsidized);
- market distortions, and particularly parastatal involvement in subsidized input delivery, tending to crowd out and inhibit private sector investment in input supply systems and hence impede sustainable development.

These concerns led to the conventional wisdom among economists and international donors in the 1980s and 1990s that input subsidies had been ineffective and inefficient policy instruments in Africa and that they had contributed to government over-spending and fiscal and macro-economic problems. From the mid 1990s, however, this conventional wisdom was increasingly challenged, with a resurgence of interest in agricultural input subsidies in Africa, new thinking about the historical and potential roles in agricultural development, and the complementary emergence of innovative subsidy delivery systems and instruments.

2.3. Resurgent interest in input subsidies

The fundamental driver for new thinking on input (and particularly fertilizer) subsidies in Africa was concern among African politicians, NGOs, and some policy analysts about the apparent failures of liberalized policies in supporting broad-based agricultural development, particularly sustainable intensification of staple food crop production. This was accompanied by continuing political demands for fertilizer subsidies in many countries; tensions among donors in resisting such demands (with increasing legitimacy of democratic governments in Africa and divergent donor views on subsidy merits); concerns about declining soil fertility, agricultural stagnation, and rural poverty in Africa; and identification of input subsidies as a potential instrument for social protection policies.

These concerns led to interest in the potential for input subsidies to deliver a wider range of (sometimes unstated) objectives than those formerly recognized in the conventional wisdom described earlier. These objectives included short-term private input market development, replenishment of soil fertility, social protection for poor subsidy recipients, and national and household food security (Morris et al., 2007).

There has also been considerable interest in the development of new instruments and approaches in designing and delivering input subsidies, as so called 'smart subsidies'. Morris et al. (2007) describe 10 features of smart subsidies: 'promoting fertiliser as part of a wider strategy', 'favouring market based solutions' and 'promoting competition' in input supply, 'paying attention to demand', 'insisting on economic efficiency', 'empowering farmers', 'involving an exit strategy', 'pursuing regional integration', 'ensuring sustainability', and 'promoting pro-poor economic growth' (Morris et al., 2007: 103–4). They recognize that 'in exceptional circumstances, poverty reduction or food security objectives may even be given precedence over efficiency and sustainability goals' (Morris et al., 2007: 104–5). Instruments proposed for implementing smart subsidies include demonstration packs, vouchers, rationing, targeting, matching grants, and loan guarantees. For all of these the details of instrument design and implementation are critical to their success, and there is continuing concern over the problems of subsidies discussed earlier and the importance of addressing wider problems in input supply chains (Jayne et al., 2009; Minot and Benson, 2009; Bumb et al., 2011).

The interest in getting input subsidies to serve new functions and objectives, and the extent to which input subsidies are the most cost-effective way of achieving these objectives, continues to be controversial. The main text of the 2008 World Development Report on 'Agriculture for Development', for example, recognized all the features of smart subsides outlined above, but its summarized position was more restricted and conventional, focusing on subsidy roles as being to provide 'sustainable solutions to market failures...through...'market smart' approaches to jumpstarting agricultural input markets....and underwriting risks of early adoption of new technologies to help achieve economies of scale...to reduce input prices...as part of a comprehensive strategy to improve productivity with credible exit options' (World Bank, 2007b).

It is, however, possible to question how important some of the objectives listed above were in successful Asian Green Revolutions (for example, replenishment of soil fertility and social protection for poor subsidy recipients) and to identify other, perhaps more important, outcomes from subsidy use in these green revolutions (see, for example, Hazell and Rosegrant, 2000) or in more recent input subsidy programmes. Such outcomes included

- long-term 'thickening' of supply chains and rural markets;
- lower staple food prices and higher wages;
- increased real incomes for poor non-recipients as well as food-insecure recipients as a result of food price and wage changes; and
- longer term structural changes in livelihoods and the rural and national economy with expanded domestic demand for higher value farm products and for non-farm goods and services, together with expanded supply capacity, due to release of land and labour as a result of increased staple crop productivity.

These debates, together with new insights into development processes, require an extension of the conventional wisdom on subsidies with a re-examination of:

- the empirical record of their success and failure;
- development opportunities and constraints facing African farmers;
- thinking on input subsidies' roles and objectives in development, on new design and implementation features, and on the conditions for inputs subsidies to be effective; and
- a more holistic conceptual framework for examining the roles, instruments, and implementation of input subsidies.

We consider each of these issues in turn to provide a basis for a review of recent experience with input subsidies in Africa in the subsequent chapter.

2.4. Input subsidies' successes, failures, and potential

The substantial success of the Green Revolution in Asian countries in driving growth and poverty and reduction is widely recognized but, implicitly or explicitly, this is often considered to have been achieved despite, rather than assisted by, input subsidies (see, for example, Economist Intelligence Unit, 2008). This position is taken despite longstanding work showing the importance of subsidies in Indonesia (see, for example, Timmer, 2004), in promoting agricultural growth in situations where subsidies should have the greatest effect (food staples in large countries, with high physical returns from input use). Djurfeldt et al. (2005) argue that input subsidies were a critical element in Green Revolution policies across a range of Asian countries. Fan et al. (2007) estimate a significant contribution of input subsidies to growth and poverty reduction in India in the early stages of the Green Revolution but not later (although estimated returns to some other investments such as agricultural research were higher). Dorward et al. (2004a) argue that sustained (but not indefinite) input subsidies were a major part of successful Green Revolution packages, making a critical contribution to thickening and thus 'kick starting' markets, first within staple food supply chains and then in the wider rural economy.

Dorward et al. (2004a) also argue that later problems with input subsidies should not obscure their initial contribution to driving growth forward, and much of the pessimism about subsidies was founded on later inefficiency of Asian subsidies and African experience of such subsidies. The Berg report criticized input subsidies as a major element in inefficient and fiscally and economically unsustainable policies that distorted market incentives, blunted competitiveness and farmer incentives, and undermined growth in private sector services in Africa. Subsidized input systems may have looked good for farmers, but the theoretical problems discussed earlier were compounded by diversion and inefficiency such that actual benefits to farmers were often very limited (World Bank, 1981). However, there are African countries that implemented input subsidy systems that had initial success in raising productivity, but for varying political and economic reasons failed to sustain the fiscal investment and market systems needed to sustain benefits (for example, Zimbabwe and Malawi).

Taking these Asian and African experiences together, Dorward et al. (2009) note that while there are egregious examples of failure with state-led approaches, there are also examples of dramatic success in fostering widespread and sustained growth in smallholder food staples (as noted above). Private market-led approaches, on the other hand, have very few examples of such success, and many failures, but the failures of continued rural poverty may be more hidden from economists working with governments and businesses than macro-economic and fiscal crises. It can also be argued, however, that private market-led approaches have never been properly tried—liberalization of food markets has proved very difficult to implement consistently—and not just in Africa. This can also be seen, however, as another challenge to private market-led approaches. An exception to this was the mid-2000s growth of smallholder fertilizer use in Kenya (Ariga et al., 2008) which, while aided by special conditions which prevent its wholesale application to other countries, nevertheless carries important lessons.

The record of input subsidies, as a major part of state-led development approaches, therefore appears to be more mixed than conventional criticisms suggest. This requires consideration of both context and programme design and implementation in appraising the potential for input subsidies as effective instruments for agricultural (and wider) development. Successful investments in input subsidies in the Asian Green Revolution cannot be simply transferred to African countries. It is important to identify situations where input subsidies could work to take opportunities and overcome constraints facing African farmers.

Poulton and Dorward (2008) and Dorward et al. (2008) consider constraints and opportunities for growth for different agricultural products in different situations in Africa and southern Africa. They suggest that while high response cereals (with roots and tubers) are the products with the greatest importance and potential for driving and/or spreading growth, they are also the crops that are most affected by interlinked challenges and failures in price instability, the price/productivity tightrope,[2] and seasonal input finance provision. In terms of conventional economic theory on subsidy gains and losses (as discussed earlier in Section 2.2), these characteristics suggest that high response cereals fulfil many of the requirements for well-designed and implemented input subsidies to have a role to play in stimulating pro-poor growth:

- the seasonal finance challenges are market failures that inhibit input use, so that the gains from subsidies addressing input affordability problems have the potential to exceed deadweight and implementation costs;

- inelastic demand for food staples means that (a) deadweight losses should be relatively low and (b) many of the gains of producer subsidies should accrue to poor consumers—if subsidies increase production on a sufficiently large scale to lower prices—and in this way input subsidies can provide a means to address the food price/productivity tightrope;

- they can, in the right agro-ecological conditions and with proper management, lead to substantial productivity and production increase.

This last point is important, in the context of arguments by Dorward et al. (2004a) that state interventionist approaches (including input subsidies) require (a) technologies, management, and agro-ecological conditions that generate sufficient productivity gains and (b) complementary infrastructure and institutions to support extension services and market activities. This ties

---

[2] The price/productivity tightrope is the dilemma in poor agrarian countries where on the one hand high food prices are needed to stimulate investment in inputs but on the other hand high prices damage poor consumers who spend a large part of their income on staple foods.

in with earlier arguments about large deadweight costs in producer-oriented subsidies in remote areas to suggest that input subsidies are more effective with favourable agro-ecological conditions for high response cereals, good market access, and higher population densities. This approach is articulated in AGRA's thinking about prioritization of investments in 'breadbasket areas' in Africa (AGRA, 2008).

2.5. Input subsidies' roles and objectives

2.5.1. Dynamic effects of subsidies on growth

The above discussion of subsidy impacts has been largely concerned with subsidies' 'static' impacts on producer costs and decisions, hence on produce supply and prices and consumer welfare (the more dynamic impacts on producer knowledge of input benefits and efficient input use contributed to these static changes). There are, however, two important potential dynamic benefits of subsidies that have been given much less emphasis in conventional discussion of subsidies' potential impacts.

First, subsidies that are effective in raising land and labour productivity (with overall increases in on-farm labour demand) and in driving down food staple prices will raise the real incomes of large numbers of poor consumers and producers, and this should expand demand for locally produced non-staple foods (horticultural and animal products) and non-farm goods and services, driving up local labour demand and wages and improving people's nutrition.[3] At the same time increasing staple crop productivity can release resources for production of the same non-staple foods (horticultural and animal products) and non-farm goods and services. These growth multipliers were critical in driving growth in Asia (Hazell and Rosegrant, 2000). Subsidies' potential contributions to the three core development processes of 'hanging in, stepping up and stepping out' (Dorward, 2009a) require particular emphasis on subsidy impacts on wages and food prices for poor consumers and producers who are net food buyers (around 50% of African farmers—Barrett, 2008) as well as subsidy implementation over a longer period, to achieve structural change rather than short-term productivity gains. The focus on staple crops—and both on labour productivity in their cultivation and on

---

[3] Effective subsidies for staple crop production offer double benefits when staple markets are relatively isolated from international markets—with both broad-based increases in land and labour productivity and increases in real incomes for net food buyers who benefit from falling staple prices. However, the dynamic benefits of broad-based productivity increases in staple production may by themselves be very significant, even if staple markets are more open to imports and exports, with a narrower band between import and export prices reducing the scope for falling prices of staple foods.

prices faced by net food buyers suggest that there can be particular benefits for women, with common gendered responsibilities in staple crop production and acquisition.

A second set of important potential dynamic benefits from input subsidies arises from their stimulation of increased input and output trade and wider economic activity (as described above) having positive spillover effects with 'market thickening'. This happens if the greater volume of economic activity stimulated by the subsidy reduces coordination and transaction costs and risks and promotes institutional and communications and transport service and infrastructure development (see Dorward et al., 2004a, 2009; Dorward and Kydd, 2004). Dynamic effects of input subsidies on the development of input supply systems (considered below) are a specific feature of this.

These potential dynamic benefits of subsidies require longer term and stable implementation of subsidies to induce behavioural and structural change, integration of subsidy policy and implementation with other policies promoting these changes, and evaluations of subsidy programmes that take account of and ideally assess these wider indirect and dynamic impacts.

2.5.2. Soil fertility replenishment

One of the reasons put forward for implementing fertilizer subsidies is the need to combat the alarming decline in soil nutrients in many parts of Africa and the need for (and benefits of) their replenishment. Crawford et al. (2006) summarize soil fertility problems in terms of declining fallows, rapid deforestation, land degradation, and declining nitrogen, phosphate, and potassium levels in arable soils. Subsidies to promote fertilizer application may then be justified in terms of positive externalities where increased fertilizer use, higher soil fertility, and higher farm yields provide a number of benefits to society rather than to individual farmers: reductions in soil erosion and downstream flooding and siltation, in deforestation and CO_2 emissions, and in soil and wider ecosystem and biodiversity loss as a result of reduced pressures to cultivate marginal and fragile land; and reductions in poverty and in rural–urban migration and hence in the wider social costs of addressing rural and urban poverty as a result of increased farm and rural incomes (Sánchez et al., 1997). It may also be argued that poverty and food insecurity cause many African farmers to place a higher value on short-term income and food production and a lower value on longer term investments in soil fertility and other types of natural capital (as compared with their value to wider society), again leading to under investment in soil fertility and a justification for subsidies to promote investments in better soil management. Negative externalities from nitrate leaching are not generally a problem with the very low rates of fertilizer application on poor farms in Africa.

2.5.3. *Effects of subsidies on input supply systems*

Effective large-scale input subsidies should lead to substantial increases in volumes of inputs purchased by farmers, and this can have a number of different impacts on input supply systems and markets. We consider a number of different processes and impacts.

First, the short-run effects of an input subsidy on the input market depend upon the nature of the subsidy and on the structure of the input supply system. If the subsidy is provided to farmers this has the effect of shifting input demand upwards. Alternatively input subsidies may be provided to input suppliers (India, for example, has used fertilizer subsidies to domestic producers to develop and protect its fertilizer industry, Fan et al., 2007). The effects of this on the input market depend upon input supply elasticity, and this in turn will depend upon the structure, conduct, and performance in domestic production and imports. This varies between countries and between different kinds of inputs. Few African countries produce fertilizer, with local fertilizer suppliers either importing blends or blending particular formulations from domestic and imported raw materials. Price elasticities for imported fertilizers should be very high, unless there are either significant importation costs and limited importation capacity (as may be the case for land-locked countries, with increased input demand bidding up importation costs and revenues (rents) in transport costs) or limited competition between importers (bidding up revenues (rents) of importers). The situation is often very different with seed supply, where imports are impeded by national seed certification controls and there is limited domestic capacity in seed production, with long multiplication lead times. Short and long run supply elasticities also differ (with greater long-run elasticity with stable policies). More elastic input supply leads to more of a subsidy accruing to producers, with gains for producers and/or consumers depending on the product elasticity of supply and demand (see Dorward, 2009b, for a graphical presentation of this). More elastic input supply leads to reduced subsidy capture by input suppliers, increased benefits to producers and/or consumers, and greater development benefits.

Input subsidies can impact beneficially on input supply systems by reducing supplier margins through economies of scale across the industry and within particular suppliers (as a result of increased volumes) and/or through increased competition if increased volumes attract new entrants into input supply. These benefits should accrue to both subsidized and unsubsidized supplies of the same inputs, and expand supply and its elasticity. The extent of improvements in economies of scale and competition depend upon the nature of the inputs and their supply systems, and upon ways in which subsidized inputs are acquired and disbursed (for example, through general price support, voucher systems or direct issue with distribution involving government institutions, input supplier cartels, or competitive input markets). Government supply is not incompatible with realization of economies of scale in subsidized input disbursement, but spillovers to unsubsidized sales are likely to be limited (unless the government also markets these) and lack of competition faced by government organizations (and by cartels) tends to undermine the achievement of such economies.

Another process by which input subsidies can impact beneficially on input supply systems is through their promotion of new relationships and forms of relationships among input sellers and buyers in poor rural areas with, for example, interlocking arrangements for linking input sellers, seasonal finance providers, and produce buyers. Again this process depends on the nature of the inputs and their supply systems, and on the ways in which subsidized inputs are disbursed. As noted earlier, this can also contribute to wider economic and market activity due to input market activities' potential spillovers into other markets (for example, expansion of a network to sell subsidized inputs may also promote buying and selling of other commodities).

The impacts of input subsidies on input supply systems are not, however, always beneficial. Damaging effects can arise in two main ways.

First, input subsidies may create considerable uncertainty and risks for input suppliers and directly undermine incentives for private investment in input supply systems. This occurs most obviously when governments intervene directly in input markets through direct supply of subsidized inputs and/or through regulation of input markets. Direct supply of subsidized inputs by government may take away business from private suppliers if there is significant displacement of unsubsidized sales by subsidized sales, leading to unsold stocks and lower sales volumes to carry fixed costs.[4] Regulation of input markets may restrict prices or volumes, or require sales of unprofitable lines or in unprofitable locations—again restricting revenues and increasing costs and risks. Inconsistent and changeable policies and interventions are particularly damaging.

Subsidies may also damage the development of input supply systems by distorting incentives so that input suppliers direct resources into competition for government contracts to supply subsidized inputs, instead of competition to expand retail sales.

The implications of this discussion are that subsidy programmes can promote input supply system development, but this needs careful consideration of input supply markets' structure, conduct and performance, careful programme design, and long-term stable but efficiency-focused

---

[4] An extreme case arises if farmers do not purchase unsubsidized inputs because they expect to obtain subsidized inputs, but subsequently cannot—in such circumstances a subsidy can not only displace unsubsidized inputs but actually depress total input use.

relationships of trust between governments and private suppliers. Quick exits and unstable, changeable subsidy programmes are unlikely to induce the private sector investments necessary for supply system development. These issues are the major concerns of many subsidy analysts (for example, Crawford et al., 2006; Morris et al., 2007; Jayne et al., 2009; Minot and Benson, 2009; Bumb et al., 2011).

2.5.4. Social protection

A number of authors (for example, Morris et al., 2007) suggest that subsidies may provide an effective way of delivering social protection. Dorward et al. (2006) locate this within an evolving relationship between agricultural development and social protection policies which they characterize as (a) social protection *from* agriculture, (b) social protection *independent of* agriculture, (c) social protection *for* agriculture, (d) social protection *through* agriculture, and (e) social protection *with* agriculture. Input subsidies fit into (a), (d), or (e) depending upon the relative emphasis on social protection and agriculture in subsidy policy design and implementation. There seems to be little empirical review of the effectiveness of subsidies as social protection instruments: we discuss issues and evidence in Malawi later (in Chapters 6 and 7) but note here that as compared with cash transfer programmes, social protection benefits from direct input subsidy transfers are reduced in a number of ways: by targeting that is only partially effective in reaching the vulnerable and marginalized; by difficulties and costs in redeeming coupons; by the difficulties that labour- and land-scarce households have in using fertilizers; and by rents or 'cuts' taken by middlemen in secondary markets for coupons and inputs. Poor, labour-scarce households may also receive limited benefits from indirect subsidy impacts on wage rates. However, poor and vulnerable households should receive more benefits from indirect impacts on staple food prices and from wider growth impacts which increase the resources available for informal social protection mechanisms.

2.5.5. Input profitability

Input subsidies are just one of four ways of improving the profitability of input use, the others being (a) raising physical productivity of inputs (through adaptation of technologies and farmers' learning how to manage them, and when—and when not—to use them); (b) reducing the costs of input purchases by increasing efficiencies (for example, in fertilizer or seed production and/or delivery systems); and (c) increasing output prices (with either high consumer prices or with subsidies funded by tax payers). As noted earlier, there are often considerable opportunities for both raising productivity and reducing costs (Crawford et al., 2006; Morris et al., 2007; Jayne et al., 2009; Bumb et al., 2011).

As we have seen, conventional thinking on input subsidies emphasizes their role in improving the profitability of input use. While *profitability constraints* on input use on food crops continue to be important, the nature of these constraints has changed, and (as will be discussed later) at the same time *affordability constraints* have become more important.

We discuss these two changes in turn, noting that different analysis may be needed for different inputs (for example, fertilizers and seeds).

Regarding constraints to farmer purchases as a result of lack of knowledge of fertilizer benefits and their correct usage, it is generally no longer the case that most farmers are unaware of fertilizers' benefits, indeed lack of access to fertilizer is commonly cited by farmers as a major constraint on their agricultural production. Although the extent of farmers' direct experience of fertilizer use varies, in most areas there are farmers with direct experience of fertilizer use, and observation and reports of fertilizer use are widespread. Farmers' ability to use fertilizers effectively and efficiently (through proper selection of fertilizer types, appropriate timing and method of application, and use of complementary investments in, for example, soil and water management and crop varieties) is more variable. Poorer farmers who do not have access to fertilizers for cash crop production may face particular problems. Input subsidy programmes continue to have a potential role in helping farmers to learn from experience here, but this requires timely provision of appropriate fertilizers supported by complementary investments in extension services and in promotion of improved soil and water management and crop varieties. Seed subsidies may have an important and more conventional 'profitability' role in promoting both achievement and knowledge of higher returns from fertilizer use and of higher returns from their own use in conjunction with fertilizer.

The high costs of fertilizers (as a proportion of crop production costs) mean that the (perceived and actual) profitability of their use is strongly influenced not only by physical responses to fertilizer use (discussed above) but also by relative fertilizer and crop prices. Relative global prices of crops and fertilizers have fluctuated over the last 40 years with a trend of falling relative cereal prices (Dorward, 2013). Relative domestic prices, however, will have changed in different ways in different countries. Although we cannot generalize as regards declining or increasing profitability of unsubsidized fertilizer use over the last 30 years, variability in food prices is a major issue in many countries. Risks of low food prices leading to the low profitability of fertilizer use may depress fertilizer use in less poor farmers' production of surplus food for the market. Fears of high food prices may make fertilizer use more profitable, but use of fertilizer by poorer food deficit farmers is more likely to be constrained by *affordability* arising from problems in accessing seasonal finance, to which we now turn.

2.5.6. Input affordability

As noted earlier, access to seasonal finance is widely considered to be a major constraint on input use on staple food crops, especially among poorer farmers (see, for example, Newberry and Stiglitz, 1981; Feder et al., 1985; Binswanger and Rosenzweig, 1986; Binswanger and McIntire, 1987; Dorward, 1996, 2006; Dorward et al., 2005b, 2009). We describe this in terms of difficulties with the *affordability* of inputs. In theory farmers can finance input purchases from farm savings, from non-farm income sources, or from borrowing. However, (particularly poorer) small farm households are rarely able to save enough to fund significant intensification, and few have access to sufficient non-farm income sources for this purpose. Credit has therefore long been recognized as a priority to support input purchases and agricultural intensification (see, for example, Feder et al., 1985) and state provision of subsidized seasonal credit services were a significant part of the bundle of subsidized services, with input provision, in successful Green Revolutions (Dorward et al., 2004a; Djurfeldt et al., 2005). Severe (and justifiable) criticism of agricultural credit programmes (for example, Adams and Vogel, 1986; Yaron, 1992) as fiscally unsustainable (with a large subsidy component and major repayment problems), and regressive (with the majority of loans going to well-connected, wealthy borrowers and limited benefits to poor households) led to their demise. The abolition of these programmes has not, however, led to their replacement by private sector and micro-finance services for staple food crop production.[5]

The absence of financial services allowing farmers to access credit to finance the significant costs of purchasing fertilizer means that only if subsidies lead to sufficiently large reductions in fertilizer prices for poorer farmers will they lead to increased access to fertilizers by such farmers. If subsidies lead to smaller reductions in fertilizer prices which do not make them affordable by poorer farmers then they are likely to mainly benefit less poor farmers whose use of unsubsidized fertilizer is less constrained by inability to finance their purchase. Such considerations are likely to be particularly pertinent for poorer women farmers, with particular shortages of working capital and difficulties in accessing credit and/or input subsidies.

---

[5] Financing of inputs for staple crop production cannot use 'interlocking' or contract farming mechanisms for loan recovery, mechanisms which have been and continue to be successful models for delivery of seasonal finance to non-staple producers where higher value crops give limited numbers of produce buyers incentives to invest in smallholder production (for example, Dorward et al., 1998; Jayne et al., 2009). Staple crops pose further difficulties for farmers' consumption, rather than sale, of the product.

Dorward (2009b) examines the issue of affordability using analysis of input use, comparing marginal value products and marginal factor costs in input use in the presence of seasonal capital constraints and financial market failures. Poor households face high interest and transaction costs when borrowing short-term capital, with limited capital of their own and high opportunity costs. These capital costs lead to much higher total marginal factor costs, and lower (often zero) input use as compared with households without affordability constraints. Dorward (2012a) presents a wider review of these issues in farm household models. Both analyses show how an input subsidy which substantially reduces the capital requirements and costs of input purchase for capital-constrained households can make input purchases possible for such households. They also show, however, how there may be substantial inefficiencies if heavily subsidized inputs are made available to farmers whose unsubsidized input use is not significantly limited by capital constraints. This suggests that input subsidies' efficiency and effectiveness in stimulating increased input use can be improved by smart subsidies that reduce the quantities of input subsidies received by less capital-constrained farmers. This can be achieved in two ways: by targeting and by rationing, topics that we consider later in this chapter and which, as we shall see in later chapters, have been major issues in the Malawi Farm Input Subsidy Programme.

An alternative and complementary perspective on the role of subsidies in overcoming affordability constraints on fertilizer use is provided in a study by Duflo et al. (2011) in Kenya. They report that a small targeted subsidy for fertilizer purchases provided shortly after harvest time is as effective in promoting fertilizer purchases among poorer households as a larger subsidy later in the season. This is because this helps farmers commit available funds to fertilizer purchase, which, once purchased, is much less fungible. This phenomenon has parallels with the popularity in Malawi of a 'fertilizer for work' programme as compared with food for work (Gregory, 2006; Devereux, 2006) and offers a potential alternative to, or graduation pathway away from, large-scale subsidies. Further investigation is needed, however, into the applicability of these findings in other contexts.

2.5.7. Political economy issues

Large-scale input subsidy programmes are extremely costly, represent very significant transfers to subsidy recipients, and offer opportunities for very substantial captures of rents by a variety of stakeholders (politicians, programme administrators, input suppliers, traders, and less poor farmers). Political economy difficulties with large-scale input subsidies are consequently found in almost all countries where subsidies are implemented. Thus, in OECD countries agricultural subsidies (not specifically input subsidies) are widely recognized to be inefficient but have continued because they serve particular political interests. Input subsidies (fertilizer and electricity, for example) persist for similar reasons in many Asian countries after they have served their role of 'kick starting' rural growth, despite being extremely costly (Gale et al., 2005; Gulati and Pursell, 2008; JiKun et al., 2011).

Political economy difficulties can, however, be particularly problematic in poorer rural economies where (a) there are very substantial economic opportunity costs from the diversion of scarce fiscal resources to input subsidies and away from other productive investments, and (b) potential personal and political gains from subsidy rents are very large relative to other income, patronage, and rent seeking opportunities in the economy. A paradox arises because substantial political commitment is needed for large-scale input subsidies to be implemented, but the political objectives behind such commitment may often focus around or be shifted towards short-term patronage opportunities.[6] Unfortunately, however, pursuit of these opportunities may undermine the economic efficiency and wider pro-poor growth benefits of input subsidies—by directing subsidies to less poor recipients with more political voice, directing subsidies towards cash crops, undermining competition and efficiency in input delivery systems, and increasing leakages and non-transparent secondary markets. These difficulties are particularly prevalent in political systems with significant neo-patrimonial elements, as is common in many poorer rural economies, particularly in Africa (Van de Walle, 1999) and may be enhanced rather than reduced by the electoral cycles of democratic government (Poulton, 2012).

Another political economy paradox arises with regard to stable, continuing, and longer term subsidies if they are to lead to supply system development and wider dynamic changes in rural economies (as discussed earlier). While this carries important benefits, it also carries important risks, as if subsidies are not set up with clear time limits and if they continue for long periods then the risks of their being politically entrenched and 'hijacked' are increased. Similarly, the longer subsidies are in place with stable subsidy systems, the greater the opportunities for fraud and subsidy diversion. There are therefore substantial challenges in promoting stability and trust for farmers and input suppliers while at the same time specifying clear exit mechanisms and rules (to reduce risks of political capture) and varying systems (to reduce fraud).

A key part of addressing these political economy issues is understanding the diverse legitimate and illegitimate interests and powers of different

---

[6] This is not intended to suggest that there are not other less self-interested and extremely important reasons for political interest in agricultural input subsidies—these are a major focus of this book. As will be discussed, subsidies may be particularly attractive to policy makers because they can lead to quick increases in food production and in some circumstances it may also be more cost-effective to subsidize fertilizer than to pay for food imports.

stakeholders (for example, farmers with different livelihoods; produce buyers, sellers, and consumers; tax payers; local and national politicians; technicians; donors; input supply businesses and employees; civil society; government and private organizations and their managers; traditional leaders), as they relate to personal, local, organizational, and wider political, financial, economic, and symbolic[7] constraints and objectives and promoting transparency and accountability.

2.6. Design and implementation features

2.6.1. Targeting and rationing of input subsidies

A subsidy is likely to be more economically efficient and effective if subsidized inputs are directed or targeted at farmers who otherwise would not use inputs (for example, due to affordability or risk aversion constraints) but who will make productive use of any subsidized inputs they can obtain. Dorward (2009b) extends the analysis of Figure 2.1 above to show that if poorer, capital-constrained farmers are targeted, then this increases the economic efficiency of the subsidy (as compared with a universal subsidy) and leads to a transfer from less-poor producers and tax payers to poorer producers and consumers (assuming that the subsidy is increasing production of a staple food crop and reducing its price relative to wages). The extent to which less poor producers (without the subsidy) actually lose from a fall in producer prices depends on the price fall (which depends upon incremental production among targeted famers and elasticity of demand) and upon alternative activities open to them (affecting their elasticity of supply).

The targeting of subsidized inputs to different groups or types of people is, however, a critical and sensitive issue, with significant costs and difficulties. In this it is helpful to distinguish between geographical targeting (between regions, districts, and different geographically defined communities) and intra-community targeting (between different categories of people or households within communities). Geographical differences between areas and communities are often correlated with socio-economic and cultural differences between these areas and communities. Costs of geographical targeting will generally be lower than intra-community targeting, with the relative effectiveness of these targeting approaches (in terms of inclusion and exclusion

---

[7] 'Symbolic' constraints and opportunities are those that while not apparently technocratically rational have significant symbolic importance. Examples include national food self-sufficiency—this may or may not be an economically efficient way of ensuring national food security, but in some countries it has significant symbolic political importance. Avoiding of weakness or devaluation of national currency is another example of a symbolic objective in some countries.

errors) and the political tensions they cause depending on inter- and intra-community differences and social, political, and cultural factors. Targeting also commonly leads to secondary markets for inputs where recipients sell subsidized inputs to non-recipients (we discuss this issue below under leakages and diversion).

The political, economic, welfare, and equity issues associated with targeting mean that targeting criteria and methods are constrained by political concerns and practicalities (at national, regional, and community levels), by programme objectives (for example, production, growth, or social protection objectives), and by the feasibility and costs of targeting. There may be arguments for comprehensive or area targeting that delivers smaller quantities of inputs (or of entitlements to inputs) to all households or farmers in a country or area (to allow greater accountability, avoid political and financial costs of attempts at targeting, and possibly even reduce targeting errors if targeting mechanisms are very ineffective).

A final comment is needed on the relative efficiencies of input use by poor and less poor producers. It has been argued above that targeting poor producers can improve subsidies' effectiveness in addressing market failures (reducing displacement, and increasing welfare and distributional benefits). These arguments, however, are undermined if poor producers make less efficient use of inputs than less poor producers. There is substantial empirical evidence supported by continually evolving theory that smaller, poorer farms tend to be more efficient users of land in the cultivation of labour intensive staple crops in poor rural economies, but larger farms tend to be more efficient users of land in the cultivation of capital and market-intensive higher value cash crops (Poulton et al., 2010). There is less evidence on relative efficiencies in use of inputs. Although poorer farmers are generally more efficient users of capital, this may not apply if there are increasing returns to capital with the use of purchased inputs (this may occur if input productivity is enhanced by complementary investments).

Targeting limits total subsidy volumes and costs by limiting access to subsidized inputs to a limited number of beneficiaries. Rationing also limits total subsidy volumes, by limiting quantities of subsidized input per beneficiary. Like targeting, it can be an effective way of reducing the total costs of a subsidy programme while at the same time allowing a higher per unit subsidy. Dorward (2009b) uses marginal analysis and supply and demand analysis (extending Figure 2.1) to show that rationing can also raise the efficiency of input use, with or without targeting, as there are commonly diminishing marginal benefits to increased input use. However, as with targeting, rationing is only effective where there are no (or limited) secondary markets in which recipients sell subsidized inputs to non-recipients.

2.6.2. Entitlement and distribution systems

Any targeting or rationing system restricts access to subsidized inputs. This requires specification of entitled beneficiaries and their subsidized input entitlement, with a mechanism allowing access to that entitlement. This may involve physical distribution of inputs against lists of entitled beneficiaries, with secure identification, or separate distribution of evidence of entitlement which is then 'redeemed' at authorized retail outlets. Evidence of entitlement is most commonly a paper voucher, but scratch cards and electronic systems involving bank cards, electronic 'smart' cards, and mobile phones may also be used. Since entitlements have considerable financial value, these must be very secure to prevent counterfeit fraud and theft (with secure printing processes and print features and/or real time, secure, and centralized monitoring of allocated and redeemed entitlements). Different systems offer different potential benefits but pose different political, technical, administrative, and social challenges (biometric information, for example, raises questions about intra-household control over input subsidy entitlements; electronic systems must be able to operate in areas with no electricity, and may require reliable mobile phone network access and expensive and/or sensitive equipment).

Entitlements may be input specific (entitling the beneficiary to a particular quantity of a particular input) or flexible (allowing choice between a limited range of specified inputs). They may also be fixed value (with beneficiaries paying a top up which varies for different locations, outlets or inputs) or associated with a fixed top up (where the top up paid by the beneficiary is constant but the redemption value to the retail outlet varies). There are important interactions between types of vouchers, secondary markets, recipient choice (of inputs and suppliers), control of fraud and of programme costs, and gendered access to and control of subsidized inputs within households.

2.6.3. Programme exits and graduation

As discussed earlier, a major criticism of input subsidies has been that for a variety of reasons they tend to continue as expensive and ineffective programmes long after their initial economic and developmental justification has become irrelevant. Consequently an important feature of 'smart' subsidies has been an 'exit strategy' (Morris et al., 2007) or 'exit options' (World Bank, 2007b). This should involve a clear understanding of the market failures that the subsidy is intended to overcome and hence of the structural changes it is intended to promote—with regard, for example, to farmers' knowledge of input use and its benefits, wider thickening of markets, soil fertility, input supply system development, input profitability, and/or input affordability. Such understanding should lead to the design of criteria and processes for 'exits' or, to use a more nuanced term, 'graduation' from the use of subsidies in promoting farmers' access to inputs to reliance on other, generally market-based, systems and processes. Graduation processes and criteria will need to consider interactions between the objectives of a programme, the particular constraints it is attempting to address, available resources, and the needs and situations of different targeting groups. We discuss this in more detail in Chapter 11.

2.7. Conditions affecting effectiveness

An effective input subsidy needs design and implementation that ensure (a) that input subsidies reach and are used by beneficiaries that would not otherwise use these inputs, and (b) that they are used efficiently and effectively to increase crop production. The design features of targeting, rationing, and entitlement and distribution systems discussed above are intended to promote (a) and, less directly, (b). We now consider three other issues affecting the reach, use, and productivity of input subsidies.

2.7.1. Leakages and secondary markets

Leakages were discussed earlier in terms of cross-crop, cross-farmer, and cross-border leakages. These are associated with the development of secondary markets where subsidy recipients sell their inputs (or input entitlements) to others, at prices normally discounted against unsubsidized inputs. Such markets may arise with targeted and rationed subsidies as a result of differences between subsidy recipients and non-recipients in access to and needs for working capital (with poorer, capital-constrained farmers selling inputs to less poor farmers) and/or differences in perceived marginal benefits to input use (with farmers with more land, for example, requiring larger quantities of inputs).

It is often argued that secondary markets should not be impeded because (a) farmers generally know what is best for them and (b) attempts to limit secondary markets generally lead to (poorer) sellers of inputs into these markets getting lower prices to the benefit of (less-poor) buyers and middlemen who capture a large share of subsidy benefits. Such arguments lead to a common related question: would it be better to give poor producers cash rather than an input subsidy and let them choose what to do with the money? This is important in the context of social protection and welfare policies' increasing use of cash transfers to avoid the inefficiencies and leakages common in subsidy administration and secondary markets.

There are, however, significant arguments that both the provision of cash transfers and widespread secondary markets fundamentally undermine input subsidy programmes' wider benefits. At the heart of arguments for input subsidies are information and market failures and externalities, all of which cause individual optimizing farmers to make decisions that are sub-optimal or inefficient in meeting the goals of wider society. A well designed and effectively implemented input subsidy programme can address four interacting sets of information and market failure and externality problems together:

- Farmers' under-valuation of the benefits of input use to themselves as individuals and to society, as a result of inadequate information on the effects of inputs when properly used and on efficient ways to use them—an information failure.

- Poorer farmers' inability to obtain seasonal working and consumption capital, or ability to obtain it only at much higher cost than the social opportunity cost of such capital—a credit market failure.

- Farmers not benefiting directly from economies of scale when increased input volumes reduce input supply costs and margins—a 'non-pecuniary' externality that arises from increasing returns to scale.

- Farmers not benefiting directly from lower output prices and consequent dynamic pro-poor growth effects of subsidies which raise staple food production and productivity—a 'pecuniary externality'.

If cash transfers replace input subsidies, or secondary markets are encouraged, then welfare transfers can be delivered more efficiently to subsidy beneficiaries (subsidy recipients and/or staple food consumers) but cash transfers are unlikely to be able to address as efficiently at least three of the four information and market failure and externality problems described above.[8] Policy choices between cash transfers and input subsidies with or without constraints on secondary market operation therefore need to take account of specific policy objectives; of the nature of the informational, market, externality, and distributional problems that need to be addressed; and of alternative instruments and combinations of complementary instruments that may be used (Filipski and Taylor, 2011).

This discussion of the role of subsidies in addressing information and market failures and externalities has important implications not only for thinking and policies on secondary markets but also on farmer choice within subsidy programmes. It is sometimes argued that voucher systems

---

[8] One would expect cash transfers to address seasonal credit market failures, but Gregory (2006) and Dorward (2006) suggest that this may not be the case as transfers as input subsidies rather than cash may help with 'enforced savings' as money savings are too fungible. Observations by Duflo et al. (2011) regarding poor Kenyan farmers' changing willingness or ability to invest in fertilizer purchase suggests further behavioural reasons for in-kind rather than cash transfers.

can and should be used to extend farmer choice, with fixed value vouchers being redeemable for different inputs which farmers may choose between. This empowers farmers, and allows them to use the subsidy to invest in inputs that they consider will make the largest contribution to their livelihoods. The effectiveness with which subsidies address information and market failures and externalities may, however, require some restrictions on farmer choice, to ensure that their choices align with wider social efficiency objectives.[9]

2.7.2. Subsistence production and net deficit producers

Our discussion of input subsidy impacts on output supply and stakeholder welfare has considered separately the subsidy impacts on output producers and consumers, linking them through market prices. This analysis is, of course, highly stylized. While there is evidence that many staple food markets in southern and eastern Africa are reasonably well integrated (Abdulai, 2007), they also tend to be characterized by high margins that inhibit exchange and incentives for surplus production (Barrett, 2008). This, together with variable staple food prices and limited off-farm income opportunities, leads to substantial subsistence production and very large numbers of African farmers who are poor deficit staple food producers and net staple food buyers (Barrett, 2008). Such farmers are both producers who can utilize an input subsidy and consumers who benefit from lower food prices.

Dorward (2009b) examines subsidy impacts on supply and demand within households and their impact on maize sales and purchases. He shows that the impacts of a subsidy on farmers will differ with the initial situation of the household as autarchic or a net buyer or seller, household composition (consumers and workers), and access to land and capital. Subsidy impacts in production and consumption by many households will not be fully reflected by changes in quantities bought and sold in food markets, and this may dampen market effects of subsidies when measured in absolute terms. However, the significant quantities of produce that are consumed within farm households without ever reaching markets also means that produce markets may be very thin, so that small percentage changes in production can lead to very large percentage changes in market supply and demand, making markets very unstable. This can be important for understanding the food market impacts

---

[9] This discussion is also relevant to suggestions that it is 'theoretically optimal' to address market failures directly, not through input subsidies, for example by providing credit services to poor farmers' production of staple foods, as argued, for example, by Wiggins and Brooks (2012). Such arguments ignore both the arguments made here about input subsidies' ability to address multiple market failures and the very great difficulties with, and lack of examples of, successful experience in providing credit services to poor farmers' production of staple foods (Dorward et al., 2008).

of input subsidies (and indeed of any policy or natural events that affect smallholder production).

2.7.3. *Complementary integration, investments and policies*

Positive impacts from input subsidies are determined by the on-farm physical productivity of inputs; by input supply system efficiency, transport and communication systems and costs; and by output market efficiency—as well as by the effectiveness and efficiency of implementation of the subsidy programme itself. Programme impacts can therefore often be enhanced by complementary investments in agricultural research and extension that can raise input productivity; by subsidies for complementary inputs (for example, seeds *and* fertilizers); and by investments in road, communications, and market infrastructure and service development. Changes in power relations—for example, in men's and women's responsibilities and control of resources—may also have critical impacts on input access and use and on direct and indirect impacts. Programme effectiveness and efficiency can also be improved by designing and implementing subsidy and other policy instruments in ways that are complementary (for example, cash transfer or cash for work programmes may be linked to subsidy entitlement systems to facilitate participation by and benefit for very poor producers; more gender aware entitlement and access systems may increase input uptake and efficiency; or subsidy entitlements may be linked to and incentivize investments in soil and water conservation). Complementary development of staple food markets is an area of complementary policy that is particularly important given the way that major subsidy benefits involve consumers' accessing food at lower prices.

2.8. Rethinking input subsidies: a conceptual framework

We now build on the integration of conventional and newer thinking in this chapter to identify key issues that need to be considered in designing, implementing, and evaluating agricultural input subsidy programmes.

The 'success' of an input subsidy programme has to be judged against the objectives of that programme. As we have seen, input subsidy programmes can and do have a wide range of different possible objectives. Most of these objectives are mutually complementary but there may be incompatibilities between some objectives (for example, there are some trade-offs between consumer and producer objectives, and between efficiency objectives and some rents—even allowing for some rents being necessary for political economy purposes to allow a subsidy to be implemented). It is also important to note that stated formal programme objectives may differ from the objectives of individual stakeholders. The balance of programme objectives should then determine the key design and implementation elements of input subsidy programmes—their focus and scale, the inputs to be subsidized, targeting and rationing systems, procurement and delivery systems, private and public sector roles, entitlement systems, graduation systems, and complementary policies and investments.

These elements have all been discussed explicitly or implicitly in earlier sections. They have suggested that input subsidies will generally (but not always) yield the greatest social and economic returns where they

- focus on consumer benefits and on indirect gains to pro-poor economic growth from increased food staple productivity;
- operate at a large enough scale (in terms of the number of beneficiaries, the subsidy per beneficiary and the total subsidized volumes) to lower staple produce prices and/or raise the productivity of substantial amounts of land and labour;
- have rationing and targeting criteria and methods with entitlement and distribution systems which direct subsidized inputs to producers whose productive input use is constrained by market failures which can be overcome or substantially reduced through the subsidy; and
- include graduation processes and criteria which encourage the achievement of structural changes which then allow the scaling down and phasing out of subsidies.

Rationing and targeting will normally be best achieved by various forms of voucher systems which enable cost-effective and timely input distribution, which support sustainable unsubsidized (commercial) input supply system development, and which limit secondary market development and leakages. Effective implementation of these various elements will normally require coordinated complementary investments and policies supporting infrastructural development, agricultural research and development, and efficient output markets offering lower and more stable staple prices to consumers.

However, as should also be clear from these sections, these elements are also highly inter-related, with many synergies and trade-offs. These interactions are most easily identified around the themes of scale and scope: large-scale subsidy programmes offer wider supply-side benefits (in input supply system development, in consumer and dynamic pro-poor growth impacts) but make effective, timely, and efficient programme management more difficult and can crowd out complementary investments needed for higher productivity of input use. Different entitlement, targeting, and rationing systems are effectively attempts to control the scale of subsidy programmes by directing limited resources to their most productive uses—but these are themselves often

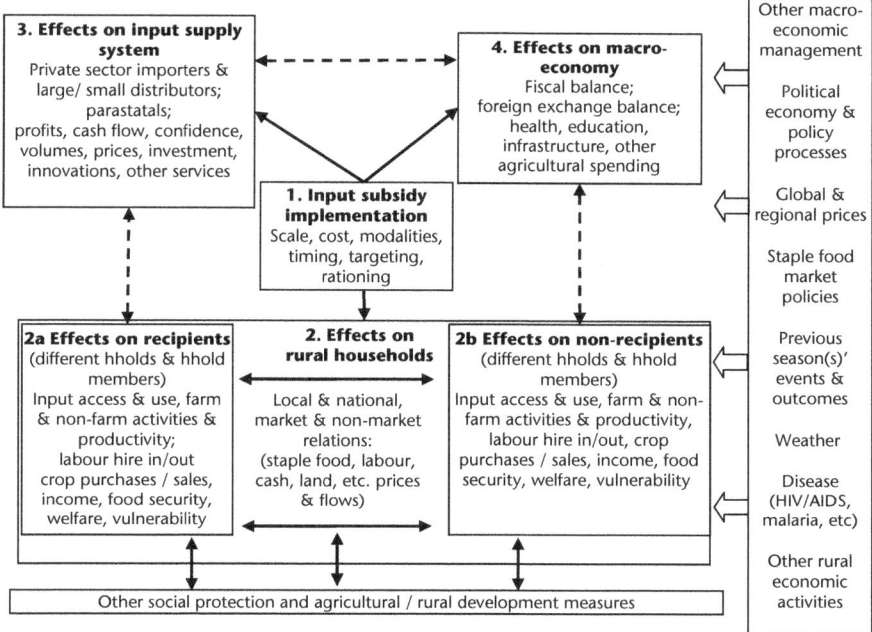

Figure 2.2. A conceptual framework for investigating agricultural input subsidies' impacts (adapted from School of Oriental and African Studies et al., 2008)

difficult and costly to implement. Indeed there is something of a paradox here, that it is in the application of targeted subsidies to input use on staple foods in poor rural areas that such subsidies both offer the greatest potential benefits and pose the greatest implementation, resourcing and coordination challenges (Dorward et al., 2009).

Figure 2.2 provides a conceptual framework that draws on the analysis and issues addressed in this chapter to identify the key variables and relationships affecting input subsidy programme impacts. It details how implementation (and its various elements) impact directly on rural households, input supply systems, and the macro-economy. Impacts on rural households can be separated into direct impacts on subsidy recipients or beneficiaries and indirect impacts on other households through the effects on the rural economy of changes in beneficiary behaviour and market activities. Direct and indirect rural economy effects, input supply system effects, and macro-economic effects all interact with and affect each other, and are also affected by and may affect other policies and processes. The figure may most easily be interpreted as an examination of short-term (say annual) effects, but longer term impacts will also arise, and may be conceptualized with a similar framework.

Table 2.2. Critical aspects of input subsidy programmes

A	Design & implementation
A.1	Basic subsidy system (objectives, focus on consumer or producer benefits, direct recipients)
A.2	Product focus—staple foods, cash crops, etc.
A.3	Input specification
A.4	Scale—beneficiary coverage
A.5	Subsidy per beneficiary
A.6	Total volumes subsidized
A.7	Procurement systems
A.8	Voucher or other entitlement systems, distribution & input access systems & timing
A.9	Rationing—objectives, methods
A.10	Targeting—objectives, criteria & methods
A.11	Input supply systems (involvement of parastatal & /or private importers & wholesale & retail suppliers) & timing
A.12	Secondary market & leakage policies (& enforcement mechanisms)
A.13	Complementary integration & investments & policies
A.14	Timing of all activities
A.15	Private & public sector incentives, resources, roles & responsibilities
A.16	Resource allocation & mobilization (finance, personnel, transport, etc.)
A.17	Auditing systems
A.18	Consistency, adaptation across areas, years
A.19	Graduation objectives, criteria, processes, etc.
B	**Outputs**
B.1	Subsidized input deliveries & receipts– quantities, locations, timing, target groups
B.2	Subsidy imports & disbursement by private sector suppliers, by type & location
C	**Outcomes**
C.1	Incremental input use
C.2	Input leakage, displacement, diversion
C.3	Incremental production
C.4	Increased productivity
D	**Impacts (short & long term)**
D.1	Output price changes (producer & consumer prices)
D.2	Input price changes
D.3	Labour market changes (hired labour demand, wages)
D.4	National/household food self sufficiency/security
D.5	Input supply system
D.6	Other market changes
D.7	Rents (supplier, producer, administrative, political)
D.8	Programme benefit–cost analysis (fiscal, economic)
D.9	Opportunity costs of programme
D.10	Macro-economic effects
D.11	Welfare & growth impacts
D.12	Wider (pro-poor) economic growth
D.13	Consumer benefits—lower output prices, access (emphasis on poorer consumers?)
D.14	Producer welfare (emphasis on poorer producers?)
D.15	Input supply system development & efficiency
D.16	Soil fertility replenishment
D.17	Sustained input adoption
D.18	Sustained input use efficiency
D.19	Soil fertility management

This framework, along with the previous discussion, helps to identify critical aspects of subsidy programmes. These are summarized in Table 2.2. The distinctions between design and implementation, outputs, outcomes, and short- and long-term impacts should not be taken as at all precise. Design and implementation must of course take into account short- and long-term objectives and the intended logical framework linking implementation to desired outputs, outcomes, and impacts. Similarly, separations between outputs and outcomes, between outcomes and impacts, and between short- and long-term impacts are by no means clear. Nevertheless, this provides a helpful guide to the gradation between on the one hand long-term impact objectives which are influenced but not controlled by programme design and implementation, and on the other hand short-term output and (to a lesser extent) outcome objectives which are directly controlled by and the responsibility of programme designers and implementers—as a direct result of their design and implementation decisions and actions.

Figure 2.2 and Table 2.2 together set out the key issues that are examined in the remainder of this book, as we consider the recent record of agricultural input subsidies in other countries in Africa (in Chapter 3) and in Malawi in Chapters 4 to 12. They also underpin the analytical framework set out in Part II for examining the Malawi subsidy programme's implementation and impacts.

3

Recent African experience with input subsidies

3.1. Introduction

Having considered key features of input subsidy programmes and a conceptual framework of their impacts in the previous chapter, we now turn to examine experience with the implementation of recent, large-scale initiatives in poorer agrarian economies. This leads to an emphasis on programmes in Africa. As noted in Chapter 2, there has been resurgent interest in input subsidies, in particular 'smart subsidies' for fertilizers in Africa. Unfortunately there are few detailed and rigorous evaluations of most of these programmes. In this chapter we review African programmes for which there is new information since an earlier review by Dorward (2009b)—but we explicitly exclude any discussion of the Malawi experience from 2005/6. In subsequent chapters we will, however, where appropriate compare Malawi's post-2005 experience with observations from this review. This review does not cover all large-scale subsidy programmes in sub-Saharan Africa since 2005, only those for which some information is available. Thus, there is no review on achievements under Kenya's National Accelerated Agricultural Input Programme (NAAIP), planned for implementation from 2008 (Dorward, 2009b). Similarly, there is very little information available on programmes in Mali and Senegal (Kelly et al., 2011) and these are therefore considered together. A number of authors comment on the lack of systematic and good quality information on subsidy programmes in Africa (Dorward, 2009b; Morris et al., 2009; Kelly et al., 2011; Druilhe and Barreiro-Hurlé, 2012).

We summarize here observations from an examination of nine fertilizer subsidy programmes in Africa selected on the basis of (a) availability of information and (b) relevance to our review of large-scale subsidy programmes aimed at boosting input use in staple crop production. We first briefly describe the main elements of each programme's history before considering what they can teach us regarding general patterns of subsidy programme objectives, design, implementation, and impacts.

3.2. Ghana[1]

In early 2008 Ghana faced high food prices and rising fertilizer prices and the government and large fertilizer importers (who had significant but high priced fertilizer stocks) discussed the potential and possible modalities for a national fertilizer subsidy programme. Press reports (Ghana News Agency, 9 June 2008, 3 July 2008) indicate that the programme was formally announced in June 2008 and operated from July to December. A total of 30,000 tons of four types of fertilizer was made available by three major importers, with pan-territorial farmer prices representing an approximate 50% subsidy, keeping farmer prices similar to the previous years', in the context of rising international prices, at a total cost of around US$15 million.[2] Large numbers of vouchers (over 1 million) were printed against planned subsidy sales of 600,000 bags. Deliveries were late for the cropping season in the south of the country (April to July), but were more timely for the north, and this may account for lower uptake and fertilizer sales in the south and use on a wider range of minor crops as compared with the north where there was more substantial uptake and use mainly on maize.

Vouchers were distributed by Ministry of Agriculture staff for redemption by distributors linked to the major fertilizer importers. There was wide variation in voucher distribution approaches, systems, and numbers across different areas, and limited information to field level staff on the total number of vouchers that they would receive for distribution. Redemption prices varied geographically to provide pan-territorial farmer prices in district capitals, but this tended to discourage suppliers from supplying fertilizers outside district capitals as neither redemption nor farmer prices covered costs of transport outside district capitals. No subsidy sales were made by (smaller) distributors independent of the major fertilizer importers (indeed in the north unsubsidized sales were reported to be banned completely) and the programme may have reduced competition and depressed sales and revenues for smaller retailers closest to farmers in rural areas. It may also have strengthened the position of importers participating in the programme (who gained from increased sales of previously imported stocks) at the expense of others. It was

---

[1] Information on the Ghana 2008 fertilizer subsidy programme is obtained from Banful (2009, 2011); Krausova and Banful (2010); Yawson et al. (2010).
[2] Total budgeted subsidy cost was $25 million but only about $15 million was directly for the subsidy inputs and voucher costs (personal communication, Afua Branoah Banful).

also widely believed that sales without vouchers were illegal. Banful (2011) reports that both political and economic efficiency considerations appear to have influenced distribution of vouchers between districts. Receipt of vouchers by farmers is reported to be associated with access to distribution points, reliance on agricultural income, hiring of labour, wealth, and years farming (Vondolia et al., 2012). There is less specific and detailed information about subsequent programmes, which appear to have operated in a similar way. However, the scale of the programme had doubled by 2011—when 150,000 tons were subsidized at a cost of US$70 million and a 50% subsidy rate— and there are continuing concerns over late implementation (Ghana News Agency, 2012; Alassan, 2012).

3.3. Zambia Fertilizer Support Programme and Food Security Pack

We consider two input subsidy programmes in Zambia, the Food Security Pack and the Fertilizer Support Programme, both confusingly known as FSP.

The Food Security Pack as reviewed by Ellis (2007) has a number of differences in design from other programmes reviewed in this chapter, but displays many similarities in its actual operation.[3] It was developed and has consistently been considered more as a social transfer programme than an input subsidy programme, aimed at 'vulnerable but viable' farming households, but attempting to address a cause of vulnerability: lack of access to productive inputs. Its main objectives have been to provide basic inputs to vulnerable households with some land and labour, but also to promote crop diversification and conservation farming. Its primarily social welfare objectives led to its implementation by a national NGO coordinating a network of district NGOs under the direction of the Ministry of Community Development and Social Services, with technical support from the Ministry of Agriculture and a domestically funded budget line from the Ministry of Finance and National Planning.

The first year of operation of the Food Security Pack was 2000/1, and it was intended to reach 200,000 households per year for three years. It has in fact operated for a much longer period on a much smaller scale as regards the number of beneficiaries served, but has been thinly spread across all 72 districts in Zambia. Budgetary provision, beneficiaries reached, and input packs have varied widely across the years (Ellis, 2007; Kodamaya, 2011), as has the composition of input packs. These were supposed to contain inputs for 0.25

---

[3] Information on the Food Security Pack is from Ellis (2007) unless another source is specifically cited.

ha of cereal (maize) production, for 0.25 ha of cassava or sweet potato production, and for 0.25 ha of legume production. Packs are provided free, but after the first couple of years the programme farmers are expected to repay 50% of the value in kind after harvest with the proceeds partly stored food security and partly sold to finance public works (Jorgensen and Loudjeva, 2005).

There have been particular difficulties with the sourcing of inputs for root crops and legumes, and in 2005/6 for example, only maize inputs were provided. Funding has often been inadequate, unpredictable, and late, and thus reached a smaller than budgeted number of beneficiaries with common late delivery of inputs. The small numbers of beneficiaries in each district have often been concentrated in small geographical areas for logistical reasons. Within these areas, targeting by local committees has been affected by local elite capture and also by widespread splitting and sharing of packs. Beneficiary selection was supposed to use primary targeting criteria focused on land-operating but land-poor households with unemployed labour, together with secondary criteria focused on favouring particular vulnerable groups (for example, households of the elderly, disabled, orphaned or unemployed youth members). However, Jayne et al. (2006) report that in 2002/3 beneficiaries under the Food Security Pack had average per capita incomes of less than half of those of beneficiaries of the Fertilizer Support Programme discussed below. There is, however, very little information available on the programme's impacts.

Turning now to consider the much larger Fertilizer Support Programme, this was initiated in 2002 as the successor to a long history of fertilizer subsidies and alongside the smaller and socially targeted Food Security Pack discussed above. Since that time the programme has grown and evolved: from 2002/3 to 2009/10 beneficiaries rose from 120,000 to 500,000 farmers, subsidized inputs rose from 48,000 to 180,000 tons of fertilizer and from 2000 tons to nearly 9000 tons of maize seed, and the subsidy rose from 50% to 75% of input costs (Ministry of Agriculture and Cooperatives, 2011). However, the same basic approach has been maintained, with fertilizer imports by private companies under government tender with distribution to farmers through cooperative societies. Our review draws on a number of studies which have examined different aspects of the programme over time.

Minde et al. (2008) report that the objectives of the programme have changed over time with it being intended at first to assist smallholders accessing inputs in remote areas which it was thought were not served by private traders. However, private sector market and service expansion, in these areas particularly, has also been stressed, with reduced government involvement in input supply. Thus, the Ministry of Agriculture and Cooperatives (2011) lists the 2011/12 programme overall objectives as 'to increase private sector participation in the supply of agricultural inputs to small-scale farmers and contribute to increased household food security and income' with specific objectives to expand private sector input markets and involvement, reduce government involvement, ensure timely and effective supply to targeted farmers, improve these farmers' access to inputs, promote competitiveness and transparency in input supply and distribution, reduce risks in farmers' inputs use, and promote rural institutional development. However, the Zambia Agricultural Consultative Forum (2009) proposed that the overall objective of the programme should be 'to increase small scale farmers' productivity in order to contribute to improved household and national household food security' (p. 14) with (as above) specific objectives to improve small-scale farmers' access to inputs with increased participation of the private sector, an expanded agro-dealer network, and timely, effective, and adequate input supply.

These multiple objectives lead to a number of different criteria by which the programme is judged. As regards private expansion, there are persistent criticisms that the programme has discouraged (or at best had mixed effects on) private trader participation due to the restricted number of companies supplying fertilizers, and unpredictable location, timing, and composition of subsidy supplies leading to uncertainty over commercial demand (for example, Jorgensen and Loudjeva, 2005; World Bank, 2010b). This is associated with concerns that there has been significant leakage of supplies from the subsidy supply chain into the commercial supply chain (Muleba, 2008; Minde et al., 2008; World Bank, 2010b; Mason, 2011) and displacement of unsubsidized sales by subsidized sales to larger farms in less remote areas where the bulk of supplies have gone (Minde et al., 2008; Xu et al., 2009a; Mason, 2011; Jayne et al., 2011).

Displacement and targeting, and widespread reports of late input delivery, also affect the programme's effectiveness in raising maize production and in improving the food security and livelihoods of poorer farmers, and again this is the subject of concern in a number of studies (Civil Society for Poverty Reduction, 2005; Jorgensen and Loudjeva, 2005; Minde et al., 2008; Zambia Agricultural Consultative Forum, 2009; World Bank, 2010b; Mason and Ricker-Gilbert, 2012). While these issues reduce the effectiveness of the programme in raising maize production, the programme's impact on increased maize production is recognized, though these increases may be smaller than the effects of good rainfall and smaller than official estimates of the programme's benefits (Minde et al., 2008; World Bank, 2010b; Mason et al., 2011). There are, however, also concerns that yield responses are limited by soil acidity and other complementary investments are needed for fertilizer subsidies to be effective (Burke et al., 2012).

There are also concerns that the programme's emphasis on maize has discouraged production of other crops such as sorghum and cassava (Haantuba et al., 2011). Coupled with these are wider concerns about poor monitoring and evaluation, expansion of the programme as regards both volume of subsidized inputs and the subsidy rate despite initial intentions to scale both back, annual budget over-runs and consequent growing programme cost—averaging nearly 40% of the Ministry of Agriculture's budget from 2002 to 2009 (Civil Society for Poverty Reduction, 2005; Jorgensen and Loudjeva, 2005; Zambia Agricultural Consultative Forum, 2009; World Bank, 2010b). Nevertheless, the programme is estimated to yield an economic cost—benefit ratio that is greater than 1 (Jayne et al., 2007) but a large number of studies comment that it is crowding out alternative and higher return investments in longer term research or infrastructural programmes (Jorgensen and Loudjeva, 2005; Jayne et al., 2007; Minde et al., 2008; Bigsten and Tengstam, 2008; Govereh et al., 2009; Xu et al., 2009a).

3.4. Nigeria

Nigeria has implemented large-scale fertilizer subsidies since the 1970s with the broad objective of promoting agricultural productivity and, latterly at least, improving food security by making fertilizers more affordable and accessible to smallholder farmers. Subsidies have been marked by wide variation in rates and modalities over time, accompanied by substantial differences between states (Akande et al., 2011). There is, however, general consistency in a very active role of the state in fertilizer delivery and widespread reports of high diversion of fertilizer, such that smallholder farmers receive only 30% of subsidized fertilizers at subsidized prices (Nagy and Edun (2002) cited by Liverpool-Tasie et al. (2010b), Banful and Olayide (2010)), with generally late delivery of subsidized fertilizers and frequent reports of concerns about quality (Nagy and Edun (2002) cited by Liverpool-Tasie et al. (2010b), Kiger and Adodo (2010), Banful and Olayide (2010)). There is, however, very little information on the impacts of subsidies in terms of increased fertilizer use, production, food security, or poverty reduction (Mogues et al., 2008). Banful and Olayide (2010) and Banful et al. (2010) report that farmers and stakeholders consider unavailability of fertilizers, late delivery, and poor quality to be much greater constraints to fertilizer use by farmers than its expense (although access to credit is also cited as a major constraint (Banful and Olayide, 2010)). Liverpool-Tasie et al. (2010b) therefore recommend that much more emphasis should be given to stable policies that encourage the development of private sector suppliers. One approach to this is the use of fertilizer vouchers to deliver subsidies. Small pilots of this approach were championed by IFDC from 2004 (Gregory, 2006) and judged to be successful in demonstrating that a voucher-based system could improve farmer access

51

to fertilizers if implemented with the private sector. Progressively larger pilots were implemented, with large programmes in two states in 2009 and 2010 reaching 194,000 and 171,000 farmers respectively with sales of 29,800 and 16,397MT (Kiger and Adodo, 2010). Kiger and Adodo (2010) report that the programme has been very successful in improving farmers' access to sub-sidized fertilizers, in reducing leakages, and in demonstrating and building private capacity in fertilizer supply, while recognizing continuing but sur-mountable challenges facing the programme. There is, however, no informa-tion on programme impacts in terms of increased fertilizer use, production, or food security, and a survey by Liverpool-Tasie et al. (2010a) find that farmers still reported late delivery and poor fertilizer quality. Their study also raises questions about beneficiary targeting—criteria seem to be very broad, with voucher distribution to members of farming or other groups, and there was some evidence of multiple receipt within households, but recipients tended to be poorer than non-recipients (Liverpool-Tasie, 2012). In this context, and with over 70% of farmers outside the subsidy programme buying fertilizer in the private market, Liverpool-Tasie (2012) do not find evidence that subsidy receipt depresses the probability of farmers buying unsubsidized fertilizer, and indeed find that for subsidy recipients who are buying unsubsidized fer-tilizers there is a significant crowding in effect, with receipt of a bag of sub-sidized fertilizer increasing unsubsidized purchases by 0.8 of a bag. This is attributed to the subsidy programme encouraging the establishment of a bet-ter private distribution network. Overall, there seems to be little doubt that the programme is a substantial improvement over the standard programmes being administered by the Federal and State governments.

3.5. Tanzania

Like many countries in Africa, Tanzania has implemented a variety of input subsidy programmes over the years. Following the withdrawal of subsidies in the 1990s, fertilizer transport subsidies were introduced in 2003 with the objective of facilitating fertilizer use in remote areas (Minot, 2009). The pro-gramme subsidized transport costs and fixed margins and prices for farm-ers, with government management of stocks and transport. Although this appeared to lead to some increases in fertilizer use, there were problems with the heavy involvement of government in managing distribution, late fer-tilizer delivery due to budgetary processes, ineffective price controls, and leakage from target beneficiaries (to local unsubsidized markets and also to neighbouring countries), with the latter problems associated with lack of skill and financial capacity among agro-dealers (Minot, 2009; World Bank, 2009).

In view of these problems, the government started piloting a 'smart sub-sidy' programme from 2007. This grew into the National Agricultural Input Voucher Scheme (NAIVS), with increasing pilots in 2008 and the develop-ment of a very large programme with World Bank support implemented from 2009 to 2012 (World Bank, 2009).

The objectives of the NAIVS are to facilitate fertilizer use in high-potential areas, to offset rising international fertilizer costs, to reduce food prices by stimulating production, and to stimulate expansion and increased capacity in the private input supply system. The main features of the programme, summarized by Minot (2009), include the use of vouchers for food crop inputs (fertilizer and maize and rice seed) and distribution to targeted ben-eficiaries with complementary support to help them improve the efficiency of input use and to expand input suppliers' financial and skills capacity. The programme is also intended to first of all scale-up and then scale-down, with a maximum of three years access by each beneficiary and termination in 2012 (although extension of the programme to other regions is under considera-tion). Vouchers, covering 50% of full input prices, are redeemed by farmers at agro-dealers who then redeem them through the large branch network of the National Microfinance Bank. Vouchers and inputs are targeted to high-poten-tial regions according to the number of maize and rice farmers per region and then targeted to full-time resident maize or rice farmers with less than one ha and the ability to part finance input purchases. Among eligible farmers, priority should be given to female-headed households and those not using improved inputs in the previous five years.

It has not been possible to source evaluation studies of the programme since 2010, but the World Bank (2009) identifies benefits and challenges from the pilot programmes. Major benefits of the targeted subsidy mechanisms over the previous transport subsidy include easier monitoring of input distribution and impacts, wider coverage and improved input affordability for farmers, and mutually beneficial links and strengthened relations with and between the National Microfinance Bank and agro-dealers. There are, however, also challenges identified from the NAIVS 2008/9 pilot where there was a need for more human and financial field resources for implementation and technical support (for the Government and National Microfinance Bank), there were insufficient inputs for all eligible farmers and late delivery of inputs to farm-ers, there were late bank payments to agro-dealers and late government pay-ments to the bank, and agro-dealers lacked sufficient working capital. Minot (2009) commends the programme design for its targeting approach and use of vouchers, intention to scale-down after 2012, and complementary support to the fertilizer subsidy (in terms of a public awareness campaign, capacity building and certification for agro-dealers, seed sector support, an emphasis on integrated soil fertility management, and investment in monitoring and evaluation). However he also questions whether it will be politically feasible to scale the programme down after 2012, and if the targeting will be effective.

Pan and Christiaensen (2012) and Patel (2011) report household survey findings in 2008 and 2009 that provide some insights into the targeting and timing of input delivery. In a sample survey in the Kilimanjaro district, Pan and Christiaensen (2012) report some difficulties with targeting in 2008. The major observation is that there are conflicts between potential targeting objectives, with an emphasis on economic efficiency in increasing production requiring targeting outcomes that favour those households with the highest marginal return to fertilizer use on fertilizer that they would not have used without subsidy receipt. These may not be the same households as those that should be targeted to reduce poverty and inequity. However, examination of actual targeting outcomes shows that elected village officials received about 60% of the distributed vouchers, and this 'substantially reduces the targeting performance...At the margin, village elected officials are usually not the more efficient input users' (Pan and Christiaensen, 2012: p. 1627).

Patel (2011) finds that cost was the most commonly cited reason for farmers not using improved inputs (cited by 69% of households not using seeds, and by 36% of households not using fertilizers), but lack of awareness was also a significant impediment. Lack of fertilizer availability was cited as problem by only 6% of farmers. They also find that the targeting criteria were not consistently followed but do not suggest that vouchers are going to the wrong farmers—contrary to Pan and Christiaensen (2012) they find no evidence of elite capture. While beneficiaries tended to be wealthier than non-beneficiaries, they note that the programme is not intended to be a pro-poor programme and targets 'middle-level farmers' most able to make good use of the inputs. They recognize, however, that this may lead to problems of displacement of unsubsidized sales. Poorer and female-headed households, which the programme also aims to prioritize, are often unable to finance the purchase cost even of the subsidized inputs. They find that in terms of programme implementation, NAIVS operations generally adhered to the guidelines, although anecdotal reports for subsequent seasons are less optimistic. However survey estimates of beneficiary coverage were much lower than indicated by MAFC's programme data, which estimate coverage above 80% in some districts. They make initial estimates of incremental production gains from input use of 147% for maize and 35% for paddy, but are not clear that this is high enough for unsubsidized input application to be profitable, raising questions about the economic returns to the programme.

As regards programme implementation, the Ministry of Agriculture Food Security and Cooperatives (2012) provides information on programme activities from 2008/9 to 2011/12: 3.5 million households are identified as eligible for voucher receipt, with actual recipients rising from 730,000 households in 2008/9 to 1.5, 2.0, and 1.8 million households respectively in the following three years. However the 2011/12 recipients excludes households who started receiving vouchers in 2008/9 and therefore 'graduated' after three years in the programme. This should give a total of some 2.5 million direct beneficiary households over the three years, each receiving three vouchers per year (two for fertilizer and one for maize or rice seed).

Activities designed to support private input supply development and more effective input use by farmers have included agro-dealer training, matching grants to guarantee agro-dealer loans from input supply companies, development of seed systems, and research and (to a lesser extent) extension on Integrated Soil Fertility Management and input use. Although some of these activities have been delayed for various reasons, significant progress has been made on others. Just under 4,000 agro-dealers have been trained and 23 agro-dealer associations formed; 2,335 agro dealers participated in the 2010/11 programme and 2,010 in 2011/12. The drop out of some agro-dealers in 2011/12 was due to discouragement from late payments in 2010/11, late delivery of the 2011/12 vouchers, phasing out of the matching grant for input supplier loans, and exclusion of a small number of agro-dealers following poor performance in 2010/11. Approximately 1,800 agro-dealers who received training did not participate in the programme in 2011/12. Some planned agro-dealer training and support activities were not implemented due to procurement process problems.

A full evaluation of the impacts of the programme on beneficiary and non-beneficiary households, on input access and use, and on the input supply system should be very informative.

3.6. Rwanda

In 2008 Rwanda responded to rapid rises in food and fertilizer prices by introducing a novel fertilizer subsidy system that involved (a) a general subsidy to fertilizers imported by the government and sold under auction to private companies obliged to sell these fertilizers at ceiling retail prices and (b) vouchers allowing farmers to buy a proportion of these at 50% of ceiling prices (Morris et al., 2009). Limited information available in 2009 suggested that both parts of the subsidy (through the ceiling price and vouchers) were broadly successful in raising productivity and in encouraging growth among private sector input suppliers (Morris et al., 2009).

3.7. Mali and Senegal

Kelly et al. (2011) and Druilhe and Barreiro-Hurlé (2012) summarize key features of programmes in Mali and Senegal, noting that in both cases information is limited due to a lack of formal monitoring and evaluation processes. The programmes started in 2008 and were largely funded from domestic resources (though in Mali donors funded just under 40% of total costs in 2008/9 and 2009/10, but a number of donors then withdrew subsequent funding due to lack of transparency and reported 'leakages'). Both programmes aimed to boost production and yields of staple food crops (for example, rice, maize, and wheat in Mali) and (in Mali) of cotton, to lower urban rice prices and to compensate farmers for high input prices. In both countries the primary objective was to promote food security, while in Mali there was an additional objective to promote exports. Programmes provided a 25 to 50% universal subsidy on fertilizers and seeds to all farmers cultivating target crops. Subsidies were provided for imports by private companies under tender and, in Mali, were administered using effectively a voucher system (a 'caution technique') through producer organizations and through agro-dealers associated with importers. In both countries fertilizer deliveries suffered from delays and importers suffered from late payments—although they benefited from growth in import volumes with, it appears, limited losses from displacement of unsubsidized sales. The lack of any apparent impact on rice prices, which remained high, calls into question both production statistics and programme benefits (Kelly et al., 2011).

3.8. Millennium Villages

The Millennium Villages Project (MVP) established integrated projects in selected villages to demonstrate the substantial changes that are possible with significant investments in health, agriculture, and community development across Africa. A major part of this is the provision of subsidized agricultural inputs (seed and fertilizer). Monitoring and evaluation systems are in place. This approach has invested in relatively small-scale, localized input subsidy programmes with much wider but generally unrealized objectives of national scaling-up.

3.9. Overall lessons

We now consider wider lessons across the eight reviewed programmes against the major issues identified in Chapter 2 as important for subsidy programme evaluation.

3.9.1. *Programme objectives*

Here, we consider how far the different possible programme objectives discussed in Chapter 2 are found in the different programmes and types of programme.

- Food security (household or national), input adoption, and producer welfare are found as objectives of all or almost all programmes (with variation as regards particular emphasis on poorer or food-insecure producers).

- Only three programmes explicitly recognize the potential for producer subsidies to benefit poor consumers, except subsistence producers. Although this is small, given the importance of consumer benefits in consideration of large-scale staple crop subsidies, it is an improvement over findings in Dorward (2009b) where none of the reviewed programmes appeared to consider consumer benefits at all. Nevertheless, there is no recognition of the potential role of subsidies in addressing the price-productivity tight rope, and only in the MVP is there a wider recognition of the potential role of subsidies in driving forward pro-poor growth: even here there is no explicit consideration of the mechanisms by which this may be achieved or of processes of structural change in the economy as a whole.[4]

- Input use efficiency and soil fertility replenishment are only explicitly considered as programme objectives in the Tanzania programmes.

- Input access and input supply system development are explicit objectives in all programmes except Mali and Senegal (and limited sources may mean that this has been overlooked), the Zambia Food Security Pack and the MVP.

- Political considerations were important for the Ghana programme and the Zambia Fertilizer Support Programme, but are not explicitly mentioned in the documentation on other programmes (though they are likely to have been important). In Nigeria the FVP's implementation is driven by an interest in depoliticizing some aspects of the existing wider Federal and state subsidy programmes, which are highly politicized.

---

[4] Other programmes may also implicitly consider that increased productivity and producer welfare may drive forward growth, but consideration of the food price, non-staple and non-farm production, and demand mechanisms is absent.

3.9.2. *Design and implementation*

As regards design and implementation features of the different programmes, there is broad commonality across the different programmes as regards

- the basic focus of subsidy systems on producers as major (and generally sole) direct subsidy beneficiaries;
- a primary focus on subsidizing inputs for staple food production (for subsistence production or for sale into domestic markets);
- very substantial subsidized input price reductions (of 50% or more for most programmes), consistent with measures to address both affordability and profitability constraints to input use;
- almost all programmes clearly rationing (or attempting to ration) the quantity of subsidized inputs to be received per household, with vouchers being a common (but not universal) means of achieving this; and
- use of private sector importers to provide basic fertilizer supplies.

There are differences across the programmes as regards

- scale, with some national programmes and others piloting potential national programmes;
- targeting, with differences as geographical targeting (in some programmes) and some programmes focusing on food-insecure/vulnerable households and others seeking to maximize production by focusing on less poor households;
- use of vouchers for targeting, rationing, and/or supply system development;
- private sector and farmer organization involvement (and nature of involvement) in distribution;
- recognition of the importance of gender awareness in targeting and entitlement and access;
- complementary policies, and their links to programme objectives; and
- graduation and exits (with the Tanzanian programme explicitly limiting farmer access to three years and with scaling-back aspirations for both the Zambian programmes, but little or no mention of exits or graduation in other programmes).

3.9.3. *Programme outcomes*

Different programme outcomes—or information gaps about particular outcomes—are closely related to the programme objectives. Thus, limited examples of subsidies leading to output (food staple) price changes and the lack of information on labour demands and markets and longer term and wider welfare and growth impacts are not surprising. Similarly, the lack of information on soil fertility replenishment is consistent with the lack of emphasis on this in programme objectives. There are, however, other similarities in outcomes that cut across differences in programme objectives, notably very common (but not universal) problems with late input delivery in subsidy programmes and common (but again not universal) leakages. Both of these are important for programme impacts, irrespective of programme objectives. There is a lack of reliable information on displacement and on production and productivity impacts, although increases in input use are reported for most programmes.

Lack of reliable information on a number of topics is associated with a paucity of programmes with monitoring and evaluation systems. Consequently, there are few estimates of economic benefits although, as will be discussed in Chapter 9, such estimates are difficult to calculate and, once calculated, often difficult to compare.

There are, of course, also substantial differences across programmes, some of these related to differences in programme objectives, as noted above. Thus, differences in reporting of input supply system impacts are related to differences in interest in these impacts. However programmes with the intention of developing supply systems may actually undermine them, if poorly designed and implemented.

3.10. Conclusions from recent experience

A number of observations from the limited programmes reviewed here warrant particular emphasis:

First, we reiterate a point made by Druilhe and Barreiro-Hurlé (2012) that the resurgence of agricultural input subsidy programmes in Africa is not a temporary phenomenon—they are attempting to address a real set of agricultural and development problems and their visibility and immediacy make them politically attractive. In this context, debates about their effectiveness and about ways to improve that effectiveness are healthy and should be welcomed. It is, however, important that such debates are based on thorough agronomic, economic, political, and administrative analysis of historic, current, and potential costs and achievements of subsidy programmes.

In this context our second observation, again supported by Druilhe and Barreiro-Hurlé (2012) is disappointing: it is notable how difficult it is to find comprehensive reviews of subsidy programmes, despite the substantial number of programmes that have been or are being implemented across Africa and the very substantial investments of public funds in these programmes.

There is a major need for country studies to document country experiences, using a comprehensive conceptual framework linking inputs, activities, outcomes, and wider impacts, as developed in the previous chapter.

Third, we note a continuing tendency for programmes to focus on production objectives and producer welfare, and to ignore the interests of consumers and the processes (and necessary conditions) for subsidy programmes to contribute to wider pro-poor economic growth. This is a critical omission, and is linked to the limited extent that the design and implementation of many programmes are integrated with complementary investments. Such integration is needed first for subsidy programmes to effectively deliver their stated objectives of incremental production, and then for them to contribute to the wider processes of pro-poor growth. Recognition of the importance of consumer price benefits and of the 'price productivity tightrope' is particularly important here. Druilhe and Barreiro-Hurlé (2012) also note the tendency to focus on producers, production objectives, and expansion of input access, and argue that there is insufficient attention paid to improved soil fertility and health, to development of private sector input supply, to complementary investments raising input productivity, to effective programme implementation (with more secure entitlement systems, better targeting, better monitoring and evaluation), and to phasing out and exits for input subsidies. However Druilhe and Barreiro-Hurlé (2012) themselves make little mention of programme benefits for consumers and for wider economic growth, and provide no discussion of farm level (as opposed to input supply) processes whereby subsidy delivery may lead to reduced need for and benefits from subsidies.

Fourth, and related to the previous two points, there appears in some programmes to be an unfortunate lack of interest in improving effectiveness and efficiency. This is evident from the limited monitoring, evaluation, and audit systems in some programmes, limited cost benefit and fiscal efficiency analysis, and limited attention to problems of late delivery, displacement, and leakage. Challenges from fiscal constraints, likely rising fertilizer prices, and the effects of climate change will make it even more important that in the future governments improve the efficiency and effectiveness of input subsidy programmes in both raising productivity and promoting wider pro-poor growth within and beyond agriculture.

Limited apparent interest in exits and graduation is also common. In the examples where this is not the case (Tanzania and Zambia) there appear to be difficulties in implementing this. This may be related to an apparent and indeed remarkable lack of attention to the question of why and how scaling back, graduation, and exit should and could occur. In the Tanzanian case, for example, farmers are to access subsidies for a maximum of three years. It is not clear how or why farmers will no long need access to the subsidy in a fourth year, but this raises important questions about the processes of change needed for this (in farmers' livelihoods and resources, in local economies, in input supply systems). Similar questions arise regarding the development of private sector input suppliers.

Two notable commonalities observed across programmes are (a) the lack or limited focus on replenishing soil fertility and (b) a strong (almost universal) prevalence of heavy subsidies (50% to 100% subsidy rates) on rationed inputs. This commonality occurs despite differences between programmes as regards first relative emphasis on improving national food security (and total input use and production) as against improving household food security (and helping food-insecure households) and second relative emphasis on supply system development. Political objectives and strong political influences on programmes are explicitly mentioned in only some of the programmes reviewed, but the scale of resources allocated to these programmes and their continued implementation suggests very strong political interest in and commitment to these programmes—even if the implications of this for programme design and implementation are not generally given very much emphasis.

When compared with the earlier review by Dorward (2009b), this review suggests that there is increased implementation of important aspects of smart subsidies, but there are still weaknesses in design and implementation, particularly late input delivery. There is also a continuing lack of emphasis on improving programme effectiveness and efficiency, limited attention to graduation processes, and inadequate attention to integration with complementary policies and programmes for improving achievements of both direct and indirect benefits of input subsidy programmes. The mixed record of input subsidies continues.

4

Malawi: political, policy, livelihoods, and market background

4.1. Introduction

This chapter sets out the background for examination of the Malawi subsidy experience in the rest of the book. We begin with some contextual information about Malawi, including a brief outline of its post-colonial history, structural characteristics, and economic and welfare indicators. This leads on to a more detailed discussion of the interactions between Malawian politics and policy. We then examine critical features of rural livelihoods and the potential impacts of input subsidies in this context.

4.2. The context

At its independence in 1964 Malawi was a small land-locked country with a population a little under 4 million largely engaged in and dependent on smallholder agriculture, with poorly developed infrastructure and little industry or mineral resources. The infrastructure and industry that was there tended to be concentrated, along with the bulk of the population, in the south and, to a lesser extent, in the centre of the country, while the north had a very low population density and very little infrastructure or industry. Cultural and historical differences between regions, however, meant that commitment to and standards of education in the north were higher than in the centre and the south.

Many long term generic features of the country have not changed much over the last 40 years or so since independence, despite major (if somewhat erratic) investments and policies to address them (see, for example, Cammack et al. (2010)). These features include high dependence on agriculture; low productivity in production of maize (the dominant staple crop which accounts for around 70% of cultivated area); lack of other exploitable natural resources; isolation and high import and export costs due to its land- locked location and poor external transport systems; poor physical infrastructure; chronic poor health, with very high infant mortality from malaria, water-borne diseases, and mal- and under-nutrition; low levels of literacy and education;[1] and broad regional differences in many of these variables. Other elements have emerged more recently as a result of development failures or wider economic, social, and natural processes. These include high population densities and small landholdings (particularly in the south), falling soil fertility, and high rates of HIV/AIDS infection, morbidity, and mortality. A further set of problems emerged from the mid 1990s due to policy and governance failures, and these include the collapse of the industrial economy due to exposure to outside competition; poor macro-economic management with large budget deficits, high interest rates, large devaluations of the Malawi Kwacha (MK), and high inflation rates; high crime rates in urban and rural areas; and weak governance.[2]

As a result, in 2004/5, Malawi was one of the poorest countries in the world, with 56% of Malawi's rural population classified as poor and 24% as ultra-poor (National Statistical Office, 2005a), a GNI per capita of around US$160, very low achievements on a range of social and economic indicators (see Table 4.1), and many people characterized by high levels of vulnerability, due to the fragility of their livelihoods, susceptibility to shocks, and large numbers of the non-poor living just above a very low poverty line (Devereux, 2006).

Understanding this depressing backdrop to the emergence of the agricultural input subsidy programme in 2005, the starting point of the programme addressed in this book, requires an understanding of agricultural and other policies in the context of wider political change in Malawi, to which we now turn.

4.3. Politics and policies

The relationship between politics and policies is best considered in relation to the periods of tenure of the three presidents of Malawi since independence: Kamuzu Banda (from 1964 to 1994), Bakili Muluzi (from 1994 to 2004), and

[1] From the mid 1990s there were major improvements in primary school enrolment and its gender balance (but not in the quality of primary education) and substantial falls in infant and under-five mortality (though these are still very high).

[2] From 2005 to 2009 there was a dramatic improvement in macro-economic management and consequent reduction of inflation and interest rates and much greater currency stability. Good weather and input subsidies also contributed to growth in food production, as will be discussed later. Macro-economic management declined, however, from 2009 to 2011.

Table 4.1. Social and economic indicators for Malawi, 1975 to 2005

		1975	1985	1995	2000	2005
Population	Population, total (millions)	5.2	7.2	10.1	11.5	12.9
	Rural population (% of total population)	92	90	87	85	88
	Rural population density (n/km² arable land)	364	368	468	465	..
Welfare	Poverty incidence (rural)					56
Health	Life expectancy at birth, total (years)	..	46	43	40	41
	Mortality rate, under-5 (per 1,000)	304	245	193	155	125
	Prevalence of HIV, total (% of pop'n ages 15–49)	..	..	..	..	14.1
Nutrition	Stunting (% children 6 to 59 months)				49	43
Education	School enrolment, primary (% gross)	..	..	..	139	122
Economy	GNI per capita, Atlas method (current US$)	130	160	160	150	160
	GDP growth (annual %)	6.1	4.6	16.7	1.6	2.8
	Inflation, consumer prices (annual %)	..	21.9	83.3	29.6	15.4
	Real interest rate (%)	..	9	-17	17	15
	Agriculture, value added (% of GDP)	37	43	30	40	35
	Industry, value added (% of GDP)	20	11	20	18	19

Table 4.1. (*continued*)

		1975	1985	1995	2000	2005
	Services, etc., value added (% of GDP)	42	35	50	43	46
Trade	Imports of goods and services (% of GDP)	46	30	48	35	52
	Food imports (% of merchandise imports)	9	8	14	10	18
Agriculture	Fertilizer consumption ('000 metric tons)	22	65	196	167	292
	Irrigated land (% of cropland)	0.93	0.97	1.50	2.46	..
	Maize growers (% agricultural households)					97

Sources: From National Statistical Office and ORC Macro (2001); National Statistical Office (2005a); Imperial College et al. (2007); World Bank (2007a).

Bingu wa Mutharika (from 2004 until his death in 2012). These three periods can be examined in terms of neo-patrimonialism where politics is centred around the president who uses the power and resources of the state to dispense patronage to sustain political power (Booth et al., 2006) and, following Cammack et al. (2010), in terms of three features of government: centralization of rent utilization and time horizons (as with stationary and roving bandits (Olson, 1993)), relations of political leaders with a more or less capable technocracy, and political inclusiveness and competition. It is also helpful to explore these using a simple distinction between three different patronage client groups: the political elite, the middle classes, and the wider masses. Regional dimensions are also important in garnering the on-going support of regional elites and, in the run up to elections, of regional masses. Poulton's analysis of the relations between political and technical considerations and processes in determining agricultural policy in different contexts also provides valuable insights (Poulton, 2012).

The first president of Malawi, Hastings Banda, held the reins of power for 30 years from independence in 1964 until he was ousted in democratic elections in 1994. He presided over a highly personalized and repressive regime, taking a strong personal interest in policy and engaging closely with a capable civil service. Two phases of policy under Banda may be considered (Booth et al., 2006; Cammack et al., 2010), the first delivering quite rapid economic growth but achieving this through a set of ultimately economically and politically unsustainable policies. These focused on developing highly import-dependent estate agriculture producing tobacco, while the smallholder sector grew much more slowly (the estate sector grew from a very small base at an average of 17% per annum from 1964 to 1977, while the much larger smallholder sector grew at less than 3% per annum (Harrigan, 2003), below the population growth rate). Smallholders were restricted to cultivation of food crops and low value cash crops, while providing a low cost labour reserve for estate agriculture. Banda used the promotion of tobacco (Malawi's 'green gold') in the estate sector as an important means of dispensing political patronage to elites and a small but emerging middle class based primarily in the central and, with time, in the northern regions. Middle class support was also garnered by investments in secondary and higher education and by growth in civil service employment, while mass support rested upon large-scale visible investments in a variety of infrastructural and development projects in all regions of the country, including fertilizer and credit subsidies channelled to better off (or less poor) smallholders, and a commitment to deliver national food security. Estate and smallholder agriculture were highly regulated, with a high degree of state intervention through generally effective parastatals and government ministries. Booth et al. (2006) characterize Banda's approach in this period as 'patronage following policy'. There was little explicit attention to welfare policies in this policy phase as government and the Malawi Congress Party played down the existence of chronic poverty.

The fragility of the growth developed under these policies became apparent when the economy was hit by a number of external shocks in the early 1980s. The government was then forced to recognize the need for different policies and to seek financial assistance, with policy conditions, from the IMF and World Bank. Malawi consequently entered its second post-independence policy phase, of liberalization, coinciding with Banda's increasing fragility and a decline in his personal policy engagement. Policies then looked to increase smallholder export crop production by increasing farmgate prices while holding down maize (food) prices (Harrigan, 2003). This encouraged the substitution of smallholder maize production by cash crops which, with removal of fertilizer subsidies and unsuccessful market reforms, resulted in a food crisis in 1987, with rapid increases in maize prices. Banda's sense of responsibility in delivering food self-sufficiency to the country (and his vulnerability to growing calls for political change and the failure of an important part of his mass patronage) led to policy reversals and the re-introduction of fertilizer subsidies and government intervention in maize markets. Despite a positive maize production response to these policy changes, maize shortages continued with two severe droughts in the 1992–4 period. At the same time access to patronage from tobacco was extended to a much larger part of the middle classes, primarily in the central and northern regions, through the promotion of large numbers of small-scale tobacco estates.

Following the transition to multi-party democracy and presidential elections in 1994, Malawi's second president, Bakili Muluzi, served two terms of office, from 1994 to 2004. A major change in agricultural policy in the mid 1990s was the repeal of the Special Crops Act, which had restricted smallholder cultivation of some crops, most notably burley tobacco. The liberalization of burley tobacco production was very successful, with rapid growth in the number of smallholders growing the crop, and without (initially at least) expected declines in quality (Harrigan, 2003). However the 10 years from 1994 were characterized by severe macro-economic mismanagement, rampant inflation, dramatic falls in the value of the Malawi Kwacha, and a weakening of government capacity. Opportunistic privatization, funding diversions, and the issue of bonds to finance budget deficits became an important source of patronage for a primarily southern region elite with commercial rather than agricultural interests, so that short-term financial interests of politicians drove policy with 'policies following patronage' (Booth et al., 2006). As the real value of civil service salaries collapsed, middle class patronage involved what Booth et al. (2006) describe as the 'democratization' of corruption. With the government's political power base in the south of the country (in contrast to Banda's base in the less populous centre), and with stagnation of the economy, growing land pressure in the south, declining soil fertility, and experience of wider use of fertilizer in the early 1990s, the politics and mass patronage of maize self-sufficiency became associated with the politics of fertilizer subsidies. In 1998 the Muluzi government introduced the universal free provision of small packs of maize seed and fertilizer under the starter pack programme. This was subsequently down-scaled to the Targeted Input Programme (TIP), and considered by donors more as a social protection programme promoting food security for vulnerable households, and less as an agricultural subsidy programme. However we note here the populist political roots of this programme and the ambiguity as to its role in promoting agricultural development, social protection, and/or short-term political patronage objectives.

'Fertilizer politics' has subsequently become a major feature of Malawi. In the 2004 presidential election, in which President Bingu wa Mutharika was elected as the United Democratic Front (UDF) candidate chosen by Bakili Muluzi, both the UDF and Malawi Congress Party (MCP) (parties of the two former presidents) campaigned with promises of different forms of fertilizer subsidy. Fertilizer subsidies continued to be a major political issue in subsequent political manoeuvring associated with the President's breaking away from former president Bakili Muluzi to form his own party, the Democratic

People's Party (DPP). Without a base in parliament, where he was vulnerable to calls for impeachment by the UDF and MCP, Mutharika introduced the highly popular Agricultural Input Subsidy Programme (AISP) to garner support from the masses, over the heads of parliament. The government also appealed to middle class professional and business people through its major emphasis and success in improving macro-economic management. This led some observers to suggest that Mutharika's term would in some ways 'be closer to the Banda tradition than to Muluzi's, with patronage being subordinated to an overall vision' (Booth et al., 2006). As time went on, however, it became apparent that Mutharika also shared Banda's autocratic tendencies, and there were increasing concerns about corruption and patronage within his government. These concerns did not prevent him from winning a broad-based landslide second term election in 2009—indeed the subsidy programme not only allowed him to garner widespread support from rural beneficiaries, diversion of resources also provided him and his party with potential opportunities to capture and use substantial resources for political patronage (Chinsinga, 2012b).The subsequent substantial parliamentary majority, however, released him from his former precarious reliance on support from the middle classes and gave free rein to both his autocratic tendencies and to increasing corruption and patronage (Chinsinga, 2012b). This led to serious political and economic problems from late 2010 until his sudden death in April 2012.

Understanding agricultural policy changes in Malawi also requires an understanding of changing donor interventions (Harrigan, 2003; Chinsinga, 2006, 2007). These were very supportive of agricultural policies in the first phase of Banda's dualistic policies as described above, making very large investments in integrated rural development projects. Concerns about the problems of Malawi's dualistic and interventionist policies, as regards both economic vulnerabilities and constraints on smallholder development, then came to the fore at the same time as a wider shift in ideology to structural adjustment and the Washington Consensus. This was a major driver of the liberalization policies in Malawi as it took on structural adjustment loans in the early 1980s. Harrigan (2003) then describes a series of 'U turns' by the World Bank in agreeing to the re-introduction of fertilizer subsidies and then later insisting on their removal and opposing their re-introduction under the start pack programme. From 2000 onwards donors placed increasing emphasis on the development of policies for social protection, and these have since evolved as regards their relationship with agricultural policies (Dorward et al., 2006) with consequences for attitudes to agricultural policies. Chinsinga (2006) describes more recent differences between donors and changes in individual donor positions. These positions have been driven by domestic donor politics, economic ideology, humanitarian concerns, changes in international development thinking and practice, and personal concerns of often short-term in-country staff. Changing donor policies have been important because (a) they have suffered frequent changes and inconsistencies, and (b) they have been unduly influential as a result both of the high dependence of the Malawian economy on foreign aid and of weaknesses (particularly under Muluzi) in government capacity and commitment to articulate consistent policies (which Sahley et al. (2005) explains in terms of political processes resulting from both Malawian understandings of state responsibilities in agriculture and social protection, and clashes with donor understandings of these responsibilities).

A number of important insights emerge from this discussion. We note that the use by different presidents of different approaches to delivering patronage to client groups with different regional interests has been a core determinant of the prominence and resources given to agricultural policies and the nature of these polices. A major challenge which all three presidents faced in this was the need to deliver short-term patronage without compromising the longer term capacity of the economy to support such patronage. Thus, 'patronage policies' were critical in the promotion of agricultural policies and investment under Banda, while failures by the policies in dealing with core poverty/vulnerability and food security problems led to their demise. Conversely, the failure of 'commerce-based' patronage polices under Muluzi led to a resurgent interest in fertilizer subsidies, which Mutharika used as a major means of garnering widespread political support in his first term. The challenges faced by Mutharika in his second term are more difficult to rationalize: as will be shown later, excessive and increasing subsidy costs up to 2009 were effectively reined in after the election, and agriculture received much less political attention—although the core elements of the subsidy were maintained. This ebb and flow of political interest in agriculture has revolved around the different regional and patronage group interests in food, fertilizer, and tobacco and has at times coincided with, and at times conflicted with, a different pattern of changing interests among donors.

It is also important to note, however, that an entirely appropriate and legitimate political preoccupation with food security arises not because of populism and patronage, but because food security is an important preoccupation for poor people, whether urban or rural, who spend a large proportion of their income on staple foods and who are very vulnerable to price changes. The emphasis on fertilizer subsidies as a response to food insecurity, however, is determined by recognition that

(a) high price volatility in relation to domestic supply shocks is a result of lack of integration of national and international maize markets (due to poor international transport links, and also foreign exchange constraints);

69

(b) the majority of poor food-insecure people and of the electorate, particularly in the south, are rural deficit producers facing particular constraints in accessing fertilizers;

(c) less-poor rural people also face difficulties in accessing fertilizer but have an interest in fertilizer access for the production of food and non-food cash crops;

(d) most urban people have strong links with rural people and rural interests; and

(e) widespread understandings among the Malawian population that fertilizers are critical to food security, that this is dependent on food self-sufficiency, and that the government has an active responsibility in ensuring food self-sufficiency and hence in enabling widespread fertilizer access.

Key to the importance of fertilizers in the food security narrative, therefore, is an understanding of severe market failures affecting rural livelihoods, an understanding which has been shared by Malawian politicians and technocrats—but less often by donors (Sahley et al. (2005) note a related divergence between donors and Malawians regarding the role of the state in maize and fertilizer provision). This difference in understanding of market failures has been an important reason for government/donor disagreements regarding instruments for pursuing the poverty reduction and agricultural development agendas of donors and the mass patronage and agriculture development agendas of domestic politics, even where their interests in these agendas appear to converge. We therefore now turn to consider briefly key features of markets and livelihoods in rural Malawi.

4.4. The livelihoods and markets context

We focus on two important features of rural livelihoods and markets in Malawi that are relevant to our analysis of agriculture policy.

First, agriculture policy is politically and economically important because of the major importance of small-scale, low productivity, and risky agriculture in the livelihoods of poor rural people. While agriculture is by no means the only source of income of poor rural people, it is critically important to their livelihoods. There are surprisingly few empirical estimates of the proportion of rural Malawians' income coming from own farm activities. The National Statistical Office (2005a) estimates agricultural activities as comprising 50% of rural household incomes and 55% of the lowest income quartile for rural and urban households, and these estimates are consistent with the commonly cited figure of 50% of income being farm income in different parts

of Africa (Ellis, 1998; Reardon, 1998; Jayne et al., 2001). Dorward (2006) estimated figures of 33% own farm income in 1998 (closer to figures of 20 to 45%
in different southern Africa case studies cited by Bryceson (1999)), although
later analysis suggests own farm incomes of 50% or more in two different rural
areas, but around 40% among poorer households (Dorward, 2007). However
such figures underestimate the wider importance of agriculture in rural livelihoods. Food expenditures are estimated to account for just over 61% of total
expenditures in the lowest income quintile in the rural population in 2004
(National Statistical Office, 2005a). A large part of the 50% or more non-own
farm income of poor people is also derived from employment on other people's farms and from providing services to other rural people whose incomes
and demand for services are also heavily dependent on agriculture (Dorward,
2006). This very large importance of agriculture coupled with the low and
risky nature of smallholder agriculture in Malawi means that agriculture is a
major source of vulnerability in rural livelihoods.

The second major feature of rural markets and livelihoods in Malawi relevant to our analysis is the very low level of market development and economic activity. Dorward and Kydd (2004) argue that a defining characteristic
of rural areas in Malawi is that low and fragile incomes and low demand lead
to limited market activity based on very small transactions. The dependence
on a relatively narrow range of risky and low productivity activities, which
leads to increased covariant risk and vulnerability in the economy within
which rural livelihoods are located, is exacerbated by poor infrastructure, services, and communications, with poor roads and transport services and poor
telecommunications, leading to high costs in physical movement of goods
and services in and out of rural areas, together with high costs of communication about market opportunities and prices.

The result of the low general level of economic activity, of the risks from
lack of diversification, and of poor communications, is thin markets, with
very low traded volumes of key commodities, manufactures, and services
(notably agricultural produce, agricultural inputs, and agricultural finance).
Thin markets are both a cause of and are caused by high costs and risks in
trading small volumes in small transactions, requiring high risk premiums
and margins to make it profitable to engage in markets. However these high
margins themselves depress demand, and the result is a low level equilibrium
trap and market failure (Kydd and Dorward, 2004). These problems are particularly acute in the input, output, and financial markets needed for intensification and increased maize productivity, and can be analysed in terms of a
'low maize productivity trap', set out in Figure 4.1.

At the heart of Figure 4.1 is low maize agricultural productivity, the direct
consequence of low yields resulting from continual cultivation of maize
on land without organic or inorganic fertilizers. Low yields then require

71

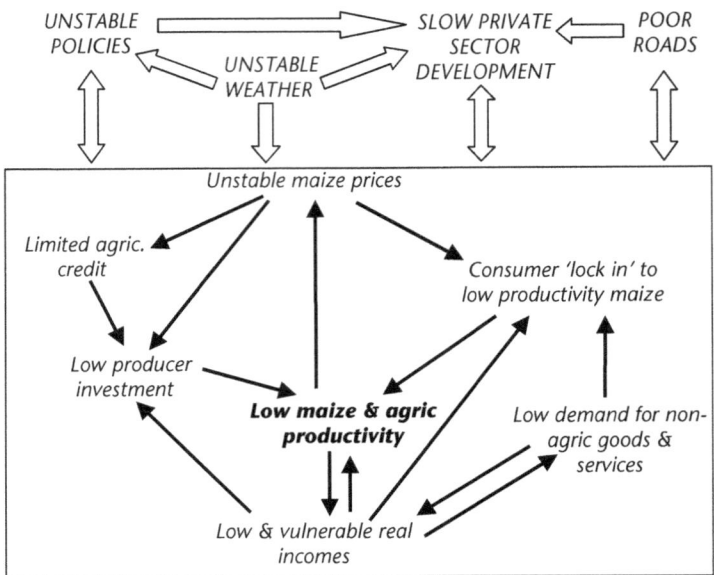

Figure 4.1. Vicious circle of the low productivity maize production trap
Source: Dorward and Chirwa (2011c).

increased areas under maize production to meet as much of household staple demands as possible (for reasons explained below). Low productivity leads to low incomes. For each farm-household this makes it difficult to afford input purchases for raising agricultural productivity. Most farmers cannot buy inputs on credit either because of under-developed credit markets and high costs of credit administration, high borrower and lender risks, consumption rather than sale of produce (with lack of cash for repayment), and high input prices and access costs due to low input demand, poor infrastructure, and high transport costs.

At the same time low maize production, low maize sales, and a high degree of subsistence consumption lead to thin markets in maize (as a large proportion of the maize produced in Malawi is consumed within households and villages, never reaching the market) and this leads to high variability in maize prices between years (as a result of good and bad rains or access to inputs) and within years (as a result of seasonality in maize stocks, input and labour requirements, incomes, and wage rates). This contributes to risks in input use, undermining incentives for investment in higher productivity by farmers with the potential to produce surpluses. However variability in maize prices also means that deficit producers seek to produce as much maize as they can to reduce their exposure to high purchase prices for maize in years when prices are high, and thus devote large parts of their cultivated land to maize. Poverty and vulnerability to shocks (low yields, high food prices, sickness, loss of employment or remittance income) further constrain productivity and productive investments—with women, who play a key role in agricultural production and rural livelihoods, particularly vulnerable to these shocks.

Low demand for inputs itself raises costs and inhibits the development of input supply systems in less accessible areas. Investments in maize market development are also constrained by low traded volumes and price risks in thin markets. High price variability for this critical commodity leads to government intervention in maize markets (with, for example, setting of minimum and maximum prices, export bans, and bans on private trade) but difficulties in designing and implementing interventions mean they often increase price variability for maize sellers, buyers, and traders; inhibit investment and participation in markets; and exacerbate the problems they attempt to address (see, for example, Tschirley and Jayne (2010)). These problems have then been exacerbated by unstable policies and unstable weather conditions (with particularly low maize production from 1992 to 1994, 2001/2, and 2004/5), lack of investment in roads, and a general policy, infrastructure, and economic context that has not encouraged long-term private sector investment and development.

The various influences and feedbacks described above lead to a vicious circle of low maize productivity and unstable maize prices inhibiting (a) net producers' investment in maize production,[3] (b) net consumers' reliance on the market for maize purchases, and (c) poor farmers' exits from low productivity maize cultivation. The result is a lock-in to widespread cultivation of low productivity maize which, because of its scale and importance in the wider Malawian economy, depresses labour and agricultural productivity and growth in the non-farm economy and of the Malawian economy as a whole.[4]

This analysis, which builds on wider understandings of coordination problems and low level traps (Rodenstein-Rodan, 1943; Hoff, 2001; Dorward et al., 2009) has important implications for understanding livelihood constraints and vulnerability, and in the design and implementation of agricultural policies and

---

[3] Profitability of and incentives for fertilizer use are commonly measured by the Value Cost Ratio (VCR) with a a general rule of thumb that it needs to be greater than 2 for smallholder investments in fertilizer use (Morris et al., 2007). School of Oriental and African Studies et al. (2008) note that with highly variable inter- and intra-seasonal maize prices and with rising nominal fertilizer prices, the VCR for maize varied markedly from the mid 1990s, with particular divergences between VCRs with peak pre-harvest and low post-harvest maize prices. In the latter case it was generally below 2, while in the former case it was generally but not always above 2. This suggests that profitability of fertilizer use on maize was a constraint to its use on maize grown for sale at or near harvest but not for maize is grown for own consumption. The divergence surplus and deficit maize producers' VCRs are exacerbated if maize price risk considerations are allowed for, as these would lead to a lower (higher) subjective valuation of maize produced for sale (purchase).

[4] This summary is not a complete account of the many issues involved. Other causes for high dependency on maize include different crops' calorific yields, dietary preferences, processing and storage considerations, farmers' familiarity with the crop, and government policies. Poor macroeconomic management also constrained wider growth before 2005.

instruments. It identifies low levels of investment and rural market development on the one hand and poverty and vulnerability on the other as interacting cause constraints to development and livelihood security. This then suggests that without the existence of established and functioning thick markets, markets cannot be relied on to deliver agricultural and food delivery services—but that such markets cannot develop, or can only develop slowly and fitfully, in the context of high levels of poverty. Two major questions emerge from this:

1. How can agricultural service markets (principally for inputs and credit) and food markets be developed in the medium to long term in order to address the problems of low productivity, poverty, and vulnerability that are endemic in Malawi?

2. How can agricultural services and food access be provided in the short term in the context of endemic poverty and low productivity and in ways that crowd in rather than crowd out market development?

These questions interact strongly with the political context discussed earlier and in particular with the different interests and ideologies of technocrats, politicians, and donors: in the first phase of policy under Banda there was a consensus recognizing that these questions, and development and patronage interests in agricultural policy, complemented each other. Subsequent agricultural liberalization policies have involved a lack of agreement regarding these questions (generally between the predominant Malawian analysis on the one hand and donor analysis on the other, but also between donors), leading to policy conflict and reversals as different views have prevailed. We examine these issues in the next section of this chapter. However, we consider a third question that emerges from the analysis above of livelihood and market constraints:

3. In what ways might a large-scale agricultural input subsidy impact on markets and livelihoods and the 'low productivity maize production trap'?

This question can be answered in two ways. First, with reference to Figure 4.1, a subsidy that substantially reduces input costs can make such inputs affordable, leading to producer investment in these inputs. If their use then leads to increased maize productivity, this can raise real incomes and then, through raising real incomes and their stimulus to demand for non-agricultural goods and services, this can break the vicious circle of the low productivity maize production trap. This will be strengthened where the subsidy is accompanied by stable policies, investment in roads, support to private sector growth, and policies that encourage more stable maize prices following weather shocks.

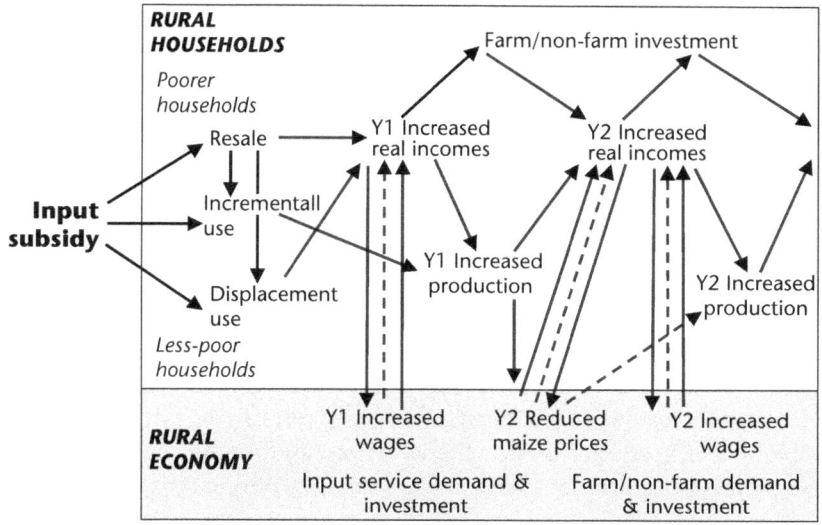

Figure 4.2. Subsidy impacts on beneficiary households and the rural economy

We can also investigate the possible impacts of a large-scale agricultural input subsidy by exploring possible effects on different households' livelihoods within the rural economy. This is set out in Figure 4.2.

Figure 4.2 identifies three possible uses of the subsidy by the recipients: reselling of coupons or of subsidized inputs, incremental use of the inputs in production, or use of the inputs with displacement of otherwise unsubsidized purchases. These different uses lead to two main types of direct benefit for recipients: immediate income transfers from reselling or displacement of some or all of the input coupons or subsidized inputs, or incremental production at harvest if the inputs are used on farm.

Immediate transfer benefits should lead to a tightening of the labour market in the season of implementation, due to contraction in labour supply by poorer households (who need to hire out less *ganyu*—casual labour—to earn food, as a result of income from reselling some or all of their coupons or subsidized inputs) and a much smaller expansion of hired labour demand by less-poor households (who have more resources available to hire labour as a result of cash saved by subsidy displacement of unsubsidized seed and fertilizer purchases). This tightening of the labour market should lead to an increase in real wages.

Increased wages lead to immediate real income and hence welfare and consumption gains to poorer households, both recipients and non-recipients. Increased on-farm labour use by the poor (as a result of reduced need to hire out labour) also means that gains from direct transfers to poor people and higher wages should lead to incremental production and welfare gains at and after harvest, even without any incremental input use (though these gains will be offset to some extent in the wider economy by losses of low cost labour to the less poor). Less-poor people who hire in labour may also incur a loss in net real income if they have to pay higher wages when hiring labour in and for purchasing local goods and services whose prices are determined largely by unskilled wage costs.

Impacts of a subsidy are, however, also expected in the season following its implementation, as a result of households having increased stocks of grain produced with the subsidy. Depending on the amount of extra production that is carried forward in these stocks, there should be two effects: decreased need for pre-harvest purchases of grain by households with insufficient stored grain and, as a result of this, decreased hiring out of *ganyu* to earn cash and food by poorer households and (slightly) increased financing to hire in farm labour by less-poor households (Dorward (2012b) provides a graphical household model analysis of this). The effects of the loosening of the grain market should be a fall in maize prices and a rise in wages.

This analysis draws out the importance of understanding different direct effects of subsidy access on different households and the different indirect effects of these as they affect labour and maize markets. Figure 4.2 shows the rather complex set of direct and indirect subsidy impacts and their relationships over time as described above. Further subsidy impacts shown in the figure are that increased real incomes should lead to greater farm and non-farm investment (in human and social capital as well as in financial, natural, and physical capital for particular enterprises), and that growing real incomes in rural areas should, through economic linkages or multipliers (Delgado et al., 1998; Dorward et al., 2002; Haggblade et al., 1989, 2007a), lead to a virtuous circle of increased demand for locally produced goods and services, including higher value non-staple foods. Increased consumption of vegetables and livestock products should lead to nutrition and health benefits and further tighten local labour demand. There will be similar human capital and welfare benefits and tightening of labour markets from investments in, for example, improved housing and sanitation, from investment in education and/ or other consumption items. Many of these benefits should accrue to both subsidy recipients and non-recipients as a result of changes in maize prices and wages.

Impacts on demand for and investment in input services will depend heavily on the way that subsidies are implemented. Understanding of these potential direct and indirect subsidy benefits should guide programme design and implementation: it should also guide investigations of programme impacts. We return to these issues later in Chapters 6 to 9. In the next section of this chapter, however, we continue our examination of evolving Malawian agricultural policies that have led to, and provide the background for, the introduction and development of the Agricultural (or later Farm) Input Subsidy Programme (AISP or FISP).

4.5. Agricultural policies

We now explore in more detail the major agricultural policies pursued in Malawi over the last 40 years or so. These policies have shaped and continue to shape infrastructure, research, knowledge, institutions, and the expectations of different stakeholders (politicians, technocrats, rural people, and voters) and, with the political analysis and context provided earlier in this chapter, are critical to understanding both the emergence of Malawi's Farm Input Subsidy Programme and its subsequent implementation and evolution.

4.5.1. Post-independence policies

Post-independence smallholder agricultural development policy revolved around the establishment and then scaling up and out of four large donor-financed integrated rural development projects (one in the northern region, two in the centre, and one in the south) to a national programme of projects covering the majority of the country. Although elements varied between projects, there were a number of common core activities: agricultural extension; subsidized supply of improved seeds and fertilizers for maize and cash crops; construction of feeder roads and market facilities; construction of offices and staff housing; and construction of health facilities. Within the context of supporting infrastructure, the core smallholder development activities involved the promotion of farming groups which took input loans for seed and fertilizer, loans which were repaid through interlocking sales at fixed prices to the parastatal marketing board, ADMARC. The system was very successful in expanding access to purchased inputs, particularly in maize production, and in achieving very high rates of credit repayment. Fundamental to this success were (a) the role of the parastatal marketing agency, ADMARC, as a sole seller of inputs to and sole buyer of produce from smallholders, (b) a major focus on facilitation of this system by extension staff, and (c) strict enforcement of penalties for non-repayment, (with the denial of access to input purchases on both cash and credit for all members of a defaulting group and, in some cases, heavy handed confiscation of assets of defaulters). ADMARC also maintained pan-territorial and pan-seasonal prices.

These policies had complex anti-poor and pro-poor elements (Chirwa et al., 2006). The interests of the poor were damaged by food prices frequently being held above import parity, and cheaper imported food prices might have allowed the large number of malnourished poor better access to food in some years (although lower maize prices would have depressed incentives for investment in improved seed and fertilizer use in maize). ADMARC also tended to tax the smallholder sector, and the proceeds of this were transferred to the estate sector, which also benefited from cheap labour in an exploitative tenant system of tobacco production.

However the smallholder development projects described above invested considerable sums in rural areas, and although the direct beneficiaries of the agricultural programmes were generally (but not always) less-poor farmers, they did promote national food self-sufficiency and local food availability (both through local production and through the network of ADMARC markets which sold maize) and stimulated economic growth in rural areas. Smallholder taxation was also mainly on cash crops, and the smallholder maize system was moderately subsidized by ADMARC (Kydd and Christiansen, 1982). Smallholder taxation was also offset, and with time eclipsed, by government infrastructural investment in the integrated rural development projects described above and by the implicit subsidies in the support of groups in obtaining credit and in marketing their produce.

This set of agricultural policies can be seen as setting up a system that addressed many of the demands made of it. Support for estates provided direct patronage to elites (and resources for dispensing patronage) and to emerging middle classes as noted earlier, particularly in the central region. Donor resources supported smallholder agricultural development that provided infrastructure and agricultural services and food access to smallholders (addressing the market development trap), meeting both donor developmental objectives and government developmental and patronage objectives (the latter being through regionally distributed visible project investments, civil service and parastatal employment, improved incomes to less poor farmers, and stable food availability in rural areas). There were also important social protection outcomes from stable pan-territorial, pan-seasonal food prices, and reliable food availability in most rural areas in the country. Although the direct beneficiaries of these policies were not generally the poorer members of rural communities, and there were differences between regions in the benefits produced by these policies, both the flow of seasonal finance to less-poor households and the increased incomes arising from the use of those inputs (and their multiplier effects) should have increased seasonal liquidity in rural communities, raising demand and wages for casual labour and increasing community resources for informal local social protection measures. The discussion of pro- and anti-poor elements of these policies also, however, illustrates conflicts over maize prices (low prices are good for poor, food-insecure consumers but high prices are needed to stimulate investment), while the longer term failure of the government to sustain these policies illustrates the difficulties governments face in allocating limited resources between the short-term demands for distribution of benefits to different interest groups on the one hand and longer term demands for investment in growth on the other.

4.5.2. Liberalization policies

As liberalization and, later, multi-party democracy and currency devaluation led to the demise of the interlocking smallholder agricultural credit system and integrated rural development approach at the core of the agricultural policies described above, subsequent agricultural policies were not part of such a comprehensive vision of rural development. Agriculture, and indeed individual crops, were seen as needing crop- and commodity-specific market solutions. The best example of this is probably the development of smallholder tobacco, which, as discussed earlier, was very successful. Harrigan (2003) reports a number of benefits from this expansion: a major cash injection with multipliers feeding through into the rest of the non-farm rural economy, the use of tobacco income to buy seed and fertilizer for maize production, and market development. However she also notes that middle income smallholders were the predominant direct beneficiaries and while there were significant numbers of poorer smallholders with very limited land growing tobacco, tobacco began to crowd out maize on these farms. This led to severe declines in maize production when devaluation of the Malawi Kwacha and the removal of input subsidies made the use of fertilizer on maize uneconomic. At the same time, growth in smallholder tobacco production was mainly in the central and northern regions, not in the southern region where the holdings are smallest and the extent, incidence, and severity of poverty are greatest (National Statistical Office, 2005a; Prowse, 2007).

A variety of social protection instruments were then introduced. Initially mainly safety nets, these were closely related to agriculture and changes in agriculture policies as they attempted to address increased food insecurity and increasing vulnerability from, *inter alia*, declining holding sizes and soil fertility and the spread of HIV/AIDS among poor rural Malawians. Over time a wide variety of different social protection programmes and instruments were implemented (Slater and Tsoka, 2007), including targeted nutrition programmes, food transfers, public works programmes, school feeding programmes, credit transfers, and more recently cash transfers.

The agricultural synergies and conflicts of many of these programmes are well known: injections of cash and food into people's livelihoods can make a critical contribution at lean times of year before harvest when labour is needed by people to work on their fields, these cash and food injections may allow them to work on their fields rather than seek work for cash or food elsewhere. These injections can also generate local economic multipliers (Davies and Davey, 2008) and build up productive capacity and assets (Covarrubias et al., 2012). However cash or food for work programmes face a dilemma in that, if they are providing work and income at the time when people need it most, then this will take people from their fields and undermine their own production (Slater and Tsoka, 2007).These programmes also face wider problems regarding the extent and value of their contributions to rural assets and most importantly to the livelihoods of participants (Devereux, 2006). A tendency for programmes to lack long-term funding and consistency has also undermined the extent to which they can be relied upon by rural households (Slater and Tsoka, 2007).

4.5.3. *Agricultural input provision programmes*

As discussed earlier, recognition of the importance of agriculture for food security, of the need for fertilizers to raise yields for poor farmers with small-holdings and declining yields under continuous maize cropping, and of difficulties in accessing maize seed and inputs led to major political, economic, and developmental interests in policies and instruments aimed at increasing poor people's access to inputs (seed and fertilizer) for maize production. Two different programmes and instruments concerned with input delivery to poor people are important for understanding the subsequent emergence of the agricultural input subsidy programme in 2005: 'inputs for work' and free input distribution (the latter under the 'Starter Pack' and 'Targeted Inputs Programme' or TIP). These programmes have operated at different scales and in different ways with different agricultural and social protection objectives of stakeholders in supporting different programmes: ambiguity and diversity in understandings of programme objectives have been widespread, and have had both benefits and costs.

'Inputs for work' describes the use of public works programmes aimed primarily at delivering social protection but, in contrast to food for work and cash for work programmes, participants are paid with agricultural inputs. 'Inputs for work' has only been implemented on a local scale by NGOs with donor funding. Payment with inputs is intended to overcome some of the difficulties with food and cash for work programmes by providing participants with work during the dry season, when there is little competition for labour with work on their fields, but benefits during the following cropping season (by easing labour and cash demands for households looking to purchase inputs) and/or by increasing subsequent maize harvests and food stocks. An evaluation of a pilot project in two districts of Malawi cited by Devereux (2006) concluded that the project was more popular with participants than food or cash for work, and yielded a very favourable return in the value of increased maize produced.

Free input distribution has been a much more widely used approach to extending access to inputs across the country, with large-scale government distributions starting from 1993 in response to currency devaluation, the removal of fertilizer subsidies, the collapse of the credit system for maize inputs, and drought (Devereux, 2006). In 1998, the government implemented a universal 'Starter Pack' programme, under which every smallholder was provided with enough seeds and fertilizer to plant 0.1 hectares of land. This, with good weather, was a contributor to an estimated 67% increase in maize output, with maize production reaching 2.5 million tonnes (Levy, 2005).

The programme, funded by DFID, was continued in 1999 amid considerable controversy, rooted in different stakeholder interests in the programme, in the political context, and different perceptions of its objectives. As originally conceived, the Starter Pack was an agricultural development programme intended to promote farmer skills in more intensive maize production, diversification out of maize, and the growth of commercial input distribution systems in rural areas. It was intended to include maize fertilizers and legume and maize seed, to be accompanied by a strong extension programme, and to address the market and livelihood constraints discussed earlier. However the programme was actually funded and implemented more as a social protection programme, with a major emphasis on fertilizer provision to promote immediate food production, and less emphasis on agricultural education, provision of legume seed, or the development of commercial input delivery systems. The programme was highly politicized, being introduced just before the 1999 presidential elections, and was seen as particularly beneficial for the southern region, the ruling party's power base.

Donors were concerned about the politicization of the programme, its high cost, its apparent emphasis on maize rather than on promoting diversification, its possible crowding out effects on input markets, and its efficiency as regards targeting and benefits to the poor. There was concern that large numbers of non-poor people were benefiting, and that receipt of inputs by such people was simply a transfer, with starter pack inputs displacing commercial purchases, although the extent of displacement is disputed. As a result DFID support of the programme was subsequently scaled back to the Targeted Input Programme (TIP).

Targeting, however, faced problems. There were considerable difficulties in the selection of beneficiaries and in the effectiveness of targeting. More fundamentally, however, Levy (2005) argues that the starter pack assisted poorer households in two ways: by increasing their own maize production and (by stimulating national maize production) reducing maize prices. The second benefit was lost when the programme was scaled back to a targeted programme. Dorward and Kydd (2005) simulate the effects of maize price and wage effects of the universal starter pack and compare this with effects under a targeted programme, and argued that even if targeting could be achieved without exclusion and inclusion problems, and ignoring both the increased costs associated with targeting and displacement effects, the wage and maize price effects of a universal subsidy could be more cost-effective than a targeted programme in delivering welfare benefits to the target group. They were concerned, however, that by depressing maize prices, the universal programme 'may undermine the important growth contributions of less poor households that engage in more intensive labour demanding maize-production' (p. 274).

4.6. The 2005/6 Agricultural Input Subsidy Programme

High food prices and food shortages following poor harvests in 2000/1 and 2001/2 (after the scaling back of the starter pack programme), led to food security and fertilizer subsidies becoming major political issues in the period leading up to the 2004 presidential elections. Both the major parties and their candidates promised fertilizer subsidies, though the UDF and Bingu wa Mutharika, its presidential candidate, offered an extension of the rationed Starter Pack approach while the MCP and its candidate, John Tembo, offered a return to price subsidies through farmer groups. After the election the new government delayed the introduction of subsidies, perhaps due to the need for controlling government expenditure to qualify for debt relief (Chinsinga, 2006). Uncertainty about a subsidy led to delays in the decision to implement another targeted input programme, and also led to delays in fertilizer imports and to farmers delaying fertilizer purchases (Sahley et al., 2005). The result was another very poor season with subsequent food shortages, high prices, very expensive importation of maize, and considerable damage to people's welfare and livelihoods and to the economy.

During 2005, therefore, the government decided to implement the Agricultural Input Subsidy Programme (AISP) as a rationed and targeted programme that would involve the partial subsidy of a much larger volume of inputs than were provided under the previous Starter Pack and Targeted Input Programme. While the impetus for this was the renewed concerns within Malawi over maize production, the decision provided an opportunity for President Bingu wa Mutharika to craft a programme that would be popular with the rural masses across the country, would provide potential resources for patronage, and was clearly different from previous subsidies or input supply programmes under Banda and Muluzi, but which also had a clear economic and welfare rationale that lay firmly in traditional domestic analysis of smallholder farmer needs. In this it was a critical strategic response to the political challenges facing Bingu wa Mutharika as he established his government without a majority in parliament. It also drew on new opportunities for independent policy afforded by the introduction of large-scale budget support by Malawi's major donors and (to a lesser extent) by ideological divisions within the donor community regarding the relative economic and welfare benefits of such a programme (with, for example, strong support from Jeffrey Sachs and the Millennium Programme).

The design, implementation, and impacts of the programme, and potential wider lessons from this, are the subject of the rest of this book.

4.7. Summary

This chapter has described the context of Malawi's introduction of its Agricultural Input Subsidy Programme in 2005. An understanding of the economic context of smallholder agriculture and rural livelihoods in Malawi is critical for understanding technical arguments for the introduction of this programme, and its subsequent implementation and impacts. The importance of, and difficulties posed by, the 'low maize productivity trap' are particularly relevant. There are important interactions here with the arguments presented in Chapter 2 about subsidies' objectives and modalities, as well as contrasts and similarities with other countries' engagement with input subsidy programmes, as discussed in Chapter 3. However Malawi's agriculture, rural livelihoods, and economy, and technical understanding of them, are themselves strongly influenced by its history of changing political circumstances and deep-rooted political influences and processes. Understanding these political issues is equally important for understanding the genesis, evolution, and impacts of agricultural input subsides in Malawi, and indeed in other countries.

Part II
Implementation and Impacts of the Malawi Programme

In this part of the book we describe the major features of the design and implementation of the Malawi Farm Input Subsidy from 2005/6 to 2011/12 (in Chapter 5) and then examine evidence for various potential impacts of the programme. Examination of these impacts and their links to prior programme design and implementation is guided by the conceptual framework set out in Figure 2.2 in Chapter 2, by the issues raised in examination of recent subsidy programme experience discussed in Chapter 3, by key political, economic, and agricultural features of Malawi discussed in Chapter 4, and by the possible impacts of a large scale agricultural inputs subsidy on different households' livelihoods within the rural economy as set out in Figure 4.2. Figure II.1 draws these strands together and restructures Figures 2.2 and 4.2 to show the causal pathway that is traced from examination of input subsidy distribution, receipts, and costs (in Chapter 5 on implementation) through to various direct and then indirect impacts (in Chapters 6 and 7), alongside and interacting with input market impacts (in Chapter 8). Chapter 9 provides an overarching consideration of the overall benefits and costs of the programme: we do not attempt to show its links across programme costs and welfare and growth impacts in the figure.

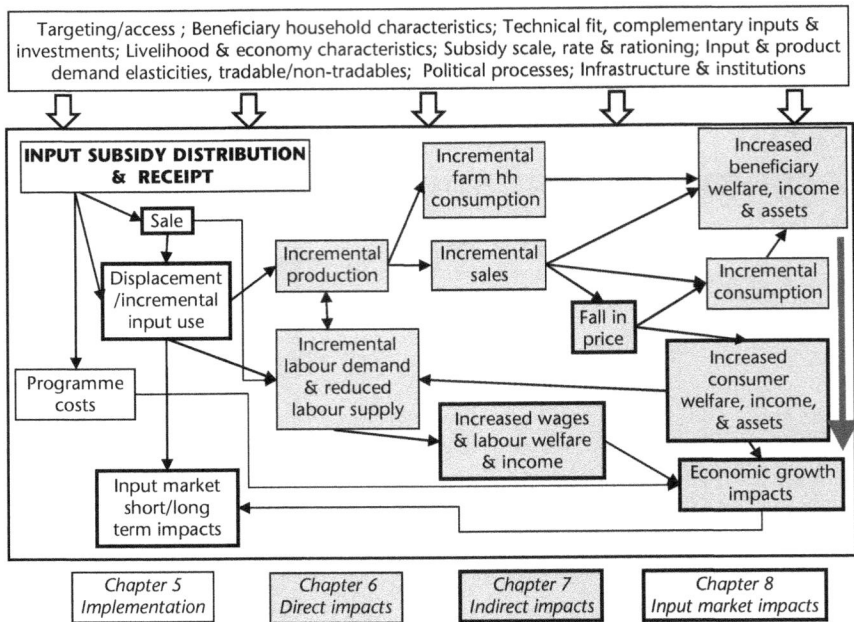

Figure II.1. Processes and influences linking and affecting inputs, implementation, and impacts

5

FISP activities and achievements

5.1. Introduction

This chapter describes the implementation of the Malawi FISP from its inception in 2005/6 to 2011/12. Our aims in this chapter are to

- set out the major activities involved in implementing the programme, and the core determinants of programme outputs which in turn determine programme impacts, as discussed in Chapters 6 and 7;
- describe the major features of the programme with regard to design and implementation features identified at the end of Chapter 2 as critical for programme evaluation (although some aspects of targeting, rationing, and private sector input supply are addressed in later chapters); and
- consider some of the political and other influences that have affected programme design and implementation.

We begin the chapter by introducing the core elements of the programme and major changes from 2005/6 to 2011/12. The bulk of the chapter then provides more detail on these, on implementation achievements and outputs of the programme, and on some of the determinants of changing practices. We go into considerable detail on some topics both to document these topics and to provide readers with information that is needed to understand issues discussed in later chapters. We conclude by discussing how consideration of the implementation of the Malawi subsidy programme fits within, extends, and/or challenges understandings of theory, practice, and policy set out in Chapters 2 to 4. We first, however, conclude this introduction with an overview of the major tasks and core activities involved in programme implementation and generation of its core outputs. A simplified summary of these is provided in Figure 5.1.

There are a number of points to note from Figure 5.1. First, following on from key lessons from the reviews in Chapters 2 and 3, programme outputs

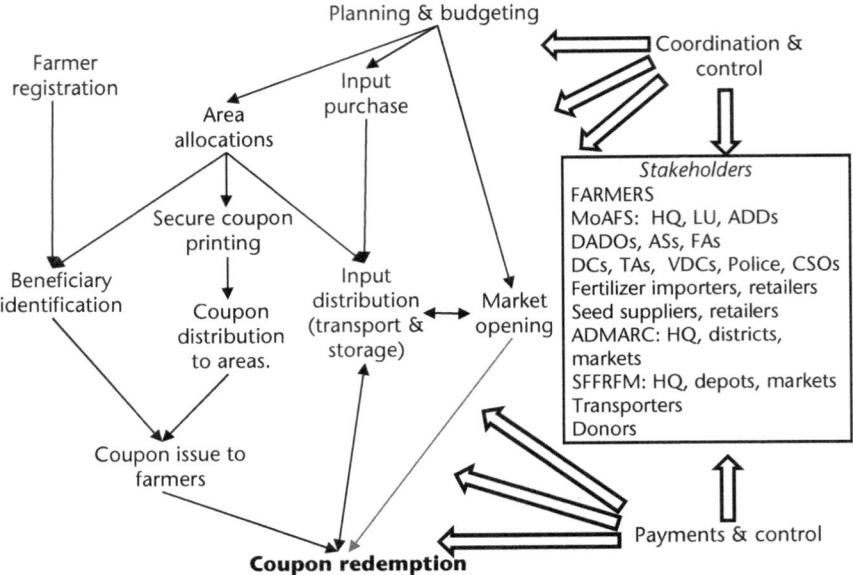

Figure 5.1. Major tasks in programme implementation
Note: see list of abbreviations for description of stakeholders.
Source: adapted from Dorward and Chirwa (2011c).

are defined as timely coupon redemption and incremental input sales. The activities and tasks required to deliver these outputs are then divided into two broad groups: input management and coupon management, with further division into input purchases and market opening on the one hand and coupon supply and beneficiary identification on the other. Across these divisions, however, there are major *planning* interactions, as coupon allocations to different areas depend upon overall planned input purchases and input distribution to different areas depends upon coupon allocations to those areas. There are also major *implementation* interactions between input and coupon management as regards timing of separate activities and of the exercise as a whole. Starting at the bottom of the figure, before coupon redemption can start in an area the markets must be stocked and open and beneficiaries must have been issued with their coupons. Similarly, input distribution to depots and markets requires the prior allocation of inputs to the areas in which markets are located. Allocations to areas, however, must follow initial decisions on the total volumes of inputs to be sold under the programme.

Finally, the figure also provides some indication of the way that the programme's complexity and scale pose major challenges in programme planning and implementation. These activities are carried out for several different sets of inputs (for example, different fertilizers and seeds), over the whole country in rural areas that are often poorly served by roads and services, serving dispersed farmers (many of whom have very low levels of literacy), without access to advanced information technology systems. There is also a wide range of stakeholders in the programme, often with different understandings of the objectives of the programme and of how it is supposed to be implemented, and different personal and professional interests in it, with some of these interests more and less 'legitimate'. Fraud and theft are also major temptations and threats (criminals are not included as stakeholders, but their influence and effects on the programme also have to be recognized). All of this occurs on a very large scale. For example, in 2008/9 more than 1.5 million fertilizer coupon beneficiaries were selected from over 2.5 million farm households, 3.5 million fertilizer coupons and 2.5 million seed coupons were printed and distributed, and 3.5 million bags of four kinds of fertilizer were purchased and distributed, together with 2.5 million bags of two different kinds of maize seed and three kinds of legume seed. These subsidized commodities were together worth around US$275 million,[1] with each fertilizer coupon's value greater than 10% of annual household income for more than around 40% of the population. Discussion of the programme's implementation, achievements, and weaknesses should take into account these considerations.

We now consider major implementation activities in turn, considering each of the activities in Figure 5.1 in terms of their structures, volume, and outputs over the period 2005/6 to 2011/12. We begin, however, with a brief overview of core programme features and of their evolution and of the context of that evolution from 2005/6 to 2011/12.

5.2. Programme design and evolution

The core stated objective of the FISP has consistently been to improve resource-poor smallholder famers' access to improved agricultural inputs in order to achieve their and national food self-sufficiency and to raise these famers' incomes through increased food and cash crop production. Later years of the programme have given greater emphasis to concerns for vulnerable farm households. Throughout this, however, there has been an emphasis on programme beneficiaries as farmers and producers, with little emphasis on beneficiaries as consumers (beyond the recognition of the programme's contribution to improving household food self-sufficiency) and there has been no emphasis on the indirect programme effects on maize prices and hence consumers.

The core of the programme has been the use of vouchers (or coupons) to target approximately 50% of farmers in the country to receive fertilizers and

---

[1] This is inclusive of transport costs and farmer redemption payments.

improved seeds for staple food (maize) production. 'Maize fertilizers' have been provided in a package of one voucher for a 50 kg bag of 23:21:0 +4S basal fertilizer (NPK) and one voucher for a 50 kg bag of urea for top dressing. Improved maize seeds subsidized under the programme were initially open pollinated varieties (OPVs) but there has subsequently been much greater emphasis on hybrid maize varieties. The seed and fertilizer packages drew on longstanding Ministry of Agriculture and Food Security (MoAFS) crop production recommendations. In the early years there were further vouchers for tobacco fertilizers, and in later years support for tobacco inputs was withdrawn and more emphasis given to provision of legume seeds. Grain storage chemicals were also provided from 2007/8 and cotton seed and chemicals provided in some years, but the disbursement and reporting channels and methods for these have been different from those for fertilizers and for maize and legume seed, and we do not report on them in any detail. The subsidization of complementary inputs (fertilizers, maize and legume seed, and maize storage chemicals) have been the main form of complementary investment in or associated with the programme, but there has also been some provision of extension messages on input use, and under the Agricultural Sector Wide Programme some investment in a nationwide set of on-farm trials of different integrated soil fertility management technologies.

Throughout the FISP, the government and other stakeholders have worked with varying success and agreement on innovations to address difficulties, improve programme performance, respond to changing political and economic conditions, and broaden impact. These changes have emerged from formal and informal discussions, reviews and lesson learning within government and with other stakeholders, and from changing policy concerns in a changing economic and political environment. Bilateral and multilateral donors have engaged substantially with the government over the programme from the 2006/7 season, with specific funding of some activities. This has involved consistent support for seed subsidies, logistics, monitoring and evaluation, and some fertilizer transport. They have also supported 'buy back' arrangements in some years (allowing the government to carry forward unused stocks from one year to the next with the costs of these stocks in the budget and accounts for the year of their use rather than purchase) and assisted with costs of auditing, anti-corruption measures, coupon printing, and exceptionally high fertilizer prices in 2008/9.

The major modifications in different years are shown in Tables 5.1 and 5.2 and involved changes in

- volumes of subsidized fertilizer and seed sales (both maize and legumes) and of grain storage chemicals and cotton chemicals and seed, with fertilizer volumes rising and then falling but seed volumes rising apart from a fall in maize seeds in 2011/12;

- reliance on private sector imports to supply parastatal fertilizer sales (generally rising) and private sector involvement in retail sales of subsidized fertilizer only in 2006/7 and 2008/9 but in seed sales for all years except 2005/6;

- programme objectives and beneficiary targeting criteria and systems placing increasing emphasis on vulnerable beneficiaries;

- beneficiary registration and beneficiary selection, voucher distribution, and market monitoring systems;

- redemption prices falling; and

- coupon design and security features and processes increasing fitfully.

Further details and explanations are provided on these changes in the following sections.

Table 5.1. Principal programme features, 2005/6 to 2011/12

		2005/6	2006/7	2007/8	2008/9	2009/10	2010/11	2011/12
Fertilizer voucher distribution (MT equivalent)		166,156	200,128	216,000	195,369	160,000	160,000	140,000
Total sub-sidized fertilizer sales (MT)	Planned	137,006	150,000	170,000	170,000	160,000	160,000	140,000
	Actual	131,388	174,688	216,553	197,498	159,585	160,531	139,901
Fertilizer voucher value, approx. (MK/bag)		1,750	2,480	3,299	7,951	3,841	5,237	6,536
Redemption price (MK/bag)		950*	950	900	800	500	500	500
Subsidy % (approx.)		64%	72%	79%	91%	88%	91%	93%
Subsidized maize seed (MT)		n/a	4,524	5,541	5,365	8,652	10,650	8,245
% Hybrid seed		0%	61%	53%	84%	88%	80%	68%
Legume seed (MT)				24	1	1551	2726	2,562
Cotton seed/chemicals		No	No	Yes	Yes	No	No	Yes
Total pro-gramme cost (MK million)	Planned	5,100	7,500	11,500	19,480	21,908	19,700	21,586
	Actual	4,480	10,346	13,362	33,922	15,526	21,868	23,455

* 950MK per bag for 'maize fertilizers' and 1450MK per bag for 'tobacco fertilizers'.

Sources: Logistics Unit reports; Nakhumwa (2006), School of Oriental and African Studies et al. (2008), Dorward and Chirwa (2009, 2011a, 2012a), Dorward et al. (2010b).

Table 5.2. Evolving programme implementation features, 2005/6 to 2011/12

	Subsidized inputs	Voucher distribution system	Voucher redemption systems	Other system features
2005/6	Maize & tobacco fertilizers, Maize seed (OPV)	First round district allocation by maize areas, distribution through Traditional Authorities (TAs), subsequent rounds less transparent	Only through SFFRFM & ADMARC	Fertilizer coupons not specific to fertilizer type.
2006/7 changes	Hybrid & OPV maize seed	Distribution through varied stakeholders	Fertilizers also through major retailers; flexible maize seed vouchers through a wide range of seed retailers	Coupons specific to fertilizer type. Fertilizer buy back system. Logistics unit involvement
2007/8 changes	Very limited legume seed; cotton seed & chemicals	District allocation by farm hh & areas, distribution through MoAFS/Village Development Committees (VDCs)	Cotton inputs through Agricultural Development Divisions (ADDs)	Reduced copies of coupons. Remote Extension Planning Area (EPA) premium
2008/9 changes	Tea & coffee fertilizers, maize storage chemicals	Use of farm household register, open meetings for allocation & disbursement led by MoAFS. Additional 'flexi-vouchers' for maize or legume seed allocated separately	Fertilizers only through ADMARC & SFFRFM; Grain storage chemicals through ADDs	Extra coupon security features & market monitoring; No remote EPA premium; ADMARC computers for voucher processing
2009/10 changes	No cotton chemicals. No tobacco fertilizers, Increased legume seed, more maize seed (hybrid & OPV) per pack	Elimination of 2nd and 3rd round distributions. Use of voter identification for registration, receipt & redemption.	Variable top up for maize seed max 100MK	Complex extra coupon security features in centre & north. Features (e.g. numbering) varied

Table 5.2. (continued)

	Subsidized inputs	Voucher distribution system	Voucher redemption systems	Other system features
2010/11 changes	No major changes	No major changes except 'flexi-vouchers' replaced by legume vouch-ers added to standard package	No major changes	No major changes
2011/12 changes	Major foreign exchange & fuel problems; cotton seed & chemicals	No major changes	Cotton inputs through ADDs	Coupons printed out-side Malawi with packs straight to Districts

Sources: Logistics Unit reports; Nakhumwa (2006), School of Oriental and African Studies et al. (2008), Dorward and Chirwa (2009, 2011a, 2012a), Dorward et al. (2010b).

5.3. Input purchases and distribution

This section describes processes, achievements, and performance in the procurement and distribution of fertilizers and of maize and legume seeds.

5.3.1. Procurement and distribution systems

The programme has used two fertilizer procurement and distribution systems in different years. The dominant system, with distribution and retailing through two parastatal corporations (ADMARC and SFFRFM—Smallholder Farmers Fertiliser Revolving Fund of Malawi), was the only system used in 2005/6 and from 2008/9, while in 2006/7 and 2007/8 this was augmented by parallel private sector retailing of subsidized fertilizers. With parastatal distribution, the government calls for tenders for the supply of specified fertilizers to three SFFRFM depots (in the southern, central, and northern regions). After a formal process of tender analysis and awards, successful bidders (both private importers and SFFRFM and ADMARC) then deliver contracted quantities to the specified depots, which also hold any programme stocks bought forward from excess supplies in the previous year. The government (working through the programme's Logistics Unit from 2006/7) then contracts private transporters to 'uplift' fertilizers from the regional depots to ADMARC and SFFRFM local area markets which act as the retail outlets for subsidized fertilizer supplies. Timely availability of fertilizers for redemption by beneficiaries requires timely award of tenders and tender deliveries, timely uplifting of supplies from depots to markets (to supply the markets and to free storage space for deliveries from importers to depots), and timely sales from markets (to supply beneficiary demand and to free storage space for deliveries from depots to markets).

Timely sales of fertilizers before or immediately on commencement of the rains are critical for a good fertilizer response, particularly for 'basal' NPK fertilizers applied at planting. However limited storage space at depots, limited transport capacity, poor feeder roads once the rainy season has started, and limited storage space at markets pose major logistical challenges in maintaining stocks for selling large quantities of fertilizers quickly after the start of the rains. Absence of such stocks leads to shortages at markets, which in turn leads to farmers wasting time and money searching and waiting for stocks. Shortages also give corrupt sales agents and others opportunities to extort extra payments from beneficiaries.

As mentioned above, a parallel fertilizer procurement and distribution system using private sector retail outlets was implemented for two years, 2006/7 and 2007/8. Under this system six input suppliers with rural chains of retail outlets were contracted to procure, store, and distribute the fertilizers that they sold under the programme, with stocks of 'subsidy fertilizers' not distinguished from stocks of fertilizers for unsubsidized sales (they were only treated differently at the point of sale, and in the subsequent submission of vouchers to the MoAFS Logistics Unit for redemption at previously agreed prices). An important part of this system was the funding by DFID of a financing agreement with Stanbic Bank to address government concerns that ADMARC and SFFRFM might be left holding unused stocks if the private sector's subsidized sales were larger than expected. Under this agreement, Stanbic bought unsold fertilizer stocks from the government at the end of the season for resale to the government at the start of the next season at the same price (plus storage and financing costs). In 2006/7 prices varied by district to reflect varying transport costs to different districts, but in 2007/8 a further 'remote areas premium' was introduced to promote companies extending their distribution network into more remote zones. Private sector sales of subsidized fertilizer were cancelled by the government at short notice in the 2008/9 season when contract negotiations were at an advanced stage, on the basis of (as far as we know) unsubstantiated reports that some private companies had been misusing fertilizer coupons and accepting them in exchange for other sales of other products.

With regards to maize and legume seeds, from 2006/7 onwards these have been supplied and distributed by private seed suppliers and sold through both private and parastatal retail outlets. A small number of seed companies negotiate annual coupon redemption prices for different seed types and packs (with the ability to charge a further 'top up' price to farmers in most years). Retailers (retail chains, small scale agro-dealers, and parastatal outlets) are then supplied with seed for sale under the programme, and have to return seed coupons redeemed by farmers back to the seed companies, who then present them to the MoAFS Logistics Unit for redemption payments.

5.3.2. Fertilizer procurement and distribution

Procurement of fertilizers for subsidized sale by ADMARC and SFFRFM is a major and critical activity in programme implementation, affecting beneficiaries' access to fertilizers (in terms of timing, volumes, and access costs), programme impacts, and programme costs (with fertilizers accounting for around 75% of net programme costs from 2009/10 to 2011/12). While procurement of fertilizers and seeds for sale through private channels is also important, this is coordinated and implemented by private companies, with critical government involvement restricted to tendering at the beginning and payment at the end. We report on these later when we consider coupon redemption and seed sales under the subsidy, and beneficiary information about delivery performance. In this section we focus on government and parastatal procurement and distribution achievements and performance for fertilizers. We discuss more on this in Chapter 8.

Figure 5.2 shows fertilizer supplies to the programme by source from 2005/6 to 2011/12 (excluding unutilized supplies carried forward). The graph demonstrates well

- the increasing volume of subsidized fertilizer from 2005/6 to 2008/9 and its subsequent decline;
- the general trend for increasing reliance on private sector supplies, but highly variable volumes of private sector supplies between years (rising year on year from 2005/6 to 2008/9, then falling back markedly in 2009/10);[2]
- government distribution of 125,000 MT or more in every year of the programme.

Given these large volumes, performance in government procurement and distribution of fertilizers is very important to programme performance as a whole. This can be considered in terms of timing and costs.

---

[2] Total private sector supplies to government in 2008/9 were greater than shown in Figure 5.2, as this excludes government purchases for winter production and purchases that were not used and then carried forward, contributing to the 2009/10 drop in new private sector supplies.

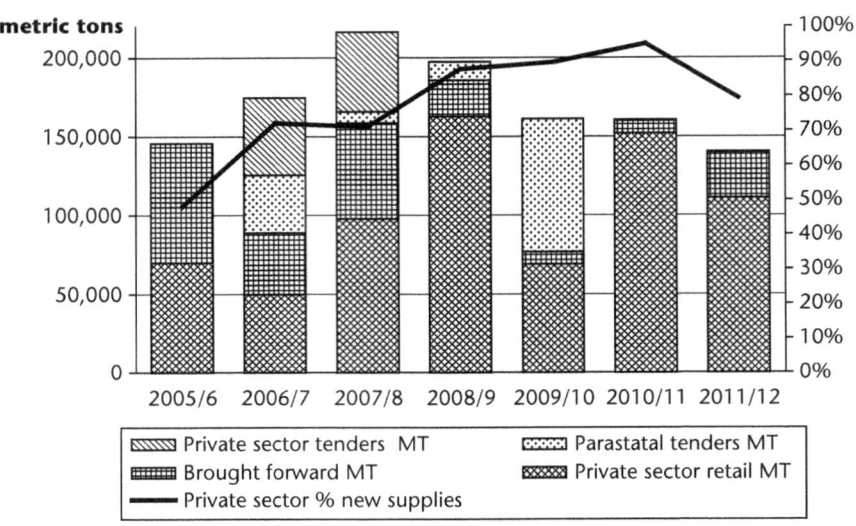

Figure 5.2. Fertilizer supplies by source, 2005/6 to 2011/12
Sources: Logistics Unit annual reports.

Procurement activities have generally been completed a little earlier each year, and this has been associated with substantial improvements in end of October and end of November deliveries in 2009/10 and 2010/11 (there were also greater carry-forward stocks in 2009/10). Despite these improvements, however, end of October deliveries have still been less than 80% of total supplies even in the best years, and have frequently been below 40%. End of November deliveries were as low as 70% of total supplies in 2008/9, and in only two years have all supplies been delivered to depots by the end of December. The limited impact of earlier tendering on deliveries is due partly to lack of firm delivery dates and late delivery penalty clauses in tender contracts, partly to the failure of some suppliers to deliver at all (with consequent late contracts with alternative suppliers), and partly to constraints on storage space at SFFRFM regional depots. This is affected by difficulties in uplifting stocks from the depots to rural markets, to which we now turn.

Earlier deliveries to depots have allowed improvements in uplifting stocks from the depots to rural markets (see Figure 5.3), with uplifts by the end of November rising steadily from a little over 64% to 86% from 2006/7 to 2010/11. However this should be 100%, indeed all supplies should be available for sale by mid November, whereas even in 2010/11 only 70% was uplifted by the end of October and 85% by end November. Although uplifts are constrained by the availability of stock in depots, they are also constrained by transport capacity, poor roads, and availability of storage space in markets, with the latter determined by the timing of seasonal markets' opening and by

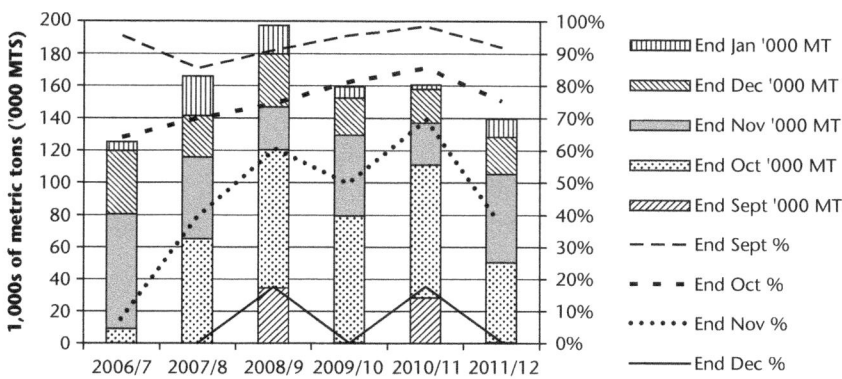

Figure 5.3. Montly uplifts to rural markets ('000 MT & % parastatal sales by end of month)

Source: Logistics Unit weekly and annual reports.

sales disruptions to stock flows. Sales are determined not only by stock availability, but also by beneficiaries being in possession of redeemable coupons. We discuss coupon distribution systems determining this later, in Section 5.4. First, however, we briefly examine another aspect of procurement performance: prices paid for inputs.

Figure 5.4 compares average fertilizer costs per metric ton (MT) for NPK (23:21:0 +4S) and urea delivered to the three depots with international prices for DAP and urea over the period 2006 to 2011 (with good data on procurement prices available for the last three years but weaker data for the previous three years). Data are shown each year from March to November, with March to April generally being the time at which tenders have been submitted (and hence the basis for tender pricing, although some contracts were established later in each season) with delivery from August to December: actual timing of different suppliers' purchases is not known, nor are the prices paid. The figure shows

- broad patterns of change in prices and in difference between delivered and international prices;
- sharp rises and falls in international prices, particularly for phosphate fertilizers in 2008, with tenders and being placed when prices were rising to their peak;
- sharp rises in urea prices from March to June 2011, with a peak in September;
- more generally, the very high volatility in fertilizer prices in recent years;
- variations in price differentials between international and landed prices and between urea and NPK prices.

The variability in international prices, with foreign exchange and other risks, and consequent exposure of suppliers to large potential losses and gains must lead to suppliers building substantial risk margins into their tenders. Measures that allow shorter bid validity periods and faster tender processing and awards should lead to lower prices. These measures would also allow for earlier delivery of supplies. Costs might also be reduced if the government took on more of the foreign exchange risks and was able to manage these risks more effectively than private suppliers.

Further insights into fertilizer prices paid by the government can be gleaned by comparing cost per MT delivered to markets with normal commercial (unsubsidized) sales prices, as shown in Figure 5.5. Here market prices include landed costs (as in Figure 5.4) and transport costs, but exclude overhead costs of ADMARC and SFFRFM. Unsubsidized prices are for November each year averaged across major centres in Malawi, and for 2008 and 2009 there is also data collected from markets around the country by the MoAFS. The figure suggests that if overhead costs were added on to the subsidized costs then unsubsidized market prices might be closer to the costs incurred by the programme through parastatal delivery (although if ADMARC is reaching more remote areas then higher average costs might also be incurred by private suppliers in reaching these).

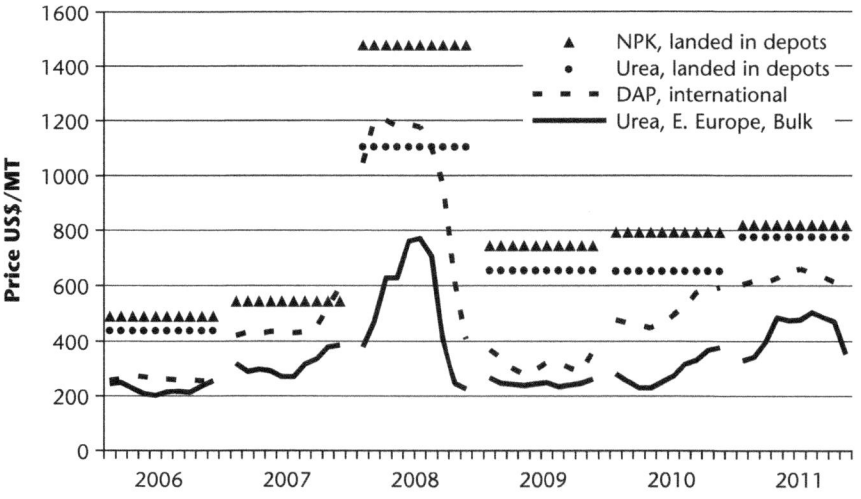

Figure 5.4. Landed and international fertilizer prices, 2006–11

Notes: 2007/8 & 2008/9 information for only part of purchases, 2009/10 excludes ADMARC b/fwd. Urea at US$1,254/MT, 2011/12 excludes ADMARC supplies of Urea at US$864/MT & NPK at US$904/MT.

Sources: Logistics Unit reports and data, World Bank commodity price data (World Bank, 2012).

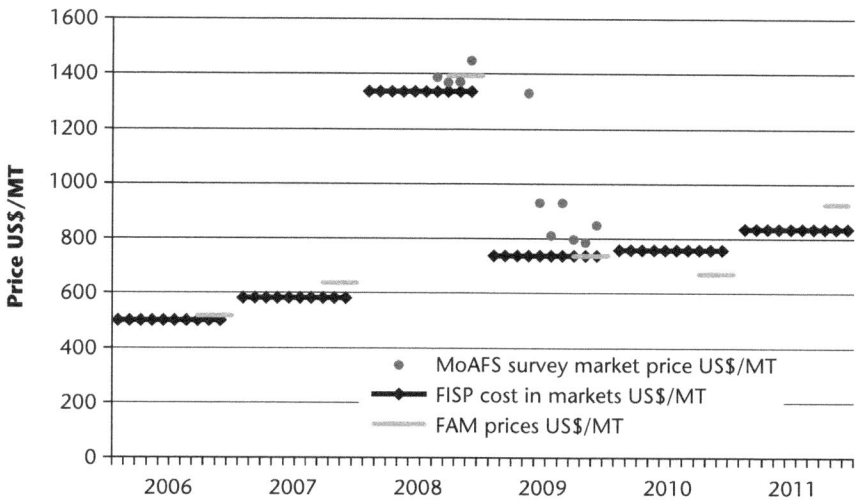

Figure 5.5. Subsidized fertilizer market costs and unsubsidized market prices, 2006–11

Notes: 2011 FAM prices are sensitive to the choice of exchange rate converting MK to US$. Prices shown are calculated with the official exchange rate, but if the widely used unofficial exchange rate in late 2011 were applied then the FAM price would be lower.

Sources: Logistics Unit reports and data, Fertiliser Association of Malawi (pers. comm.), MoAFS market reports.

The effectiveness of the programme in obtaining low-priced fertilizer supplies may also be investigated by examining the patterns of tender prices. Table 5.3 presents the range of prices paid from 2008/9 to 2011/12. Price ranges are high, although they have generally been falling and in some years (such as 2009/10) cannot be explained by wide variation in international prices during the buying period. Some suppliers appear to have been paid consistently higher prices (for example, Simama and, notably for a large urea consignment in 2009/10, ADMARC). On the other hand there is no evidence of higher prices being paid to SFFRFM (indeed the low outlier prices for NPK and urea in 2008/9 were both for supplies from SFFRFM). Price ranges remain high even after removal of outliers, but again have generally been falling since 2008/9.

5.4. Coupon distribution

We now examine the activities involved in coupon distribution, which, as shown earlier in Figure 5.1, run in parallel with input procurement and distribution activities. We again first provide an overview of systems and then consider

Table 5.3. Fertilizer procurement prices before and after removal of high outliers

Year	Fert.	Price ($/MT)		After removal of high outliers				Outlier price	% supply
		Mean	Range ($/MT)	Mean price	Range ($/MT)	% change mean	Suppliers removed		
2008/9	NPK	1,453	407	1,450	348	0.2%	Mulli Bros	1,649	1.3%
	Urea	1,121	313	1,090	239	0.4%	Simama	1,246	3.0%
2009/10	NPK	744	390	736	287	3.1%	Simama, Coin	886	5.1%
	Urea	715	670	647	221	8.4%	ADMARC	1,246	9.2%
2010/11	NPK	791	202	779	192	1.5%	Various inc Simama	870	13.0%
	Urea	650	236	645	103	0.7%	Masina Investments	830	2.5%
2011/12	NPK	824	124	817	51	0.7%	ADMARC	904	7.1%
	Urea	776	200	775	135	0.2%	ADMARC	864	1.4%

Source: Author calculations from Logistics Unit Annual reports

achievements and performance over the life of the programme, drawing on information from programme records and from farm household surveys.

5.4.1. *Systems*

Coupon distribution to beneficiaries involves a number of activities, as set out in Figure 5.1: allocations to different areas, beneficiary identification, and then actual distribution of coupons. These activities are conditional on the quantity of subsidized inputs set in the national budget, the registration of all farm families, the printing of coupons, and then their distribution to districts and communities.

The formal process and criteria for determining budgeted quantities of subsidized inputs are not clearly documented. Starting from 2005/6 there has been an aspiration to provide enough inputs to provide a core maize fertilizer package for roughly 50% of Malawian smallholder farmers. Budget decisions for subsequent years are likely to have been made on an incremental rather than zero budgeting basis, with increases and decreases determined by political objectives, funding availability, competition for funds between ministries, and budgeted prices and costs.

Formal area allocations of coupons then involve the division of the national budget for subsidized inputs between Extension Planning Areas (EPAs) within districts. From 2005/6 to 2008/9 allocations of the total across EPAs were made in two or more rounds. In 2005/6 and 2006/7 the first allocation was reported to be proportionate to the previous year's MoAFS estimates of maize and tobacco hectarage in each EPA, but from 2007/8 onwards EPA allocations were increasingly, and from 2009/10 exclusively, reported to be proportional to MoAFS estimates of the number of farm families per EPA, with, again from 2009/10, annual registration of farm families by villages within each EPA.[3] Within EPAs, processes and formal stakeholder roles in coupon allocations between and within villages have varied between years and areas and have also differed from actual, informal roles. Overall, they have involved Traditional Authorities (TAs), local government and MoAFS staff, Village Development Committees (VDCs), and local stakeholders identifying beneficiaries to receive coupons for redemption for different inputs at very reduced cash prices.

Printing of coupons has been funded and managed by the MoAFS and carried out in Malawi in all programme years except 2011/12 (when DFID funded printing outside Malawi). A requirement that coupons be clearly identified with unique beneficiary serial numbers by district and (in some years) EPA, has meant that printing has been conditional on district and EPA allocations. Once printed, with security features that have varied from year to year but have generally become more stringent with time, packs of coupons are bundled and distributed to each EPA, via District Agriculture Development Officers (DADOs). Coupon distribution to beneficiaries has involved the same parties as allocation, with the addition of a police presence to keep law and order and to safeguard the valuable packs of coupons.

A constant feature of programme design has been that intended recipients of maize fertilizers should each receive two coupons, to allow subsidized purchase of one 50 kg bag of basal fertilizer (23:21:0 +4S) and one 50 kg bag of urea. However, there has also been considerable variation over time and between areas in allocation and distribution processes and criteria determining selection of beneficiaries and the numbers of coupons of different types actually received per recipient.

Supplementary rounds of coupon allocations to areas and beneficiaries from 2006/7 to 2008/9 were much more opaque as regards systems, criteria, and numbers of coupons distributed. These were nominally intended to address problems of unmet demand in the first round of distribution but were widely considered to allow opportunities for often politically driven allocations outside formal systems.

5.4.2. Total coupon receipts

Two sources of information on coupon distribution and receipt can be compared: programme records on coupon disbursement, and farm household survey estimates of coupon receipt. These can also be compared with input sales records on coupon redemption. There is, however, a major difficulty

---

[3] Initial allocations based on crop areas or farm families were commonly modified for a variety of generally undocumented technical, administrative, political, and other reasons.

with this as the estimation of total coupon receipts from farm household survey data requires the multiplication of mean receipts per household (estimated from the survey) by the total number of farm households—but there are major discrepancies between the estimates of the number of rural households based on the National Statistical Office (NSO) 2008 census on the one hand and MoAFS estimates of farm families on the other. The extent of these discrepancies is shown in Figure 5.6.

These differences may have a number of causes:

a. the definitions of farm families and of rural households may be different, with a larger number of smaller-farm families;

b. MoAFS processes may lead to households splitting for the purposes of registration, to increase the number of coupons that they may be able to receive;

c. 'ghost' families and villages may have been created by corrupt field staff or traditional leaders to enable them to obtain coupons;

d. the NSO may have missed some households in the census;

e. the NSO rural households listing excludes all households residing in cities or in urban areas, but many urban households are also engaged in agriculture and may receive coupons.

It is possible that the discrepancies in Figure 5.6 result from all these causes. Examination of the figure certainly suggests that there has been some 'inflation' in MoAFS farm family estimates. The central region appears to have had a remarkable growth in farm families from 2005/6 to 2009/10 (reaching 20% in 2009/10), with numbers then flattening off and actually declining from 2010/11 to 2011/12. Combined with a spurt in growth in the southern region from 2008/9 to 2009/10, this resulted in an estimated increase of 14% in Malawian farm families in 2009/10. Northern region

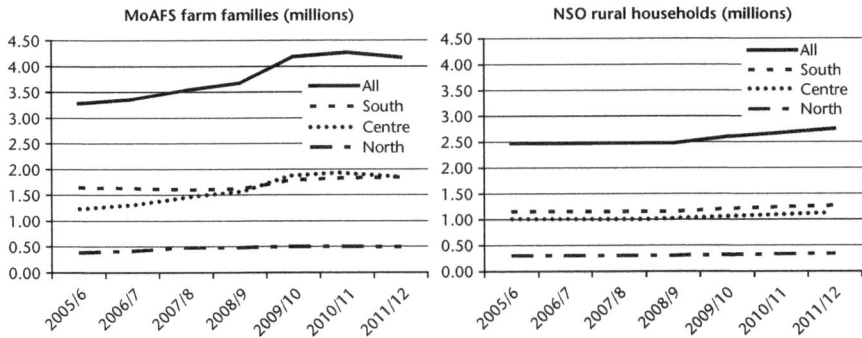

Figure 5.6. MoAFS farm families and NSO rural households

growth rates were also high from 2005/6 to 2007/8 and then flattened off. These regional and temporal variations pose questions regarding the reliability of the farm family estimates, and suggest that the NSO estimates may be more reliable—although they may also exclude some urban farm households.[4]

Table 5.4 compares estimates of coupon issues and receipts from these different sources. Higher MoAFS farm family estimates lead to higher estimates of total coupon receipts, exceeding MoAFS formal allocations in 2008/9 and 2010/11 (although there may have been substantial informal supplementary allocations in 2008/9, this was not the case in 2010/11 when the excess is greatest). Lower NSO-based rural household estimates, however, lead to lower estimates of total coupon receipts, considerably below MoAFS formal allocations in all three years.

Following the discussion above of Figure 5.6 and the use of NSO rural household definitions in the farm household estimates of coupons received per

Table 5.4. Estimates of fertilizer coupon issues and receipts from different sources[5]

	2006/7	2008/9	2010/11
A. Households receiving one or more coupons	54%	67%	79%
B. Coupons received per recipient household	1.7	1.5	1.4
C. Coupons received per household (all households)	1.01	1.12	1.13
D. Estimate of total coupons received, NSO based rural household estimates (millions)	2.51	2.79	2.73
E. Estimate of total coupons received, MoAFS farm family estimates (millions)	3.32	4.11	4.42
F. MoAFS voucher allocation (millions)	3.48	3.91	3.20
Discrepancy as % of missing coupons as % MoAFS allocations			
G. Using NSO rural household estimates (D as % of F)	28%	28%	15%
H. Using MoAFS farm family estimates (E as % of F)	5%	−5%	−38%

Sources: 2006/7, 2008/9, and 2010/11 household surveys; Logistic Unit reports; author calculations from National Statistical Office (2008a) and data supplied by MoAFS.

[4] The small increase in the NSO rural household growth rates from 2008/9 is due to post-2008 estimates relying on 2008 rather than 1997 census data.

household, we may expect more reliable estimates of total coupon receipts using the NSO rural household estimates. This suggests that a total of 3.3 rising to 4.4 million fertilizer coupons were distributed to rural households in the 2006/7, 2008/9, and 2010/11 seasons. We discuss later the implications of this for estimates of diversion and fraud in the programme.

Comparable analysis for seed coupons is difficult, as a result of changing systems and quantities of seed coupon allocations. However, 2008/9 and 2010/11 survey estimates of coupon receipts per household multiplied by estimated rural household numbers give total coupon receipt estimates that are close to MoAFS records of total allocations.

5.4.3. *Coupon distribution processes and performance*

Section 5.4.1 has described broad processes for coupon distribution. In this section we examine these in a little more detail, comparing formal procedures adopted by the programme with those actually reported in 2006/7, 2008/9, and 2010/11 farm household surveys and focus group discussions. We consider how procedures and criteria for coupon allocation and distribution have changed, the timing of these activities, their outcomes in terms of the numbers of coupons distributed, and perceptions of these processes.

Formal instructions for coupon allocation and distribution have specified who should be involved and procedures to be used. These instructions have changed over time in response to both difficulties and complaints on the one hand and examples of success on the other. Thus, in 2005/6 Traditional Authorities (TAs) were tasked with allocating coupons between villages within EPAs, and Village Development Committees (VDC) with allocating coupons between households within villages. Complaints that some TAs and VDCs were subverting allocations led to instructions in 2006/7 that allocations be made by district, area, and village committees in accordance with standard local government structures, with detailed terms of reference and membership for each committee. Beneficiaries, were supposed to be 'full time smallholder farmers who cannot afford to purchase one or two bags of fertilizer at prevailing commercial prices, as determined by local leaders in their areas'. Guidelines also specified that coupons should be issued to beneficiaries 'just before they go to a market point to purchase inputs, to minimize chances of abusing them'.

---

[5] Estimates of the percentage of households receiving coupons are in broad agreement with survey results for six districts in central and southern Malawi reported by Holden and Lunduka (2010b) with 68 and 75% of households receiving coupons in 2007/8 and 2008/9 respectively, and 1.4 and 1.5 coupons per recipient household in the same years. Chibwana et al. (2010) estimate that 77% of households received fertilizer coupons in 2008/9 in samples from two districts in central and southern Malawi.

In 2007/8 programme objectives and formal targeting criteria were amended to give greater emphasis to concerns for vulnerable households. Systems for allocation and distribution of coupons within districts were also modified to give less power to TAs and more responsibility to MoAFS staff, following support from communities to disburse vouchers through MoAFS staff following the 2006/7 programme experience. 'Flexi-seed' vouchers were also introduced, allowing households who were not given a set of vouchers for the maize seed and fertilizer package to nevertheless benefit from subsidized maize, legume, or cotton seed. This was not, however, particularly popular as there were very limited supplies of legume seed, cotton seed was wanted by relatively few farmers, and many farmers saw it as a poor substitute for receipt of fertilizer coupons. Flexi-seed coupons were discontinued in 2009/10 and replaced by specific legume seed coupons.

In 2008/9 all farm families were registered and the list of registered farm families was used in subsequent identification of beneficiaries in 'open village meetings' led by teams involving MoAFS staff, local government staff, religious leaders, VDC members, and civil society representatives. Beneficiary lists were compiled by village and EPA and district. These lists were then checked by the Logistics Unit against allocations before distribution registers were printed with beneficiary names by village and delivered to the MoAFS. Similar procedures were followed from 2009/10 to 2011/12 except that beneficiaries were also supposed to have voter ID cards from the 2009 elections and there were further increases in emphasis on beneficiary targeting to focus on more vulnerable households—emphasizing child-headed, female-headed, or orphan-headed households, those infected or affected with HIV and AIDS, and guardians or carers of vulnerable people (all of whom should be also be Malawians owning land).

Key informant interviews, information from community questionnaires, and anecdotal evidence suggest that a wider variety of coupon allocation and distribution procedures has been followed than would be expected from consistent implementation of the formal instructions. Thus, in 2006/7 the involvement of the DDC (District Development Committee) and VDC was almost, but not quite, universal with, for example, in one surveyed district only one committee level under the DDC organizing bulk transport of fertilizers for farmers. The extent and nature of involvement of the TAs in the process varied widely, and was strongest in the central region where there were reports of TAs subverting the process in various ways. Targeting criteria reported also varied markedly between districts with, for example, different emphases on farmers' inability to otherwise afford fertilizer purchase.

Wide variations in practice were also associated with the introduction of open meetings from 2008/9. First the extent of their adoption varied, with 81 and 96% of respondents reporting open meetings for allocation and distribution of fertilizer coupons in 2008/9, and similar figures for 2010/11. Where open meetings were adopted, some FGDs described them as meetings where pre-determined beneficiary lists were announced, while others reported actual participatory selection of beneficiaries. Some respondents recognized their value in informing people about the programme and consequently helping to reduce struggles and conflicts, but perceptions also appear to be conditional on perceptions about changing numbers of available coupons compared to the previous year.

As regards the second, supplementary allocation of coupons, a large proportion of respondents reported that these were distributed based on the choices of traditional leaders and, in other cases, by politicians mainly targeting their supporters and party sympathizers. However, Chinsinga (2012b) documents reports of some more general political interference in coupon allocation.

A significant and widely practiced variation from official procedures has involved 'redistribution' of coupons. Coupon allocations should lead to all beneficiaries getting two coupons for 'maize fertilizer' (one for NPK and one for urea). However, substantial numbers of respondents report receipt of one coupon (or even the proceeds of a part of a coupon). This is also reported by Holden and Lunduka (2010b) and we discuss this further with regard to targeting outcomes in Chapter 10.

We now turn from a description of coupon allocation and distribution processes to consideration of performance in these activities as regards timing and respondents' perceptions of effectiveness. Discussion of diversion and fraud in coupon allocation is deferred to its own section later in this chapter, while targeting is considered later in Chapter 10.

Information on the timing of beneficiaries' receipt of coupons is available from the 2006/7, 2008/9, and 2010/11 household surveys. This is summarized across all regions in Figure 5.7 and shows a clear improving trend over the three surveys, but with only 40% of beneficiaries receiving their coupons by the end of October in 2010/11 (70% in the south, 11% in the centre, and none in the north) there is still need for considerable improvement. Community survey respondents reported similar patterns.

Survey respondents have also been asked to rate different aspects of programme implementation from very good to very bad. In Table 5.5 scorings on timing show small but steady annual improvements in perceptions of timing since the start of the programme, with overall ratings moving from 'bad' to 'not good, not bad' from 2005/6 to 2010/11. Ratings of methods of coupon distribution and of criteria for coupon distribution have not changed much, and are broadly 'not good, not bad'. Perceptions of numbers

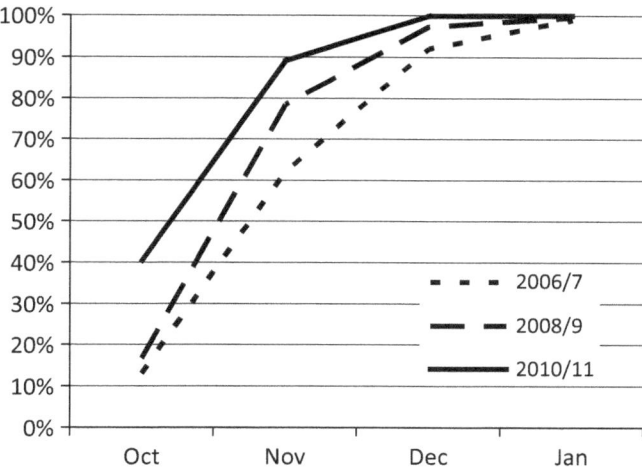

Figure 5.7. Percentage of beneficiaries reporting receipt of maize fertilizer coupons by end of each month

of coupons distributed have been declining. This may result from changes in the average number of coupons received per recipient (see Table 5.4) as a result of the increasing redistribution of coupons discussed earlier. Holden and Lunduka (2010b) find that 28% of respondents in 2008/9 reported 'insufficient coupons' as the main problem with the programme, while 42% considered corruption to be the main problem. However Holden and Lunduka (2010a) also report that 31% of respondents from the same survey suggested that more or enough coupons should be supplied, with 20% suggesting that the coupon distribution system need to be improved, 10% each suggesting providing more inputs and introducing a general fertilizer subsidy, and 9% suggesting that chiefs be removed from involvement in coupon distribution.

The final issue to be discussed on coupon distribution is the extent to which farmers had to pay for coupons. We may expect some under-reporting of this. Five per cent of fertilizer coupons were reported as being obtained with some payment in both 2006/7 and 2008/9 (this is lower than the estimate of 14% for 2008/9 survey reported by Holden and Lunduka (2010b)). Reported sources of such fertilizer included TAs and headmen, agricultural staff, VDC members, traders, and fellow farmers. A much lower figure of 2% was found in 2010/11. Reported prices varied dramatically, with medians of 600MK per coupon in 2006/7, 2000MK in 2008/9 (when prices for unsubsidized fertilizer were very high) and 1000MK in 2010/11 (Holden and Lunduka (2010b) reported median prices of 1500MK for 2007/8 and 2500MK for 2008/9).

Table 5.5. Scoring on different programme elements by year

	2005/6	2006/7	2007/8	2008/9	2009/10	2010/11
Timing of distribution	2.73	2.73	2.56	2.01	2.20	1.93
Methods of coupon distribution	2.89	2.94	2.97	2.81	2.69	2.74
Criteria for coupon allocation		2.95	2.92	2.83	2.79	2.83
Number of coupons	2.96	3.02	3.07	3.16	3.20	3.36

Scores: 1 = very good; 2 = good; 3 = not good not bad; 4 = bad; 5 = very bad.

5.5. Coupon redemption

As with input and coupon distribution, we consider coupon redemption with an overview of systems and then consider achievements and performance over the life of the programme.

5.5.1. Redemption systems

Redemption of coupons for subsidized inputs essentially involves the presentation of a valid coupon and any necessary payment to an authorized retailer who, after checking the validity of the coupon, issues the specified input. Three main systems have been used over the life of the programme: redemption of fertilizer coupons by parastatals (SFFRFM and ADMARC), redemption of fertilizer coupons by approved private retailers in the 2006/7 and 2007/8 seasons, and redemption of seed coupons by parastatals or private retailers from 2006/7.[6] We describe core features of each of these systems: a description of more detailed changes between years is provided in Section 5.5.3.

Under the parastatal system for fertilizer redemption, fertilizer stocks are distributed to ADMARC and SFFRFM markets (some of which are specially opened during the input supply season) as described earlier. Beneficiaries then present their coupons with the required farmer payment and the parastatal issues the fertilizer. ADMARC and SFFRFM were then supposed to return to the government both the money and coupons received from farmers. The

---

[6] Some subsidized OPV maize seed was supplied through ADMARC and SFFRFM under the 2005/6 programme without coupons with a 70% subsidy, but there is no further documentation of this.

extent to which coupons have been returned has varied between years, while information on reimbursement of farmer payments is not available. From 2006/7 onwards fertilizer subsidy sales information has been reported by the Logistics Unit on the basis of stock reconciliations and, from 2006/7 to 2010/11 on the basis of weekly market reports.

Redemption of fertilizer coupons by approved private retailers in the 2006/7 and 2007/8 seasons was identical to redemption of coupons by parastatals as regards transactions with farmers. However, reimbursement for sales (of the retailer's own stocks) was obtained by submission of invoices to the MoAFS supported by redeemed coupons, with reimbursement per coupon at a previously contracted price covering subsidy costs (with retailers keeping farmer payments as the unsubsidized part of the overall payment).

The seed coupon system has been based on annual agreements between the MoAFS and seed supply companies in the Seed Traders Association of Malawi (STAM). Under these agreements individual companies contract with different retailers to supply them with seed approved for subsidized sale, and then to receive from these retailers the details of subsidized sales, with supporting coupons. The seed companies subsequently invoice the MoAFS for each seed coupon returned to them as a result of its use in purchasing their seed. The distribution between retailers and seed supply companies of MoAFS payments and of any farmer payments are a matter for negotiation between retailers and seed supply companies and are not a matter for MoAFS.

An important issue in coupon redemption is the setting of redemption fees to be paid by farmers. As indicated earlier in Table 5.1, while fertilizer prices have risen over the life of the programme, farmer contributions through the redemption price have fallen by almost 50% in nominal terms (more in real terms), from 950MK per bag to 500MK/bag for 'maize fertilizers', and the subsidy has therefore increased from around 65% to over 90%. Fertilizer redemption prices have been politically determined, generally announced by the president in political statements or at rallies. There is little evidence of any technocratic involvement in the setting of these prices, which are very low: when a price of 500MK/bag was announced for the 2012/13 season it was widely criticized as a contributor to high and unsustainable and distortionary programme costs undermining budgets for other MoAFS activities. Politics has generally played a smaller role in the setting of seed prices, which have been negotiated by seed companies and the MoAFS. However in 2007/8 agreement that farmer redemption payments ('top ups') of up to 100MK could be charged per 2 kg pack of hybrid seed had to be abandoned following a political statement that all subsidized maize seed was free. Seed redemption prices are less important than fertilizer prices, both politically and in their impact on the programme budget.

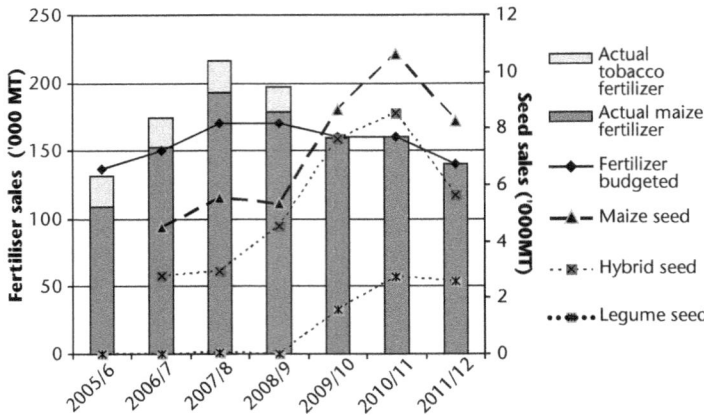

Figure 5.8. Subsidized fertilizer and seed sales by year
Source: Calculations from Logistics Unit (2011) and earlier reports.

5.5.2. Total redemption

Figure 5.8 shows the total volumes of fertilizer and seed redemptions by year. Subsidized fertilizer sales increased from 2005/6 to 2007/8, and were considerably over budget from 2006/7 to 2008/9 (with budgeted fertilizer sales of 150,000 MT in 2006/7 and 170,000MT in 2007/8 and 2008/9). The lower sales from 2009/10 were almost exactly on budget. Maize seed sales increased from 2006/7 to 2010/11 but fell back in 2011/12. Hybrid maize seed sales increased dramatically from 2007/8 to 2009/10, with reduced sales of OPV seed, but OPV sales then grew again in 2010/11 and 2011/12—with hybrid seed sales hardly growing in 2010/11 and then declining in 2011/12. There were also dramatic increases in legume seed sales in 2009/10 and 2010/11, with 2011/12 sales a little lower than in 2010/11.

5.5.3. Coupon redemption performance

Apart from the introduction of private sector seed and fertilizer sales in 2006/7 and the withdrawal of private sector fertilizer sales in 2009/10, the only major changes in redemption processes between years have been variation in redemption payments required from farmers. These are set out in Table 5.6. Variation in pack sizes for hybrid and OPV seed packs and in farmer top up payments required for different varieties led to some competition and farmer choice, where different seed stockists accessible to beneficiaries carried different or a range of stocks.

Performance in coupon redemption can be considered in terms of availability of inputs for redemption, and timing and costs of redemption. These are all related.

Table 5.6. Coupon redemption parameters, 2005/6 to 2011/12

	Fertilizers top-up payment (MK per 50 kg)	Maize seed pack			Legume seed	
		Size (kg)	Top up farmer payment (MK)	Redemption value (MK)	Size (no farmer top up)	Redemption value (MK)
2005/6	*	OPV pack size	n/a*	n/a*	-	-
2006/7	950	2 kg hybrid seed or 3 or 4 kg OPV seed	0	400	-	-
2007/8	900	2 kg hybrid seed or 4 kg OPV seed	0**	400	2 kg	400
2008/9	800	2 kg hybrid seed or 4 kg OPV seed	0	680	2 kg	680
2009/10	500	5 kg hybrid seed or 10 kg OPV seed	<=100MK	1500	2 kg	350
2010/11	500	5 kg hybrid seed or 7.5 kg OPV seed	<=100MK	1650	2 kg	740
2011/12	500	5 kg hybrid seed or 10 kg OPV seed	<=100MK	1815	0MK for 2 kg	815

* 950MK per bag for 23:21:0 and urea, 1450MK per bag for Compound D and CAN.

** Farmer top ups agreed initially but subsequent political announcements led to confusion and inconsistent payments.

Lack or limited availability of inputs when needed has been a major difficulty that has frequently delayed purchase and use of subsidized inputs. We have discussed in earlier sections how for fertilizers this has been caused by late opening of seasonal markets, late distribution of inputs to markets, and late distribution of coupons to beneficiaries—and how these three factors interact—as late market opening and coupon distribution makes timely input distribution to markets more difficult, and hence fertilizer stock-outs more likely. Farmers and sellers have no flexibility in substituting between types of fertilizer since coupons are specific to each type of fertilizer. With seeds, however, there has been more flexibility, with opportunities to exchange maize seed coupons for different varieties of hybrid and OPV seed, if different stocks are available.

Table 5.7. Reported distances to buy inputs, time spent buying inputs, and costs for transport and miscellaneous expenses

	Hours travel & waiting		Transport and misc expenses (MK)		Distance to nearest ADMARC (km)		Distance to nearest private selling point (km)	
	Mean	Median	Mean	median	Mean	Median	Mean	Median
2006/7	13	7	247	150	7	5	7	5
2008/9	17	9	304	200	9	5	14	8
2010/11	23	12	270	200	5	4	8	6

Stock-outs have been relatively common in all years of the programme, have affected all inputs, and in 2006/7 were experienced by both private and parastatal retailers.[7] However when they manage to get their inputs farmers are generally pleased with the fertilizers they get, but are sometimes disappointed by lack of availability of hybrid maize seed and specific types of legume seed. We discuss access to maize seed further in Chapter 8.

Stock-outs lead to increased time and cost for farmers travelling to and from and waiting at markets, and while it appears that hours travelling and waiting have increased over the life of the programme there is no clear evidence of changes in transport and other costs or in distances to markets (see Table 5.7).

Stock-outs also provide sales clerks with opportunities to demand extra payments for access to limited stocks. This is a problem that is widely reported in the media and in focus group discussions and key informant interviews. Table 5.8 provides survey estimates of the extent and nature of these extra demands.

Table 5.8 shows no clear trend in the frequency or size of extra payments. In 2006/7 the percentage of coupons requiring tips and mean redemption price were lower at ADMARC/SFFRFM than at all other distributors, but this masks considerable variation between different distributors, with some having a slightly lower reported incidence of tipping than ADMARC/SFFRFM. In 2008/9 and 2010/11 community survey respondents, focus group discussions, and key informant interviews all suggested that the payment of bribes to redeem inputs was more widespread than is suggested by the survey results, with focus groups suggesting that this was closely related to problems of queuing. Chinsinga (2009) also reported extra payments of 200MK to 800MK per bag of fertilizer being demanded by some ADMARC staff (with

---

[7] Holden and Lunduka (2010b) find that only 7% of respondents in 2008/9 reported 'insufficient inputs' as the main problem with the programme. However data from the same survey indicate that 19% of households considered fertilizer to arrive too late, 6% considered it was on time but insufficient, and 8% considered it both late and insufficient (equivalent figures for 2007/8 were 37%, 6%, and 6%, respectively) (Holden and Lunduka, 2010a).

Table 5.8. Reported extra payments for coupon redemption (MK/bag fertilizer)

Year	Retailers	% coupons paid tips	Median price	Mean price	Mean extra payment	Median extra payment if paid
2006/7	Private	27%	950	1,223	273	n/a
2006/7	Parastatal	18%	950	983	33	n/a
2008/9	Parastatal	14%	800	827	27	200
2010/11	Parastatal	9%	500	536	36	250–500

those unable to pay being required to wait two or three days before they were served); extortion of cash from beneficiaries by criminal elements to 'facilitate' input acquisition; and organized theft through tricking farmers. The Farmers Union of Malawi (2011) report that 5% of their sample of registered beneficiaries reported being asked to pay bribes for input redemption although 42% considered it common or very common to be asked for such a bribe.[8] However, only 20% of those asked for a bribe reported that they had paid it. The Farmers Union of Malawi (2011) FGDs also reported that women were particularly vulnerable to these demands

It is difficult to determine if extra payments made for hybrid seed are corrupt, as extra payments have been supposed to be made for some hybrid varieties in some years. However, no payments should have been required for OPV or legume seed, but 12% and 11% of respondents reported making some payment for OPV and legume seed in 2010/11, respectively.

5.6. Diversion and fraud

Diversion of subsidized inputs away from intended beneficiaries is an issue that has been raised in Chapters 2, 3, and 4. Diversion takes several forms, from inclusion errors in targeting (whereby inputs go to smallholder farmers who were not supposed to get them) through leakages (for example, as a result of sales of vouchers or subsidized inputs at low prices) to outright fraud and corruption, where people capture subsidized inputs as a result of direct criminal activity or as a result of political influence (and of course illegal political capture is itself criminal). We make a distinction here between mis-targeting within the smallholder sector and diversion outside the smallholder sector.

---

[8] This divergence between perceived frequency and reported experience is interesting and may inform interpretation of FGD information—perhaps suggesting that the incidence of these problems is overstated in FGDs.

Targeting is the subject of Chapter 10. We consider here evidence regarding the extent of leakage or diversion outside the smallholder sector.[9]

Illegal activities are inevitably clandestine and difficult to trace. There have been numerous media reports of cases of theft and fraud regarding FISP coupons and inputs (Tambulasi, 2009), successful prosecutions, and on-going police, audit, and Anti-Corruption Bureau investigations. There are also frequent allegations of fraud by village officials and extension agents in focus group discussions and key informant interviews. It is, however, very difficult to obtain objective and comprehensive estimates of the extent of these activities. The lack of transparency in coupon allocation when combined with excess demand for coupons leads to perceptions of and complaints about corruption and diversion of coupons, and this may occur even in situations where these perceptions and complaints may not be warranted. In addition, while there may be many cases that are not discovered, acute interest in those cases that are discovered may lead to over-estimates of their occurrence and scale.

Fraud may arise in a number of ways: through voucher allocation to non-existent ('ghost') beneficiaries (or villages), with theft of the allocated vouchers by Ministry of Agriculture staff and/or Traditional Authorities, diversion of vouchers to people with power (government staff, traditional leaders, or politicians) or to criminals for sale, direct allocation to non-beneficiaries, and printing of extra or counterfeit vouchers within or outside the system. There may also be thefts of inputs. Another type of corruption is operated by some who act as gatekeepers, with village headmen or sales clerks demanding bribes (extra payments or services) in exchange for coupons or coupon redemption which beneficiaries are entitled to without such bribes. This last form of corruption was discussed in Sections 5.4.3 and 5.5.3.

Although there should be control systems that prevent or at least monitor these different types and sources of fraud, the existence and operation of these systems have not always been clear, or, as with some audits, their implementation has been slow and a full picture has still to emerge. The extent and investigation of diversion has also been affected by changing political conditions, as discussed in Chapter 4.

The divergence in estimated number of households between the NSO census and the MoAFS farm registry (discussed in Section 5.4.2) poses difficulties in using household surveys to investigate this issue. For example, with the NSO farm family estimate it appears that 2.7 million fertilizer coupons were received by smallholder farmers in 2010/11 against a recorded allocation of 3.2 million, leading to an estimate of 0.5 million 'missing' coupons (15% of those issued, compared to 28% in 2008/9). However, with the MoAFS farm

---

[9] It should be noted that some apparent targeting errors within the smallholder sector also involve the abuse of power and influence by people who are smallholder farmers.

family estimate it appears that 4.4 million fertilizer coupons were received by smallholder farmers in 2010/11 against a recorded allocation of 3.2 million, leading to receipts exceeding issues by 38% (compared to 5% in 2008/9). These difficulties are compounded by the lack of a nationally representative sample for the 2010/11 FISP survey. However, they do suggest that if the NSO figures are taken as being closer to the to the true population with the NSO (as opposed to MoAFS) household definition (as suggested by earlier examination of the differences in regional changes in MoAFS figures and by the survey using NSO households for sampling and the NSO household definition) then high losses in 2008/9 have been substantially reduced in 2010/11.

We can, however, go further than this to make some very broad estimates of leakage and diversion of subsidy vouchers and inputs outside the smallholder sector. The basis of these is the diagram of possible voucher and subsidized input flows in Figure 5.9. The diagram shows on the left hand side the legitimate flows of vouchers and inputs within the smallholder sector, and on the right the illegitimate flows of vouchers and inputs outside the smallholder sector. Boxes in bold represent variables for which we have estimates from household surveys or administrative records (although estimates for smallholders' cheap purchases are not available for 2006/7). This then allows some estimation of the scale of diversion first of vouchers (by comparison of estimates of voucher receipts and use by smallholders against programme voucher redemptions) and then of subsidized seed and fertilizers (by comparison of estimated input acquisition and use by smallholders against total programme supply). These estimations are prone to error, first as a result of uncertainty regarding the total number of farm households (as discussed earlier) and second as a result of making estimates by subtraction, which tends to magnify percentage errors. Nevertheless, these estimates may be taken to provide some broad indications of the changes in the scale of diversion in the programme. These are set out in Table 5.9 for the 2006/7, 2008/9, and 2010/11 years when survey data were available. As in Section 5.4.2, we take the NSO-based estimates of the number of rural households to be most reliable and consistent with the sample surveys.

The results of this analysis are presented in Table 5.9 (capital letters in each row refer to the framework in Figure 5.9). This suggests that there were very high leakages or diversions outside the smallholder sector in 2006/7 and 2008/9, with smallholders receiving only 63 and 68% respectively of recorded coupon issues. Despite their smaller share of disbursed coupons in 2006/7, it appears that smallholders redeemed a higher percentage of their coupons as compared with others, and as a result bought a greater share of the subsidized fertilizers than in 2008/9. Of the fertilizers bought by others under the subsidy in 2008/9, however, a large proportion (about 50%) appears to have been sold to smallholders at lower than unsubsidized prices,

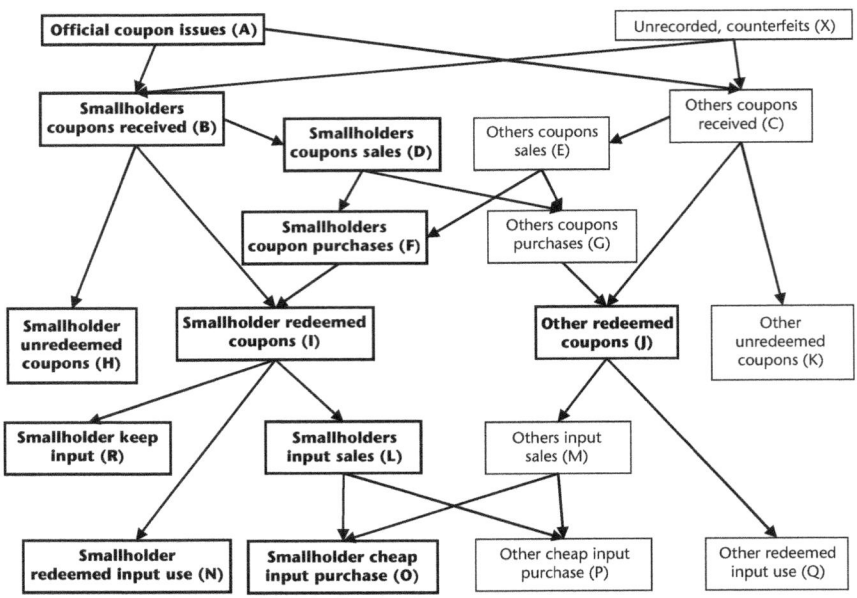

Figure 5.9. Flows of coupons and subsidized inputs

so that the smallholder sector ended up using about 80% of the subsidized supplies—though a little over 25% of this was not purchased with the full subsidy. This is broadly comparable with Holden and Lunduka (2010b) who estimate that in 2008/9 21% of total household fertilizer use was obtained through cheap purchases of fertilizer (and 25% through purchased coupons). In 2010/11, however, smallholder farmers received a higher, but still not high enough, proportion of voucher issues (85%) and it is also estimated that in addition almost all the diverted subsidy fertilizer sales were then resold to smallholders (again at prices between full and zero subsidy). If smallholders are assumed to have received around 50% of the subsidy when buying originally subsidized fertilizers from other sellers then the proportion of fertilizer subsidy captured by others fell from a little under 30% of the subsidy in 2008/9 to a little over 10% in 2010/12. Since the subsidy volume was approximately 25% higher in 2008/9, and the price of fertilizers was approximately 65% higher, the estimated loss through diversion fell by just under 80% from 2008/9 to 2010/11.[10]

---

[10] A similar analysis for maize seeds in 2010/11 (Dorward and Chirwa, 2011) and administrative records suggests substantial numbers of counterfeit maize seed coupons that year. These have less national and political significance and less individual and aggregate value than fertilizer coupons, but nevertheless offer substantial income opportunities for criminal activities.

Table 5.9. Estimated shares of coupon and subsidized fertilizer receipts by smallholders and others[1]

	2006/7	2008/9	2010/11
Coupons % recorded issues			
Recorded issues (from MoAFS and Logistics Unit)—A	100%	100%	100%
Received by smallholders, exc. purchases—B	63%	68%	85%
Received by others (by subtraction)—A-B = C-X	37%	32%	15%
Redemptions Total (from Logistics Unit)—I + J	87%	102%	100%
Smallholders—I	63%	69%	78%
Others (by subtraction)—J	25%	34%	22%
Counterfeits/extras redeemed (min.)	-13%	2%	0%
Fertilizers % subsidy sales			
Total subsidy sales (from Logistics Unit)—I + J	100%	100%	100%
Smallholder redemption & use—N	72%	58%	78%
Others' redemption—J by subtraction	28%	42%	22%
Smallholder low price purchases—O	n/a	21%	21%
Total smallholder use—N + O	n/a	79%	99%
Others' low price/redemption use—P + Q	n/a	21%	1%

[1] Smallholder low price purchases (O) are estimated as all purchases below a cut-off price. In 2008/9, there was a much greater range of fertilizer prices reported by respondents, and the cut-off point for 'low price' purchases was set at 150MK/kg, around 70% of the standard commercial price. For 2010/11 examination of the data suggested a cut-off point of 85MK/kg, around 85% of the standard commercial price. However some of the higher price purchases could be for stock from the subsidy if some traders bought subsidized fertilizers and sold it as if it were commercial, particularly when selling in smaller quantities. Allowance for this might suggest somewhat higher reselling of subsidized purchases than estimated above, in which case estimates of 'others low price redemption and use (P + Q)' would fall. However, the broader conclusions of this section would not be significantly changed—indeed some would be strengthened.

Source: Author calculations from survey data.

Despite the apparently precise estimates presented here, these should be taken as illustrative—sampling error will affect survey estimates and, as discussed earlier, there is uncertainty regarding the number of farm families and the subtractions in the calculations may magnify errors. Nevertheless, the broad conclusion that there were substantial reductions in the extent and value of diversion of subsidized fertilizer from 2008/9 to 2010/11 is likely to be robust. While it appears that there is still substantial diversion of fertilizer subsidy benefits away from smallholders, it is instructive to compare this with, for example, the UK Income Support Allowance, which in 2009/10 suffered from estimates of over-payments (estimates which are unlikely to be complete) of a little over 5% as a result of fraud and error (Department for Work and Pensions, 2012).

These conclusions regarding levels and changes in diversion and fraud are compatible with the continued reports of variable but widespread diversion of fertilizer coupons in rural areas (by government staff, TAs, headmen, and VDC members). The apparent reduction in diversion of coupons and fertilizers that never reach rural areas ('Others' low price/redemption use—P+Q' in Table 5.9 is dramatically reduced in 2010/11) is also compatible with a reduced and changed political significance and role of the programme after the 2008/9 election, as mentioned earlier in Chapter 4. Further information on these matters may become available in the future as ongoing audit investigations continue (but these tend to be slow with, for example, media reports in 2012 regarding audit investigations of the 2007/8 and 2008/9 programmes) and with the change in government in 2012 opening up the political space for investigations of prior fraud.

5.7. Farmer support

Proper use of subsidized seed and fertilizer is an important determinant of the impact of the FISP, and this would suggest that access to extension advice on use of fertilizer and improved seeds should be an important component of the programme. The household surveys in 2006/7, 2008/9, and 2010/11 do not show any consistent changes by year but between 15% and 20% of farmers (beneficiaries and non-beneficiaries) received extension advice on fertilizers and maize varieties, with advice on average being considered moderately useful. A greater proportion of farmers in the north received advice than in the other two regions, while a somewhat lower proportion of female-headed households and poorer households receiving advice (as compared with male-headed households and less-poor households).

5.8. Programme finance and costs

The final major implementation issue that we address in this chapter is the cost of the programme. We consider overall programme cost to provide a measure of fiscal resources used by the programme and of its sources. Examination of the cost breakdown and comparison of actual and budgeted costs provides further information on resource use and financial management.

Constructing a consistent set of financial information about the programme over the period 2005/6 to 2011/12 faces a number of difficulties:

1. There are difficulties with the treatment of farmer payments for fertilizer sold though ADMARC and SFFRFM. For inputs supplied through the private sector, the government reimburses the supplier at an agreed rate which is calculated as the cost of input supply less farmer payments. However, for fertilizers supplied through ADMARC and SFFRFM, the government bears the whole cost of supply and requires reimbursement of farmer payments from ADMARC and SFFRFM. There are no publicly available accounts of this, though anecdotal information suggests that

SFFRFM has been repaying these monies in full for a number of years while ADMARC only began to increase its payments in later years.

2. There are substantial gaps in reported costs in different years, leaving analysis with decisions to make about estimating these in some years but not others, and with doubts about their completeness when they are included.

3. Fertilizers may be bought one year and carried over to the next as stock. These costs have been handled in different ways in different years, and when there are large price rises and falls between years these pose difficulties for allocating costs between years.

4. There are substantial programme costs that do not appear in any accounts—for example, the costs of extension staff time allocated to the programme, for at least three months of the year, are not included in any financial costs for the programme.

5. Finally, and expanding on the previous two points, there are differences between annual fiscal accounts of the programme on the one hand (important for consideration of the programme's fiscal impacts) and economic analysis of the programme's opportunity costs. While this difference may be conceptually clear, this is often not the case in practice.

As a result of these practical and conceptual difficulties in recording programme costs, different statements of aggregate costs may be found in different contexts.

Our best estimates of programme costs from 2005/6 to 2011/12 are set out in Table A5.1. This provides some detail on different information available and unavailable in different years and is the basis for information presented in Figure 5.10.

There are a number of points of interest in Figure 5.10. First, we note how programme costs appeared to be increasing exponentially from 2005/6 to 2008/9, while the programme budget was supposed to rise more slowly and steadily. This led to an increase in estimated expenditure from US$74 to US$250 million from 2006/7 to 2008/9, with the programme accounting for 68% and 16% of the MoAFS and national budgets and 6.6% of GDP in 2008/9. However, while the 2009/10 budget continued to rise, 2009/10 actual programme costs fell dramatically below the budget, and although costs rose again above the budget in 2010/11 and 2011/12 they remained below half of the 2008/9 levels in relation to the national budget and GDP (at or below 8% and 3% respectively). The major cost item causing programme cost changes is clearly the cost of fertilizer (which here includes procurement and transport to markets), as seed and other costs are responsible for a small proportion of programme costs and show a steady increase

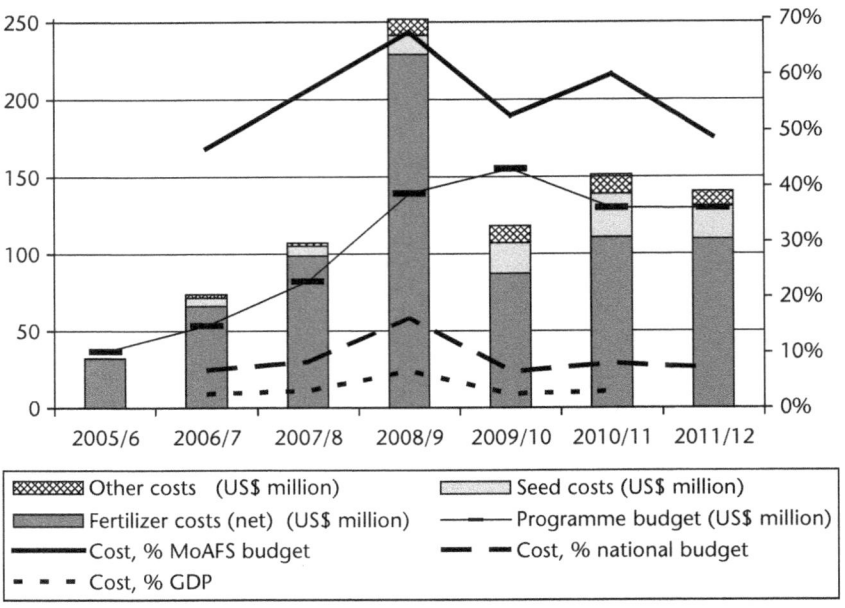

Figure 5.10. Budgeted and actual programme costs
Sources: see Table A5.1.

over the life of the programme (due to increases in seed volumes and prices and greater reporting of other cost items). Fertilizer costs are then the product of volumes and prices, as shown earlier in Figures 5.4, 5.5, and 5.8, respectively. Figure 5.8 shows that fertilizer volumes increased dramatically from 2005/6 to 2007/8, and then fell back somewhat in 2008/9 (though they were still above 2006/7 volumes) before being rigorously cut and held to budget from 2009/10 onwards. The major cause of the price spike in 2008/9 was therefore high international fertilizer prices, as clearly shown in Figures 5.4 and 5.5. The pattern of rising fertilizer volumes from 2005/6 to 2008/9, the commitment to these volumes despite very high prices and costs in 2008/9, and then the rigorous cut in volumes after 2008/9 have to be seen in the context of the changing political circumstances before and after the May 2009 presidential and parliamentary elections, as discussed in the previous chapter.

5.9. Summary

This chapter has set out the main features of the evolving design and implementation of the Farm Input Subsidy Programme from 2005/6 to 2011/12. This has emphasized the scale and complexity of the programme, and ways in which design and implementation have evolved in response to lessons learnt and, importantly, changing political conditions. Key programme elements as set out in Chapter 2 concern its stated food security and productivity objectives, its focus on producers of staple crops, the importance of political commitment to its establishment and operation, and the consequent effects of that on targeting, rationing, and diversion. Other ongoing challenges are noted, with regard to timeliness of input delivery to farmers and involvement of the private sector in the fertilizer supply system, although cost comparisons for private and public sector distribution are not clear cut. The changing fiscal costs of the programme illustrate both the political pressures for programme continuation and expansion (and resource diversion), and the potential for scaling the programme back when political conditions and strategies change. Implementation of the programme has clearly been affected by continuation of the political considerations that led to its establishment, as discussed in Chapter 4. Chinsinga (2012b) reports considerable frustration among senior MoAFS staff at the way that the president's political interest in the programme inhibited discussion and implementation of technical suggestions for programme improvement. These sensitivities also affected relations between donors and programme management within MoAFS and engagement with monitoring and evaluation activities. The high costs in 2008/9 also highlight the vulnerability of the programme to international fertilizer prices (a vulnerability that is again likely to be evident in the 2012/13 season, following the major devaluation of the Malawi Kwacha in 2012).

The programme shares many of the design and implementation features of other recent subsidy programmes in Africa, as reviewed in Chapter 3. As regards objectives, there is a focus on producer gains and on household and national food self-sufficiency, with a lack of regard for consumer interests and wider growth processes. There is also limited attention to improving input efficiency, soil fertility replenishment, and fertilizer supply system development. This focus is consistent with switching attention to monitoring and evaluation and auditing over the life of the programme and associated with the political management of the programme by the president. It is also consistent with a relative lack of integrated attention paid both to complementary investments that will raise programme efficiency and to 'graduation', the process by which beneficiaries and the economies in which they are embedded may grow out of the need for agricultural input subsidies.[11] As regards implementation, the programme involves heavy reliance on private sector

---

[11] Some of these issues are addressed in the 2011–16 Medium Term plan for the programme (Government of Malawi, 2011) which has as its goal 'to increase food security at household level through agricultural output growth' and its purpose 'to increase agricultural productivity and input market development'.

fertilizer imports and a substantial targeted and rationed subsidy distributed using vouchers, but limited success in household targeting. It also faces the widespread problem of late delivery of inputs to beneficiaries.

These issues are the subject of Chapters 6 to 11 which consider beneficiary, wider and private sector impacts of the programme, targeting, and graduation.

Table A5.1. Estimated programme costs, 2005/6 to 2011/12 (US$ million)

	2005/6	2006/7	2007/8	2008/9	2009/10	2010/11	2011/12
Exchange rate, MK/US$	140.00	140.00	140.00	140.00	141.31	151.55	166.71
Recorded costs							
Seeds—flexi/ legumes	0.00	0.00	1.89	5.24	2.83	6.66	6.26
Seeds—maize	0.00	5.23	4.58	7.33	17.13	21.64	15.12
Cotton chemicals	0.00	0.00	0.24	n/a	0.00	0.00	n/a
Fertilizer b/f from y-1	0.00	0.00	11.82	24.88	35.17	0.00	0.00
Fertilizer—new supply	51.62	61.16	77.60	237.63	57.18	115.28	112.63
Fertilizer— private retail	0.00	17.43	24.53	0.00	0.00	0.00	0.00
Transport costs	n/a	4.76	5.99	9.24	6.33	5.95	5.54
Logistics Unit operations	n/a	0.37	0.42	0.24	0.21	0.34	0.28
ADMARC operations	n/a	n/a	0.00	0.06	1.06	2.24	1.57
SFFRFM operations	n/a	0.75	1.41	n/a	n/a	2.05	0.98
District financing	n/a	0.19	n/a	n/a	n/a	n/a	n/a
Coupon production	n/a	0.11	0.09	n/a	n/a	n/a	n/a
Communications	n/a	0.20	n/a	n/a	n/a	n/a	n/a
Input quality monitoring	n/a	0.05	n/a	n/a	n/a	n/a	n/a
M&E	n/a	0.29	n/a	n/a	n/a	n/a	n/a
Buyback finance fees	0.00	0.39	n/a	0.00	0.00	0.00	0.00
Total recorded costs	51.62	90.92	128.58	284.63	119.92	154.16	142.38
Less: Farmer redemption due	19.62	17.02	21.32	23.12	11.43	10.59	8.39
Unused stock (exc. buyback) 0.0	0.00	0.00	19.83	0.00	0.00	0.00	

Table A5.1 (*continued*)

	2005/6	2006/7	2007/8	2008/9	2009/10	2010/11	2011/12
Net recorded Costs	32.00	73.90	107.26	241.68	108.49	143.57	133.91
Estimated other costs							
Brought forward stocks	0.00	0.00	n/a	0.62	1.76	0.00	0.00
MoAFS operations	n/a	n/a	n/a	7.86	7.78	7.26	6.60
ADMARC/ SFFRFM	n/a	n/a	n/a	1.26	n/a	n/a	n/a
Voucher printing	n/a	n/a	n/a	0.14	0.14	0.13	0.00
Other agencies' costs	n/a	n/a	n/a	0.23	0.23	0.21	0.19
Total est. other costs		n/a	n/a	10.11	9.91	7.60	6.79
Total net costs, recorded & estimated	n/a	n/a	n/a	251.79	118.40	151.17	140.70
Total costs, recorded & estimated exc. cf stock	n/a	n/a	n/a	274.91	129.83	161.76	149.09
Programme budget	36.43	53.57	82.14	139.14	155.04	129.99	129.48
Funding							
Direct donor support	0.00	9.51	7.13	37.75	17.48	22.05	44.85
Balance: Malawi Govt.	n/a	64.39	100.13	214.04	100.92	129.12	95.84
Cost, % MoAFS budget	n/a	46.8%	57.2%	67.6%	52.7%	60.1%	48.9%
Cost, % national budget	n/a	6.8%	8.2%	16.2%	6.5%	8.0%	7.1%
Cost, % GDP	n/a	2.5%	3.1%	6.6%	2.5%	3.0%	n/a

Notes: Farmer redemption due on ADMARC and SFFRFM fertilizer sales. Malawi Government contribution based on recorded and estimated costs shown.

Sources: Author calculations from Logistics Unit Annual reports, Nakhumwa (2006), School of Oriental and African Studies et al. (2008), Dorward and Chirwa (2009, 2011a, 2012a), Dorward et al. (2010b), Malawi Government Annual Budget Statements.

6

Direct impacts of input subsidies

6.1. Introduction

In this chapter we examine evidence on the direct impacts of the subsidy following the causal chain set out in Figure II.1 in the introduction to Part II. The most direct benefit of the subsidy programme is to increase maize production at household level. This is also consistent with the programme's objective of increasing maize productivity and national and household food security in Malawi as discussed in Chapter 5. Given difficulties in obtaining maize production and productivity data (as mentioned in Chapter 1, see also Dorward and Chirwa (2010b)), we discuss various estimates of programme maize production impacts. We then draw on work reported in Chirwa et al. (2011d) to look at the contribution of the subsidy programme on welfare indicators for beneficiaries—food consumption, self-assessed poverty, income, assets, incidences of shocks and stresses, health, and education. The collection of panel data in the periodic evaluation of the subsidy programme and the incorporation of the second Integrated Household Survey (IHS2) questions in the design of 2006/7, 2008/9, and 2010/11 surveys allows comparison of the same households from the 2002/3 or 2003/4 season and thus estimation of the impact of the subsidy programme on direct beneficiary households, as compared with non-beneficiaries, over time. Impacts are also assessed using a partial equilibrium model (Dorward and Chirwa, 2012b) and with related findings in other studies.

There are, however, two main caveats to the household level analysis of direct beneficiary impacts. First, some of the indicators are subjective assessments by households: thus with difficulties of calibration and differences in the timing of interviews, caution must be exercised in interpreting the panel level results. Second, if economy-wide effects (discussed in Chapter 7) are very strong, with the subsidy benefiting many households which have not been beneficiaries, the differential impacts at household level may be weak regardless of direct benefits or the number of times a household has had access to subsidized fertilizers in the past six agricultural seasons. In such cases the econometric analysis may not be able to pick up small differences between beneficiary and non-beneficiary households. It should also be noted that although improved seeds are part of the subsidy programme, the analysis of the impacts is focused on receipt of subsidized fertilizers as these are generally correlated with receipt of subsidized seed and involve a much larger subsidy.

The chapter is organized as follows. The next section presents the methods that are used to evaluate the direct impacts of the fertilizer subsidy on beneficiary households. In Section 6t.3, we examine direct impacts on maize production and food security. Section 6.4 evaluates the impacts on human capital (health and education). Section 6.5 assesses the impacts on incomes, self-assessed poverty, assets, and shocks, and Section 6.7 presents evidence from qualitative beneficiary interviews. Finally Section 6.8 presents concluding remarks.

6.2. Methods of evaluating direct beneficiary impacts

We report on three main methods to assess direct beneficiary impacts of the Farm Input Subsidy Programme.[1] The first, reported in Chirwa et al. (2011d), is panel regression, which exploits matched panel data for different rounds of data collection: the second Integrated Household Survey (IHS2) covering the 2002/3 and 2003/4 agricultural seasons, the Agricultural Input Subsidy Survey (AISS) for the 2006/7 and 2008/9 seasons, and the Farm Input Subsidy Survey (FISS) for the 2010/11 agricultural season. This is analysed using a fixed effects panel data strategy with the following specification:

$$Y_{it} = \alpha_i + \delta_t + \sum_{k=2}^{k=5} \beta_k (\delta_t * FISP_{ik}) + X_i + \varepsilon_{it} \qquad (6.1)$$

where i is the individual household, t is the wave of the survey (2004/05, 2006/7, 2008/9, and 2010/11), k indexes the household categorization of access to subsidies over the past six years, α_i are individual fixed effects, δ_t is a dummy variable equal to 1 for each round of the survey (with 2004/5 as the base category), otherwise equal to 0, and $(\delta_t * FISP_k)$ is the interaction dummy that is equal to 1 only for households that received fertilizer subsidy in access category k, Y is the impact indicator, and X is a vector of household characteristics. The coefficient $\hat{\beta}$ gives the impact of the subsidy programme. The FISS in 2010/11 tracked access to fertilizer subsidy since the programme

---

[1] Estimation of maize production impacts also uses other methods, as explained in Section 6.3.

started, and this has enabled us to account for the number of times the household has had access to fertilizer subsidies between the 2005/06 and 2010/11 seasons. Households are categorized into five groups represented by dummy variables: never had access (base category), accessed 1–2 times, accessed 3–4 times, accessed 5 times, and accessed 6 times (continuously). The impact indicators used in the regression model include food security, education and heath, assets and welfare, and shocks.[2] Alternatively, we measure access to the subsidy programme by the quantity of subsidized fertilizers in place of dummy variables. The panel analysis is based on the full panel sample (461 households) and a sub-sample of panel households that were identified as poor based on per capita expenditure in the IHS2 (227 households). The latter allows us to investigate the impact of the subsidy programme on households that had the same initial condition prior to the subsidy programme.[3]

Table 6.1 presents the various indicators reported from Chirwa et al. (2011d) for testing various hypotheses on the direct beneficiary impacts of the subsidy programme. In addition to the broad hypothesized relationships in Table 6.1, we also expect the subsidy to have larger impacts on households that have had access to subsidized fertilizers in all the past six seasons compared to those that have had less access. This implies that there should be a positive trend in the value of the coefficients of times of receipt of subsidy as the frequency of receipt increases from 1 to 6 times.

Table 6.2 presents the distribution of the panel sample of households in Chirwa et al. (2011d) by the number of seasons the households have had access to subsidized fertilizer. It is helpful to identify three groups regarding households' subsidy receipt: a small proportion who never had access to subsidized fertilizer (no access), a much larger group who had access to subsidized fertilizer at least once and up to five times in six seasons (intermittent access), and those had access to subsidized fertilizer six times (continuous access). These groups accounted for 4%, 51%, and 45% of households, respectively. Most of the households are, therefore, repeat beneficiaries.[4] In terms of headship of households in 2010/11, 66% and 34% of the sample households were male and female headed, respectively. The distribution of household by the poverty status in IHS2 also shows that the overall sample has equal numbers of households that were poor and non-poor.

---

[2] Panel data on education and health is only available from IHS2 and the 2010/11 FISS and the panel analysis is based on two periods.

[3] Ricker-Gilbert (2011) shows that OLS cross-sectional data analysis finds apparently significant direct subsidy impacts when regressing some measures of beneficiary impact against subsidy receipt, but that these relationships are not significant when investigated using fixed effects or first difference models. We therefore rely on our own and others' results only when they take account of the effects of possible endogeneity of subsidy receipt.

[4] However, these figures reflect receipt of subsidized fertilizers and do not account for the quantity received and the last time it was received for those that received it less than six times.

Table 6.1. Beneficiary household level impact indicators and hypotheses

Welfare category	Impact indicators	Impact: Alternative hypothesis
Food security	1) Adequacy in food consumption in past month	Positive
Schooling and health	1) Primary school enrolment at household level	Positive
	2) Incidence of under-5 illness	Negative
Subjective poverty	1) Subjective assessment of poverty status	Positive
Shocks and stresses	1) Number of shocks experiences by household	Negative
	2) Incidence of severe agriculture-related shocks	Negative

The second approach used to investigate direct beneficiary effects is qualitative analysis based on focus group discussions, key informants, and life stories of some beneficiaries, collected in the 2006/7, 2008/9, and 2010/11 periods. In each of these rounds of surveys, and each of the 8–14 districts of the surveys, detailed qualitative interviews were conducted covering systems of implementation of the subsidy programme, cropping patterns and livelihoods, and local peoples' and beneficiary's perceptions of the impacts of the programme on their welfare. The number of qualitative interviews varied with the number of districts covered in the surveys. For instance, in the 2010/12 survey, which had the smallest number of districts (8 districts), qualitative data was collected through 8 focus group discussions, 24 key informants' interviews, and life histories from 64 households.

The third method used to investigate direct beneficiary effects is a partial equilibrium model, informal rural economy modelling (Dorward and Chirwa, 2012b), with analysis for two of the largest livelihood zones in Malawi from 2005/6 to 2010/11. These two livelihood zones, Kasungu–Lilongwe Plain (KAS) and Shire Highlands (SHI) between them include just over 40% of rural households in Malawi and also represent examples of less and more densely populated areas in the centre and south of the country, respectively. Cluster analysis of data from the IHS2 was used to develop a household/livelihood classification within the livelihood zones.[5] We report results from simulations based on two scenarios. The basic scenario, simulated in both zones, compares model outcomes 'with subsidy' with actual prices against outcomes 'without subsidy' with equilibrium prices. The 'basic with household savings' scenario, only simulated in the SHI livelihood zone, is the same as the basic

[5] Dorward and Chirwa (2012b) provide details of the informal rural economy modelling and specification of household types and construction of individual household livelihood models.

Table 6.2. Distribution of sample and number of seasons with access to subsidized fertilizer

Number of seasons	Panel households		Headship, 2010/11		Poverty status in IHS2		Proportions of poor & non-poor	
	Number	%	Male	Female	Poor	Non-poor	Poor	Non-poor
0	19	4	75	25	33	67	2	5
1	42	9	75	25	57	43	7	8
2	35	7	72	28	48	52	7	6
3	33	7	60	40	48	52	8	10
4	45	10	66	34	45	55	97	9
5	80	17	55	45	49	51	16	16
6	208	45	68	32	52	48	50	47
N	461	100	66	34	50	50	100	100

Note: Weighted figures.
Source: Chirwa et al. (2011d).

scenario except that it assumes 20% incremental savings carried forward by each beneficiary household from increased income as a result of subsidy receipt.

6.3. Impacts on maize production

The main justification for implementing the Farm Input Subsidy Programme has been to improve maize productivity and achieve food security at household and national level. Discussion in Chapters 2 and 4 of likely subsidy impacts and linkages in Figure II.1 also suggest that increases in staple food production and productivity should be one of the major drivers of indirect subsidy impacts, through domestic price and real income effects. Determination of subsidy impacts on maize production is therefore fundamental to the assessment of programme impacts.

Subsidy impacts on maize production have been estimated in a variety of ways. The simplest and most commonly quoted indicators of impact have been changes in estimated national maize production before and after the subsidy (see, for example, Dugger (2007) and Denning et al. (2009)). These show dramatic increases in estimates of national maize production, with estimated maize production of 1.2 million MT in 2004/5 (before the subsidy) followed by estimates of 2.6, 3.2, 2.8, 3.8, 3.4, 3.8, and 3.6 million MT in the seven subsidy years 2005/6 to 2011/12 (these estimates are presented in Figure 6.1 in terms of incremental production above pre-subsidy estimates). There are, however, a number of difficulties with the use of increases in national production estimates as estimates of subsidy impacts, or even as indicators of subsidy success. First, there is no way of separating the impacts of the subsidy on maize production from the impacts of other variables. The most obvious of these is the weather, but other variables may also be important—thus, poor production in 2004/5 was caused by a combination of poor rains and late and limited commercial fertilizer deliveries and sales.

Second, it is not clear why estimated production should have increased so dramatically during the life of FISP (as opposed to increasing mainly following its inception). This appears to be the result of increasing estimated hybrid maize yields (which rise by 20% from around 2,500 to around 3,000 kg/ha from 2005/6 to 2011/12), an increasing proportion of maize area under hybrid varieties (with a 70% increase in hybrid maize area over the same period), by a small increase in overall maize area (7%), and by a very large differential between hybrid and local maize yields (with hybrid maize yields increasing from 160 to 240% of local maize yields). However, although hybrid maize areas may have increased with increased volumes of subsidized seeds, it is not clear what can have driven the large increases in hybrid maize yields when volumes of subsidized fertilizer were falling back from 2007/8, although Holden and Lunduka (2010b) estimate rising maize yields for both local and hybrid maize from 2006 to 2009. A possible explanation for this is that fertilizer use in one year has dynamic effects on yield in the following year. Thus, Ricker-Gilbert and Jayne (2011) estimate that 100 kg of subsidized fertilizer receipt increases immediate maize yield by 165 kg and receipt of 100kg fertilizer per year over three years yields an extra 316 kg of maize in the fourth year. Holden and Lunduka (2010b) also estimate that rising maize yields are associated with small falls in overall maize area and maize area share (with a net increase in maize production). Chibwana et al. (2012), however, estimate increases in maize and tobacco area with the subsidy.

Third, the hybrid yield estimates are not consistent with other estimates of farmers' hybrid maize yields (Government of Malawi and World Bank, 2006; Ricker-Gilbert et al., 2009; Chibwana et al., 2010; Holden and Lunduka, 2010c; National Statistical Office, 2010a). While these are admittedly very variable, they are almost all below 2,000 kg/ha (Dorward and Chirwa, 2010a).

The very high national production figures are not consistent either, with very high domestic prices from early in 2008 through much of 2009. These discrepancies are illustrated in Figure 7.4 in Chapter 7, which plots estimated maize availability against price by market season, with remarkably high prices in many of the marketing seasons when production estimates would have suggested that greater maize production and availability would have led to low prices. We discuss possible reasons for this in Chapters 8 and 9, but note here that one likely partial explanation is that production was over-estimated in these years, most notably following the 2006/7 harvest with export of a little over 300,000MT of maize to Zimbabwe in the 2007/8 season. Dorward and Chirwa (2010a) also show that there are difficulties in reconciling national production figures with estimates of consumption and export—national production figures suggest that there should be greater availability of maize than required by the population, and this in turn is not consistent with high levels of food insecurity and child malnutrition (as shown for the latter, for example, in Table 7.5)

Finally, there are doubts regarding the methodology used in deriving these figures. This involves field extension workers taking samples of fields and estimating yields for these and crop areas, and then the aggregation of yield and area estimates up to district, Agricultural Development Division (ADD), and national estimates. Sampling and estimation methodologies actually employed by field extension workers are not very clear, and aggregate estimates are subject to technical adjustments. Given past examples of over-estimation of cassava areas and yields, tendencies for crop production figures to be used in judging extension performance, the political importance of national figures, and instances of apparent attempts in President Mutharika's government to influence sensitive statistics,[6] there appear to be considerable risks of upward bias of these estimates.

With estimates of national maize production therefore not being able to provide estimates of the impacts of the subsidy programme, a better alternative should be to estimate incremental production from the use of subsidised inputs, fertilizer, and improved seeds. Here we would ideally use estimates of maize yield responses to incremental fertilizer and seed inputs resulting from the subsidy programme. These could then be multiplied and added across seed types for beneficiaries and for the programme as a whole. Estimates of incremental input use as a result of the programme are examined later in Chapter 8. We briefly consider here estimates of incremental production per unit incremental input use made in a number of studies.

A number of studies have attempted to estimate yield responses to nitrogen on farmers' fields and on-farm yield differences between varieties, from on-farm trials and from farm surveys. School of Oriental and African Studies et al. (2008) reviewed a number of these and concluded that 12, 15, and 18 kg grain per kg of N were reasonable estimates of responses of local (or traditional), Open Pollinated (OPV) and hybrid varieties respectively, under reasonable farmer management, with further gains of 100 and 200 kg per ha for OPVs and hybrid varieties over local varieties, in the absence of fertilizer.

---

[6] See, for example, the delayed and very limited release of yield estimates in National Statistical Office (2010a), the 2012 Malawi Revenue Authority (MRA) scandal (where the MRA borrowed money to inflate its reported cash holdings), and apparent downward estimates of the consumer price index noted in National Statistical Office (2012) and discussed in Chapter 7.

A small number of studies since then have specifically examined fertilizer and seed yield responses. School of Oriental and African Studies et al. (2008) and Dorward and Chirwa (2010b) report that attempts to gather sufficiently reliable information from farm household surveys in 2006/7 and 2008/9 had not been successful, and the latter reported very wide differences in yield estimates from different surveys with little attempt to reconcile differences.

Nevertheless, triangulation across national yield, production, and consumption estimates does provide some guidance on which estimates are likely to be more or less reliable.

- Chibwana et al. (2010) estimate from farm survey mean yield differences of around 210 kg/ha between hybrid and local varieties, with fertilizer responses of 11.5 and 9 kg grain per kg N for local and hybrid maize respectively.[7] While the basic differential between local and hybrid is broadly consistent with other findings, the higher response to local than to improved maize is not, and may be the result of the parsimonious production function employed with no fertilizer/variety interaction terms.

- Holden and Lunduka (2010c) report an average difference of 323 kg/ha between 'matched' local and hybrid maize yields in their farm surveys, and a fertilizer response of 9 kg grain per kg N.

- Makumba et al. (2012) derive fertilizer response estimates of 16.8 kg grain per kg N for hybrid maize farmer-managed trials across the country. These were achieved with high rates of fertilizer use (over 250 kg/ha), but comparison of high and low fertilizer rates on researcher-managed on-farm trials suggests that response rates might be considerably higher than this with lower fertilizer rates. Questions about how marginal response rates depend upon overall fertilizer rates, upon incremental application of subsidized inputs, and upon other aspects of crop management (such as the time of planting, fertilizer application, and weeding) further complicate the issue.

The approach taken by School of Oriental and African Studies et al. (2008), with an approximate +/- 20% range to allow for the effects of over- or under-estimation, therefore still seems as reasonable as any. This discussion, however, highlights the importance of improving maize yield and production estimates in Malawi, not only for consideration of the direct impacts of the subsidy programme, but for wider economic, agricultural sector and food security planning and management.

---

[7] These figures are calculated from figure 2 in Chibwana et al. (2010) and assume that fertilizer is applied as 50% 23:21: 0 and 50% urea.

Figure 6.1 therefore compares estimates of incremental maize production for each year of the programme using first national production estimates and then the approach taken by School of Oriental and African Studies et al. (2008), with a +/- 20% range allowing for possible over- or under-estimation and downward adjustments in some years (2005/6, 2007/8, and 2011/12) to allow for the effects of poor rainfall in some parts of Malawi. It should be noted that all these estimates ignore the impacts of storage losses (Denning et al., 2009). Also for the purpose of obtaining a relatively simple estimate of production impacts, the approach taken by School of Oriental and African Studies et al. (2008) assumes that the nutrients in subsidized tobacco fertilizers from 2005/6 to 2008/9 provided benefits equivalent to those that would have been obtained if the nutrients had been applied to maize, and benefits from these nutrients are therefore measured in maize production. This should lead to a limited over-estimate of incremental maize production but not, when these figures are used in the benefit–cost analysis in Chapter 9, an over-estimate of the value of programme benefits. Over-estimates of maize production should be limited because tobacco fertilizers accounted for between 10% and 17% of total subsidized fertilizers in these three years, and suffered from much higher estimated displacement rates (School of Oriental and African Studies et al., 2008). Figure 6.1 shows that if incremental national maize production estimates are all attributed to the effects of FISP then this requires a fertilizer response approximately double the responses used in the School of Oriental and African Studies et al. (2008) estimates.

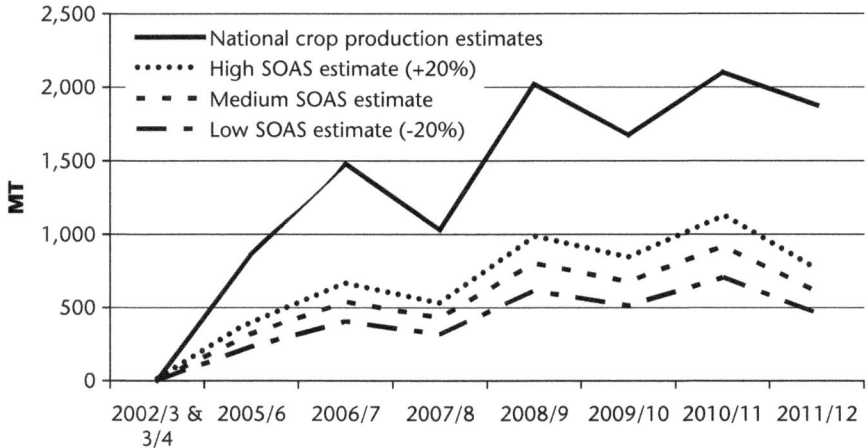

Figure 6.1. Increases in maize production estimates above 2002/3 and 2003/4 base
Source: MoAFS Annual Crop Estimates, author calculations.

Estimates of increased maize production among beneficiaries are also consistent with qualitative evidence from focus group discussions and life stories of beneficiaries in Chirwa et al. (2011d) and discussed later in Section 6.7. These suggest that the subsidy has increased food (maize) production at household level. However, most of the more positive stories came from households that were already buying commercial fertilizers before the programme and those that received two bags of subsidized fertilizers (rather than those that received less as a result of sharing of fertilizers).

6.4. Impact on food consumption

Improvements in maize production should lead to improved food availability and food security for beneficiary households. In all the panel surveys, households were asked whether they considered their food consumption in the month before the survey inadequate or adequate. In order to assess the impact of food security, Chirwa et al. (2011d) created a dummy variable representing adequacy in food consumption equal to one if the household revealed that food consumption was adequate or more than adequate, and to zero if it was inadequate and to investigate, using fixed effects, the impact of the subsidy programme on food security. Estimation of the impact of the number of times that subsidized fertilizer is received (as outlined earlier) indicates that among households that received subsidized fertilizers continuously (six times) about 22% more reported adequate food production as compared with non-recipients, with the coefficient being statistically significant at the 5% level. Among those who had received subsidized fertilizers less than six times, increasing frequency of fertilizer use also led to increasing frequency of reported adequate food production. Separate estimation of the impact of the quantity of subsidized fertilizer received also provided evidence of a positive and significant impact on food consumption adequacy. These findings are consistent with the evidence of increased maize production reported above, with qualitative reports from focus group discussions (School of Oriental and African Studies et al., 2008; Dorward and Chirwa, 2010a; Chirwa et al., 2011d) and with the findings of Holden and Lunduka (2010a). They report that receipt of subsidized inputs increases the probability of households being net sellers rather than net buyers of maize, and also that 66% and 69% of surveyed households reported improvements in household and community food security as a result of the subsidy programme (although 60% of the households in their sample were still net buyers of maize despite the subsidy programme). However, only 30% of households reported that the subsidy programme led to increased maize consumption.

6.5. Impacts on education and health

6.5.1. *Primary school enrolment*

Chirwa et al. (2011d) also investigate the impact of beneficiaries' access to subsidized inputs on schooling based on enrolment of the primary school age group between 5–13 year olds, while controlling for household characteristics. This analysis uses a two-period panel, IHS2 (in 2003/4 and 2004/5) and FISS (in 2010/11), in which members of households that were more than 5 years old were asked whether they were in school. This enabled the generation of an indicator of primary school enrolment at household level, computed as the number of primary school age children in school divided by the total number of primary school-going age children in the household. The results indicate that the subsidy has a positive impact on schooling. Across all households, there was a general increase in school enrolment between the two periods, a change that was universally confirmed in focus group discussions and key informant interviews. The coefficients of the dummies for receipt of subsidized fertilizer 1–2 times, 5 times, and 6 times are statistically significant at the 5%, 1%, and 10% level, respectively, although there is no clear trend in the value of the coefficients of the number of times of receipt and primary school enrolment. Similar but weaker relationships are observed for the model estimated only for households categorized as poor in the IHS2.

The estimated positive impact of subsidy receipt on educational enrolment is consistent with anecdotal reports on programme impacts, with focus group discussion reports (School of Oriental and African Studies et al., 2008; Dorward and Chirwa, 2010a), and with Holden and Lunduka (2010a) who report that 65% of respondent households perceived that there was a positive impact of subsidy receipt on school attendance.

6.5.2. *Health and nutrition*

Improvements in food availability at household level due to access to subsidized fertilizers may improve beneficiaries' health in a number of ways—through improved food security and nutrition from increased own production and income, and from increased ability to finance health care. This can be investigated in a number of ways. Chirwa et al. (2011d) examine the impact of subsidy receipt on incidence of illness using data for households that had under-5 members in 2004/5 and 2010/11. On average, about 59% of households in 2004/5 had under-5 members who were ill in the two weeks before the survey, but this fell to 49% in 2010/11. The econometric evidence of the impact of the subsidy programme on the health of children in beneficiary households shows a negative relationship between access to subsidy and incidence of under-5 illness: households that had access to subsidized fertilizer five or six times were significantly more likely (at the 5% level) to have under-5 children that had not fallen ill in the two weeks before the survey.

This impact was not commonly articulated in focus group discussions and key informant interviews. However Holden and Lunduka (2010a) also explored people's perceptions of subsidy receipt on health, and report that 40% of respondents perceived that subsidy receipt improved health. Further evidence on the impacts of subsidy access on health, but not of access to FISP itself, is provided by Ward and Santos (2010), who examined the impact on stunting from access to Targeted Input Programme inputs prior to 2004/5. They found a significant reduction in stunting for each year of receipt of TIP inputs, and based on strong international evidence on the relationship between adult height and wages, discuss possible long-term beneficial effects of increased adult height on earnings.

6.6. Welfare impacts

We now consider evidence for direct impacts of subsidy receipt on a number of different variables related to welfare: subjective assessment of well-being, real incomes, assets, and shocks and stresses.

6.6.1. Subjective wellbeing assessment

The panel surveys collected consistent information on self-assessment of well-being, using households' subjective assessment of their poverty status based on a ladder ranging from 1 representing the poorest to 6 representing the richest. As reported in Chirwa et al. (2011d) we use these subjective measures as outcome indicators of participation in the Farm Input Subsidy Programme. The mean self-assessment of well-being for panel households increased from 1.66 in 2004/5 to 2.34 in 2010/11(Chirwa et al., 2011d). After controlling for household and year effects, households' self-assessments were higher by 54%, 69%, and 68% in the 2006/7, 2008/9, and 2010/11 surveys, respectively as compared with the pre-subsidy survey.[8] However, the estimated impacts of subsidy receipt by beneficiaries' households are small and not statistically significant (with some estimates marginally negative).

---

[8] Estimates for model (1) for all households and with dummies for the number of times subsidized fertilizer was received. Similar positive coefficients of the year dummies were also found with models (a) estimated only for households categorized as poor in the pre-subsidy survey and (b) assessing subsidy receipt in terms of the total quantity of subsidized fertilezer received from 2005/6 to 2010/11. Coefficients were statistically significant at 1% or (for 2010/11 with the poor households sample) at 5%.

We therefore cannot reject the null hypothesis that receipt of the subsidy does not statistically affect changes in self-assessment of poverty among beneficiaries, and this suggests that the subsidy programme may have only weak direct income effects on beneficiary households.

These results are consistent with sentiments expressed in qualitative interviews in which most households report that they are not able to produce surplus maize which could be sold to earn extra cash income. As discussed below, life histories with selected households revealed that although some have had access to subsidized fertilizers continuously they may still struggle to produce maize that takes them to the next harvest and have to rely on *ganyu* to earn income to purchase food. Small but insignificant positive effects are consistent with small direct improvements from subsidy receipt which may be overshadowed by wider positive changes affecting all households through indirect market effects of the subsidy and other positive changes from 2002/3 and 2003/4 to 2006/7 and subsequent years. However, the differences between the estimated dummy coefficients for 2008/9 and 2010/11 are very small, suggesting that after a substantial improvement in perceived well-being from the pre-subsidy to 2006/7 surveys, and a smaller improvement from 2006/7 to 2008/9, there may have been little or no further improvement in perceived well-being from 2008/9 to 2010/11. We discuss these issues in Chapter 7.

In contrast with these results, however, Ricker-Gilbert and Jayne (2010b) do find a significant increase in satisfaction with life with increased receipt of subsidized fertilizer between the pre-subsidy and 2008/9 surveys.

6.6.2. *Household real incomes*

Reliable estimates of real incomes are difficult to obtain in survey data, without extensive and thorough analysis of expenditure data. Ricker-Gilbert (2011) reports an analysis of the impact of subsidy receipt on reported incomes using the same panel data set as Chirwa et al. (2011d), but excluding the 2010/11 panel. He finds no significant impacts of subsidy receipt on non-farm income or on total household income, although net value of rainy season crop production (a measure of farm income) is positively affected by subsidy receipt in the year of receipt (but not subsequent years), with each extra kg of fertilizer received increasing net crop income by 174MK (p = 0.01). While net crop income is estimated from production estimates, non-farm income is derived from respondent estimates, and total income is the sum of farm and non-farm income. National Statistical Office (2005a) estimate mean (median) household expenditure and consumption for 2002/3 to 2003/4 years as 99,532MK (72,000MK) and reported income as 50,000MK (36,123MK): reported incomes are approximately 50% of reported expenditure and consumption suggesting considerable under-estimates in reported incomes. Mean (median) non-farm incomes for 2002/3 to 2003/4, 2006/7, and 2008/9 reported by Ricker-Gilbert are 31,000MK (9700MK), 10,000MK (2600MK), and 39,000MK (13,000MK), respectively. The extraordinary drop in 2006/7 (which is also reflected in total household income estimates) is not explained and does not match patterns of self-assessed well-being reported above or asset holdings reported below. This raises serious questions about the reliability of non-farm and total household income data and hence of the findings reported by Ricker-Gilbert (2011) on the impacts of subsidy receipt on non-farm and total household incomes.

These concerns about the reliability of data on reported income suggest that other analytical approaches may be preferred for estimating subsidy impacts on real incomes. Changes in real incomes of targeted poor households were therefore examined using the informal rural economy model introduced in Section 6.2 and described more fully in Dorward and Chirwa (2012b). This allows comparison of real income estimates for 'target households' (that is poor male- and female-headed types) with and without the subsidy (with an average receipt of 75 kg and 2 kg of subsidized fertilizer and hybrid maize seed respectively per household) but with constant prices (that is without any wider market equilibrium effects). Gains averaging around 7% (just under 1000MK) across poorer beneficiary households are estimated in the Shire Highlands with lower gains (around 4%, just under 450MK) in the Kasungu–Lilongwe Plains where poverty is less severe and poor households are less capital constrained and have lower returns to capital. School of Oriental and African Studies et al. (2008) also state that increases in beneficiary incomes were reported in a number of focus group discussions in 2007.

6.6.3. *Assets*

Increased productivity and incomes resulting from subsidy receipt may allow beneficiary households to increase their investment in assets. Increases in human capital or assets (in education and health) were considered earlier in Section 6.5. Here we examine evidence on investment in physical and livestock assets.

Holden and Lunduka (2010a) examined the impacts of subsidies on the value of assets and on livestock ownership measured in tropical livestock units. They find a general build-up in the real value of assets from 2006 to 2009 (particularly from 2007 to 2009), suggesting 'that welfare has improved on a broad scale' (pp. 20), but they find no evidence of direct impacts of subsidy receipt on asset accumulation. They conclude that their results 'strengthen the impression that the direct targeting effect of the subsidy program is less important than the economy-wide effect of the program when it comes to growth effects in the economy' (pp. 21–2). There is no evidence of a general increase in livestock endowments, nor of direct subsidy impacts on this.

Ricker-Gilbert (2011) also explores possible direct impacts of subsidy receipt on asset holdings. He reports no significant impact of subsidy receipt on household livestock and durable assets for subsidy received in the survey year or in each of the previous three years. However, in an earlier presentation Ricker-Gilbert and Jayne (2010b) report positive but weak impact of subsidy receipt aggregated over the previous three years on household total assets, consumption, and productive assets (p = 0.12, p = 0.36, and p = 0.16, respectively). Ricker-Gilbert (2011) also finds a very large increase in the value of assets in the sample as a whole, with an increase of 73% in mean value of assets per household and 27% in median value of assets per household, although mean values show a large increase from 2002/3 and 2003/4 to 2007, while median values show a large increase from 2007 to 2009. The large increase from 2007 to 2009 was also observed by Holden and Lunduka (2010a).

6.6.4. Shocks and stresses

Changes in the vulnerability of households to shocks and stresses are another possible impact of subsidy receipt on household welfare. Households experience a number of shocks and stresses and many of these are agricultural related.

Simple comparison of the frequency of reported shocks from the IHS2 (pre-subsidy) survey to the FISS (2010/11) survey shows a decline from 24% to 13% in households that experienced lower crop yields due to weather or rainfall as the most severe shocks between IHS2 and FISS, respectively. Other agriculture-related shocks whose incidence declined were large falls in the sale price of crops and a large rise in the price of food. The relative importance of chronic and acute illnesses appears to have risen as a result of the decline in importance of severe agricultural shocks.

Using the panel surveys we investigate whether there is a relationship between the extent of subsidization and shocks experienced by households. Chirwa et al. (2011d) estimate two fixed-effect regression models using IHS2 and FISS survey data, one using all panel households in the sample, the other only using households that were classified as poor in the IHS2 survey before subsidy implementation. Both models show that the number of shocks declined between 2004/5 and 2010/11. However, with respect to the relationships between shocks and frequency of subsidized fertilizer receipt, the estimated coefficients for dummy variables show that recipients of fertilizer subsidies tend to experience more shocks than non-recipients (with all coefficients statistically significant at the 10% or 1% levels and larger coefficients for recipients that access subsidized fertilizer less than five times). A possible explanation for this is that there is some season specific targeting of the subsidy to households who have experienced shocks.

These issues were explored further with examination of the relationships between frequency of access to subsidized fertilizers and the incidence of severe agricultural related shocks (identified where these were reported as the most severe shock). This analysis gave mixed results. For results obtained with all panel households, subsidy receipt is not significantly related with the incidence of agricultural shocks (estimated coefficients are positive but not significant), but the overall incidence of severe agriculture-related shocks has declined over time (with the decline significant at 5%). However, for the sub-sample of panel households identified as poor in IHS2, there is no evidence that severe agricultural related shocks have declined (the coefficient is marginally positive but not significant). In contrast to the results above, however, it is striking that among poor households those with access to subsidized fertilizers are less likely to have agriculture-related shocks as their most severe shock (estimated coefficients are negative and significant at 1%, 5%, or 10%), but there is no clear trend suggesting that higher frequency of access to subsidized fertilizer is associated with more or fewer agricultural related shocks.

In summary, the evidence on changes in shocks and stresses is rather mixed. Overall, the number of shocks experienced by beneficiary households has fallen significantly over time, although those with access to subsidized fertilizers continue to experience shocks and stresses like other households. However, among poor beneficiary households, agriculture-related shocks are less likely to be the most severe shocks; hence the subsidy appears to have helped poor households to become cushioned or resilient against agriculture-related shocks.

6.7. Impacts in life stories of beneficiary households

Analysis of beneficiary life stories gathered in 2010/11 reveals a mix of perceived impacts of subsidy receipt on their well-being. While there are positive stories about the increase in food production at household level among most households that receive subsidies, the life histories illustrate the challenges of the programme in delivering sustained direct benefits to beneficiary households. In most life histories of beneficiaries, particularly among the most vulnerable groups (female-headed, elderly-headed, and child-headed households), the stories were that the subsidy programme has enabled them to produce 'a bit more food' than when they had no access to the subsidy. The qualitative analysis points to the following issues:

- In most cases, households that report success with the subsidy programme are those that are already relatively well-to-do and purchased commercial fertilizers before the subsidy programme. For instance, one of the beneficiaries who has had access to the subsidy over five seasons, was also buying coupons that enabled him to profit from tobacco cultivation, and claimed that together this transformed his life from the 'poor' to the 'well-to-do' category.

- Households that reported receipt and use of two fertilizer coupons, are likely to talk positively about the extent to which the subsidy improved their food production for such years compared to households that received less than two bags of subsidized fertilizers.

- Sharing of coupons is widespread, and most households that have participated in the subsidy programme attribute the perceived failure of the programme to significantly change their lives to inadequate amounts of fertilizers. This is particularly the case for households that have never used fertilizers prior to the subsidy programme. There are many life stories that described how the full package of the subsidy was beginning to change their lives, only to experience drifting back to poverty due to the dilution of the subsidy as a result of the redistribution that takes place at village level.

- There is also a tendency for beneficiaries to thinly spread the subsidized inputs over a larger parcel of land. Even among households that received two bags of subsidized fertilizers, the sentiments were that the subsidized fertilizer was not adequate for the amount of land the household had for maize cultivation. This is exacerbated by the lack of technical advice on the appropriate use of fertilizers, with most households reporting lack of access to agricultural extension services.

- There is widespread recognition that the subsidy has helped beneficiary households to produce a 'bit more maize' and more importantly has reduced the purchase price of maize even in the lean months of January and February. Most of the beneficiaries interviewed, particularly those that were still not able to produce enough own maize to last them to the next season, consider the low price of maize as one major benefit of the programme.

- Households that are not able to produce maize to last to the next harvest tend to purchase from the market. Most poor households engage in *ganyu* to earn incomes to buy maize and most reported that *ganyu* wage rates have been increasing while maize prices have been falling and maize is locally available. This has enabled the poor to afford purchase of maize based on *ganyu* incomes which have also improved over time. Due to higher wages, households reported that they have reduced the amount of time they spend on *ganyu* and there has also been an increase in opportunities to operate off-farm income generating activities.

- Poor and vulnerable households such as female- and/or elderly-headed households that received subsidy fertilizers rarely supplement the supply of fertilizers with commercial purchases, leading to application of subsidized fertilizers on larger parcels of land. Generally, where subsidized fertilizers are supplemented by commercial fertilizers, such households were buying commercial fertilizers prior to the subsidy or they are better off households that are also receiving subsidies. The quantitative analysis also shows that among beneficiaries there is much lower use of supplementary commercial fertilizers by poor households as compared with non-poor households.

As Chirwa et al. (2011d) note, the case studies of beneficiaries highlighted two challenges that have implications on direct beneficiary impacts of the subsidy programme: targeting and sharing of coupons at village level. We discuss these issues in Chapters 10 and 11.

6.8. Summary

This chapter has reviewed the direct beneficiary impacts of the subsidy programme using quantitative and qualitative data collected over time in a variety of different studies. Use of a partial equilibrium model also helped to triangulate the results from the analysis of the quantitative and qualitative data. A broadly consistent picture of direct subsidy impacts emerges from this, which we summarize in Table 6.3 and discuss below.

As Table 6.3 shows, the evidence examined in this chapter suggests that subsidy receipt has immediate or current season beneficial impacts on beneficiaries' maize production, net crop income, food consumption, and household income (though impacts may be limited, particularly with food consumption). There appear to be no immediate impacts on ownership of physical assets, estimates of immediate impacts on subjective well-being are mixed (one study finding positive impacts, the other finding no impacts) and the observed positive relationship with shocks is counter-intuitive and perhaps best explained by reverse causality. There is then evidence of lagged impacts on beneficiaries' maize production and food consumption (again with limited impacts). There appear to be no lagged impacts on ownership of physical assets, on net crop income, or on subjective well-being, there is no evidence from sufficiently robust data to draw any conclusions on lagged impacts on household income, and the observed positive relationship with shocks is again counter-intuitive and possibly due to reverse causality. The models estimated for examining direct subsidy impacts on school enrolment and child health do not allow examination of immediate impacts separately from lagged impacts.

The finding of lagged impacts on maize production is consistent with residual effects of fertilizer application on soil nutrients (as suggested by Ricker-Gilbert (2011)) and/or with reduced cash flow constraints as postulated earlier in Chapter 4. Lagged impacts on food consumption are then consistent with

Table 6.3. Summary of findings on direct subsidy impacts

	Current season impacts	Lagged season impacts	Wider seasonal changes
Maize production	+ve	+ve	+ve
Net crop income	+ve	X	+ve
Food consumption	+ve but limited	+ve but limited	+ve for 2006/7 & 8/9
School enrolment	?	+ve	+ve
Child health	?	+ve	+ve
Subjective well-being	Mixed (+ve, X)	X	+ve
Household income	?, +ve	?	?
Physical assets	X	Mixed (weak +ve, X)	+ve
Shocks	+ve*	+ve*	-ve

Notes: * Possible reverse causality.

+ve: evidence for positive change; X: evidence does not suggest change.

-ve: evidence of negative change; ?: lack of evidence.

this. The lack of lagged impacts on net crop income, despite these impacts on maize production, are consistent with the observed lack of lagged impacts of subsidy receipt on tobacco production despite the existence of immediate positive impacts (Ricker-Gilbert, 2011). If the limited immediate and lagged gains from increased maize production are invested in food consumption, school enrolment, and health, this may explain the lack of direct lagged impact on subjective well-being and on investment in physical assets. The ability of econometric models to identify direct impacts may also be limited by the widespread practice of sharing of subsidized fertilizer (as described in Chapter 5) and by general increases in maize yields and production, net crop income, food consumption, school enrolment, child health, subjective well-being, and asset ownership (as summarized in the last column of Table 6.3).

As regards the impact of sharing of subsidized fertilizer, it was certainly the opinion of a number of respondents in focus group discussions and life histories that this severely reduced the scale and persistence of subsidy impacts, raising questions about possible thresholds for persistent impacts. However, the absence of apparent impacts on accumulation of physical assets should not obscure the important long-term social and economic benefits of investment in 'consumption' that lead to increased school enrolment and improved child health.

It is also important that the possible roles of the subsidy in driving general improvements should not lead to under-estimates of overall subsidy impact, through a narrow focus on direct beneficiary impacts. This is therefore the focus of Chapter 7.

7

Economy-wide effects of input subsidies

7.1. Introduction

Examination of economic theory on subsidy impacts in Chapter 2 stressed the importance of considering wider market effects of large-scale input subsidy programmes for staple crops. This was set out in the conceptual frameworks at the end of Chapter 2, in discussion of possible impacts on Malawian farmers' livelihoods in Section 4.4 of Chapter 4, and in the Introduction to Part II. Nevertheless, it was noted in Chapter 3 that these impacts have been largely ignored in consideration of both the objectives and impacts of recent subsidy programmes in Africa.

This chapter follows on from discussion of direct subsidy impacts in Chapter 6 and considers evidence of the economy-wide impacts of the FISP. It builds on observation of a range of general beneficial changes summarized in Table 6.3 (increases in maize production, net crop income, food consumption, school enrolment, child health, subjective well-being and physical assets, and decreases in *ganyu* labour supply). The chapter is organized into six sections after this introduction. The next section outlines different sources of evidence and analytical methods considered in subsequent sections, which consider in turn the main potential economy-wide impacts identified in Figure II.1. We then consider in turn the evidence on subsidy programme impacts on macro-economic stability (in Section 7.3), on maize trade (in Section 7.4), on maize prices and wages (in Section 7.5), and on other variables (in Section 7.6). Section 7.7 then provides concluding remarks.

7.2. Sources of evidence and analytical methods

There are two main tasks in determining both direct and economy-wide impacts of the subsidy programme: first the identification of changes associated with the programme, and second attributing or determining the causal dependence of these changes to or on the programme. For direct impacts, there are often opportunities to compare households or areas 'with and without' and 'before and after' subsidy receipt. A variety of experimental and analytical approaches can then be used to address problems of selection bias—for example, using panel data and fixed effects analytical methods as outlined in Section 6.2 in the previous chapter.

Such approaches are not available when considering economy-wide impacts of a large-scale programme such as the Malawi Farm Input Subsidy Programme, as economy-wide effects spread through the economy 'with and without' comparisons cannot be made. We therefore draw on four different approaches when examining possible impacts of the programme:

- examination of changes in variables where an economy-wide subsidy impact is expected, with consideration of likely changes that might have been expected in the absence of the programme;

- regression analysis (using panel data) relating the extent and nature of subsidy access in an area to area wide variables;

- computable general equilibrium (CGE) models; and

- a partial equilibrium model linking different household livelihood models to maize and labour markets.

These approaches all have their own strengths and weaknesses, and there are different challenges in their implementation and application in different contexts. We discuss each briefly.

Examination of changes is a starting point for any analysis of possible economy-wide programme impacts. Apart from difficulties in obtaining relevant and reliable data on some variables, the major issue here is the problem of attribution of change to a particular cause—or indeed the recognition that where there has been no change this could be the result of the subsidy programme counteracting the effect of some other change. We identify three broad changes that roughly coincide with the implementation of the subsidy programme from 2005/6 to 2011/12 and that would be expected to have widespread benefits: improved macro-economic management, good tobacco prices, and generally favourable rainfall—although there is some variation in each of these within the period. Thus, there were major improvements in macro-economic management from 2004 onwards, which are perhaps best demonstrated by the fall in interest rates, debt, and debt servicing from 2004/5 to 2007/8, but resurgent debt in 2008/9 and subsequent raised interest rates (National Statistical Office, 2011).[1] Rainfall was also generally

---

[1] We do not discuss rates of inflation here as National Statistical Office (2012: p. 207) casts some doubt on the reliability of inflation figures.

favourable over the period 2005/6 to 2010/11. Although there were local incidences of flooding and dry spells that caused local production shortfalls, these did not lead to widespread lowering of yields and production. There were more widespread dry spells in 2011/12: these did not lead to a major reduction in national production estimates by the MoAFS, but substantial areas were affected, leading to estimates of 1.63 million people affected by serious food shortages (FEWS NET, 2012). Similarly, burley tobacco prices rose in 2007 with high prices continuing in 2008 and 2009 before falling back in 2011 and recovering somewhat in 2012. Total burley tobacco incomes follow a similar pattern though sometimes with a lag as farmers expand (contract) tobacco areas following high (low) prices (see Figure 7.1).

Improved macro-economic management and good rainfall are probably best considered as necessary but not sufficient conditions for rapid positive change in the rural economy and in rural people's livelihoods, and it is therefore necessary to look elsewhere for drivers of such change. World Bank (2010a) argues that Malawi's growth is export-led with weak linkages between maize production and economic growth due to limited sales and thus limited multipliers. This is supported by high correlation between annual per capita export volumes and per capita GDP from 1960 to 2007, and low correlation between annual per capita maize production and per capita GDP from 1990 to 2005. This argument places considerable emphasis on the role of tobacco in driving broad-based growth. It ignores,

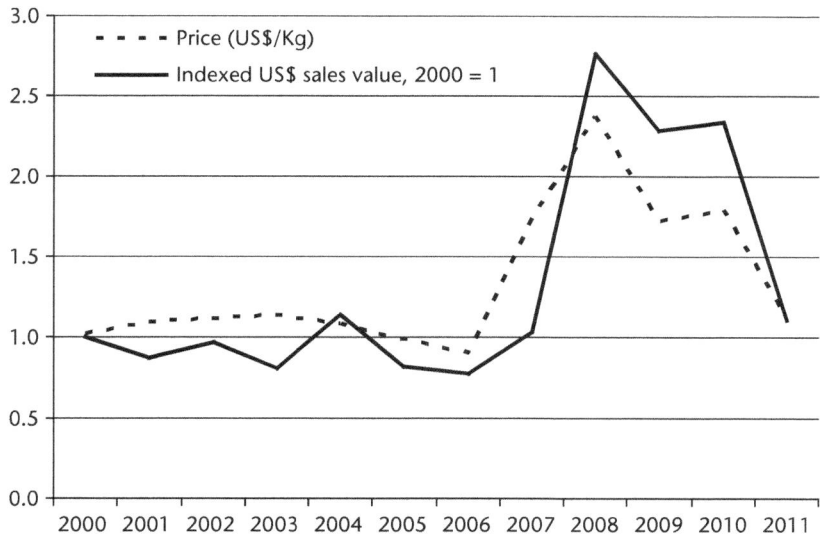

Figure 7.1. Burley tobacco prices and sales values, 2000–11
Source: Tobacco Control Commission.

however, the importance of low maize prices and high maize productivity to real incomes of large numbers of net food-buying farmers. It may well be the case that in the past there has been very limited correlation between per capita maize production and per capita GDP. However, low growth in maize productivity may be one of the causes of Malawi's low GDP growth, with exports the major driver of the limited growth that there has been. In teasing out the effects of high tobacco prices from those of the subsidy programme it may be instructive to note that tobacco prices started to rise with the 2007 harvest, whereas the subsidy programme affected the 2006 harvest. This suggests that changes prior to the middle of 2007 are unlikely to have been driven by improved tobacco prices.

Regression analysis relating area wide subsidy access and other variables is the second approach that may be used to investigate some of the subsidy programme's economy-wide impacts. This approach only works for changes in relatively local markets that are not well integrated. There are a number of studies that show that Malawian maize markets are relatively well integrated (Chirwa and Zakeyo, 2006; Meyer, 2008). Less is known about the integration of labour markets, but one would expect integration to be low in markets for *ganyu* labour (with intermittent demand, the importance of social relations, and relatively immobile suppliers of *ganyu*). Ricker-Gilbert (2011) exploits this to investigate the impact of subsidy receipt on wages across different communities. This approach has not, to our knowledge, been applied to investigate other possible economy-wide subsidy impacts, but it would appear to have potential application in studying impacts of subsidy-induced labour market changes, but not subsidy-induced maize market changes. There are challenges to the collection of reliable data on rural wages. However, these are reduced where panel data are employed since analysis of changes in wages among respondents between surveys demands consistency in wage measurement within responses by the same households at different times, rather than consistency in wage measurement across households (where standardized definitions of tasks are very problematic).

Computable general equilibrium (CGE) models should in principle be the best approach for investigating economy-wide programme impacts. Apart from the costs involved in developing such models, there are two main difficulties in the use of this approach: obtaining reliable data on the wide range of variables and relationships that make up such models, and constructing models to properly capture key features of the livelihoods, markets, and economies modelled. These challenges are also discussed in Chapter 9, where possible uses of CGE models in benefit–cost analysis are examined. We note here, however, that more conventional CGE models, including those that have been developed for Malawi, may be considered 'top down' models in the sense that in broad terms they start from analysis of national accounts to develop a Social Accounting Matrix (SAM) for the economy as a whole, and then work down to model in fairly broad terms the main sectors in the national accounts (Dorward et al., 2004b; Benin et al., 2008; Douilleta et al., 2012). This approach does not, however, adequately describe the seasonal constraints and market failures affecting poorer households and hence the potential role of the subsidy in addressing the low productivity maize production trap, as argued earlier in Chapter 4 (see also Dorward et al., 2004b). An alternative approach, the 'Local Economy-wide Impact Evaluation' or LEWIE model, is currently being developed to address this problem (Taylor, 2012) with an illustrative application to analysis of the Malawi subsidy programme (Filipski and Taylor, 2011). Although this method is expected to provide valuable insights into economy-wide impacts of the subsidy in the future, existing information from CGE models is limited. Nevertheless, the use by Buffie and Atolia (2009) of a 'standard' CGE model to investigate FISP impacts provides useful insights given its assumptions, and these insights are made more useful by Filipski and Taylor (2011) in their examination of potential changes in analysis when some of these assumptions are changed.

Partial equilibrium models that link different household livelihood models to maize and labour markets are the fourth broad approach used in investigating economy-wide subsidy impacts. These suffer from similar but narrower challenges as CGE models as regards the need for reliable data on a wide range of variables and relationships. We use an Informal Rural Economy' or IRE model (described briefly in Chapter 1 and more fully in Dorward and Chirwa, 2012b) to explore both the direct impacts of the programme (as described in Chapter 6) and economy-wide impacts which arise from impacts on maize and labour supply and demand and hence on maize prices and wages.

7.3. Macro-economic environment and role of input subsidies

The contribution of the subsidy programme to economic growth and macro-economic aggregates is difficult to disentangle as there are so many factors that affect macro-economic stability. However, we compare macro-economic developments between 2000 and 2005 (the pre-FISP period) with those between 2006 and 2011 (the FISP period).

The macro-economic environment since the introduction of the Farm Input Subsidy Programme has remained relatively stable with high growth rates and low inflation (Chirwa et al., 2011d). Table 7.1 shows the average performance of the economy between 2000 and 2011. With respect to growth in gross domestic product, the official figures record average growth between 2000 and 2005 (pre-FISP period) of 1.7% per annum compared to 7.8% per annum in the subsidy period, with the agricultural sector an important driver

Table 7.1. Economic growth performance, 2000–10 (% per annum)

Indicator	2000–5	2006–11	2005	2006	2007	2008	2009	2010
Real GDP growth	1.7	7.8	3.3	6.7	8.6	9.7	7.7	6.7
Real agricultural growth	2.1	10.3	7.8	12.3	12.3	11.8	10.4	6.6
Manufacturing growth	0.1	5.4	4.3	4.6	3.6	9.9	4.8	4.2

Source: Chirwa (2011) and Chirwa et al. (2011d).

of recent growth: in the pre-FISP period, the agricultural sector GDP only grew by 2.1% per annum compared to 10.3% per annum during the subsidy period. Allowance for bounce-back in 2006 following the bad rains in the previous year lowers this figure by a little over 1%.

However data on GDP growth in the FISP period need to be interpreted cautiously for two reasons. First, annual crop production estimates are used in the calculation of GDP. As was discussed earlier in Chapter 6, there are concerns that crop production estimates in the FISP period may be somewhat over-estimated. If this is the case then GDP will also be over-estimated, given the close relation between the performance of the agricultural sector and the economy. Determining the possible scale of such over-estimates is difficult but it is unlikely to lead to an inflation of GDP by more than 1.5% over the FISP period as a whole. This could then be a small contributor to higher GDP growth in the FISP period. Possible distortions to the GDP deflator as a result of under-estimates of CPI are, however, possibly much larger. National Statistical Office (2012) use an unexplained revised estimate of inflation of just under 130% between the 2003/4 and 2010/11 Integrated Household Surveys. Comparison of the published CPIs for 2003 and 2010, 154.3 and 319.8, (Reserve Bank of Malawi, 2012) suggests inflation of approximately 107%, in which case the real GDP in 2011 might be some 17% lower than indicated by current published estimates. This could reduce annual GDP growth estimates by some 2.5 percentage points.[2] If these calculations are broadly correct, they have very serious implications for Malawi's growth record since 2005. Nevertheless, agricultural sector performance in the FISP period would still be impressive, averaging a little under 8%—or a little under 7% if the 2006 recovery from bad 2005 rains is factored in.

---

[2] Although for ease of explanation the effects of possible under-estimation of CPI are averaged across the 2006 to 2011 period, in fact distortions are more likely to have arisen from 2008 onwards when maize prices started rising.

The agricultural sector has therefore grown consistently during the subsidy period, and this has helped overall economic growth. Growth rates in both gross domestic product and in agricultural output may be partly attributed to the subsidy programme, although as discussed earlier they may also be partly attributed to high tobacco prices and to improved macro-economic management, and have been aided by the good rains experienced in most seasons since 2005/6. The dry spell that hit some parts of the country in 2009 and lower tobacco prices and higher interest rates since then have contributed to the marked decline in agricultural growth after 2009.

There have also been fiscal implications of the subsidy programme, particularly as much of the financing comes from domestic revenues. As detailed in Chapter 5, the high costs of the programme have increased resource allocations to the agricultural sector and the subsidy accounts for a significant proportion of the national budget. Chirwa et al. (2008) note that due to the subsidy programme, Malawi became one of the first African countries to achieve a 10% budgetary allocation to the agricultural sector, in accordance with the African Union (AU) and New Partnership for African Development (NEPAD) target for stimulation of agricultural growth. However, this increased spending on the agricultural sector has come at the expense of increasing budget deficits and increasing debts. Figure 7.2 shows official figures for trends in fiscal deficit/GDP ratio and public debt/GDP ratios from 1999 to 2010. The deficit as a proportion of gross domestic product has worsened during the period of implementation of the subsidy programme. The deficit after grants increased substantially in 2008 and 2009, in line with the very high expenditures on the

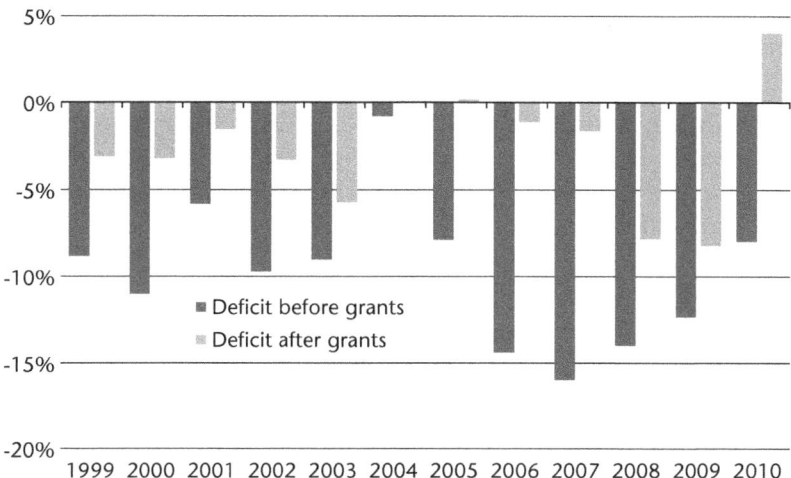

Figure 7.2. Fiscal deficit/GDP ratio, 1999–2010

Source: Computed by authors based on Reserve Bank Database.

FISP in 2008/9 reported in Chapter 5 (with other expenditures related to the 2009 elections) before a surplus was registered in 2010.

There has also been some worsening of domestic debt, which increased from 8.2% in 2006 to 15.7% in 2010. The rising costs of the subsidy programme from 2006/7 to 2008/9 and, as noted earlier in Chapter 5, its general failure to keep within budget (except for 2009/10) may have contributed to these trends—together with other pressures on public expenditure associated with the 2009 election. However it is also important to consider the budgetary implications of possible maize import and humanitarian distribution costs for government if the absence of the subsidy would have led to lower and possibly insufficient national maize production.

7.4. Maize exports and imports

There are difficulties in obtaining good data on international maize trade flows in Malawi, partly due to the restrictions imposed on maize exports and imports and due to informal and hence unreported trade across borders with Mozambique, Zambia, and Tanzania. There are conflicting estimates of trade across different reports (for example, Jayne et al., 2010; FAOStat; and FEWS NET reports). In broad terms, however:

- Malawi is more commonly a maize importer than exporter, with relatively small annual informal imports and no formal imports in most years, unless there is a national food shortage demanding large-scale formal imports and increasing informal imports.

- Informal imports have been fairly constant during the subsidy years, after major imports in 2006 following the poor 2004/5 harvest.

- Following the large estimated harvest in 2007, the government allowed formal exports of maize amounting to around 400,000 tonnes through the granting of licenses for export, particularly to Zimbabwe (licenses were granted to exporters that had unsold stock from the 2006 harvest, with permission for ADMARC to export up to 100,000 metric tons of maize, with the rest exported by private exporters).

- This was followed by a dramatic maize price surge, peaking at 90MK/kg and formal imports from South Africa of around 40,000 MT in 2008/9 (Jayne et al., 2010).

- According to FEWS NET (2011) the government also issued export licences from July 2010 to August 2011, allowing an increased export of maize mainly to Kenya and Zimbabwe, although it has been difficult to track records of these exports.

This suggests that the overall domestic maize supply has improved except in 2008/9 (following the 2007/8 harvest). However these figures need to be interpreted together with information on domestic maize prices, to which we now turn.

7.5. Impacts on maize prices and rural wages

Maize is the main staple food in Malawi. The price of maize has the largest weight in the food price index of the consumer price index. Increased maize production as a result of the subsidy programme should push maize prices down and promote more general price stability and benefit net maize buyers among both beneficiaries and non-beneficiaries of the subsidy programme. Changes in maize prices are therefore a critical determinant of real wages and consideration of changes in real wages thus requires consideration of changes in both maize prices and nominal wage rates. We examine these in turn.

7.5.1. Maize prices

One of the expected benefits of the farm input subsidy is to reduce both the price of maize relative to rural incomes (Dorward, 2013) and its intra- and inter-seasonal price variability. Figure 7.3 shows nominal and real maize prices between 2001 and 2011 in Malawi Kwacha and US dollars per kilogram. Both inter-seasonal and intra-seasonal variability of prices are evident, and prices have not behaved as might be expected. The FISP period has experienced higher average and peak nominal maize prices than the pre-FISP period

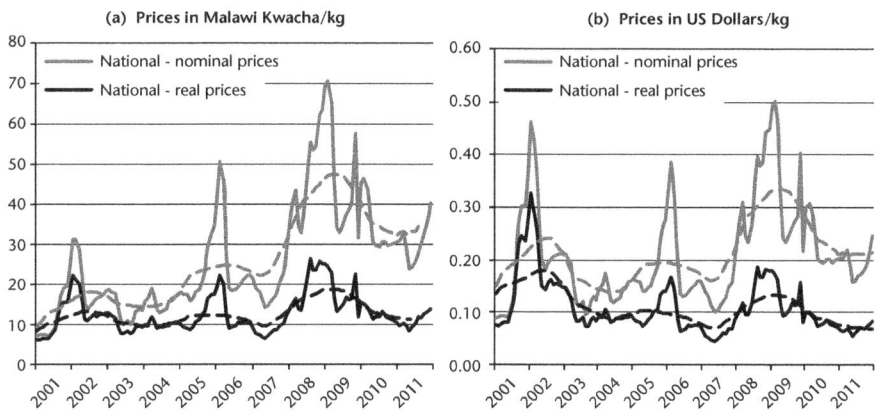

Figure 7.3. Nominal and real maize prices in Malawi, 2001–11
Source: Computed by authors based on MoAFS Price Monitoring Data.

with prices in the FISP period reaching a peak of 70MK per kilogram (US$.50 per kilogram) in January/February 2009 compared to a peak of 50MK per kilogram (US$0.39 per kilogram) in February 2006. As regards real prices (deflated by the CPI), averages in the pre-FISP and FISP period are not substantially different: as the moving averages show they are a little higher in the FISP period when measured in Malawi Kwacha and a little lower when measured in US$.

Between 2001 and 2011 there were three surges in the price of maize: in 2001/2, 2005/6, and 2008/9. Chirwa (2009) notes that price surges in 2001/2 and 2005/6 are mainly explained by reductions in maize production owing to poor weather conditions (with heavy rains in March and dry spells and floods in some areas exacerbated by low input uptake in 2000/1; and late distribution of inputs and poor rains in many areas in 2004/5).

The surge in maize prices in the 2008/9 market season should not be attributable to such supply-side issues because of relatively good rains and improved access to subsidized seeds and fertilizer. High prices in 2008/9 (and other market seasons) also raise questions about MoAFS' high national maize production estimates. Figure 7.4 shows 1993/4 to 2010/11 maize prices (average annual prices from MoAFS market surveys, in US$) against estimated quantity consumed per capita, calculated from Ministry of Agriculture and Food Security crop production estimates, census data, and exports and import estimates compiled from various sources.[3] This perspective on prices and supply estimates draws attention to an apparent shift in the relationship between net supply and prices from around the 2006/7 production season.

Chirwa (2009) suggests several reasons for the high maize prices in 2008/9 despite estimated high maize production levels in the 2007/8 production season.

1. Poor quality of information about domestic supply from the government, both in terms of domestic production and stocks in reserves, created speculative behaviour. Even with record reported maize production levels, maize prices remained high, creating uncertainty about domestic supply, with asymmetric information among different agents.

2. The unsatisfied contract to export to Zimbabwe from the 2006/7 harvest also fuelled speculation that there was a domestic maize shortage. By February 2008, only 302,000 metric tons of maize had been exported to Zimbabwe by the private sector through the National Food Reserve Agency (NFRA), and Malawi failed to satisfy the contract of maize exports to Zimbabwe (FEWS NET, 2008). In addition, there was speculation that

---

[3] Production estimates from a production season are linked to prices in the following marketing season. Thus, for example, the very high prices experienced in the 2008/9 market season are shown in Figure 7.4 against the 2007/8 production season.

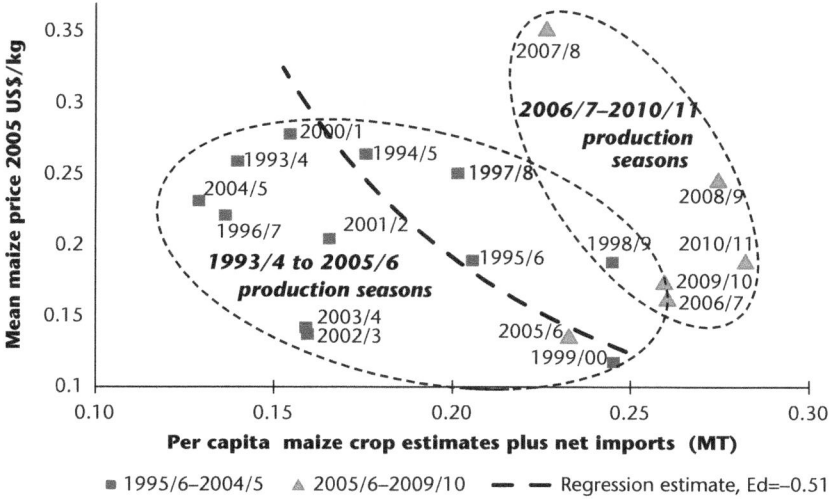

Figure 7.4. Maize prices and estimated quantity consumed per capita from 1993/4 to 2010/11 production seasons[7]

Source: Adapted and updated from Dorward and Chirwa, (2011c).

exports to Zimbabwe would continue from the 2007/8 harvest, which was also a surplus year according to the MoAFS crop estimates. The private sector was having difficulty in sourcing maize from the market and this sent signals that there were supply shortages and prices began to increase substantially.

3. The behaviour of state agencies, ADMARC and the National Food Reserve Agency (NFRA), who were offering higher purchase prices to farmers than the private sector, and the government's imposition of a ban on private trader purchases, also appeared to signal domestic supply shortages.

4. High international maize prices, amid continued reported surplus maize production, created speculation that the export market for maize would be lucrative, leading to stockpiling and purchasing maize from farmers at higher prices by the private sector.

5. A further possible cause of tighter markets could be government purchases of maize for stockpiling of the national grain reserve following the construction of a 60,000 MT new storage capacity.

Table 7.2 shows average nominal maize prices in Malawi and major cities between 2001 and 2011, and suggests that during the FISP period the average national prices and the prices of maize in the major cities have almost

---

[7] The regression estimate is discussed in Chapter 9.

Table 7.2. Average nominal maize prices, 2001–11

	Malawi Kwacha per kilogram				US Dollars per kilogram			
Period	National	Mzuzu	Lilongwe	Blantyre	National	Mzuzu	Lilongwe	Blantyre
Pre-FISP	18.12	17.32	18.43	19.16	0.19	0.18	0.19	0.2
	(8.84)	(8.48)	(8.66)	(10.03)	(0.09)	(0.07)	(0.09)	(0.09)
Post-FISP	33.53	35.13	35.6	38.02	0.23	0.24	0.25	0.26
	(13.83)	(12.12)	(14.07)	(19.56)	(0.1)	(0.09)	(0.1)	(0.14)

Note: Figures in parenthesis are standard deviations in monthly prices.

Source: Computed by authors based on MoAFS Price Monitoring Data.

doubled in Malawi Kwacha terms. Monthly variability of maize prices (measured in standard deviations) has also increased in the FISP period, although the coefficient of variation has fallen slightly. Prices and price variability have also increased in US$ terms, though not as dramatically. It appears therefore that the subsidy programme has not significantly reduced either prices or food price risks.

It seems clear then that maize prices have not fallen in real or nominal terms over the period of FISP implementation. However, this does not necessarily mean that the FISP has not exerted downward pressure on maize prices but rather that other pressures pushed prices up in 2008/9 (as discussed above). In the absence of such pressures maize prices did fall and remain low throughout the 2006/7 marketing season, following the introduction of FISP in 2005/6 and before government interventions tightened the market after the 2007 harvest. Prices were also low throughout the 2010/11 market season, prior to the macro-economic problems that surfaced in mid 2011.

CGE and partial equilibrium models also suggest that FISP should lead to maize price falls in the absence of interventions or macro-economic or other changes affecting maize prices. Simulations by Buffie and Atolia (2009) estimate long-run falls in domestic food prices of 2% to 5%, with higher short-run falls of up to 9%. Filipski and Taylor (2011) estimate that the 2005/6 subsidy would have led to a 5% increase in maize production in a model that assumes perfectly competitive markets (they also unfortunately assume that maize prices are determined exogenously on the world market and therefore do not estimate any price changes). The introduction of credit constraints on input purchases (one part of the low maize productivity trap discussed earlier in Chapter 4) reduces the overall agricultural production impacts of the FISP to a little over 2% (specific impacts on maize production are not stated) but an alternative specification that introduces unemployment and efficiency wages results in the FISP increasing agricultural production by over 13%. The Informal Rural Economy partial equilibrium models also give consistent estimates of increases in maize production of 10% to 20% across all households with the FISP, although direct beneficiary impacts tend to be higher (Dorward and Chirwa, 2012b). Aggregate production increases lead to lower maize prices, with median falls across different years varying from 8% to 40% under different scenarios. Given the clear endogeneity of Malawian maize prices, the large maize production impacts of the FISP in these simulations should have substantial price impacts.

It is, therefore, surprising that falls in real maize prices are not observed, despite the upward pressures on maize prices discussed above. This discussion, however, has examined only nominal prices and real prices deflated by the CPI. As noted by Dorward (2011) and Dorward (2013), real consumer prices are often best examined in relation to incomes, and in this regard there is evidence that real maize prices have fallen relative to wages. We therefore turn now to consider evidence of changes in nominal wage rates.

7.5.2. Wages

One of the expected economy-wide benefits of such a large-scale input subsidy programme is its influence on rural wages relative to maize prices. As outlined in Chapter 4, rural wages may increase due to the low supply of casual labour and high demand for labour among labour-hiring farming households. With low and stable maize prices, the increase in rural wages should increase real incomes of poor households. We discussed maize price movements in Malawi before and after the introduction of the FISP in Section 7.5.1. We now consider wage rates in both nominal terms and relative to maize prices.

Despite difficulties in obtaining reliable data on rural wage rates, there is evidence of rising wage rates in rural areas following the introduction of FISP. School of Oriental and African Studies et al. (2008) report survey data findings that median wage rates rose by 33% from 2005/6 (following a poor 2004/5 crop production season) to 2006/7 (following the 2005/6 subsidy and better rains) per day across the two years. Focus group discussions and key informant interviews also reported increases in wages and increased bargaining power for sellers of labour in a tighter market, with a shift from price setting by buyers of *ganyu* to sellers of *ganyu* and wage increases of 50% or more in some areas. School of Oriental and African Studies et al. (2008) also report anecdotal evidence of increased *ganyu* rates from commercial farmers who faced difficulties in obtaining hired labour without paying higher wage rates. FEWS NET (2007) also reported reduced search for employment by *ganyu* labour in November 2007 with increased scarcity and cost of hired labour reported by farmers wishing to hire labour.

As noted earlier in Chapter 6, Ricker-Gilbert (2011) reports contractions in labour supply over the period 2003/4 to 2008/9, with a large contraction in labour supply before 2006/7 followed by a smaller expansion before 2008/9. He does not report changes in wage rates, although with relatively stable labour demand (and he only reports agricultural labour demand) higher real wage rates would be expected. Dorward et al. (2010a) state that focus group discussions and key informant interviews in 2008/9 reported continued improvements in *ganyu* wage rates and bargaining positions for sellers of *ganyu* (as in 2006/7). Household survey estimates of changes in nominal wage rates from 2006/7 to 2008/9 suggest increases of around 70%, so that over the period 2005/6 to 2008/9 they just about kept abreast with maize price increases, although this involved a dramatic increase in real wages from 2005/6 to 2006/7 and then a smaller decline from 2006/7 to 2008/9.

Chirwa et al. (2011d) find that nominal wages have continued to increase in rural areas since 2009, and when coupled with falling maize prices this implies increased real wages among households participating in the labour market. Figure 7.5 shows mean farm-gate purchase prices for maize, selling prices for tobacco prices, and *ganyu* wage rates between 2009 and 2011, as reported by survey respondents in 2011. With respect to maize prices, the overall prices at which households buy maize show strong seasonal effects in all districts (with January prices considerably higher than June prices) and falling prices from 2009/10 to 2010/11 (Figure 7.5a). This is consistent with maize market prices shown earlier in Figure 7.3. Tobacco prices generally fell slightly between 2009 and 2010 (Figure 7.5b), although in Blantyre and Zomba households reported improved tobacco prices. Again this is consistent with national data on tobacco prices in Figure 7.1. With respect to wages (Figure 7.5c), there is a steady increase in *ganyu* cropping season wages reported by households over the period January 2009 to January 2011, and these increases occurred in all the districts that were surveyed. Wage increases are broadly similar across all districts in percentage terms.

These wage rates and maize price developments were also widely reported in focus group discussions and in life histories of some of beneficiaries. In most life histories of beneficiaries, engaging in *ganyu* to earn income to purchase food is a common strategy among poor households and improvements in wages and reduction in maize prices made maize more affordable even for poor households. This is confirmed in Figure 7.5d which shows real increases in *ganyu* wages in terms of its maize grain purchasing power (variability in prices between areas may be due to bias and reporting inconsistencies, but data collection methods attempted to minimize changes in bias between surveys, and hence estimates of percentage change in wages within in each area should be and appear to be more consistent). Overall, the reported maize purchasing power of daily *ganyu* wages increased by 47% between January 2009 and January 2010, with the highest reported increase of 80% in Ntcheu district and lowest increase of 34% in Phalombe district.

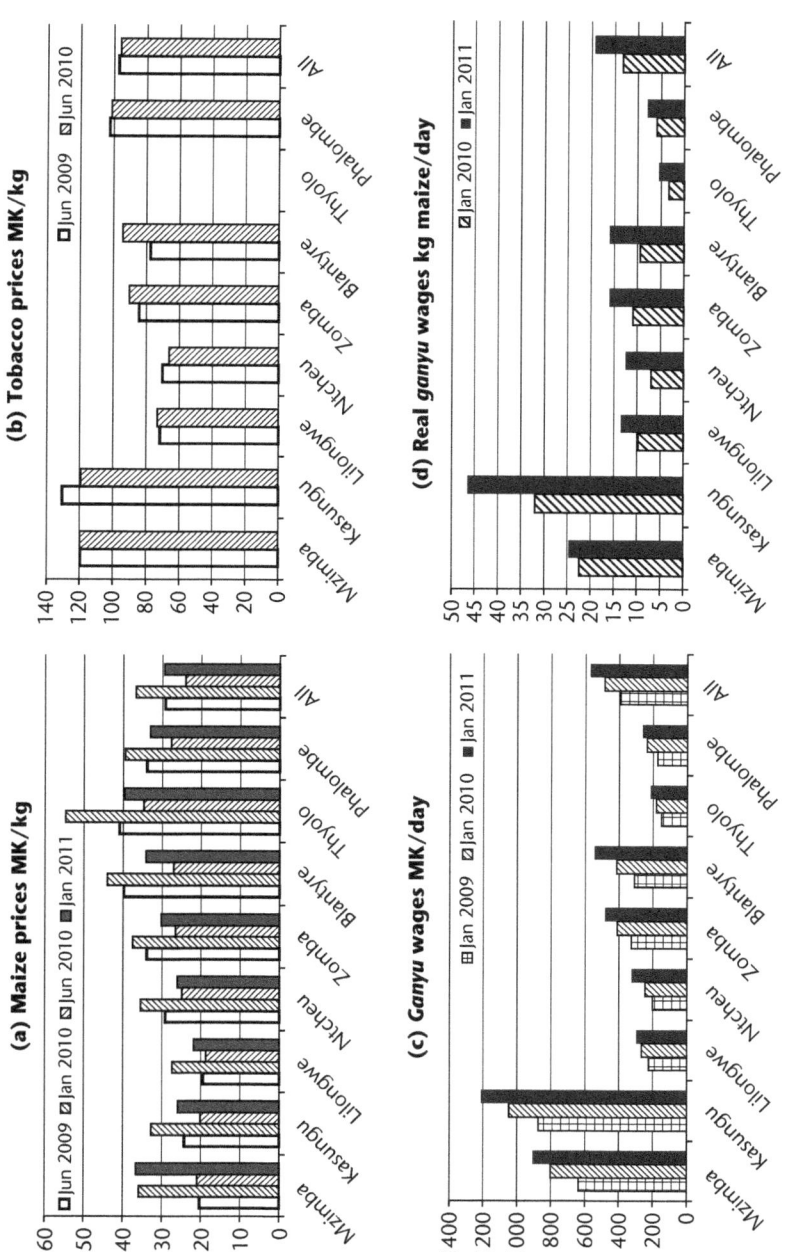

Figure 7.5. Average farm-gate maize prices, tobacco prices, and *ganyu* wages, 2009–11

Source: Chirwa et al. (2011d), computed from FISS3survey data.

It appears then that real wages increased from 2005/6 to 2006/7, fell back somewhat from 2006/7 to 2008/9, and then increased again from 2009 to 2010. How far can this be attributed to the impact of FISP? The four approaches set out in Section 7.2 may be examined to investigate this, in addition to focus group discussions and key informants attributing increased wage rates to the impact of FISP in household surveys (School of Oriental and African Studies et al., 2008; Dorward et al., 2010a; Chirwa et al., 2011d).

Considering first general patterns of change, the two primary explanations for improved rural wages are improved tobacco prices and earnings, and the FISP. It appears that while nominal wage rates increased over the period 2005/6 to 2009/10, real wage rates improved from 2005/6 to 2006/7, fell back somewhat from 2006/7 to 2008/9, and then rose again from 2009 to 2010/11. Tobacco prices rose in 2006/7 and therefore cannot explain increases in nominal or real wage rates from 2005/6 to 2006/7. These increases might be explained by improved crop production in 2005/6 as compared with 2004/5 as a result of both the FISP and improved weather. Increased nominal wage rates from 2006/7 to 2008/9 would be consistent with the effects of increased maize production as a result of relatively good weather and the FISP and/or the effects of higher tobacco prices received from 2007 onwards. Increased nominal wage rates from 2008/9 to 2010/11 would be consistent with the effects of falling maize prices as a result of the removal of maize market distortions with continued high production (with good weather and the FISP) and with continuing relatively high tobacco prices (these remained above 2005/5 levels: as Figure 7.1 shows 2009 and 2010 prices were similar to 2007 prices, higher than 2006 prices, but lower than 2008 prices).

Further evidence of the impact of the FISP on wage rates is provided by Ricker-Gilbert (2011) in his use of regression analysis to examine the relationship between the amount of subsidy received in communities and median *ganyu* wage rates in these communities. He finds significant ($p = 0.01$) positive relationships between wages and subsidy receipt, commercial fertilizer price, hybrid maize price, tobacco price, and coefficient of variation of rainfall. He also finds significant ($p = 0.01$) negative relationships between wages and the standard deviation of subsidy receipt per household and long-run average rainfall. The estimated effects of subsidy receipt and of maize and tobacco prices are particularly interesting, with an average of 50 kg per household estimated to increase nominal wages by 10%, and an increase in 1 standard deviation decreasing nominal wages by 0.1%. An increase in tobacco prices by 50MK/kg (very approximately the increase in 2007, 2008, and 2009 above 2005/6 and earlier prices) is estimated to also raise nominal wages by 10%. An increase in maize prices of 30MK/kg would lead to an increase in nominal wages of a little over 4%. However, since a 30MK/kg increase in maize prices represents an increase of 100% or more over 2003/4 or 2006/7 maize prices, and maize accounts for a significant proportion of expenditure of the poorer people who hire their labour out for *ganyu* work, the small increase in nominal wages will not be enough to prevent a fall in real wage rates.

Positive impacts of FISP are found in both the CGE models discussed earlier in the chapter. Buffie and Atolia (2009) find real unskilled wages rising by up to 5% immediately after the introduction of FISP, and then declining slightly or significantly depending in later years on the sources of programme finance. Filipski and Taylor (2011) also report FISP leading to an increase in rural wages with their 'perfect competition' model, although the scale of this increase is not reported. There is no specific mention of wage effects with the model allowing for liquidity constraints. Where they postulate efficiency wages, the impact of the subsidy is not on wage levels but on employment, and the impact of the subsidy on labour income is very large.

The importance of economy-wide effects on real wages is also supported by informal economy model simulations of the two largest livelihood zones (Shire Highlands and Kasungu–Lilongwe Plain) in Malawi between 2005/6 and 2010/11 (Dorward and Chirwa, 2012b). Small increases in wages and larger post-harvest falls in maize prices combine to give increases in the wage to maize price ratio, with average increases in the pre-harvest period of 19% and 5% for the Shire Highlands and Kasungu–Lilongwe Plain respectively, and 73% and 32% in the post-harvest period. These 'basic scenario' simulations are consistent with the earlier discussion of potential impacts in Section 4.4, with differences between the two zones explained by the greater proportion of poor households in the Shire Highlands livelihoods zone.

7.6. Other variables

The previous section considered different sources of information on possible subsidy impacts on maize prices and wages. This reflected both the importance of these impacts (indicated, for example, by their central position in the causal impact chains set out in Figures 2.2, 4.2, and II.1) and the availability of information and analysis on these impacts. There are, however, a range of other potential FISP impacts that are important for welfare and economic benefits, but where there is less evidence on impact. In this section we review changes in these variables over the period in which FISP has been implemented. Arriving at firm conclusions regarding change is difficult. A number of data sources are supported by anecdotal evidence in suggesting improvement on many variables over the period 2005 to early 2011, after which there were increasing political and economic difficulties associated with a number of President Mutharika's policies. However the third Integrated Household Survey (IHS3, National Statistical Office, 2012), reporting on the situation

Table 7.3. Household food consumption over the past 1 month, 2006/7–8/9 (%)

Season	Less than adequate	Just adequate	More than adequate
2006/7	38	51	10
2008/9	10	63	27

Note: Interviews with households were conducted in May and June, shortly after harvest.
Source: Dorwarc et al. (2010a).

in 2010/11, contains a number of statistics that present a much less positive picture. Finding consistency across these estimates and other data sources, including those on estimated FISP impacts, is problematic.

7.6.1. *Food availability and consumption*

National food production and per capita availability indices show increases in national food security in Malawi since the implementation of the FISP in 2005/6. As discussed earlier in this chapter, there are questions about the reliability of some of the national crop production estimates on which these are based (possible discrepancies between maize production estimates and prices were discussed earlier, and there are longstanding queries about inconsistencies between national crop estimates and survey estimates of root crop areas and production).[4] Nevertheless, there is general agreement that the food security situation has improved in the country partly owing to incremental use of fertilizers and improved seeds provided under the subsidy programme and partly owing to the good weather conditions that Malawi has had during this period. These trends of national food security are consistent with household survey findings that show improved self-assessment of food security. Table 7.3 shows the proportion of households with different food consumption between the 2006/7 and 2008/9 seasons from a survey of beneficiaries and non-beneficiaries of FISP. Overall, there is a shift to more households reporting adequate and more than adequate food consumption.

However, National Statistical Office (2012) finds that 33% of households experienced situations on food insecurity, with 42% of the rural population being food insecure in 2010/11. Concerns also arise about the large numbers of people continuing to experience food insecurity and needing emergency humanitarian support. This appears to be particularly serious in 2012/13 with estimates that about 1.6 million people in 15 districts, mainly in southern Malawi, will be unable to meet adequate basic food requirements (FEWS NET, 2012). This is mainly due to prolonged dry spells and poor rains: similar situations in previous years have been associated with local droughts or floods and are arguably unrelated to the FISP.

---

[4] This is illustrated by the divergence between estimates in Ministry of Agriculture and Food Security (2007) and National Statistical Office (2010a).

7.6.2. Incomes and poverty

Earlier discussion of FISP focus group discussion and key informant reports of FISP impacts on real wages implicitly or explicitly linked this to improved real incomes. Estimates of subsidy impacts on nominal wages (Ricker-Gilbert, 2011) when combined with estimates on maize production also suggest increases in real incomes for poorer non-beneficiaries as well as beneficiaries. There are explicit results from the different CGE models of Buffie and Atolia (2009) and Filipski and Taylor (2011), with Buffie and Atolia (2009) estimating short-term real income increases of the poor (many of whom may not receive subsidized inputs) rising by 4% to 8%, and Filipski and Taylor (2011) estimating that the introduction of liquidity and labour market imperfections into their model increases the income gains of non-beneficiaries from spillover effects. The IRE partial economy model of Dorward and Chirwa (2012b) also estimates substantial real income gains from wage and maize price change impacts, averaging 10% and 3% across all households in the 'basic scenario' in the Shire Highlands and Kasungu–Lilongwe Plains respectively. In this, poor non-beneficiary households gain most, non-poor beneficiaries, and poor non-beneficiaries gain direct and indirect benefits respectively, and non-poor non-beneficiaries generally lose from the indirect impacts through higher wages and low maize prices. In the Shire Highland Livelihood Zone (SHI), simulated 'indirect gains' to real incomes for target households are considerably higher than the direct gains from subsidy receipt (13% as compared with 7%). These indirect gains are higher than simulated for the Kasungu–Lilongwe Plain (KAS) because of the former's high rates of poverty incidence, high land pressure, and larger numbers of poor people relying more on sales of *ganyu* labour and spending a higher proportion of their income on maize purchases.

If the farm input subsidy raises the income of the poor then it should also play a role in poverty reduction. Indeed evidence of the impacts of the FISP on the wage to maize price ratio and the impact of tobacco prices on wages (as reported earlier) should have led to falls in poverty from 2005/6 to 2010/11. Given the scale of the FISP, these should show up in national poverty statistics. Evidence on changes in poverty at the national level is, however, mixed. Table 7.4 shows the trend in different estimates of the poverty head count ratio between 1998 and 2011. The national head count poverty rate in 2005, prior to the implementation of the subsidy programme, was estimated at 52% while in the rural areas it was estimated that 56% of the population were living below the poverty line. Seasonally adjusted model-based estimates from welfare monitoring surveys suggest that the poverty rate increased in 2005/6 following the poor 2004/5 crop season and subsequent food shortages, then declined sharply between 2006 and 2007 before stabilizing from 2007 to 2009 (Chirwa et al., 2012). The urban poverty rate is estimated to have fallen by almost half in this period. However, recent poverty estimates based on the 2010/11 integrated household survey suggest that between 2004/5 and 2010/11 the national poverty rate was much higher than predicted by the WMS estimates, and only fell by 2% between 2004/5 and 2010/11, suggesting only a marginal change in the well-being of the population. This would be consistent with high maize prices putting a brake on growth in real incomes in these years: one would then expect low maize prices in 2010/11 to stimulate further growth in real incomes and falling poverty. However, poverty incidence in rural areas is estimated at over 56% in 2010/11 (National Statistical Office, 2012), much higher than expected, with a fall of only 1.5% from 58.1% in 2004/5 to 56.6% in 2010/11.

The very limited fall in estimated poverty incidence from 2004/5 to 2010/11, as reported by National Statistical Office (2012), is difficult to reconcile with estimates of wider changes (in labour supply, wages, crop income, school enrolment, child health, subjective well-being, asset ownership, and experience of shocks) reported in different surveys discussed in this and the previous chapter. However the continued high reported poverty incidence in 2010/11 (with high incidence of ultra-poverty) is consistent with a number of other estimates of change from 2004/5 to 2010/11 (National Statistical Office, 2005a, 2012): increases in moderate stunting, wasting, and underweight and small reductions in ownership of tables, radios, and sickles. On the other hand, these findings are less easy to reconcile with other estimates from these surveys: falls in severe stunting, wasting, and underweight; increases in ownership of beds and bicycles; increases in permanent and semi-permanent housing with decreases in traditional housing; increases in access to improved water sources and use of improved sanitation; and decreases in the proportion of people reporting inadequate food, clothing, and health care.[5] Furthermore, examination of changes in poverty incidence across districts shows a wide range of changes.[6] These apparent inconsistencies pose important questions that need to be resolved, suggesting inconsistencies in either the IHS2 or the IHS3.

7.6.3. Nutrition

As with the poverty incidence estimates, one would expect economy-wide FISP impacts on real incomes to lead to national improvements in the nutrition status of children in Malawi. Anthropometric indicators, however, present an

---

[5] These improvements are found across all income quintiles.

[6] These, for example, range from an astonishing almost halving of poverty incidence in six years in Thyolo and Rumphi Districts, from 65 to 37% and from 62 to 37% respectively, to a rise in poverty incidence from 38 to 57% in Lilongwe, from 66 to 82% in Chikwawa, and from 51 to 61% in Mzimba District (next to Rumphi).

Table 7.4. Trends in poverty headcount in Malawi, 1998–2011 (%)

	1998	2004/5	2005*	2006*	2007*	2008*	2009*	2010/11
National	54.1	52.4	56	58.4	41.3	41	40	50.7
Urban**	18.5	25.4	24	25	11	13	14	17.3
Rural**	58.1	55.9	53	47	44	44	43	56.6

Note: * Predicted poverty rates based on an econometric model using welfare monitoring survey data (Mathiassen, 2006 and National Statistical Office, 2005b) with seasonal adjustments as in Chirwa et al. (2012).

**WMS urban and rural figures are not seasonally adjusted.

Sources: Government of Malawi and World Bank (2006), National Statistical Office (2005b, 2007, 2008b, 2009, 2010b, 2012), Chirwa et al. (2012)

apparently confusing picture (Table 7.5). This expectation requires first that the FISP has raised the real incomes of poorer households, and second that such increases in real income lead to improved child nutrition. We consider here first evidence of wider changes in children's nutritional status, and then, more briefly, evidence that higher incomes do lead to improved child nutrition. There are, however, difficulties in interpreting anthropometric measures across different surveys as a new standard population reference for the calculation of under-nutrition measures was developed by the WHO in 2006, replacing the 1977 NCHS/CDC/WHO reference. Estimates calculated using the different reference populations are not comparable (de Onis et al., 2006; National Statistical Office and ICF Macro, 2011), but the 2010 Demographic and Health Survey (National Statistical Office and ICF Macro, 2011) usefully provides estimates derived from both standard population references, and we include both of these in Table 7.5 to provide some indication of the way that the different standard population references may affect comparisons across surveys.

Stunting is the measure that should provide the best indicator of longer term child nutrition, as it is less affected than underweight and wasting by seasonal variations in food intake and disease. Simple comparison of the estimates in Table 7.5 suggests that there has not been much of a fall in under-nutrition from 2000 to 2011. However, allowance needs to be made for the change in standard reference population for the 2010 DHS and 2010/11 IHS3 surveys. These two surveys give similar estimates using the 2006 WHO reference population (47.1% and 48.1% prevalence of moderate stunting, respectively). The DHS2010 estimate translates into a much lower prevalence when calculated using the 1977 NCHS/CDC/WHO reference. There would presumably be a similar adjustment to the 2010/11 IHS3 (making it something like 42.5%) providing no evidence of any increase in stunting and suggesting that if anything it may have fallen. Similar arguments apply with regard to estimates of severe stunting, with much stronger evidence for a fall in the prevalence of severe stunting.

Table 7.5. Nutritional status of children under 5 years, 2000–11 (%)

Indicator	2000	2004/5	2006	2009	2010		2011
	(DHS*)	(IHS2*)	(MICS*)	(WMS)	(DHS*)	(DHS**)	(IHS3**)
Stunting	49	43.2	46	36	41.5	47.1	48.1
Severe stunting	-	17.8	20.5	-	15.4	19.6	14
Wasting	5.5	4.6	3.5	1	3.7	4	11.4
Severe wasting	-	1.3	0.5	-	0.9	1.5	1
Underweight	25.4	22.2	20.5	17	17.8	12.8	30.6
Severely underweight	-	7.4	3.6	-	3	3	1.2

Note: DHS = Demographic and Health Survey, IHS = Integrated Household Survey, MICS = Multiple Indicator Cluster Survey, WMS = Welfare Monitoring Survey.

*: compared against 1977 NCHS/CDC/WHO reference.

**: compared against WHO Child Growth Standards adopted in 2006.

Sources: National Statistical Office and ORC Macro (2001), National Statistical Office and ICF Macro (2011), National Statistical Office (2007, 2010b, 2012), Government of Malawi and World Bank (2006).

Measurement of wasting and being underweight requires accurate weighing of children. On both these indicators the 2010/11 Integrated Household Survey (IHS) stands out for very high prevalence estimates as compared with other surveys (even allowing for adjustments for the different reference populations, which are very small for wasting). This contrasts with the percentage underweight estimates in the 2010 Demographic Household Survey (DHS), estimates which are particularly low compared to earlier surveys when standardized against the same reference population. The 2010/11 IHS estimates of the prevalence of severely wasted and underweight children are however relatively low, particularly when possible adjustments are made to the prevalence of severe wasting to standardize the reference population.

Overall, it is difficult to drawn any firm conclusions on changes in children's nutritional status from these different estimates. There are, however, possible indications that the prevalence of moderate stunting has fallen a little (although it is still very high) but that there has been a more substantial reduction in the prevalence of severely stunted and of moderately and severely underweight children (if we ignore the 2010/11 Integrated Household Survey estimate of the prevalence of moderately underweight children as an outlier).

The various surveys reported in Table 7.5 also have the potential to provide evidence on links between income and child nutrition. Both the IHS surveys report anthropometric results by consumption quintile, and all surveys report estimates separately by region and for urban and rural areas. Neither the 2004/5 nor 2010/11 IHS show any clear decline in stunting or severe stunting in higher income quintiles. However in the 2010/11 IHS the proportion of children who are moderately or severely wasted or underweight falls in higher income quintiles. This is the case for the 2004/5 IHS2 estimates of moderate and severe wasting but not for estimates of the prevalence of underweight children. Both the 2006 MICS and the 2010 DHS show declining stunting and underweight prevalence (moderate and severe) with higher wealth quintiles, but only the 2010 DHS shows this for wasting. International cross-country analysis (for example, Headey, 2011a; Webb and Block, 2012) suggests a stronger relationship between income growth and stunting and a weaker one between income growth and wasting at lower income levels.

Examination of regional differences in anthropometric measures in Malawi may shed a little more light on the relationships between these measures and income and on the consistency between different surveys. Both the IHS2 and the IHS3 estimate highest median incomes and lowest poverty incidence in the central region, and lowest median incomes and highest poverty incidence in the southern region, with the northern region in between. With regard to anthropometric measures the different surveys present somewhat inter-regional comparisons as regards particular measures, but in broad terms the northern region seems to have a lower prevalence of under-nutrition while the central region tends to have the highest prevalence, despite higher median income and lower poverty incidence than the other regions.

7.7. Summary

The chapter set out to review the economy-wide impacts of the Farm Input Subsidy Programme in Malawi. These are important to arguments put forward in Part I regarding the importance of such impacts for large-scale input subsidy programmes supporting staple crop production. Examination of these impacts involved identification of changes potentially associated with the implementation of the FISP and consideration of the attribution of these changes to the FISP and to other potential influences (such as macro-economic management, rainfall, and tobacco prices) using four principle approaches: consideration of patterns of change in different variables; regression analysis; simulations with CGE models; and simulations with a partial equilibrium Informal Rural Economy model.

Although most macro-economic indicators show an environment of macro-economic stability, some of the indicators—such as fiscal deficits and domestic debt—have been unfavourable within the period of implementation of the subsidy programme. While good macro-economic management made the implementation of the FISP possible, the FISP may have then contributed both to good agricultural growth and to fiscal deficits and domestic debt (in and following years when FISP costs were not well controlled). There are possible difficulties with published estimates of GDP growth, but even allowing for these, agricultural sector performance in the FISP period would still average a little under 8%—or a little under 7% if the 2006 recovery from bad 2005 rains is factored in.

The analysis of the economy-wide effects of the input subsidy programme must recognize some mixed and puzzling results. While there are multiple sources of evidence for the positive effect of the subsidy programme on production, high maize prices from 2007 to 2009 are not obviously consistent with this, but a number of explanations for this are put forward. Evidence for rising nominal and real wages (as measured against maize prices) is very strong, derived from a variety of different information sources and analytical approaches. Regression analysis linking wage rates to subsidy receipts in different areas is particularly revealing as it also provides insights into the effects of changes in tobacco prices and maize prices on nominal and real wage rates. Evidence of the FISP causing increases in real wage rates and consequent rises in real incomes is also provided by qualitative date from rural people and by CGE and IRE modelling. These sources also suggest that there have been or should have been increases in real incomes, especially among poor buyers of maize and sellers of *ganyu* labour, and consequent falls in poverty incidence. However while there is a substantial body of evidence suggesting that this has been the case, the very recently released Integrated Household Survey poverty incidence estimates for 2010/11 are only very slightly lower than the 2004/5 estimates. We are not currently able to resolve the inconsistencies between these conflicting sets of information.

8

Impacts on input market development

8.1. Introduction

The implementation of the Farm Input Subsidy Programme (FISP) in Malawi since the 2005/6 agricultural season has involved the interaction of the government of Malawi, the private sector, the development partners, Civil Society Organisations (CSOs), non-governmental organizations, traditional leaders, and smallholder farmers. These have played various roles in the implementation and success of the programme. The private sector has played a critical role in the procurement, transportation, and retail of farm inputs, but their involvement in the programme has changed over time. The private sector is involved in several aspects of the subsidy programme including the procurement of fertilizers, the transportation of fertilizers to various markets, the retail sale of fertilizers, and the production and sale of improved seeds.

There are potential benefits from the inclusion of the private sector in the implementation of a large and nationwide agricultural input subsidy programme, as noted in Imperial College et al. (2007). First, it is believed that most of the activities can be done more efficiently by the private sector, which is less prone to the bureaucracy associated with state delivery of services. Second, the involvement of the private sector is seen as a strategy for developing the private market system, especially in remote areas where the incentives for private sector investment in markets are weak. Third, the involvement of the private sector may allow the government to use scarce resources on other activities, by reducing the cost of the subsidy to the government. Fourth, the participation of the private sector in input retailing may reduce the displacement effects of the input subsidy programme.

This chapter assesses the impact of the Farm Input Subsidy Programme on the development of the private sector. The next section reviews the roles and nature of private sector participation in the input supply systems and the subsidy programme. Section 8.3 highlights the overall input purchases and use. Section 8.4 analyses the changes that have occurred in the fertilizer market and the experiences of private sector participation in the subsidy programme. Section 8.5 looks at the impact of the subsidy programme on the seed industry. Section 8.6 highlights the challenges and opportunities for greater private sector participation in the implementation of the subsidy programme. In Section 8.7 we conclude and highlight the issues and options for improving private sector participation in the implementation of the subsidy programme.

8.2. Roles of various players in input supply systems

The public and private sectors play various roles in the supply of farm inputs in Malawi, from procurement of inputs to retailing of inputs to farmers. The Malawi Government is directly involved in the supply of farm inputs through its two state-owned firms, the Agricultural Development and Marketing Corporation (ADMARC) and the Smallholder Farmer Fertilizer Revolving Fund of Malawi (SFFRFM). These state-owned firms compete with private sector enterprises comprising large-scale enterprises, cooperative, retail chain stores, and small-scale agro-dealers. With the introduction of the farm input subsidy, state enterprises and private firms have played varying roles over the life time of the programme. The input suppliers have a number of associations and networks including the Fertilizer Association of Malawi (FAM), the Seed Traders Association of Malawi, Agricultural Input Suppliers Association of Malawi (AISAM), and a network of input suppliers under the Citizen Network for Foreign Affairs (CNFA)/Rural Market Development Trust (RUMARK). In addition, the National Association of Smallholder Farmers of Malawi (NASFAM), a farmer cooperative, also provides input access to smallholder farmers on a commercial basis through a network of input supply shops. While state-owned enterprises have had consistency in the supply of inputs, the private sector participates in the subsidy programme in various ways in the fertilizer and seeds components of the programme. On the one hand, the relative roles of the private sector in the fertilizer component of the programme have varied over time as regards their participation in and exclusion from retail sales while remaining important partners in the procurement of fertilizers for the programme and commercial sales. On the other hand, private sector participation in the seed component of the programme has been consistent. Apart from participation in the subsidy programme, the private sector also procures fertilizers and seeds for commercial sales in various market outlets across the country.

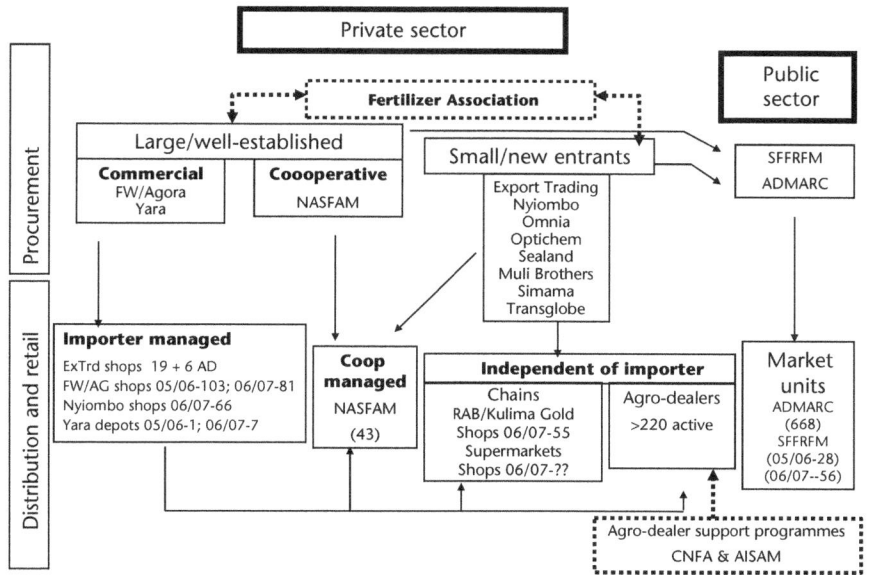

Figure 8.1. Structure of the fertilizer industry in Malawi in 2010
Source: Kelly et al. (2010) and School of Oriental and African Studies et al. (2008).

8.2.1. *Fertilizer markets under FISP*

The structure of the fertilizer industry in Malawi has evolved since the introduction of the input subsidy programme, with exits and entries, but it remains dominated by a few players with vertical and horizontal relationships. Figure 8.1 shows the characteristics and level of participation of various players in the supply of fertilizers in procurement, distribution, and retail. At procurement level, the private sector players can be categorized into large/well-established private firms (commercial firms and cooperatives) and small/new entrants, while in the public sector there is SFFRFM and ADMARC. The private sector firms and SFFRFM import fertilizers for both the subsidy programme and commercial sales while ADMARC has only procured for the subsidy programme. The private sector firms participate in the procurement of fertilizers for the programme in a competitive tendering process. In addition, the two state-owned enterprises, ADMARC and SFFRFM, also take part in the fertilizer tendering process.

Over time, the business opportunities in the supply of fertilizers to the programme have led to new entrants in the importation of fertilizers. Dorward et al. (2010b) note that there has been increased participation of the private sector in the supply of fertilizers to the programme, be it in terms of number of players and the relative volume handled by the private sector relative to volumes handled by the state-owned enterprises or parastatals. Most importantly, private sector participation in the procurement of fertilizers has been consistent since the programme started in 2005/06. There has been growing interest in the supply of fertilizers to the programme. Logistics Unit (2012) shows that in the 2011/12 season, 65 enterprises submitted bids to supply fertilizers to the subsidy programme of which 20 were awarded contracts, an increase from 11 companies in the 2007/8 season (Logistics Unit, 2008).

Procurement is vertically linked to the distribution and retail of fertilizers to farmers, with some of the private sector firms and the two state-owned enterprises owning retail outlets in different parts of the country. The large private firms and some small to medium-scale new entrants also supply unsubsidized fertilizers to a network of agro-dealers and retail chain stores or supermarkets. However, the participation of the private sector in the retailing of subsidized fertilizers has been limited. Although the private sector plays a dominant role in the procurement of fertilizers, its participation in fertilizer retailing to smallholder farmers under the subsidy programme has varied, with the private sector participating only in the 2006/7 and 2007/8 agricultural seasons (Dorward and Chirwa, 2011c). In these two seasons, smallholder farmers were able to redeem fertilizer coupons at some of the major retailers of fertilizers, but smallholder agro-dealer sellers were excluded from the redemption of fertilizer coupons. Otherwise, ADMARC and SFFRFM have been the only market outlets through which smallholder farmers have redeemed their subsidy fertilizer coupons.

The other important role played by the private sector in the implementation of the subsidy programme is the transportation of fertilizers from the national depots to retail outlets in various parts of the country. There is no participation of state-owned enterprises in this activity, and this service is purely provided by private transporters through competitive bidding. The transporters of fertilizers from depots to unit markets are selected by the Ministry of Agriculture through a bidding process (Logistics Unit, 2008). In the 2011/12 season, a total of 23 transporters participated in the distribution of fertilizers from SFFRFM depots to various unit markets across the country (Logistics Unit, 2012) compared to 16 transporters in the 2008/9 season (Logistics Unit, 2009).

8.2.2. Seeds market

In contrast to the fertilizer market, the seeds market is a private sector-based system, with no state-owned enterprise playing a role in the procurement of seeds. Figure 8.2 shows the structure of the seed industry in Malawi at various levels of the supply chain. The seed industry comprises the growers and retailers. The growers form the Seed Trade Association of Malawi (STAM) and

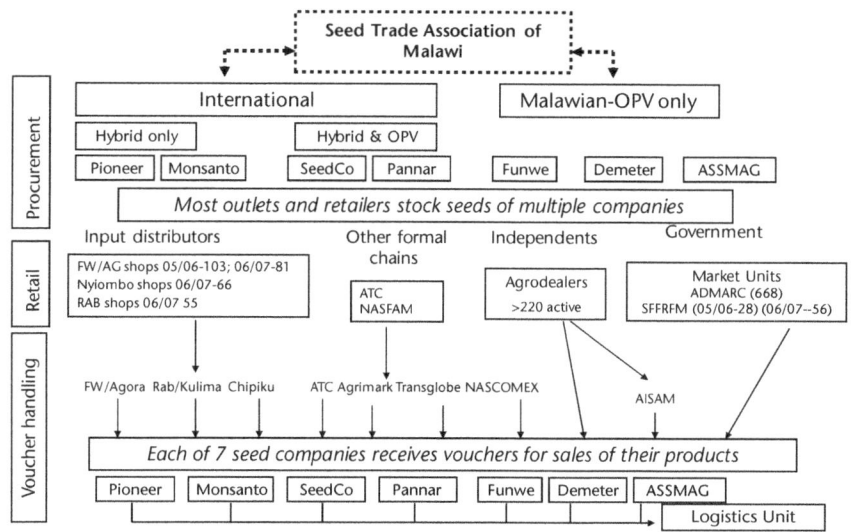

Figure 8.2. Structure of the seed industry in Malawi in 2010

Source: Kelly et al. (2010) and School of Oriental and African Studies et al. (2008).

are classified by ownership into international firms and domestic firms; by 2011/12 there were18 seed growers in Malawi. The international companies are involved in the production of hybrid and open pollinated varieties while Malawian-owned companies tend to specialize in open pollinated varieties and legume seeds. The international firms include Pioneer and Monsanto who specialize in hybrid maize, and Pannar and Seed Co specializing in both hybrids and open pollinated varieties (OPV). The domestic firms specialize in OPVs and legume seeds and include Funwe, Demeter, and the Association of Smallholder Seed Multiplication Group (ASSMAG). The retail sector of the seed industry consists of seed growers' distributor outlets, agro-dealers, cooperatives, supermarkets, and parastatals (ADMARC and SFFRFM).

The private sector has been a major player at all stages of seed supply and distribution of seeds in the subsidy programme. Its exclusive role in seed procurement and retail has been consistent since the commencement of the programme in 2005/6. Both large international and smaller domestic firms (including smallholder seed multiplication groups) have been awarded contracts to supply hybrid and OPV maize seeds and legumes to the programme. In the 2007/8 season, for instance, six growers of seeds participated in the supply of maize seeds to the subsidy programme with one specializing in hybrid seeds, two in both hybrids and OPV, and three specializing in OPV seeds. More recently, as we observe below, the number of companies for supplying maize and legume seeds to the subsidy programme has increased.

The delivery of the seed component of the programme has, since 2006/7, been consistent with the promotion of private sector development in input markets. In the 2005/6 season, all the distribution and retailing of seeds under the subsidy programme was done through ADMARC and SFFRFM (Imperial College et al., 2007). However, beginning with the 2006/7 season, seed procurement has been handled purely by the private sector, and seed suppliers have been distributing the seeds to retailers (parastatal and private sector retailers) across the country. The 2006/7 season also saw the inclusion of small-scale agro-dealers in the redemption of seed coupons (Dorward and Chirwa, 2011c) and Logistics Unit (2008) notes that maize seed dealer outlets were unrestricted and seed producers entered into various arrangements with small-scale input agro-dealers and retail chain stores in addition to ADMARC and SFFRFM outlets.

8.3. Overall input purchase and use

There are difficulties in estimating the overall purchases and use of fertilizers due to lack of consistent data on commercial sales of fertilizers. However, we use import figures to estimate fertilizers available for commercial sales after accounting for subsidized fertilizers. The official import data include fertilizers for both estates and smallholder farmers. Figure 8.3 shows the trends in imports, disaggregated between subsidy fertilizers and fertilizers available for commercial sales, using industry data from 2004 to 2006 (School of Oriental and African Studies et al., 2008) and NSO import data from 2007. The trend in the fertilizers available for commercial sales after subtracting the subsidy from imports shows a marginal increase between the 2004/5 and 2005/6 season and a sharp decrease in 2006/7.[1]

After falling in 2006/7, the trend from 2007/8 is for increasing availability of commercial fertilizers in addition to increases in total imports of fertilizers. However, available commercial fertilizer in 2010/11 is still below the 2004/5 level (the year before the commencement of the subsidy programme). A small reduction in subsidized fertilizer between 2007/8 and 2008/9 is associated with a substantial increase in the quantity of fertilizer available for commercial sales in 2008/9. There is a decline in importation of fertilizers and availability of commercial fertilizers in 2009/10 but an increase in imports and available commercial fertilizers in 2010/11 while the subsidy levels remained

---

[1] Industry data on total fertilizer sales from 1998 to 2006 as reported in School of Oriental and African Studies et al. (2008) are not consistent with NSO import data over the same period, and are on average around 80,000 MT per year higher. If this continues from 2007 then commercial sales from 2007 would be around 80,000 MT higher than indicated in Figure 8.3. It should also be noted that annual estimates on sales may not be accurate due to carry forward of stocks, but these should average out over two or more seasons.

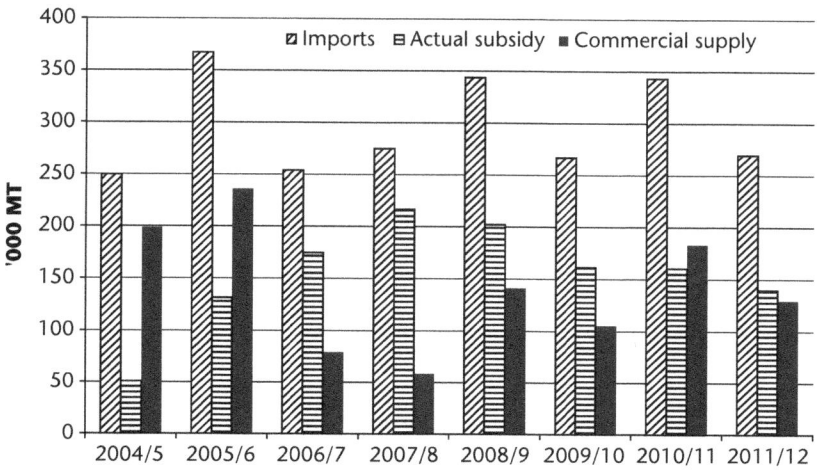

Figure 8.3. Fertilizer imports and fertilizer use, 2004/5–11/12[2]

Sources: National Statistical Office (2009)—Statistical Year Book Data Set; Dorward and Chirwa (2011c) and School of Oriental and African Studies et al. (2008).

unchanged. The decline in 2009/10 is also associated with a sharp decline in the previous season's price for burley tobacco. Chirwa et al. (2011a) note that 2008/9 prices for burley were significantly low towards the end of the marketing season compared to three previous seasons. This might have led to reduced demand for commercial fertilizers.

Interestingly, available commercial fertilizer in 2010/11 was more than subsidized fertilizer. The subsidy programme in the 2010/11 season excluded tobacco fertilizers, and the increase in the available commercial fertilizers may reflect lower displacement due to the focus of the programme on maize fertilizers. As noted in School of Oriental and African Studies et al. (2008), the subsidy on tobacco fertilizers had higher displacement than the subsidy on maize fertilizers. Then, in 2011/12 there is another drop in imports, subsidized fertilizers, and available commercial fertilizers. Tobacco was also excluded in 2011/12 but the decline in available commercial fertilizer may be partly due to the collapse of tobacco prices in 2010/11 season which led many smallholder farmers to abandon tobacco production in the 2011/12 season. The 2011/12 crop estimates show that tobacco production was expected to decline by more than 36%. Except for bad years for tobacco, these results show that there has been an overall increase in fertilizer importation and an increase in the fertilizers available for commercial use, suggesting that after an initial decline the subsidy programme might have stimulated fertilizer use.

---

[2] 'Commercial supply' estimated by subtraction of subsidy from imports for 2007/8 and thereafter.

Table 8.1. Household survey estimates of total seed purchases ('000 metric tons)

Season	Subsidized		Unsubsidized		Total	
	Hybrid & OPV seed	Legume seed	Hybrid & OPV seed	Legume seed	Hybrid & OPV seed	Legume seed
2007/8	1.7	-	4.3	-	6.1	-
2008/9	4.7	-	5.4	-	10	-
2009/10	5.4	0.9	3.6	1.6	10.9	2.5
2010/11	8.2	1.6	4.8	2.8	15.9	4.4

Note: Estimates based on NSO population estimates.

Source: Dorward and Chirwa (2011a).

Data on overall purchases and use of seeds are not readily available. However, national estimates from household surveys show that the quantity of hybrid maize seeds used increased. Table 8.1 shows that total hybrid and OPV maize seeds use has increased by 160% between 2007/8 and 2010/11 season, while legume seeds use almost doubled between 2009/10 and 2010/11 largely due to increased levels of seed subsidization.

8.4. Developments in the fertilizer markets

8.4.1. *Changes in competition in fertilizer procurement*

The introduction of the Farm Input Subsidy Programme has attracted a number of entrepreneurs in the fertilizer import sector. Figure 8.4 presents the trend in the number of firms that participate in the procurement of fertilizers under the subsidy programme. There are two parastatals involved in the procurement of fertilizers, ADMARC and SFFRFM, but only SFFRFM has been active in the bidding while ADMARC has benefited from uncompetitive allocation as a parastatal, except in 2011/12 where it also participated as a bidder. There are increasing trends in both the number of private sector bidders interested in procuring fertilizers and the number of bidders who were awarded contracts to supply subsidy programme fertilizers, particularly from the 2009/10 season. The number of interested private bidders increased from 24 companies in 2009/10 to 65 companies in 2011/12. The subsidy programme has over time attracted new companies whose traditional business is not importation of agricultural inputs. Similarly, the number of successful awards of contracts has also increased from 10 private companies in 2009/10 to 20 private companies in 2011/12. Some of the new companies, as well as the more established ones, have had links with different political parties, and

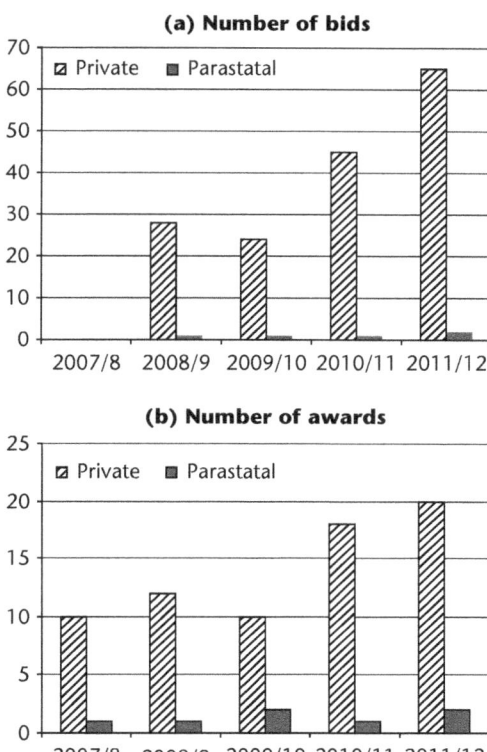

Figure 8.4. Number of bids and awards in fertilizer procurement, 2008/9–11/12

Source: Logistics Unit (2008, 2009, 2010, 2011, 2012).

these may have affected their participation in the programme. With respect to parastatals, SFFRFM has always participated and succeeded in the supply of subsidy fertilizers while ADMARC has only been awarded contracts to supply in the 2009/10 and 2011/12 agricultural seasons. However, what is not clear is whether the new entrants in fertilizer imports are also importing fertilizers for commercial sales.

Apart from the entry of other players in the supply of fertilizers under the programme, there have also been notable exits, such as the National Association of Smallholder Farmers of Malawi (NASFAM), Rab Processors, and Yara who participated in 2006/7 but have not since continued to participate in the programme (Kelly et al., 2010). Yara closed down its international representation in Malawi, turning over an exclusive right to import Yara fertilizers to Agricultural Resources Limited. These exits are therefore only in

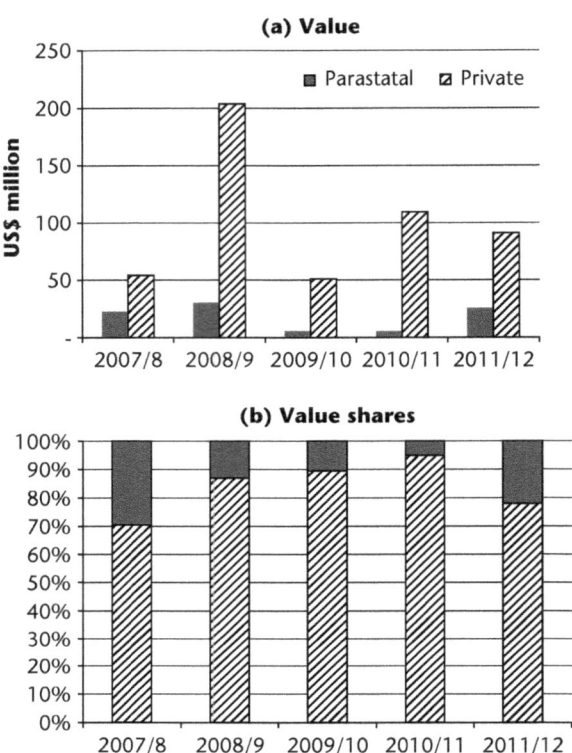

Figure 8.5. Value and value share of subsidized fertilizers supplied by sector, 2007/8–11/12

Note: The figures are new procurement during the season.

Source: Logistics Unit (2008, 2009, 2010, 2011, 2012).

subsidized fertilizers; the firms have continued to supply fertilizers in the market on commercial basis.

Figure 8.5 shows the share of fertilizers supplied to the programme by the private firms and parastatals in terms of value of supplies. Panel (a) shows large annual variations in the value of fertilizer purchases by the private sector between 2007/8 and 2010/11. In panel (b), however, there is a steady increase in the share of the value of supplies accounted for by the private sector, increasing from 71% in 2008/9 to 95% in 2010/11, but falling to 78% in 2011/12. In monetary terms, the highest realized value to the private sector occurred in 2008/9, amounting to $203.75 million, consistent with the high volume procured by the private sector but also reflecting high international fertilizer prices.

8.4.2. *Changes in competition in the fertilizer retail market*

There are several kinds of players in the fertilizer retail market including importer-managed outlets, cooperative-managed outlets, chain stores and supermarkets, agro-dealers, and parastatals' unit markets (Kelly et al., 2010). The participation of the private sector in the retail marketing of subsidized fertilizers has been the most difficult aspect in relation to the development of the private input markets across the country. As noted above, the private sector was allowed to redeem fertilizer vouchers only in the 2006/7 and 2007/8 seasons.

In the 2006/7 season, a total of 174,688 metric tons of subsidized fertilizers was sold to smallholder farmers with ADMARC and SFFRFM sales accounting for 72% of fertilizer sales and the private retailers accounting for 28% (School of Oriental and African Studies et al., 2008). The private sector continued to participate in retail of subsidized fertilizers in 2007/8, with the innovation of a remote market premium. According to Logistics Unit (2008), 'in certain extension planning areas (EPAs) within the districts where private sector involvement had been limited in the previous year, it was agreed to pay the retailers an additional sum of either 100MK or 200MK per voucher depending based on last year's sales figures for each EPA'. Kelly et al. (2010) find that the 'remoteness' premium encouraged the private sector to provide inputs in more locations in 2007/8 than in the previous season, although there was no evidence that such outreach was on a medium to long term basis.

Those in favour of private sector participation in fertilizer subsidy retail sales point to several benefits, including efficiency, freeing government resources, facilitating a strategy for promoting input markets in remote areas, broadening of choice of and competition between outlets for smallholder farmers, and reducing transaction costs and costs of queuing. However, opponents of private sector participation in the subsidy fertilizer retail market argue that the private sector cannot be trusted as they may be exchanging coupons for other merchandise rather than fertilizers in the absence of an audit system,[3] the available stocks held by private sector firms cannot be verified, that there is a high incidence of fraud in the private sector, and that private sector sales make it difficult to control the cost of the subsidy programme. These arguments were cited as grounds for the government's decision to exclude the private sector from retail sales of subsidized fertilizer from 2008/9 onwards.

Counter-arguments are that there is also evidence of fraud and corruption by some parastatal sales clerks, and that effective cost control should be achieved through control of coupon issue—as has been achieved from the

---

[3] There were anecdotal claims in the media that some farmers were obtaining iron sheets in exchange for fertilizer coupons in some private sector input outlets.

2009/10 season (although difficulties are also illustrated by major problems with excess seed costs in 2010/11 as a result of problems in detecting large numbers of counterfeit seed vouchers).

8.4.3. *Fertilizer sales trends: evidence from household surveys*

The household surveys shed light on the trends in the commercial sales of fertilizers among smallholder farmers. Figure 8.6 shows the various retail channels from which households reported purchasing their commercial fertilizers in the 2006/7, 2008/9, and 2010/11 seasons. The proportion of households accessing private company market outlets for commercial purchases has increased significantly from about 6% in the 2006/7 season to about 30% in 2010/11. This increasing trend is also evident in the use of club or farmer cooperatives as a source of commercial fertilizers. The purchase of fertilizers on a commercial basis from parastatals has been falling, from 18% in 2006/7 to about 13% in the 2010/11 season. These figures suggest that commercial sales of fertilizers have flourished in the presence of the subsidy programme. Although, the private sector has been excluded in the retail of subsidized fertilizers, the subsidy programme might have stimulated demand for commercial fertilizers, thereby promoting private sector development.

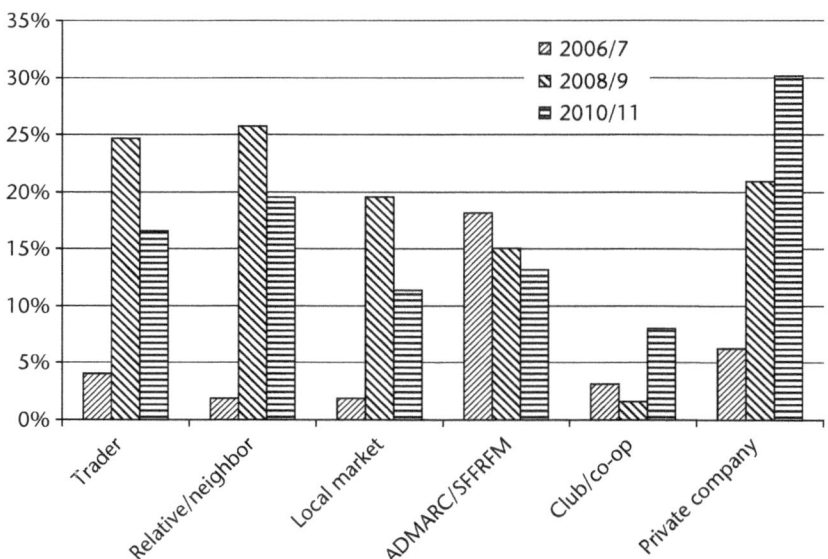

Figure 8.6. Sources of households' commercial fertilizer purchases, 2006/7–10/11
Source: Computed by authors based on AISS1, AISS2, and AISS3.

The evidence on household use of different marketing channels for purchase of commercial fertilizers in Figure 8.6 is also supported by information on the average volumes of commercial fertilizers purchased by households, shown in Figure 8.7. On average, the volume purchased from traders has fallen significantly from about 50 kg in 2006/7 to about 10 kg in 2010/11. Sourcing fertilizers from relatives or neighbours increased, but this may be fertilizer that could either have been subsidized and resold or received through remittances. There is an increase in average volumes purchased from the local market initially, but this declined between 2008/9 and 2010/11. There is a declining trend, however, in average commercial purchases from parastatals (ADMARC and SFFRFM). The increasing trends in the volume purchased from farmer cooperatives and private company outlets suggest positive private sector market development. For instance, in the 2006/7 season, households purchased on average 9 kg of commercial fertilizers, but this increases to 42 kg in 2008/9 and 60 kg in 2010/11, despite fertilizer price increases. This further suggests that the subsidy programme may have helped in stimulating commercial demand for fertilizers, and certainly has not depressed it over the longer term, as private marketing activities have continued to flourish in the medium term.

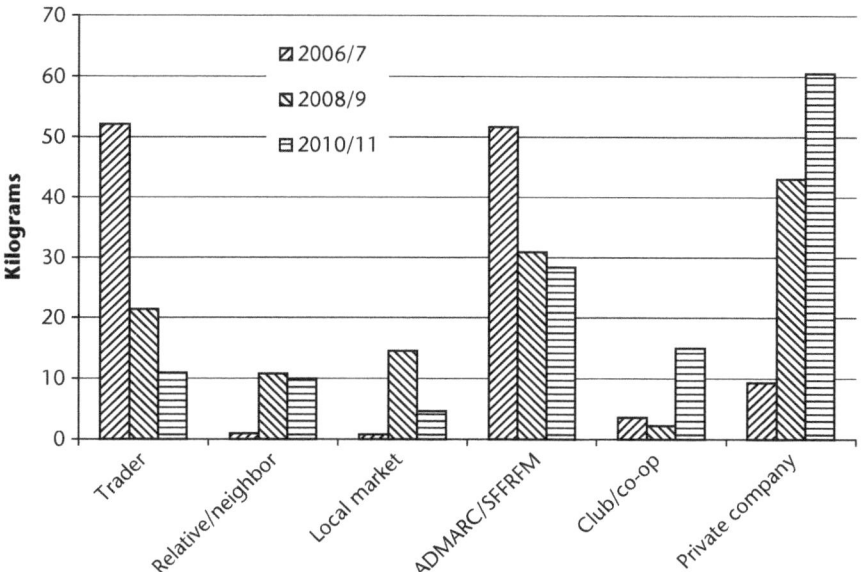

Figure 8.7. Mean quantities of commercial fertilizer purchases per household, 2006/7–10/11

Source: Computed by authors based on AISS1, AISS2, and AISS3.

Interestingly, although the international fertilizer price almost tripled in the 2008/9 season (Dorward and Chirwa, 2011c), there was an increase in the purchase of commercial fertilizers from private company retail shops. This is also consistent with the lower estimated displacement in 2008/9 season (Ricker-Gilbert and Jayne, 2010a). Similarly, Chirwa et al. (2011d), using a matched panel, note general increases in the purchase of commercial fertilizers between 2008/9 and 2010/11 among poor and non-poor households and a decrease in average subsidy fertilizers received by households.

These positive changes in private sector market development are also consistent with earlier studies. For example, Kelly et al. (2010) note that the perceived number of retailers selling only fertilizers increased, while those selling both seeds and fertilizers fell between the 2006/7 and 2008/9 agricultural seasons, although community surveys revealed little change in the number of input suppliers. Nonetheless, there were also a number of exits from seed and fertilizer markets during the period. Similarly, a higher proportion of retailers revealed that their business performance in terms of sales and profits had increased between 2007/8 and 2008/9 (Kelly et al., 2010).

8.4.4. *Displacement of commercial fertilizer sales*

The Farm Input Subsidy Programme could have several impacts on the input market system depending on the scale, targeting, and other implementation modalities. On the one hand, a poorly-targeted large-scale programme results in displacement of commercial sales and introduces disincentives for private investments in input markets. On the other hand, a well-targeted programme can stimulate additional demand for commercial fertilizers among subsidized households by improving the productivity and profitability of their farming activities and their ability to finance fertilizer purchases. The displacement effects are a function of targeting among other factors such as fertilizer prices and prices of agricultural produce: where subsidized fertilizers are provided to farmers that can afford commercial purchases, the displacement of commercial sales is likely to be high, thereby depressing incremental production. Thus, poor targeting, in which better-off farmers also tend to be recipients of subsidized fertilizers, may lead to substantial displacement of commercial sales by subsidized sales, resulting in a reduction of production and welfare impacts of the subsidy programme.

The relative promotional and displacement effects are examined in Table 8.2 which shows the quantity of subsidized and commercial fertilizers acquired by households in the 2009/10 and 2010/11 seasons by IHS2 poverty status (2002/3 and 2003/4) compared with commercial fertilizers in the IHS2. Among poor households the average quantity of subsidized fertilizers

Table 8.2. Quantity of subsidized and commercial fertilizers by IHS2 poverty status (kg)

| Years with subsidy access | Poor households in 2003/4 | | | | | | Non-poor households in 2003/4 | | | | | |
| | Subsidy | | | Commercial | | | Subsidy | | | Commercial | | |
	N	2009	2010	2003/4	2009	2010	N	2009	2010	2003/4	2009	2010
0	4	0	0	82	58	55	11	0	0	691	132	128
1	17	3	12	37	61	79	18	10	17	123	246	250
2	15	44	20	176	126	92	13	32	17	221	157	181
3	18	52	36	68	29	80	23	35	44	174	98	99
4	22	59	50	130	54	70	22	49	39	79	141	151
5	37	51	38	52	31	51	37	54	40	162	72	102
6	114	70	66	72	40	51	112	75	74	116	61	63
All	227	54	47	78	48	61	236	53	49	165	100	109

Source: Computed by authors based on IHS2 and FISS3 data.

declined from 54 kg in 2009/10 to 47 kg in 2010/11, while commercial fertilizers increased from 48 to 61 kg. A similar trend is observed among non-poor households, and may be related to economy-wide impacts of the programme. The data also shows that both poor and non-poor households supplement subsidized fertilizers with commercial fertilizers, but among the poor the higher the number of seasons a household benefits from the subsidy, the lower the supplementation with commercial fertilizers. No consistent pattern emerges with respect to non-poor households that are subsidized.

A comparison of the 2009 and 2010 commercial purchases with the 2003/4 purchases shows a mixed picture among different households. On the one hand, among the category of poor households, only those that have had access to the subsidy in seasons 1 and 3 are on average purchasing more in 2010 than in 2003/4. On the other hand, among the non-poor households, only for households that have had access to the subsidy in seasons 1 and 4 do we witness purchases above the 2003/4 levels. This suggests some crowding out of commercial fertilizer sales due to the subsidy programme, although the decline in commercial purchases also occurred among households that have never received subsidized fertilizers. However, it should also be noted that the average prices of commercial fertilizers substantially increased from 37MK per kg in 2003/4 to 97MK per kg in 2010/11, an increase of 162% over the period; this might have dampened the demand for commercial fertilizers.

School of Oriental and African Studies et al. (2008) using national fertilizer sales data and taking into account the price effects, estimated displacement rates of 20% and 42% in 2005/6 and 2006/7, respectively, without any allowance for the effects of fertilizer and maize or tobacco price changes on demand. The displacement rates were substantially higher for tobacco fertilizers compared to maize fertilizers. Using household survey data and a matched sample of smallholder farmers, Ricker-Gilbert et al. (2010) note that the proportion of smallholder farmers purchasing commercial fertilizers fell from 40% in 2003/4 to 16% in the 2006/7 season. The regression results, from a double hurdle model allowing for fertilizer and maize or tobacco price changes, revealed a displacement rate of 22%, with 18% among poorer households and 30% among non-poor farmers (Ricker-Gilbert et al., 2010). Using a similar model, Ricker-Gilbert and Jayne (2010a) estimate an average displacement rate of 3% in 2008/9.

Chirwa et al. (2011d), using household data for 2002/3, 2003/4, and 2010/11 seasons, find that for a matched sample of households that bought commercial fertilizer in the 2002/3 and 2003/4 seasons, a 1% increase in sub-sidized fertilizers led to a 0.39% reduction in commercial sales, but this fell to an elasticity of –0.15 (or a net displacement rate of 15%) for the whole sample of panel households who bought commercial fertilizers in either of the seasons. The decrease in the elasticity suggests that the subsidy programme does not only have displacement effects, but also promotional effects when one accounts for households that did not initially purchase commercial fertilizers.

The displacement rates in the seed market tend to be higher, although there is also anecdotal evidence suggesting that the subsidy programme is stimulating demand for improved maize seeds. School of Oriental and African Studies et al. (2008) note that in 2006/7 one of the major suppliers of improved seeds reported a sales increase of 52% over 2005/6 levels, with many suppliers qualitatively indicating improvements in sales. Kelly et al. (2010) also find evidence of the positive impact of the subsidy programme on seed sales in the 2007/8 and 2008/9 agricultural seasons. In addition, a large proportion of retailers surveyed were in favour of the continuation of the seed subsidy: 95% of those that participated and 76% of those that did not participate in the 2008/9 agricultural season (Kelly et al., 2010). However, Mason and Ricker-Gilbert (2012) find that a 1 kg increase in subsidized seed acquired by the household reduces commercial improved maize seed purchases by 0.56 kg in Malawi (a displacement rate of 56%), higher than in Zambia where the displacement rate is 49%. Improved seeds are substantially cheaper than sub-sidized fertilizers, and relatively more households can afford to buy commercially thereby increasing displacement rates relative to the displacement rates in fertilizer markets. However, it must be recognized that estimation of both fertilizer and seed displacement rates involves difficulties in categorization of some purchases as subsidized or unsubsidized. This is likely to be particularly difficult for seeds, where purchases of recycled hybrid seed may be difficult to distinguish from purchases of new seed.

Table 8.3. Number of seed suppliers to the subsidy programme, 2006/7–11/12

Seed type	2006/7	2007/8	2008/9	2009/10	2010/11	2011/12
Hybrid maize	3	3	3	4	3	5
OPV maize	5	5	4	4	4	6
Tested bean	-	-	-	4	2	5
Tested groundnut	-	-	-	4	4	10
Soya bean	-	-	-	2	2	3
Pigeon pea	-	-	-	1	1	5
Cow peas	-	-	-	1	1	1
Cotton	-	-	2	-	-	-
Number of firms	6	6	8	8	9	12

Note: Some firms supply more than one type of seed, so the total number of firms is not the total for the columns.
Source: Logistics Unit (2008, 2009, 2010, 2011, 2012).

8.5. Developments in the seed market

8.5.1. *Changes in competition in the seed market*

The private sector has, from 2006/7, consistently participated in the distribution and retailing of seeds under the subsidy programme, as noted above. Improved maize seeds and legumes have been made available to the programme by the private sector in all years, though the retailing of seeds under the programme was implemented from the 2006/7 season. This has meant players in the seed value chain—including seed producers, agro-dealers, and supermarkets—have been participating in the subsidy programme. Previous evaluation reports such as School of Oriental and African Studies et al. (2008) and Kelly et al. (2010) have pointed to the positive impact of the subsidy programme in promoting private sector businesses in input provision.

In terms of the structure of the seed industry, there have been some limited changes in the number of seed growers, but the major changes in the structure seem to have occurred at retail level. Table 8.3 provides the distribution of firms supplying various seeds to the subsidy programme and shows that the number of firms supplying seeds has increased from 6 in 2006/7 to 12 in 2011/12. Two new growers entered into the market in 2009/10: Seed Tech supplying maize hybrid and OPV, and National Association of Smallholder Farmers of Malawi (NASFAM) supplying groundnut seeds (Logistics Unit, 2010). In 2010/11 the number of firms supplying seeds to the programme increased to nine, with the exit of Agricultural Input Suppliers Association of Malawi (AISAM) and entry of Panthochi supplying OPV maize seeds and Peacock supplying tested groundnut seeds to the programme (Logistics Unit, 2011). In 2011/12, 12 companies supplied seeds to the programme with the re-entry of AISAM, ASSMAG, and Seed Tech and a new entry, Pindulani (Logistics Unit, 2012). Although the number of firms has increased over the years, Kelly et al. (2010) note that this has not resulted in competitive pricing as the supply prices to the programme are negotiated between STAM and the government: this competition has just broadened the choice of seeds for the farmers.

Nonetheless, the seed industry is highly oligopolistic, with new entrants just providing fringe competition. Data from the Logistics Unit shows that the two largest suppliers of seeds to the subsidy programme account for 71% of maize voucher redemption and the three largest suppliers account for 87% of maize voucher redemptions. Similarly, in the legume seed market, the two and three largest suppliers to the subsidy programme account for 65% and 75% of voucher redemptions, respectively.

There is, however, an increase in the level of competition at retail level in terms of the number of competitors in the local communities. Kelly et al. (2010) find that agro-dealers reported a 15% increase in competitors between 2005/6 and 2008/9, while distributors reported a 3% increase in the number of competitors. However, community surveys revealed that only 22% of the communities believed that the number of seed sellers accessible in their community had increased, while 57% maintained that the numbers had remained the same between 2006/7 and 2008/9 (Kelly et al., 2010).

8.5.2. Trends in subsidized seeds sales

As described in Chapter 5, under the subsidy programme, smallholder farmers are provided with maize seed vouchers and flexible vouchers that they can use to purchase legume seeds. In 2007/8 and 2008/9, flexible vouchers were also allowed for maize seed redemption, but they have been restricted to legumes since the 2009/10 season. Table 8.4 presents the size of the seed component of the subsidy programme, which provides indicators of private sector participation. In terms of coupons redeemed, maize is the main component and when flexible vouchers were also accepted for maize seeds a high proportion of them were also redeemed for maize seeds. One reason for this was the problem of availability of legume seeds in the earlier seasons of the programme (School of Oriental and African Studies et al., 2008).

On average, the programme has distributed to smallholder farmers 5840 MT of hybrid maize seeds, 1,837 MT of OPV maize seeds and 2,256 MT of legume seeds per year. As discussed in Chapter 5, there has been a steady increase in hybrid seeds obtained by smallholder farmers since 2007/8 until a fall in 2011/12. The volume of OPV maize seeds dropped substantially in 2008/9 but then increased steadily from the 2009/10 season. The consequent value of private seed business promoted directly by the subsidy amounted on

Table 8.4. Size of the seed component of the subsidy programme, 2007/8–11/12

Variable	2007/8	2008/9	2009/10	2010/11	2011/12
Coupons redeemed (N)					
Maize coupons	1,603,302	1,561,329	1,614,070	1,988,066	1,376,216
Flexi coupons—maize	518,264	929,382	-	-	-
Flexi coupons—legumes	142,043	87,228	1,142,738	1,310,420	1,245,172
Seeds distributed (MT)					
Hybrid maize seeds	2,944	4,532	7,619	8,521	5,586
OPV maize seeds	2,597	833	1,033	2,129	2,591
Legume seeds	-	-	1,551	2,727	2,490
Cost of seeds ($ millions)					
Maize seeds	8.18	11.94	17.171	23.237	16.487
Legume seeds	0.99	0.63	2.837	7.147	6.734

Source: Logistics Unit (2008, 2009, 2010, 2011, 2012).

average to US$19.1 million per year over the five agricultural seasons (excluding farmer top up payments for hybrid maize). Figure 8.8 shows the values and value shares of this seed business and the increasing share of legumes in the cost of the seed supplies obtained by smallholder farmers from the subsidy programme. This reflects substantial improvements in the availability of legume seeds in the market under the programme, such that legumes accounted for nearly 30% of the seed component in the 2011/12 season compared to only 5% in the 2008/9 season.

With respect to the relative cost of maize seeds and legume seeds (Figure 8.8(b)), there is an increasing share of legumes in the cost of the seed supplies obtained by smallholder farmers from the subsidy programme. With the increase in the number of seed growers providing legume seeds, the trend reflects substantial improvements in the availability of legume seeds in the market under the programme, such that legumes accounted for nearly 30% of the seed component in the 2011/12 season compared to only 5% in the 2008/9 season.

8.5.3. *Seed purchases, use and preferences: evidence from household surveys*

The role of the private sector in the marketing of seeds can be deduced from household survey data obtained in the 2006/7, 2008/9, and 2010/11 seasons. Figure 8.9 shows the use of various market channels to access improved maize

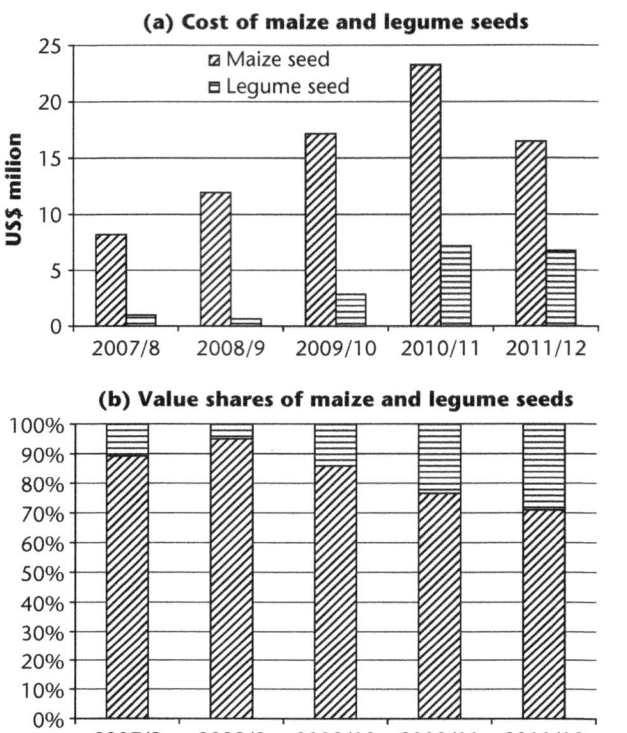

Figure 8.8. Values and value shares of subsidized maize seed sales, 2007/8–11/12

Source: Computed based on Logistics Unit (2008, 2009, 2010, 2011, 2012).

seeds (hybrid and OPV) by households in the survey years.[4] The parastatals, ADMARC and SFFRFM, are the main retail markets from which smallholder farmers obtained their improved seeds, with about 70% of farmers utilizing these outlets. With respect to private outlets, use of private companies by households to obtain improved seeds has been increasing from 10% of households in 2006/7 to 17% in 2010/11. There is also increasing use of relatives or neighbours as a source of improved seeds, from 4% of households in 2006/7 to 13% in 2010/11. These sales through relatives or neighbours could be of recycled seeds or remittance seeds offered for resale or subsidy seeds offered for resale.

---

[4] For each market channel, we compute the proportion of households using the market channel, and due to multiple uses of markets by some households the total for the year is more than 100%.

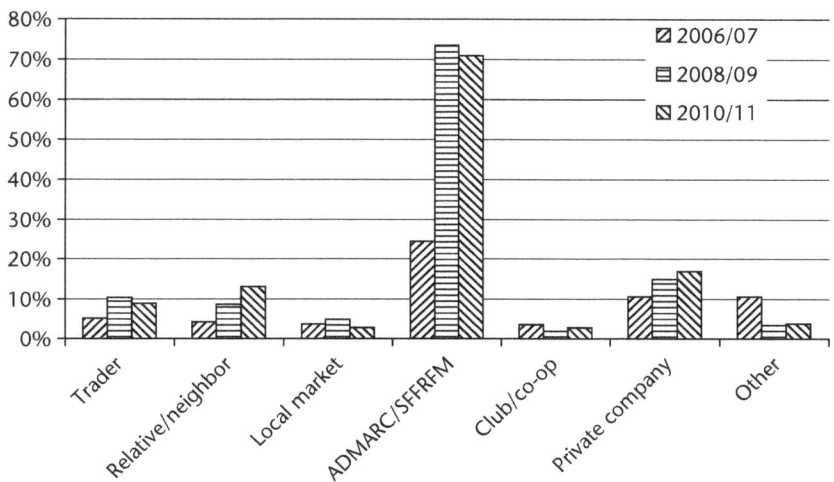

Figure 8.9. Households accessing improved maize seeds by retailer, 2006/7–10/11
Source: Computed by authors based on AISS1, AISS2, and AISS3.

With respect to quantities of seeds bought commercially or using the seed subsidy vouchers, Figure 8.10(a) shows first for total hybrid and OPV seed purchases and then for each type separately an average decline per household of commercial purchase and an increase in subsidy purchase between 2008/9 and 2010/11. The 2010/11 figure also reflects the increase in the number of seed coupons provided under the programme compared to the 2008/9 season. Farmers are also purchasing more hybrid maize seeds both commercially and under the subsidy programme compared to OPV maize seeds. While commercial purchases of OPV maize seeds have remained the same, for hybrid maize seeds commercial purchases declined from an average of 2.1 kg in 2008/9 to 1.6 kg in 2010/11 per household. In both cases of hybrid and OPV maize seeds, there is an increase in subsidy redemption. These declining trends suggest that the subsidy programme is crowding out commercial purchases, as discussed above with regard to displacement estimates, although the overall use of improved seeds has been increasing.

With respect to the relative participation of state and private retailers between 2008/9 and 2010/11, Figure 8.10(b) shows that there was a substantial decline in average purchases of commercial seeds through private retailers but a greater increase in subsidized seed purchases by households. Similarly, average commercial purchases of hybrid maize seeds fell but average subsidized purchases of hybrid maize seeds increased. In contrast, average purchases of commercial seeds from state marketing outlets marginally declined (from 0.16 kg to 0.07 kg) between 2008/9 and 2010/11 largely due to a fall

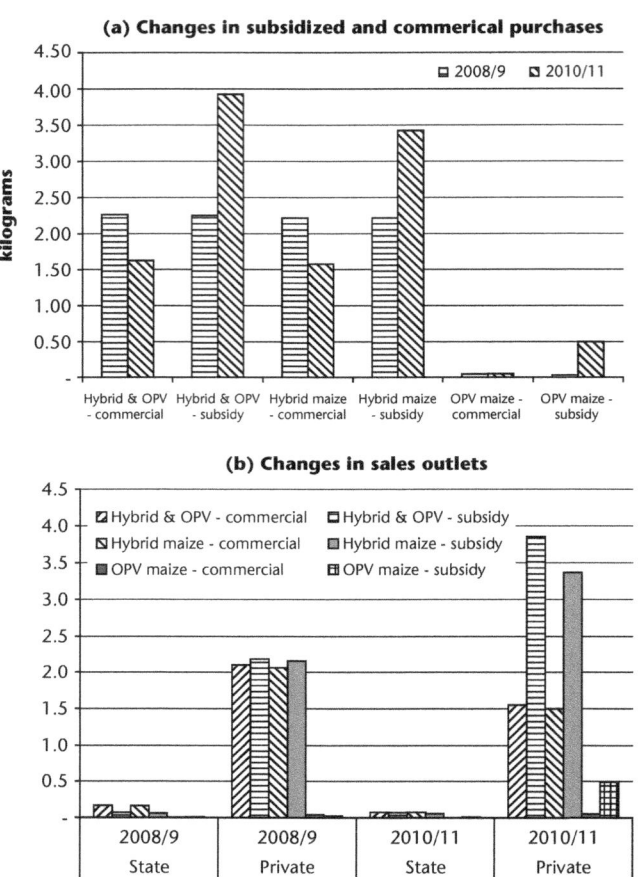

Figure 8.10. Volumes of improved maize seeds purchased per household, 2008/9 and 2010/11

Source: Computed by authors based on AISS2 and AISS3.

in hybrid maize purchases. Although, the proportion of households accessing the private market system is small relative to households accessing state markets, as observed above, the average purchases of seeds per household purchasing is higher from private market outlets than from parastatal outlets. Agro-dealers have played an important role in facilitating access to inputs in rural areas. Chinsinga (2011) notes that with FISP there has been an increase in the number of seasonal agro-dealers, a situation that has been supported by the practice of seed companies who collect the unsold inventories from contracted agro-dealers during the off-peak FISP period.

There has been a proliferation of maize seeds varieties in the market, which has broadened the choice for farmers. However, under the subsidy programme this

Table 8.5. Inputs actually obtained against those wanted by farmers in 2010/11(%)

Inputs obtained	As wanted	Other inputs wanted				
		Hybrid maize	OPV maize	Soya	Groundnut	Beans
Hybrid maize	84	13	1	0	0	0
OPV maize	58	40	0	2	0	0
Soya	56	0	0	0	35	9
Groundnut	94	0	0	0	2	4
Beans	85	0	0	0	15	0

Source: Dorward and Chirwa (2011a)

choice is constrained by the availability of preferred seeds and seed varieties in different markets and times when farmers require the seeds. Table 8.5 illustrates the seed preferences by farmers in the 2010/11 season. For maize seeds, there is higher preference for hybrid maize seeds with 84% getting the hybrid variety they wanted and 13% getting alternative hybrid varieties. This preference for hybrid maize is also reflected in the 40% of those that got OPV seeds but wanted hybrid seeds. Lunduka et al. (2012) find that farmers prefer hybrid maize seeds in Malawi due to high yields and their drought tolerance, while OPV maize seeds are preferred due to their early maturity. Among the legume seeds, farmers tend to prefer groundnuts and bean seeds and a higher proportion of them got what they wanted. The higher preference for groundnut seeds is also reflected in the additional 35% that got soya seeds who wanted groundnut seeds.

There are regional variations in seed preferences, but most farmers in different regions usually got the seeds and the seed varieties that they wanted (Dorward and Chirwa, 2011a).These figures suggest that hybrid maize seeds are the preferred maize seeds for smallholder farmers. The differences between what was obtained and what farmers wanted were, however, noticeable for legume seeds, with groundnut seeds being most in demand, but due to scarcity many farmers having to opt for soya seeds. Groundnuts and bean seeds are the legume seeds most wanted by smallholder farmers.

8.6. Challenges and opportunities of private sector participation[5]

The participation of the private sector in the input subsidy programme is challenging but can also provide opportunities for improving the implementation and efficiency of the programme. For instance, on the one hand,

[5] This section draws heavily on Chirwa and Dorward (2012).

major challenges are the exclusion of the private sector from the retailing of subsidized fertilizers and policy inconsistency in its role in the subsidy programme. On the other hand, however, private sector participation could provide opportunities for achieving multiple development objectives and for improving efficiency in the implementation of the programme.

8.6.1. *Challenges in private sector participation*

Several challenges have been experienced with regard to the roles of the private sector in the implementation of the subsidy programme. First, the timing of the award of tenders, particularly for supply of fertilizers to the programme, has been a major source of difficulty, as discussed in Chapter 5. The longer the time between submission of tenders and the awards of tenders the more likely the prices are to change and this can lead to protracted negotiation about supply prices for fertilizers. There have been cases in which companies awarded tenders have been unable to supply at the tender prices due to increased costs of supply. However, there is evidence that this has improved over time. Kelly et al. (2010) note that most stakeholders in 2008/9 were of the view that the announcement of tenders improved but the tenders were awarded late. Dorward et al. (2010b) argue that the delays in award of tenders increased private sector risks as both the prices of fertilizers and fuel had risen dramatically in the period between June 2006/7 and June 2008/9. There have been improvements in the timing of announcement of tender awards more recently (Dorward and Chirwa, 2011c).

Second, there is often a problem of trust between the private sector and the government and this has contributed to the continued exclusion of the private sector in the retailing of subsidized fertilizers. The lack of trust emerges from both sides. From the government side, there are some in government that believe that private sector firms with their profit motive are likely to exploit their engagement to the detriment of smallholder farmers and public welfare. Chinsinga (2011) documents some of the profit and quick-gain motives of some of the agro-dealers in input supply markets. There have been allegations, based on anecdotal incidents reported in the media but not substantiated, that some private sector retailers were accepting fertilizer coupons in exchange for non-fertilizer items. This reinforced the views of those sceptical of the private sector that the private sector was unable to self-regulate its behaviour in the programme. Others have also argued that when the private sector was involved in the retailing of subsidized fertilizers, there was high incidence of tips paid by farmers. However, Kelly et al. (2010) find that the incidence of tips and malpractices was higher in parastatals than in private sector retails, although the differences were not statistically significant, and the incidents of accepted fake vouchers were higher in parastatals outlets.

Furthermore, even with exclusion of the private sector in subsidized fertilizer retailing, smallholder farmers still report an increased incidence of tips from ADMARC and SFFRFM outlets (Dorward et al., 2010b; Dorward and Chirwa, 2011c). The mistrust of the private sector is also exacerbated by the absence of an audit system on the stock movement of inputs as a way of detecting malpractices. From the private sector's point of view, the government's inconsistent decisions on private sector participation in retail of subsidized fertilizers, and delays in making inclusion or exclusion decisions, characterize policy instability, creating uncertainty for private input market development. This was particularly the case in 2008/9 when a decision was made about private sector involvement and contracts for inclusion provided, but the government reversed the decision without prior notice (Kelly et al., 2010). By the time the government had made the decision to exclude the private sector, the private companies had already stocked their retail shops in readiness for redemption of vouchers.

Third, the subsidy programme has attracted new entrants that were hitherto uninterested in the fertilizer business, particularly from domestic companies, some just created to bid for contracts to supply fertilizers to the programme (Holden and Tostensen, 2011). Some of these companies were highly connected to the political establishment, but when awarded contracts they had difficulties in fulfilling their deliveries. For non-established agricultural input suppliers, their main interest is the short-term gains from participation in the programme rather than the medium to long-term development of the input supply market. Chinsinga (2012a) notes that most of the contracts in the provision of transport services were awarded to companies politically linked to the ruling party. Logistics Unit (2012) notes that although it became clear in the 2011/12 programme that some of the suppliers were unlikely to supply, the government continued to grant extensions and the final deliveries occurred in February 2012 instead of the end of October 2011. The existence of vested interests is one reason for non-compliance with the terms of the fertilizer supply. Although there have been improvements in the timing of deliveries, late deliveries were evident and this problem has been attributed to the lack of penalty clauses in the contracts (Dorward et al., 2010b; Dorward and Chirwa, 2011c; Logistics Unit, 2011). Large numbers of new entrants in seed sales may also be associated with poor service to farmers (Chinsinga, 2011) and in 2010/11 may have contributed to the use of large numbers of fake vouchers in subsidized purchases.

Fourth, in the seed component of the subsidy programme, there is some collusive behaviour of seed suppliers in deciding the supply price of seeds offered to the programme. Although the subsidy programme has attracted a number of players in seed production and supply, the pricing arrangement is tantamount to collusive pricing due to the desire by the government to have a uniform top up for farmers (Kelly et al., 2010).There is no competitive tendering in the seed supply to the subsidy programme, in contrast to the fertilizer supply system, although in recent years, a variable 'top up' payment by farmers on subsidized hybrid seed packages has provided some competition and benefited some smallholder farmers. Thus, in 2010/11, seed companies were allowed to apply a discretionary maximum farmer payment of 100MK per maize seed voucher topping up the government redemption value of 1,650MK, and all hybrid seeds providers applied the maximum top up while only one OPV provider made a top up charge (Logistics Unit, 2011, 2012).

Finally, there is evidence that the payment system used by the government for supplies and services rendered to the programme by the private sector is inefficient. Logistics Unit (2012) reports some companies waiting six months to be paid after delivery of fertilizer supplies. Similarly, seed companies had outstanding invoices for three months in the 2010/11 season (Logistics Unit, 2012). The Logistics Unit final weekly report for the 2011/12 programme indicated that the government still owed seed companies, fertilizer companies, and transporters for supplies and services provided during the 2010/11 subsidy programme. These delays in payment are likely to lead to the high supply price of inputs and services as suppliers factor in the risk of delayed payments in their prices.

8.6.2. Opportunities from greater private sector participation

Greater involvement of the private sector in the subsidy programme not only promotes private sector development in input markets but can also improve efficiency in the implementation of the programme. There are several ways in which the private sector can play a positive role in input market development. First, increased involvement of the private sector provides the opportunity for increasing the efficiency of implementation of the programme. This can be achieved by increasing the number of outlets from which smallholder farmers can redeem their input coupons and broadening their choice of markets. The increase in the competition may consequently improve the quality of services at market outlets and reduce the incidence of tips at the markets. Kelly et al. (2010) note that although the incidence of tips was not significantly different between parastatals outlets and private sector outlets, smallholder farmers were more likely to 'never pay tips' in private sector outlets. The increase in the number of outlets can also reduce the opportunity cost of queuing—a phenomena that has been evident in the programme.

Second, the involvement of the private sector can also encourage private investment in rural input markets. This requires consistency and transparency in the government's decisions to build the confidence needed for investment. There are also opportunities for designing future private sector participation on the basis of performance-based indicators, such as verifiable expansion of retail outlet coverage. Alternatively, the private sector could bid to supply specific quantities of subsidized fertilizer in under-served areas identified by the government. These areas could be served directly by the private companies or through private company sub-contraction to agro-dealers. As the analysis above has shown, private sales of fertilizers have flourished suggesting an increased demand for fertilizers, but it is not clear whether this has also facilitated the expansion of the private sector into poorly served areas. Such performance rewards, combined with increased demand for fertilizers, could provide the incentives needed for the private sector to invest in more input market infrastructure on a permanent or seasonal basis.

The third area in which the subsidy can exploit opportunities of private sector involvement is storage facilities. With the exclusion of the private sector from subsidized fertilizer retailing, all the programme fertilizers have to be delivered at one of three SFFRFM depots for uplifting to SFFRFM and ADMARC markets. The exclusion of the private sector has thus created pressure on storage facilities at both the depots and parastatals unit markets. This has introduced inefficiencies and increased the incidence of stock-outs in unit markets. Logistics Unit (2012) notes that the shortage of storage space in markets in the critical early months of the programme in 2011/12 meant that although 63% of total annual fertilizer supply was available in the central depots, only a little over 60% of this was uplifted to unit markets. The limited storage capacity of SFFRFM depots in the past years of private sector exclusion from subsidized fertilizer retailing has led to congestion (Logistics Unit, 2011, 2012), a situation that could be alleviated by more involvement of the private sector in retail markets.

Fourth, better methods of targeting that reduce displacement and therefore increase demand for commercial purchases could help in input market development. In Chapter 10 we discuss some targeting options that have the potential to reduce displacement and the practical difficulties associated with these options. Fifth, improvements in the timing of coupon distribution, that is distributing earlier, can help farmers to plan for commercial purchases and thereby help commercial sales and encourage investment in input markets. Earlier distribution of coupons can bolster input sales as those that do not receive coupons and those that receive coupons but want to top up would be certain about their commercial purchases. In this case, involvement of the private sector could also offer opportunities for earlier purchase of inputs by farmers and hence more effective yield gains. Finally, there are also opportunities that may arise with the use of electronic vouchers, which could enable the private sector to invest in an electronic system resulting in shared costs, benefiting both government and private suppliers.

8.7. Summary

This chapter set out to review the impacts of the subsidy programme on the development of the private sector in farm input supply. The private sector has played a major role in the subsidy programme since 2006/7. It continues to play an increasing role in the importation and procurement of fertilizer for the subsidy programme, but was only allowed to retail subsidized fertilizers in the 2006/7 and 2007/8 seasons, and agro-dealers were excluded even then. Otherwise, the retailing of subsidized fertilizers has been monopolized by the two parastatals, ADMARC and SFFRFM. In the seed sector, however, various players in the seed value chain, including agro-dealers, have been allowed to participate in seed production and retailing of subsidized improved maize seeds and legumes, and indeed the production and distribution of subsidized seeds has been managed entirely by the private sector.

Overall, although the subsidy has had some negative impacts on private sector development in the form of short-run displacement of unsubsidized commercial sales, in the medium to long term it appears to have been catalytic in raising the demand for fertilizers and improved seeds. In the fertilizer markets, the private sector is increasingly the main supplier of fertilizers to the programme, and their exclusion from the retail market for subsidized fertilizers does not appear to have dampened demand for commercial fertilizers in the medium term. In the seeds market, the increase in the seed subsidy from 2009/10 seems to be crowding out commercial sales. However, like the fertilizer market, in the medium to long term the massive seed subsidy may stimulate demand for improved seeds as farmers witness the benefits of technology adoption. In addition, there is an increase in the number of private sector players in both the fertilizer and seed markets, although exits, especially in the fertilizer market, are evident. However, the challenge is to translate the increase in competition into reasonably priced inputs and high quality services offered to smallholder farmers in under-served areas.

There are benefits from expanding the role of the private sector, in reducing programme costs, increasing efficiency, and alleviating problems of storage capacity in parastatal markets. However the involvement of the private sector will require mutual trust among stakeholders, systems of transparency and accountability, and policy consistency and credibility. These conditions could create an environment that is conducive to private sector investment in input markets. As the demand for commercial fertilizers increases, assuming current trends continue, there may be scope for a gradual reduction in the subsidy programme. However, this will require strategic investment in input markets by the private sector to sustain such demand and a strategic approach to programme graduation, an issue we discuss later in Chapter 11.

While the volume of subsidized fertilizers has been falling from its peak in 2007/8, the growing demand for commercial purchases by smallholder farmers should also provide incentives for private companies to strategically position themselves by expanding their networks in under-served areas. One way this could be achieved might be by developing sustainable partnerships within the agro-dealer network that exists in rural areas. There is also scope for increasing private participation in the fertilizer retail market through performance-based contracts to supply under-served areas.

Nonetheless, it is important to continuously monitor the impact of the subsidy programme on private sector markets and to monitor the integrity and efficiency of the private sector in input supply. As we argue later in Chapter 11, improving the efficiency and competitiveness of input suppliers is one of the conditions that can facilitate graduation from the subsidy programme, at household, area, and national levels. In particular, periodic surveys tracking programme effects on smallholder farmers' commercial purchases and on input markets should generate useful information for evidence-based decision making about private sector roles and government engagement with and policy for input market development. An important element of this engagement should be the monitoring of market efficiency through analysis of market structure (considering the number and characteristics of players, their market power, and vertical restraints), behaviour in the market, and resultant benefits in terms of efficiency that promotes smallholder development and welfare.

9

Benefit–cost analysis, 2006/7 to 2010/11[1]

9.1. Introduction

In this chapter we develop benefit–cost estimates for the FISP, using methods that have relatively simple analytical and data demands (to allow their application in practical policy analysis) but nevertheless yield reasonably robust estimates that allow valid comparisons with estimates of the costs and benefits to potential alternative investments.

The chapter is structured as follows. After this introduction we first consider the purpose and principles for benefit–cost analysis (BCA) and common methods used in BCA. We then review problems and challenges identified with previous BCA on the FISP. This leads on (in Section 9.5) to technical suggestions for methodological improvements in estimating benefit–costs of FISP and we then apply these methodologies to estimate returns to investment over the life of the programme. Readers without a particular methodological interest in benefit–cost analysis may like to skip this section. We conclude with a discussion of the implications of the analysis for FISP's design and implementation.

9.2. Benefit–cost analysis purposes and principles

Benefit–cost analysis (BCA) of input subsidy programmes has two main functions.

- It gives an indication of the returns to specific programmes as compared to returns that might be achieved from alternative investments, and can thus guide overall government investment and spending decisions. Estimates of such returns are also commonly used for more

---

[1] This chapter draws heavily on Dorward and Chirwa (2011b).

general comparisons of the returns to different types of investments (for example, between agricultural input subsidies, research, and infrastructural development) in order to guide investment choices between programmes.

- It provides information about the variables that are important in determining costs and benefits of a specific programme or type of programme, and hence can guide programme design and implementation decisions to increase benefits relative to costs.

These two uses of BCA are both important, but they present analysts with something of a dilemma. The first requires the use of common standards across different programmes, perhaps in different sectors, to give comparable results across investment alternatives. These standards generally involve standardized methods, but it is often difficult to apply such methods across programmes that affect people and the economy in different and complex ways and in different policy contexts. These difficulties need to be recognized when making comparisons between BCA results obtained for different programmes. The second purpose of BCA requires not so much standards for comparable estimates of returns, but accurate estimates of the relative importance of different variables affecting these returns in particular investments— and here there may be more value in tailoring methods to match specific programme features. This, however, leads to a danger that the results may not be comparable with results from analysis of other investments, but may nevertheless be (wrongly) used for making such comparisons.

Taking these two purposes together with an overall objective that BCA should provide rigorous, reliable, and objective estimates of benefits and costs, we suggest the following seven principles for the choice and implementation of BCA methods (these are not set out according to any prioritization). BCA methods applied in any situation should be

1. *Practicable*: They must be applicable to the data and analytical resources (skills and software, for example) that are available (or can reasonably be obtained).

2. *Externally consistent*: They must provide measures that are comparable with generally accepted good practice in definitions of costs and benefits (for example, in definitions of financial and economic benefits).

3. *Contextualized*: They must take account of particularities that affect the benefits and costs of a programme as regards the processes by which costs and benefits are linked, the effects of other policies and investments on these, and the conditions affecting these.

4. *Holistic*: They must take account of all the significant benefits and costs associated with a policy or investment programme, both direct benefits and costs to recipients or beneficiaries and indirect benefits and costs to others.

5. *Internally consistent*: They must properly represent the significant relationships between investments and behaviours by different stakeholders, taking account of 'counterfactuals' (comparing actual behaviours and outcomes under a programme or investments against those that would have occurred in its absence).

6. *Transparent*: Assumptions, measures, data sources, shortcomings, and possible bias and inaccuracies in methods and their results must be stated and discussed.

7. *Cost-effective*: BCA methods should be chosen, developed, and implemented to ensure that costs of analysis are commensurate with the value of the information provided.

The cost-effectiveness of methods is of course affected by the costs of BCA methods in providing information and in value of the information provided.

- Costs are determined by resource demands for gathering extra information needed and for analysis (as discussed above under *practicability* and as we discuss below as regards demands for different methods).
- The value of the information provided is determined by its quality and by the scope for its use.
  - The determinants of quality are *external and internal consistency*, *holism*, and *contextualization* (as discussed above) and the strengths and weaknesses of analytical methods (which we discuss below).
  - Scope for use of information is determined by *transparency* of results (as discussed above), by the strengths and weaknesses of different methods (which we discuss below), and by the potential 'decision space' for changes in policy choices, design, and implementation in the light of new information provided by BCA.

There are particular challenges in applying the first four of the principles above to the specific situation in which the FISP operates.

1. *Practicable.* There are severe limitations in data availability (for example, on crop areas and yields, the yield and production effects of subsidized seed and fertilizer, and the number of farm families in the

country). There are also limited financial and human resources available for analysis, but the determination of the 'counterfactual' situation of what would have happened without a subsidy is very complex, properly requiring consideration of changes throughout the whole economy as a result of changes in farm incomes, in food prices, and in the real incomes of consumers. The data and resource limitations lead to a fundamental question about the practicability of making any reliable estimates without substantial improvements, particularly in data availability.

2. *Externally consistent.* Limited availability of good quality data poses problems for the application of good practice in BCA. A further difficulty arises with the longstanding history of policy interventions inhibiting maize imports and exports, as this makes it very difficult to identify true economic prices for maize—conventionally, import and export parity prices should be used in economic analysis, but one may legitimately ask if liberalized market policies are a real policy option for the Malawian Government (see Tschirley and Jayne (2010) for a nuanced discussion of these issues). If import parity prices are to be used in the analysis then it is very difficult to determine what national prices would actually have prevailed with and without the subsidy (this adds to the already difficult task of estimating counterfactual 'without subsidy' prices for comparison against the 'with subsidy' situation—a 'double counterfactual problem').

3. *Contextualized.* The effects of the subsidy on livelihoods are complex, widespread, and in many ways specific to the problems faced by poor Malawian smallholders (with the low maize productivity trap and policy context discussed in Chapter 4). Analysis has to take account of these contextual issues—but this may lead to conflict with the two previous principles—requiring more complex, non-standard analysis.

4. *Holistic*: The scale and nature of the FISP means that it has widespread, complex, and varied effects on the livelihoods of different farm households, on consumers, and on maize and labour markets. Ideally this requires holistic consideration of dynamic and interacting changes in rural livelihoods and in rural and national markets. This presents very large data and analytical challenges. This is clearly related to the problems of contextualization, with similar potential for conflict with the principles of practicality and external consistency—for example: can simpler methods be modified to represent key effects of wider, complex changes and also generate results that allow meaningful comparison with BCA on other investments?

9.3. Benefit–cost analysis methods

Investment and policy analysis methods can be classified according to the extent to which they focus on direct, 'partial equilibrium' effects of an investment or policy on the beneficiaries in the relevant sector as against wider, indirect 'general equilibrium' effects on beneficiaries and non-beneficiaries across all sectors in an economy. Increasing consideration of wider indirect effect increases the analytical complexity and data requirements. However although these effects may not be important for smaller scale interventions, they may dominate the direct effects for large-scale investments in the agricultural sector if these affect food prices and the productivity of large areas of land and large amounts of labour. Where more complex and demanding general equilibrium methods are used, these should properly represent markets' and different stakeholders' behaviours and interactions. Where more simple partial equilibrium methods are used, then these should where possible build in simple adjustments to simulate possible wider economy effects.

It is helpful to distinguish between three basic methodological approaches to BCA for large-scale policy investments:

a) *Regression models* which estimate returns to investments by analysing comparative data sets across different regions in a country, for example, and estimate the impacts of investments on welfare measures or economic growth (for example, Fan et al. (2007)), implicitly taking account of multipliers and wider general equilibrium market effects.[2]

b) *Computable general equilibrium (CGE) and multi-market models* that analyse the effects of investments by simulating economic behaviour with and without investments—with general equilibrium models simulating economy-wide effects, and multi-market models examining effects across a more restricted set of markets (for example, Buffie and Atolia (2009) use a CGE analysis of the Malawi FISP to consider the relative benefits of investment in the FISP against investment in infrastructure, but do not undertake a formal BCA of the FISP).

c) *Partial equilibrium models* that examine investment's welfare impacts on producers and consumers (see, for example, C. P. Timmer (1989) for Indonesia).

---

[2] These regression models are different from those discussed earlier in Chapter 7. The models discussed there can provide insights into economy-wide impacts, but their use in capturing all the major economy-wide impacts of a programme are limited if there is substantial market integration and price transmission across different areas. This will often be the case for cereal markets within countries.

Table 9.1. Broad characteristics of three model types

	Regression models	CGE/Multi-market models	Partial equilibrium models
Data demands	Very challenging: time series data for different & relatively independent regions: investment, welfare & other variables	Very challenging: national & multi-sectoral data on supply, demand, productivity, market performance, & factor ownership; direct productivity impacts of investment/policy interventions	Demand (& ideally supply) information on specific commodity/ies of interest; direct productivity impacts of investment/policy interventions
Capacity to describe multi-market, indirect effects	Good: intrinsic in analysis of broader welfare effects	Good: the key benefit of these models, but depends on quality of model formulation & data	Weak: no explicit consideration, but can introduce *ad hoc* adjustments to allow for these effects
Capacity to describe differential market failure effects	Good: should be intrinsic in analysis of broader welfare effects but may not capture some spillovers	Weak: very challenging as regards data demands & model formulation	Weak: no explicit consideration, but can introduce *ad hoc* adjustments to allow for these effects
Capacity to isolate effects of specified intervention(s)	Depends on range of conditions in data set—difficult if covariant changes or if there are varying spillovers across regions	Good, depending on quality of model	Can be good, depending on context & processes
Strengths	Good data sets & properly executed analysis can give very holistic empirical analysis	Multi-market effects, counterfactuals	Relatively simple data & methodological demands
Weaknesses	Very demanding requirements as regards historical/empirical data sets—this can limit breadth of application of models; assumptions/context may not be explicit or generalizable; may not account for some spillover effects	Complex & demanding; proper representation of market failures & differential behaviour of producers & consumers very challenging—otherwise misleading; assumptions/context may not be explicit	Does not take account of market effects—these can only be addressed with simple relatively *ad hoc* adjustments

These models differ as regards their data demands, the nature of the analytical challenges they present, and their ability to allow for market failures, differential effects on different types of consumers and producers, linkages and multipliers across markets, and the interactions between these. Table 9.1 sets out the broad characteristics of these three types of model.

It is clear from Table 9.1 that the three different approaches have different and in many ways complementary features, strengths, and weaknesses. We can conclude from this that

- In different contexts there will be different choices of method to best follow the principles outlined earlier.

- In all cases analysts must recognize and take account of the limitations of their methods and data, and document these to ensure that those using their results are able to properly interpret them.

- Those using BCA results to compare returns from different investments or to guide policy or investment design and implementation must take great care to ensure that differences in analytical methods, issues, and data quality are properly allowed for in their considerations.

- In the particular situation of the Malawi FISP

  - it is impossible to conduct regression analysis as the empirical situations and data available do not allow this;

  - CGE and multi-market models are very demanding of analytical resources and data, and consequently these models may be used for stylized analysis of possible effects, but will be too expensive in implementation, too complex in application/interpretation, and too reliant on weak data to provide a practicable method for regular and detailed year by year analysis;

  - the more limited data and analytical demands of simpler partial equilibrium models mean that they are the most practicable (though there are still significant challenges here).

9.4. Problems and challenges with benefit–cost analysis (BCA) of the FISP

Dorward and Chirwa (2009, 2010a) and School of Oriental and African Studies et al. (2008) have used standard partial equilibrium methodology for estimating the economic benefit–cost ratio and fiscal efficiency of the subsidy programme. They recognize, however, that this method does not take account of wider benefits to poor consumers from lower food prices, and that paradoxically a greater fall in the price of maize provided a lower estimate of programme benefit when in fact larger price falls should lead to wider growth and poverty reduction benefits. They also consistently identify a number of concerns with the use of their results in comparing estimated returns from subsidies and from other investments. These concerns are also relevant to the limited reports of benefit–cost and related analysis by others (For example Buffie and Atolia (2009) and Denning et al. (2009)) and to discussion of these results.

The concerns may be broadly classified into related problems first with data, second with methodology, and third with wider theoretical issues. These problems are of course related, as

- methodologies embody theory and require, and are limited by, data, and
- theories require, and are embodied in and limited by, methodologies.

The three major theoretical questions concern

(a) the measure of benefits,

(b) the extent of benefits and processes of change, and

(c) the valuation of incremental production.

The measure of benefits: Ideally benefits should represent welfare changes to recipients and non-recipients. This, however, raises questions about the nature of welfare, methods of measurement or estimation, and the relative importance and weighting of welfare changes for different stakeholders (for example, questions about the relative importance of welfare changes in poorer and less-poor people, and about the relative importance of welfare changes in people now and in the future). Economic theory provides widely used measures of welfare changes through the concepts of consumer and producer surplus. There are, however, severe methodological and data difficulties in the estimation of supply curves needed for the estimation of changes in producer surplus. As a result, changes in real income are commonly used as proxy measures of welfare in benefit–cost analysis, and generally provide similar answers (Sadoulet and de Janvry, 1995; Alston et al., 2000). The relatively simple analysis in School of Oriental and African Studies et al. (2008), Dorward and Chirwa (2009), and Dorward et al. (2010a) provides reasonable estimates of changes in aggregate real income across producers and consumers, but no information about the distribution of these benefits between producers and consumers or between beneficiaries and non-beneficiaries. This differentiation is important for the use of weights to address distributional questions about welfare changes for different types of people.

The extent of benefits and the processes of change: We argued in Chapters 2 and 4 that subsidy programme benefits can have wide-ranging and far-reaching dynamic effects where they directly overcome financial market failure and investment affordability problems of recipients, and address these same problems for poor non-recipients through staple food prices and higher wages;

and that they should also generate more conventional multiplier growth effects (where, for example, increases in recipients' income lead to increases in consumption of locally produced goods and services, and hence increases in incomes for local providers of these goods and services). Haggblade et al. (2007a) suggest agricultural multipliers (excluding dynamic effects from overcoming market failures) range from 1.3 to 1.5 in sub-Saharan Africa, while Davies and Davey (2008) report estimated multipliers of 2 to 2.45 from conditional cash transfers in Dowa (though these fixed price estimates may be reduced by 30% to allow for supply constraints, to give estimates of 1.4 to 1.7). Diao et al. (2003) estimate a multiplier of 1.5 from increases in grain productivity in Malawi while Benin et al. (2008) estimate a multiplier of 1.1 from increases in maize productivity in Malawi.

Dynamic effects and multipliers are implicitly allowed for in BCA using regression analysis (for example, Fan et al. (2007)), and they should be explicitly modelled in general equilibrium analysis, although this is seldom the case for the dynamic effects of overcoming market failures. Multipliers and dynamic effects are not allowed for in estimates derived from partial equilibrium methods, and this leads to a biased under-estimate of returns when these estimates are compared with estimates of other investments' returns if these estimates are derived from regression or general equilibrium analyses.[3]

The valuation of incremental production: The concerns discussed above about the measure of benefits and their extent and distribution are concerned with the valuing of incremental production, in a very broad sense. Here, however, we discuss two narrower issues: first the choice of prices for valuing output and second the discount rate to use.

As noted earlier, there are legitimate questions about the feasibility of liberalized market policies as a real policy option for the Malawian Government, and hence if economic analysis should use border or domestic prices. Either way there are then serious methodological challenges in determining 'counterfactual' prices for a situation without the subsidy (with a 'double counterfactual' problem if combinations of domestic and border prices are to be used). Dorward et al. (2010a) and School of Oriental and African Studies et al. (2008) use information on border prices with informed judgement to address the 'double counterfactual' problem to estimate what border prices would have prevailed with and without the subsidy in the absence of policies restricting imports.

---

[3] We do not attempt to consider the health and education benefits discussed in Chapter 7 in the benefit–cost analysis in this chapter. In using market prices as the basis of valuation we are also ignoring questions raised about the value of maize to people who cannot afford to buy it at higher prices.

They also do not use an explicit discount rate when comparing programme benefits and costs. However any comparison of the programme's benefit–cost ratio with internal rates of return estimated for longer term investments involves an implicit assumption that benefits are achieved one year after investment. It might, however, be argued that costs are incurred in December to January (when seeds and fertilizers are paid for and applied to the field) but benefits are obtained in June (when crops are harvested), giving a return after 6 or 7 months. It might also be considered, however, that benefits from lower maize prices and increased consumption are enjoyed over the period June to May, yielding a return over an average of around 12 months. These two alternatives have major implications for estimates of internal rates of annual return, as the former has a net Internal Rate of Return (IRR) 70–80% higher than the net benefit–cost ratio (BCR, net benefits divided by costs).

The discussion above addresses theoretical and related methodological concerns with the standard use of partial equilibrium analysis in BCA for the FISP. These concerns are exacerbated by and linked to difficulties with the quality and availability of critical data on yield responses to subsidized inputs, on overall production data, and on the number of rural and farm households—difficulties that have been noted repeatedly in earlier chapters.

9.5. Improving FISP benefit–cost estimates[4]

Consideration of these theoretical, methodological, and data difficulties together with the earlier discussion of purposes and principles for BCA suggests a number of approaches to improving the BCA of the subsidy programme. These involve

1. Continued use of partial equilibrium analysis, with its relatively limited demands for data and analytical resources, but with more formal counterfactual price estimation.

2. Extension of the method to distinguish between producer and consumer gains and, among producers, between subsidy recipients and non-recipients.

3. Consideration of possible dynamic effects of growth and liquidity multipliers.

4. Consideration of results with alternative estimates of the time period for returns.

---

[4] This section contains quite detailed consideration of methodological issues in improving BCA methods. Readers without specific technical interests in this may prefer to skip the section and go straight to Section 9.6.

All these approaches involve elaboration of the estimation of programme benefits, as estimation of programme costs is not conceptually problematic (although, as discussed in Chapter 5, there are difficulties in obtaining reliable data on some cost items). Total costs incurred in input acquisition (including transport and distribution costs) are added to programme administration costs, with application of shadow exchange rates to non-tradable costs in the later years of the programme when the Malawi Kwacha is generally considered to have been over-valued. Costs of acquisition for subsidized inputs that displace unsubsidized inputs are subtracted from the programme costs, as these provide no incremental benefits and are simply a transfer from government to the recipients of those subsidized inputs. Although they consequently have little effect on the benefit–cost ratio of the programme (being excluded from both benefits and costs), they do affect the Net Present Value (NPV) of the programme, and hence its fiscal efficiency (which we define as NPV/fiscal costs).

9.5.1. Methodology for formal estimation of prices and producer and consumer gains

To improve on existing estimates of programme benefits we therefore begin by formalizing price estimation, focusing on the effects of the subsidy programme on maize production.[5] Figure 9.1 shows how for an autarchic economy[6] a production subsidy causes a downward shift in the market price supply curve (S to S*) and this leads to an expansion in supply (from Q to Q*) and a fall in consumer price for the product (from P to P*).

The change in real income for producers is analysed in terms of the effects of changes in output prices, costs, and volumes produced and sold.

$$\Delta Y_P = \left[QP^* + (Q^* - Q)P^* - \Delta Q_F C^* - (Q^* - \Delta Q_F)C \right] - [QP - QC] \tag{9.1}$$

$$\Delta Y_P = (Q^* - Q)P^* - Q(P - P^*) - \Delta Q_F C^* - (Q^* - Q - \Delta Q_F)C \tag{9.2}$$

---

[5] The 2006/7, 2008/9, and 2010/11 household surveys reported in Dorward et al. (2010a) and School of Oriental and African Studies et al. (2008) show that almost all the incremental fertilizer use as a result of the subsidy programme was applied to maize and there is no evidence of shifts in cropping patterns in 2008/9 as a result of the subsidy programme. (Holden and Lunduka (2010c) also find no evidence of shifts in cropping patterns, although Chibwana et al. (2012) suggest some shifting into maize by subsidy recipients.)

[6] The assumption of autarchy is a reasonable analytical starting point for the Malawi maize market, given the high transport costs in exporting to or importing from the world market. We consider later the effects of informal imports from surrounding countries (notably Mozambique), actual or potential price ceilings from potential imports from South Africa, and exports to Zimbabwe in 2007/8.

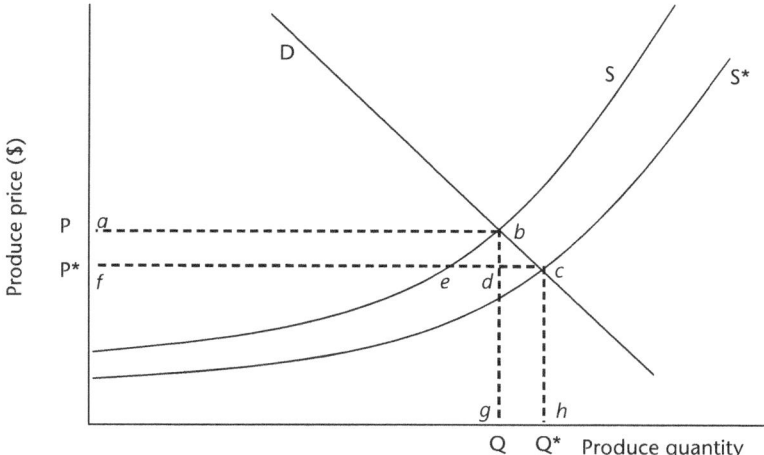

Figure 9.1. Input subsidy impacts on output supply and price
Source: Adapted from Dorward (2009b).

where Y_p * = producers' income after subsidy
Y_p = producers' income before subsidy
Q* = production after subsidy
Q = production before subsidy
P* = output price after subsidy
P = output price before subsidy
ΔQ_F = increase in production from use of subsidized inputs
C = producers' average unit costs for output before/without subsidy
C * = producers' unit costs for extra output (i.e. excluding subsidized costs)

The change in producers' income therefore consists of changes in sales value less the costs of production with the subsidy, plus the savings on unsubsidized production where this has been displaced by subsidized production. The change in sales value is made up of a loss due to the fall in product price for the original amount produced (area *abdf* in Figure 9.1), but a gain from extra production at the lower price (area *dchg* in Figure 9.1).[7] With totally elastic demand there would be no price loss and all the subsidized production would be extra production, hence under these circumstances

---

[7] In the long run the loss of producer incomes from falls in unsubsidized maize production and in prices may be smaller than estimated here as rising real incomes for consumers will raise prices for non-maize and non-farm goods and services, which can replace their lost and/or lower value maize production.

$\Delta Y_p = (Q*-Q)P*-\Delta Q_F C*$. With totally inelastic demand there would be no increase in production and all the subsidized production would displace unsubsidized production, hence $\Delta Y_p = -Q(P-P*)+\Delta Q_F(C-C*)$. Under these circumstances $\Delta Y_p = 0$ and hence

$$Q(P-P*)=\Delta Q_F(C-C*)$$

The change in real income for consumers consists of the savings on existing purchases due to the price fall (*abdf* in Figure 9.1) plus the savings in extra purchases which are best valued in terms of savings on previous expenditures (area *bcd* in Figure 9.1).

$$\text{Change in consumer real income} = \Delta Y_C = (P-P*)Q + \frac{1}{2}(P-P*)(Q*-Q) \quad (9.3)$$

Total change in producers' and consumers' real income can be estimated by the sum of changes in producer and consumer incomes:

$$\Delta Y_T = (Q*-Q)P*-\Delta Q_F C*-(Q*-Q-\Delta Q_F)C + \frac{1}{2}(P-P*)(Q*-Q) \quad (9.4)$$

The method for estimating overall benefits in equation 9.4 is broadly that used in Dorward et al. (2010a) and School of Oriental and African Studies et al. (2008). They use analysts' informal judgement of 'double counterfactual' prices with and without the subsidy respectively to estimate P* and P in the absence of government bans on formal imports. P can, however, be estimated using formal estimates of price elasticity of demand (E_D), together with information on prices and production with the subsidy. $(P-P*)$ can then be substituted as follows:

$$(P-P*)=\frac{1}{E_D}\frac{P*}{Q*}(Q*-Q) \quad (9.5)$$

We can then substitute for $(P-P*)$ into equations 9.2, 9.3, and 9.4 as follows:
Change in producer real income

$$\Delta Y_p = (Q*-Q)P*-Q\frac{1}{E_D}\frac{P*}{Q*}(Q*-Q)-\Delta Q_F C*-(Q*-Q-\Delta Q_F)C \quad (9.6)$$

Change in consumer real income

$$\Delta Y_C = \frac{1}{E_D} \frac{P^*}{Q^*}(Q^* - Q)(Q + \frac{1}{2}(Q^* - Q)) \tag{9.7}$$

Change in producer and consumer real income

$$\Delta Y_T = (Q^* - Q)P^* - \Delta Q_F C^* - (Q^* - Q - \Delta Q_F)C + \frac{1}{2E_D} \frac{P^*}{Q^*}(Q^* - Q)^2 \tag{9.8}$$

Equations 9.6 to 9.8 still present problems in that we require an estimate of $(Q^* - Q)$. However, the seasonal separation of supply and demand means that if we can initially ignore farmers' expectations of lower prices in the following season then incremental production will be equal to the increase in production from use of subsidized inputs, so that $(Q^* - Q) = \Delta Q_F$. Introducing this into equations 9.6 to 9.8 gives the following estimates of changes in real income:

Change in producer real income $\Delta Y_P = \Delta Q_F(P^* - C^*) - Q\frac{1}{E_D}\frac{P^*}{Q^*}\Delta Q_F \tag{9.9}$

Change in consumer real income $\Delta Y_C = \frac{1}{E_D}\frac{P^*}{Q^*}\Delta Q_F\left(Q + \frac{1}{2}\Delta Q_F\right) \tag{9.10}$

Change in producer and consumer real income

$$\Delta Y_T = \Delta Q_F(P^* - C^*) + \frac{1}{2E_D}\frac{P^*}{Q^*}\Delta Q_F^2 \tag{9.11}$$

All of the analysis in this section has been derived from our initial consideration of a closed economy (Figure 9.1). It does, however, also apply to a small open economy with a wide band between import and export parity prices. Thus, if increased production causes an economy to eliminate imports of Q_M so that the price falls to P*, below import parity P_M, then this can be handled by estimating gains in consumer and producer real incomes allowing for these prices.[8]

---

[8] Note that where producers outside an economy export into that economy but at prices largely determined within the economy (as is broadly the case with Mozambican exports to Malawi), then the loss of producer income suffered by these producers due to the price fall is not a loss to the domestic producers and the domestic economy.

In these circumstances then assuming that $(Q*-Q)=\Delta Q_F$ as above then

$$\Delta Y_P = \Delta Q_F P * -(Q - Q_M)(P_M - P*) - \Delta Q_F C * \tag{9.12}$$

$$\Delta Y_C = Q(P_M - P*) + \frac{1}{2}(P_M - P*)(\Delta Q_F - Q_M) \tag{9.13}$$

and

$$\Delta Y_T = \Delta Q_F P * + Q_M(P_M - P*) - \Delta Q_F C * + \frac{1}{2}(P_M - P*)(\Delta Q_F - Q_M) \tag{9.14}$$

Use of equations 9.9 to 9.11 or 9.12 to 9.14 depends on the relative values of P_M and P: equations 9.9 to 9.11 are used if $P_M > P$, and equations 9.12 to 9.14 are used if $P_M < P$, where P is estimated from equation 9.5. If, in addition, $P_M < P*$ then P_M replaces P* in equations 9.12 to 9.14, and there are no consumer benefits or producer losses from price changes. The equations above can also be adjusted to allow for exports if P* is below the export parity price P_X. In this case P_X replaces P* in equations 9.12 to 9.13 if the subsidy would move domestic prices from above import parity to below export parity prices, or in equations 9.2 to 9.3 (with replacement of $(Q*-Q)$ by ΔQ_F) if the subsidy would move domestic prices which are already import parity to below export parity.

The methodology developed in this sub-section demonstrates the basic validity of the BCA approach used in Dorward et al. (2010a) and School of Oriental and African Studies et al. (2008), but also allows a breakdown between producer and consumer benefits with more formal estimates of P and Q* if estimates of ΔQ_F and of price elasticity of demand (E_D) are available.

9.5.2. Estimation of price/quantity demand relations and of incremental production

We now develop estimates of overall returns to the subsidy and of separate producer and consumer benefits using the methodology developed above. First, however, estimates are needed of price elasticity of demand (E_D) and of ΔQ_F. These estimates are unfortunately not without their own difficulties.

We first consider the estimation of price elasticity of demand (E_D) or (more generally) of the relationship between price and quantity demanded. Figure 7.4 in Chapter 7 shows maize prices and estimated quantities consumed per capita. This highlights an apparent discrepancy between the 1993/4 to 2005/6 and 2006/7 to 2010/11 data sets, with higher prices in the latter set. Possible explanations for this were discussed earlier in Chapter 7, but it raises wider questions regarding the impact of increases in production on maize prices. If production estimates from 1993/4 to 2005/6 are broadly correct, then this suggests that the 1993/4 to 2005/6 data should provide a reasonable estimate of price elasticity of demand with constant wages—although there may be upward shifts in demand when wages rise.

Three regression models were estimated of log quantity on log price quantity from maize price data and supply estimates from 1993/94. The first is derived from data from the 1993/4 to 2009/10 seasons with the inclusion of a dummy variable for subsidy effects from 2005/6 onwards and a time variable to allow for changing base per capita demand over time. This gave an estimate of price elasticity of demand of –0.24 (n = 17, t = 1.5, R^2 = 0.56). Given concerns about the reliability of data from 2006/7 to 2009/10 as discussed above, and implausibly high estimates of 'without subsidy' prices when subsequently applying this model, it was rejected. The second model regressed log quantity on log price quantity from the 1993/4 to 2005/6 seasons[9] and gives an estimate of price elasticity of demand of –0.38 (n = 13, t = 1.9, R^2 = 0.24). The third used the same data set with the inclusion of a time variable to allow for changing base per capita demand over time, and gives an estimate of price elasticity of demand of –0.51 (n = 13, t = 2.2, R^2 = 0.33). The third model was preferred as regards its better fit and inclusion of a time effect, and was therefore used in the analysis that is reported below and is shown in Figure 7.4.

Having considered the estimation of the relationship between price and quantity demanded and hence of price elasticity of demand (E_D), we now consider the estimation of ΔQ_F, incremental production from the subsidy programme. The difficulties of obtaining reliable and precise estimates of ΔQ_F were discussed earlier in Chapter 6. As noted there, Dorward et al. (2010a) and School of Oriental and African Studies et al. (2008) have therefore estimated incremental production assuming that every kg nitrogen (N) in incremental fertilizer application leads to 12 kg incremental grain production when applied on local maize and to 18 kg incremental grain production when applied on hybrid maize.[10] This approach was also followed here, with incremental fertilizer application as a result of the subsidy programme estimated from 2006/7, 2008/9, and 2010/11 survey estimates of displacement of unsubsidized fertilizer sales by subsidized fertilizer sales.

---

[9] Restriction of the data series to the 1993/4 to 2005/6 seasons (a) provides more consistent estimates than are obtained from the 1993/4 to 2009/10 series and (b) standardizes for the effects of possible inconsistency in production estimates and of higher nominal wages in later years.

[10] See School of Oriental and African Studies et al. (2008) for summary of a range of different studies from which these estimates were derived.

Table 9.2. Base benefit–cost analysis, 2005/6–10/11

Year	ED	P	P*	PM	PX	BASE BENEFITS		
						Net benefit	BCR	FE
		US$/kg				(US$ mill)		
2005/6	0.51	0.24	0.14	0.29	0.14	12.4	1.17	0.34
	AE	mean =	0.14	n/a	n/a	-7.6	0.90	-0.21
2006/7	0.51	0.25	0.13	0.32	0.17	47.8	1.49	0.65
	AE	mean =	0.15	n/a	n/a	6.0	1.06	0.08
2007/8	0.51	1.83	0.35	0.30	0.15	39.4	1.30	0.41
	AE	mean =	0.25	n/a	n/a	8.9	1.07	0.09
2008/9	0.51	1.16	0.25	0.28	0.13	-39.0	0.87	-0.16
	AE	mean =	0.28	n/a	n/a	-40.2	0.87	-0.16
2009/10	0.51	0.46	0.17	0.28	0.13	31.9	1.18	0.23
	AE	mean =	0.26	n/a	n/a	35.4	1.20	0.25
2010/11	0.51	0.95	0.19	0.35	0.20	127.9	1.55	0.88
	AE	mean =	0.30	n/a	n/a	106.0	1.46	0.73

Notes: E_D, P, P*, P_M and P_X represent respectively demand elasticities, without and with subsidy maize prices (in current US$), and import and export parity maize prices (calculated from SAFEX prices with import and export transport costs of $100/MT and $50/MT respectively). BCR (benefit–cost ratio) is calculated as total economic benefit divided by total economic costs; FE (Fiscal Efficiency) as net benefit (total economic benefit less total economic costs) divided by total fiscal costs. Under E_D, 'AE' stands for Analyst Estimates as reported in Dorward et al. (2010a) and School of Oriental and African Studies et al. (2008). 'n/a' indicates 'not applicable'

9.5.3. *Formal estimation of prices and producer and consumer gains*

Using these estimates of the relationship between price and quantity available and of the incremental production from the subsidy we can now estimate changes in overall incomes from equations 9.11 and 9.14 over a range of assumptions, as shown in Table 9.2 for the years 2005/6 to 2010/11.[11]

Table 9.2 presents for each year the border adjusted prices estimated in one row with the demand elasticity discussed earlier (and shown in Figure 7.4) and, in another row, using analysts' judgements. Different columns then show estimates of net benefits, benefit–cost ratios (BCRs) and fiscal efficiencies (FEs) without any growth multipliers.

The main point of interest in Table 9.2 is the differences between results obtained by prices estimated using demand elasticity calculations and those

[11] Elasticities of demand *per se* were not used in these calculations, due to averaging problems over price and quantity ranges; instead the estimated equations were used to calculate price and quantity changes.

obtained by analysts' judgements:[12] estimated returns are generally higher with prices estimated using demand elasticity calculations than with those obtained from analysts' judgements. This arises partly from lower prices in analysts' estimates, particularly in the earlier years, due to more weight being given to the possibility of substantially lower price imports from Mozambique in 2005/6 and 2006/7 and (to a lesser extent) in 2007/8 and 2009/10.[13]

9.5.4. *Effects of growth and liquidity multipliers*

There is no particular methodology for the building of growth and liquidity multipliers into partial equilibrium analysis. We use equations 9.9, 9.10, 9.12, and 9.13 to estimate producers' and consumers' relative gains and losses, and then multiply these by relevant estimates of agricultural multipliers. As discussed earlier, a number of studies estimate agricultural multipliers of around 1.4 in sub-Saharan Africa and Malawi. We therefore initially multiply farm benefits and costs by 1.4. In order to allow for possible multiplier effects of alternative use of resources invested in the programme, we use a multiplier of 1.2 for alternative investments (the lower number to allow for the high multiplier effects of increases in income to poor rural people). Table 9.3 shows the results of this analysis together with results without the use of multipliers (also shown earlier in Table 9.2).

The table shows that estimates of net benefits, benefit–cost ratios, and fiscal efficiencies generally increase when the effects of multipliers are allowed for, and these increases can be substantial. Further analysis (summarized in Table 9.4) using different multipliers for different types of people (producers, consumers, and subsidy recipients) shows that if poorer households have higher multipliers (as they normally do) and account for a higher share of national maize consumption than of national maize production, then subsidies that lead to domestic price falls will, other things being equal, generally lead to higher returns, as will greater targeting of the poor as subsidy recipients (Dorward and Chirwa, 2011b).

---

[12] Differences in results across different years are due to variation in maize prices (with high domestic prices from 2007/8 requiring analysis using import parity prices for the 'without subsidy' situation—and even for the 'with subsidy' situation in 2007/8), and in fertilizer prices (which rose steadily from 2005/6 to a peak in 2008/9). Differences in some results from those presented in Dorward and Chirwa (2011b) are due to allowance here for weather-affected yields, as set out in the incremental production estimates presented in Chapter 6.

[13] Where 'without subsidy' domestic prices would be higher than import parity, the formal price estimation also allows for part of the subsidized production to substitute for imports (so that consumer benefits are not derived from a simple average of import parity and 'with subsidy' domestic price).

Table 9.3. Benefit–cost analysis without and with growth multipliers

Year	ED	BASE			Growth multiplier		
		Net benefit	BCR	FE	Net benefit	BCR	FE
		US$ mill			US$ mill		
2005/6	0.51	12.4	1.17	0.34	23.0	1.24	0.63
	AE	-7.6	0.90	-0.21	-3.7	0.95	-0.10
2006/7	0.51	47.8	1.49	0.65	77.5	1.61	1.05
	AE	6.0	1.06	0.08	14.7	1.15	0.20
2007/8	0.51	39.4	1.30	0.41	71.6	1.42	0.75
	AE	8.9	1.07	0.09	22.7	1.17	0.24
2008/9	0.51	-39.0	0.87	-0.16	-9.8	0.97	-0.04
	AE	-40.2	0.87	-0.16	-9.2	0.97	-0.04
2009/10	0.51	31.9	1.18	0.23	69.1	1.31	0.49
	AE	35.4	1.20	0.25	58.8	1.34	0.42
2010/11	0.51	127.9	1.55	0.88	204.5	1.69	1.41
	AE	106.0	1.46	0.73	134.8	1.58	0.93

Notes: E_D represents demand elasticities. BCR (benefit–cost ratio) is calculated as total economic benefit divided by total economic costs. FE (Fiscal Efficiency) is calculated as net benefit (total economic benefit less total economic costs) divided by total fiscal costs. Under E_D, 'AE' stands for Analyst Estimates as used in BCA reported in Dorward et al., (2010a); School of Oriental and African Studies et al., (2008). AE multiplier estimates derived from multiplier effects on base estimates with $E_D = 0.51$. Economic costs exclude costs of displaced fertilizers. Data from Dorward et al., (2010a); School of Oriental and African Studies et al., (2008) and Table 9.2.

Table 9.4. Alternative estimates of returns to FISP investments, 2005/6–10/11

Estimation	ED	Annual return			Annualized return over 10 months	
		Net benefit US$ mill	BCR	FE	AIRR	FE
Basic estimate	0.51	36.72	1.26	0.39	1.32	0.49
	AE	18.09	1.09	0.13	1.11	0.16
Simple multiplier	0.51	46.30	1.31	0.58	1.39	0.73
	AE	16.65	1.12	0.14	1.14	0.17
Differentiated multipliers (a)	0.51	36.56	1.34	0.60	1.42	0.76
	AE	11.45	1.13	0.19	1.16	0.23
Differentiated multipliers (b)	0.51	63.41	1.44	0.84	1.55	1.07
	AE	27.86	1.22	0.30	1.26	0.37

See notes on previous tables. Simple (unweighted) averages. Differentiated multipliers with consumer multiplier of 1.4, producer multiplier of 1.2, and recipient multiplier of 1.1 (a) or 1.4 (b). Annualized return if BCR is achieved over 10 months.

9.5.5. *Sensitivity of BCA estimates to time of return, yields, and displacement*

It was noted earlier that the use of benefit–cost ratios implies an annual return on investment. However, it might be argued that returns are achieved over a shorter period, for example 7 months from fertilizer purchase and application to harvest. This can lead to substantial increases in the Annual Internal Rate of Return (AIRR), depending on the BCR—for a BCR of 1.2 the AIRR would increase by 14% to just under 1.4, while for a BCR of 1.3 the AIRR would increase by 21% to just under 1.6. Allowance for returns over 10 months (as illustrated in Table 9.4) gives smaller increases in BCR.

For a given initial 'without subsidy' situation, returns to investment are also affected by changes in yield and displacement effects with the subsidy. Higher yields lead to higher returns from increased volumes of incremental production, but they also tend to lead to lower prices—increasing returns to consumers and losses to producers. The latter effect becomes important where differential multipliers are used. Where prices are very high and remain above import parity price then there are no price effects.

Increased displacement reduces incremental production, with opposite effects to those discussed above with increasing yields. Reduced returns are, however, counteracted to some extent by reduced costs, and this means that the BCR falls less than the Fiscal Efficiency (indeed if costs fall by a smaller proportion than benefits then the BCR may rise slightly while the FE falls significantly). Dorward and Chirwa (2011b) provide more detailed information on the sensitivity of investment returns to these changes.

9.6. Summary

We conclude with a brief summary and review of the findings in this chapter and discuss their wider relevance to the economic viability, design, implementation, and evaluation of the Malawi FISP and other subsidy programmes.

9.6.1. *Review of findings*

This chapter has considered purposes, principles, and alternative BCA methodologies against particular theoretical, methodological, and data challenges faced in BCA of the FISP. We have then put forward a formal methodology for improving the estimation of producer and consumer gains and losses and used this to provide alternative estimates of the programmes' annual net benefit, benefit–cost ratio, and fiscal efficiency from 2005/6 to 2009/10, with further investigation of the effects of multipliers (from growth linkages and liquidity benefits for poor households). The results (using a simple average over the five years) are summarized in Table 9.4.

Without consideration of any growth multipliers, the estimated average BCR of the six years of the subsidy programme ranges from 1.09 (the estimates using analysts' estimates of prices) to 1.26 (with formal estimation of demand and an elasticity of demand of 0.51). Adding in multipliers raises the estimated BCRs to between 1.12 and 1.22, using analysts' price estimates, and between 1.31 and 1.44 with more formal demand estimation. Further allowance for returns over 10 months raises the range of the AIRR to between 1.14 and 1.55 (with multipliers). These are high estimated returns and suggest that returns estimated using simple partial equilibrium analysis are downwardly biased by, in particular, exclusion of the effects of growth multipliers.

However, precise estimation of the BCR remains difficult, for reasons that are set out in this and previous chapters. Nevertheless, leaving aside the possibility of achieving returns in less than a year, and taking formal price estimation as more reliable than analysts' estimation, suggests that the average BCR is likely to be around 1.35 after allowing for the effects of multipliers, with fiscal efficiency of around 0.6. Lower estimates using analysts' price estimates give an estimated BCR of around 1.15 and fiscal efficiency of 0.2. These estimates are sensitive to yield responses (and hence both programme implementation and weather), and international maize prices. The latter have been higher in recent years, and are likely to remain high, and there is considerable potential for higher yield responses than those assumed here. Higher displacement would not affect the BCR very much but would lower fiscal efficiency.

9.6.2. *Economic viability of the Malawi FISP*

Overall these returns are high and suggest that the FISP has provided a good return on investment—with scope for improved efficiency and effectiveness to make returns much higher in the future. However there are, of course, also risks of poor implementation, unfavourable weather, and changes in prices that depress returns.

The extent to which the FISP represents the best use of investment funds depends upon competition for funds between different investments and their relative returns. Buffie and Atolia (2009) find, using CGE analysis, the net benefits of the FISP depend critically upon the relative returns to fertilizer use and to investments in roads, and upon the extent to which investment in FISP crowds out investments in infrastructure. They conclude that a strategy of mixed investments is probably best. However Filipski and Taylor (2011) find that CGE model results are sensitive to model formulation regarding seasonal finance constraints on input purchases—which were not allowed for by Buffie and Atolia. Fan et al. (2007) report that investments in education, roads, agricultural research and development, credit subsidies, and input subsidies (in that order) all yielded high returns in such a mixed investment strategy in the early stages of the Green Revolution in India.[14]

There is very limited specific information on returns to alternative investments, such as in roads and in agricultural research and development in Malawi, and it is common to rely on estimates from other African countries or from Asia. These tend to show very high returns to these investments. Buffie and Atolia (2009) use returns to infrastructure investment of between 10 and 30% (a BCR of 1.1 to 1.3), citing evidence from Fan et al. (2003) and Pohl and Mihaljek (1992). Alston et al. (2000) report a modal rate of return of 43% to agricultural research from a meta-analysis of studies but report very wide ranges in estimates with some possible biases indicated by lower estimates in peer reviewed and *ex ante* (as opposed to *ex post*) studies and in studies in LDCs. Estimated returns from the FISP are comparable with these estimates. None of these returns allow for wider impacts, such as the health and education benefits discussed in Chapters 6 and 7 and the long-run effects of reduced food shortages and malnutrition on children's mental and physical development and subsequent adult productivity. Any such allowance would have to take into account likely differences across the different investments being compared, as other investments may also yield such benefits without including them in the estimation of returns to investment.

9.6.3. *Implications for subsidy programme design and implementation*

The formal price analysis and introduction of multipliers in the BCA in this chapter reinforces previous studies' discussions of the lessons from BCA for FISP and other subsidy programme design and implementation: returns will be improved by measures that increase yield responses to fertilizer (for example, earlier input delivery, greater emphasis on integrated soil fertility management, improved application, more cost effective formulations, more technical advice, more targeting to the poor) and that reduce displacement (for example, better regional and household targeting, better control of diversion and fraud, earlier registration and input delivery). The inclusion of multipliers in the BCA strengthens the importance of all of these issues, as gains from improved efficiency and effectiveness are multiplied. It also adds further weight to the importance of targeting, of ensuring that maize marketing

---

[14] Rationing of large unit subsidies in the FISP should make it more efficient than India's universal subsidies; and its impact on liquidity constraints in the absence of a credit programme should mean that it generates some of the benefits that Fan et al. report for credit subsidies in India. Fan et al.'s estimates of returns to subsidies relative to roads may be under-estimated to some extent as a result of higher cross-region spillover effects from subsidies, not captured in the model.

policies allow increased maize production to lower maize prices (as benefits to poorer subsidy recipients and consumers tend to have higher multipliers) and suggests that to maximize linkages and reduce leakages (Dorward et al., 2003) there should be complementary investments in measures facilitating the growth of the non-farm economy and of non-staple agriculture (for example, horticulture, legumes, and livestock) in response to subsidy-led growth real in real incomes.

9.6.4. Implications for future data collection and benefit–cost analysis

The partial equilibrium methods developed in this chapter have sought to follow and find appropriate compromises between the seven principles set out in Section 9.2: being practicable, externally consistent, contextualized, holistic, internally consistent, transparent, and cost-effective. The method is relatively simple in terms of its data needs and the calculations required but nevertheless it takes account of the context and complex processes affecting FISP returns, and it also addresses the key questions that policy makers and technicians ask (regarding both FISP's overall returns—for comparison with other investments—and the critical variables that determine its effectiveness and efficiency). It could be improved by further research leading to better estimates of maize price determinants and of growth multipliers, and by more robust estimation of (quite probably changing) demand elasticity for maize and better information on yield and production effects of subsidized inputs.

Its application does, therefore, highlight the need for good data in Malawi's agricultural sector. This is a major challenge. Malawi has excellent data on market prices, and the biennial FISP evaluation surveys have provided valuable information on targeting and use of subsidized inputs. However there are continuing difficulties with data on the total number of farm households, on cropping areas and yields, and on yield responses to inputs and agronomic management. Improved data on these variables is critical not just for the evaluation of the FISP, but for much wider policy development, monitoring, and evaluation.

Part III
Strategic issues

The final part of the book, before the conclusion, consists of two chapters that look at two strategic issues relevant to all agricultural input subsidy programmes: targeting and graduation.

Targeting is an issue that has received attention in the theoretical and analytical literature on agricultural subsidies, as evidenced in Chapters 2 and 3. Targeting systems and outcomes of the Malawi FISP were considered briefly in Chapter 5. Chapter 10 examines these issues in more detail and considers challenges and options for improving targeting systems and outcomes in the Malawi FISP.

Like targeting, graduation has received considerable attention in the design, implementation, and analysis of social protection programmes. It has, however, received very little attention in agricultural input subsidy programmes where it has been considered largely in terms of the need for and difficulties with 'exits'. The processes by which the need for subsidies becomes redundant and the criteria and mechanisms for programme exits have received much less attention. Chapter 11 takes the concept of graduation as used in social protection and develops it for application in the specific context of the Malawi FISP.

10

Targeting and access to input subsidies

10.1. Introduction

Targeting, the process of directing subsidized inputs to particular areas and households within those areas, plays a critical role in the Farm Input Subsidy Programme and is a hotly debated issue in its implementation. It is widely recognized that efficiency in targeting is one of the critical factors determining the effectiveness and impact of the subsidy programme. Targeting also has implications for private sector input market development, actual graduation, and sustainability of the programme. A well-targeted farm input subsidy programme should lead to incremental use of inputs, by minimizing displacement of commercial sales and ensuring that only those that need production support access the inputs. The choice of the types of targeting systems which are intended to deliver particular targeting outcomes depends on the targeting objectives and the objectives of the programme. Targeting objectives are determined by technical and political programme objectives and by an understanding of how subsidized inputs are used in different contexts and of how this affects input productivity and its economic and social impacts. Targeting, therefore, is not only important, it is also controversial, highly political (at national and local levels), and difficult to implement in a large-scale programme due to challenges and costs in its implementation and supervision.

This chapter sets out a conceptual framework for examining alternative targeting objectives and methods and their applicability in different situations. It then uses this conceptual framework and household survey analysis to examine the practice and outcomes of targeting in different programme years. The next section of the chapter reviews the framework for targeting farm input subsidies at national, district, and beneficiary levels. Section 10.3 examines factors that determine access to subsidized farm inputs, focusing on household characteristics and programme processes. Section 10.4 analyses how the subsidy programme affects or is affected by gender relations by investigating intra-household allocation of farm inputs to different plots. Section 10.5 reviews the difficulties experienced by the most vulnerable groups in accessing subsidized farm inputs. Section 10.6 offers proposals for alternative targeting options and their implications. Finally, Section 10.7 provides concluding remarks.

10.2. Targeting at national, district, and beneficiary levels[1]

10.2.1. *Targeting objectives and impacts*

Targeting objectives depend on the objective of the programme and Table 10.1 illustrates how these may be related. It neither attempts to provide a comprehensive description of the range of possible programme objectives nor to explore in any depth their implications for targeting and targeting objectives. It does, however, introduce key issues that need to be considered about the impacts of targeting and the critical outcomes that targeting systems attempt to influence. In the case of the farm input subsidy, programme objectives might include increasing national and household production and food security, national food self-sufficiency, beneficiary asset building and graduation, environmental protection improving welfare of vulnerable groups, and wider, inclusive social and economic growth. There is therefore a link between programme objectives and targeting objectives.[2] For instance, if the programme objective is to increase production then the targeting objective may be to maximize input use (minimizing displacement) and productivity of incremental input use. This would entail identifying geographical areas and household types with low displacement and high input use efficiency, such as poorer, able-bodied, good farmers in productive maize growing areas. Similarly, if the programme objective is to improve beneficiary household food self-sufficiency, then the targeting objective would be to target food deficit or insecure households in productive maize growing areas who are able to redeem coupons and use them effectively.

Different objectives may be related in two ways. First, some of them may be complementary (as, for example, between maximizing production, as discussed above, and promoting national food self-sufficiency). A different set of relationships between targeting systems, outcomes, and impacts is presented in Figure 10.1. This distinguishes between the *targeting system* (intentions, implementation, and costs), *targeting outcomes* (the number of beneficiaries, the inputs received per beneficiary, the characteristics of beneficiaries, and

---

[1] This section draws heavily on Dorward and Chirwa (2012c).

[2] Dorward and Chirwa (2012c) provide a detailed analysis of the links between programme objectives and targeting objectives and their implications.

Table 10.1. Programme objectives and their implications for targeting

	Programme objective	Targeting objectives	Implications
A1	Increased production	Maximize incremental input use (minimize displacement) & productivity of incremental input use.	Identify geographical areas & household types with low displacement (i.e. unable to buy unsubsidized inputs) & high input use efficiency— poorer, able-bodied, 'good' farmers in productive maize growing areas?
A2	National food self-sufficiency	As above	As above
B1	Beneficiary household food self-sufficiency	Target *food deficit/insecure* households in productive maize growing areas & able to redeem the coupons & use the inputs effectively—complementary safety nets to aid financing of redemption by poor targeted households	Identify such households
B2	Beneficiary household food security	As in B1 above	As in B1 above
B3	Social protection for beneficiaries	Target *most vulnerable* households in productive maize growing areas & able to redeem the coupons & use the inputs effectively	Identify such households. Complementary safety nets to aid financing of redemption
C1	Wider household food security	As in (A1) above	Complementary policies to promote access to maize markets with low & stable prices in rural and urban areas, higher *ganyu* wages, complementary social protection (e.g. cash transfers)
C2	Social protection for all households	As in (C1) above	As in (C1) above
C3	Poverty reducing broad-based growth	Some combination of (B2), (B3), and (C1) above,	Combination depends on the relative effectiveness/efficiency of direct impacts for targeted beneficiaries and indirect impacts benefiting the poor more generally
D	Programme graduation—area	As in (C3)	Together with development of (private sector) input supply systems and produce markets

(continued)

Table 10.1. (*continued*)

	Programme objective	Targeting objectives	Implications
E	Programme graduation—households	As in (B1)	May need mechanisms to help beneficiary household saving/other forms of affording input access to enable graduation (ability to afford unsubsidized fertilizer) after specified time as programme beneficiary
F	Environmental protection	As in (C3)	Together with focus on areas with fragile and sloping soils, particular land pressure and pressure on forested hills. Complementary promotion of integrated soil fertility management

Source: Dorward and Chirwa (2012c).

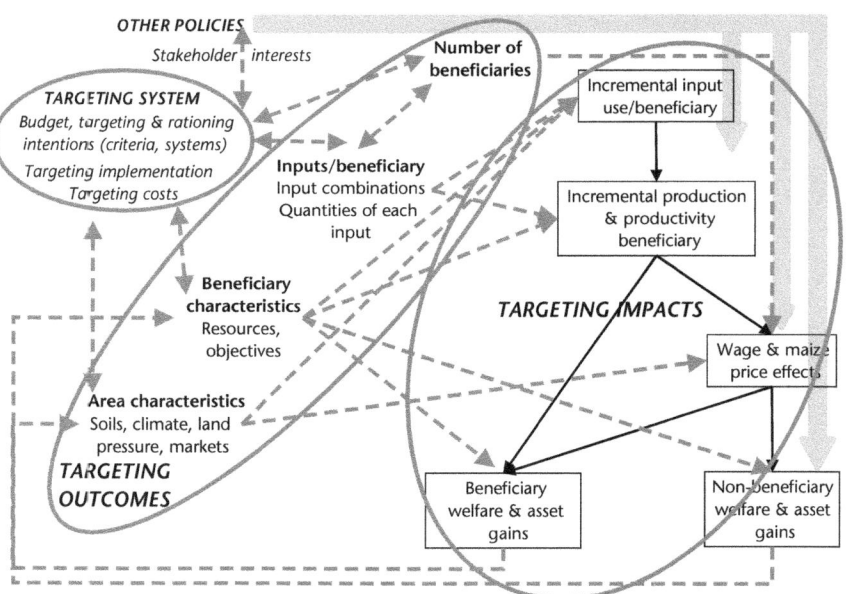

Figure 10.1. Targeting variables and impacts
Source: Dorward and Chirwa (2012c).

the characteristics of areas in which the beneficiaries reside and farm), and *targeting impacts*. These interact with other policies and stakeholder interests. The targeting system influences targeting outcomes through broad targeting design and implementation (determining the quantities of subsidized inputs in different areas, and hence the characteristics of areas receiving inputs and of potentially eligible beneficiaries) and through more detailed processes of coupon allocation, issue, and redemption (determining the quantities of subsidized inputs received by different individuals and households, and hence the characteristics of beneficiaries and the number of beneficiaries receiving different input combinations). These of course interact, and intentions are commonly modified or subverted to some extent during implementation. This needs to be explicitly allowed for in targeting system design.

The major targeting impacts are affected by four issues which determine the effectiveness of the Farm Input Subsidy Programme: displacement, input productivity, economy-wide effects, and graduation. First, displacement implies that a household's access to subsidized inputs reduces their purchase of unsubsidized inputs such that the incremental input use from the subsidy is less than the amount of subsidized inputs. Displacement rates are affected by beneficiary characteristics, with higher displacement rates among non-poor beneficiary households and lower rates among poor beneficiary households (Ricker-Gilbert et al., 2010). It is also likely that displacement will be lower in areas where market access is poorer and inputs more expensive.[3] This suggests that to reduce displacement, targeting should be aimed at areas with poorer market access and a greater proportion of poorer households, and, within those areas, at poorer households. Second, input productivity is affected by beneficiaries' farming skills and knowledge, crop management, application of complementary inputs, timely planting and weeding, and overall rates of input application, rainfall, and soils. This implies that targeting should focus on areas with higher productivity potential in order to maximize production and on possibly less-poor households able and keen to make the most productive use of the inputs. Third, as argued in earlier chapters, economy-wide effects of the subsidy result from falling maize prices and higher wages benefiting the poor, and helping to achieve pro-poor growth objectives. Linkage or multiplier effects are also likely to be higher where poorer households are the main income beneficiaries (as argued in Chapters 7 and 9). The implications for targeting are that inputs should be focused on households yielding the greatest incremental production benefits (allowing for possible trade-offs between higher input productivity and displacement if

---

[3] Ricker-Gilbert et al. (2010) report that participation in unsubsidized fertilizer purchase is depressed with increasing distance to a paved road, whereas subsidized purchases increase with distance to a paved road. Chirwa et al. (2011b) do not find any significant effect of distance to paved road on participation in unsubsidized fertilizer purchases.

less poor households use inputs more productively), with concerns for wage and linkage impacts strengthening arguments for more targeting of poorer households and poorer areas Finally, graduation (described in Chapter 11 as the process by which programme benefits to poor, vulnerable households and areas enable them to improve assets and livelihood opportunities sufficiently to allow withdrawal of subsidies without reversion to their former vulnerable state) is affected by both beneficiary and area characteristics. As discussed in Chapter 11, this is critical for promoting programme impacts and controlling costs and involves the crossing of thresholds by beneficiary households and/or areas. Targeting for graduation should then try to concentrate resources on households and/or areas for whom graduation, the crossing of thresholds, is easiest. Determination of these is, however, very difficult.

It is clear that even if programme objectives have a relatively simple focus on national food self-sufficiency, targeting has to address difficult trade-offs between higher displacement and possibly higher incremental input productivity among less poor beneficiaries. There are greater and more complex trade-offs if wider pro-poor growth and graduation objectives are also important, requiring more attention to welfare gains, growth linkages, and complex graduation processes among poorer beneficiaries. Determination of ideal targeting outcomes is also made more difficult if objectives are unclear, contested, highly variable, and changeable; if there is limited information about differences in displacement, input productivity, labour market, and graduation effects of different subsidy allocations to different households and areas; and if the effectiveness of subsidies in meeting different objectives for and through different households and areas is also affected by a range of other policies and by macro-economic and other changeable and uncertain conditions.

10.2.2. *Targeting criteria and processes*

If targeting desirable outcomes are determined by programme and hence targeting objectives then, as set out in Figure 10.1, targeting criteria and processes should be designed and implemented to deliver these outcomes. It is helpful to consider targeting within the FISP in terms of six main stages: (1) setting of targeting criteria; (2) identification of areas and beneficiaries; (3) allocation of coupons; (4) distribution of coupons; (5) redistribution of coupons; and (6) redemption of coupons. Processes and criteria within each of these activities are formally defined by the government through the MoAFS, and Table 10.2 presents the major changes in targeting processes and criteria in the FISP from 2005/6 to 2009/10 (systems and criteria have been largely unchanged from 2009/10 to 2011/12).

Table 10.2. Major changes in targeting processes, 2005/6–9/10

	2005/6	2006/7	2007/8	2008/9	2009/10
Area targeting criteria	District allocation nominally by EPA maize & tobacco areas, but highly variable between districts. *Ad hoc* district allocation of supplementary coupons.	District & EPA allocation by maize & tobacco areas, but highly variable between districts. *Ad hoc* district allocation of supplementary coupons.	Initial district & EPA allocation by farm household & maize & tobacco areas, highly variable between districts. *Ad hoc* allocation of supplementary coupons. Overall criteria opaque.	Initial district & EPA allocation by farm household& maize & tobacco areas, but highly variable between districts. *Ad hoc* district allocation of supplementary coupons. Overall criteria opaque.	District & EPA allocation criteria not clear, variable between districts. Overall criteria opaque but more in line with farm households/district.
Beneficiary targeting criteria	Beneficiary selection criteria unclear.	Full time smallholder farmers unable to afford purchase of 1 or 2 unsubsidized fertilizer bags.	n/a	Resource poor local resident with land; guardians looking after physically challenged. Vulnerable households (child- or female-headed, PLWHA)	Resource poor local resident with land; guardians looking after physically challenged. Vulnerable households (elderly-, child-, or female-headed, PLWHA)
District/TA/Village coupon allocations	District allocation by MoAFS HQ. Village allocation by TAs,	District allocation by MoAFS HQ. Village allocation by DDC, ADCs, TAs.	District allocation by MoAFS HQ. Village allocation by DDC, ADCs, TAs.	District allocation by MoAFS HQ. EPA/village allocation by MoAFS staff, DDC, ADCs, TAs.	District allocation by MoAFS HQ. EPA/village allocation by MoAFS district staff, DDC, ADCs, TAs.
Beneficiary identification/coupon allocation	Largely by TAs, VDCs	Systems highly variable between areas—by 'local leaders' TAs, VDCs, MoAFS staff. Reallocation by VH common.	Systems highly variable between areas—by 'local leaders' TAs, VDCs, MoAFS staff. Reallocation by VH common.	Use of farm household register, open meetings for allocation led by MoAFS (participation unclear). Reallocation by VH common.	Farm household register, allocation in MoAFS led open meetings (unclear participation). Voter reg. nos & ID required. Reallocation by VH common.

(Continued)

Table 10.2. (*continued*)

	2005/6	2006/7	2007/8	2008/9	2009/10
Coupon distribution system	See above: allocation and distribution simultaneous	See above: allocation and distribution simultaneous	Distribution varied, more by MoAFS and VDCs. Open disbursement led by MoAFS. Redistribution by VH common	Open meetings for disbursement led by MoAFS (degree of participation unclear). Redistribution by VH common	Open meetings led by MoAFS (unclear participation). Voter reg. numbers & ID required for receipt & redemption. Redistribution by VH common
Coupon redemption systems	Only through SFFRFM & ADMARC	Fertilizers also through major retailers; flexible maize seed coupons through wide range of seed retailers	Fertilizers also through major retailers; flexible seed coupons through range of seed retailers; cotton inputs through ADDs	Fertilizers also through major retailers; flexible seed coupons through range of seed retailers; cotton inputs through ADDs	Fertilizers only through ADMARC & SFFRFM; separate maize & legume seed coupons through retailers, variable top up for maize seed max 100MK

Coupon targeting and distribution processes were described in Chapter 5, Sections 5.4.1 and 5.4.3, and are not described here although they are summarized in relevant rows of Table 10.2. Here we discuss in more detail the criteria used in beneficiary selection.

Selection of beneficiaries is supposed to be guided by targeting criteria. In 2008/9, for example, beneficiaries of FISP were supposed to meet any of the following criteria (Ministry of Agriculture and Food Security, 2008)

- resource poor Malawian that owns a piece of land;
- guardians looking after physically challenged persons;
- *bona fide* resident of the village;
- vulnerable, such as child-headed, female-headed, or orphan-headed and those infected or affected with HIV and AIDS.

However, there have been a number of changes in beneficiary and area targeting criteria over the life of the programme. For instance, beneficiary targeting criteria have shifted from an initial focus on 'full time smallholder farmers unable to afford purchase of 1 or 2 unsubsidized fertilizer bags' to put more emphasis on poor and vulnerable groups. There are, however, difficulties in applying these criteria due to ambiguities and tensions among different targeting criteria, difficulties in establishing measures for these criteria, large numbers of deserving households, and lack of understanding and other interests among those conducting beneficiary targeting. As a result even with the best will in the world there is considerable ambiguity and inconsistency in the application of these criteria, and this creates space for abuses by those able to control the selection processes. Political considerations further complicate matters. As noted earlier in Chapter 5, from 2005/6 to 2008/9 the 'supplementary distribution' of coupons provided major opportunities for politically motivated targeting of coupons to particular districts, to particular areas within them, and to particular individuals (Chinsinga, 2012b).

Overall, despite significant changes to improve beneficiary targeting criteria and processes, there are continuing fundamental difficulties with the lack of clarity in targeting criteria, the large numbers of households satisfying the criteria, and inconsistent application of criteria by local leaders and government staff. These difficulties continue to limit the achievement of desired beneficiary targeting outcomes.

10.2.3. *Targeting outcomes*

Targeting outcomes can be considered in terms of area and beneficiary targeting. Changes in area allocation criteria have led to changes in coupon distribution between regions, with increases in coupons redeemed in the

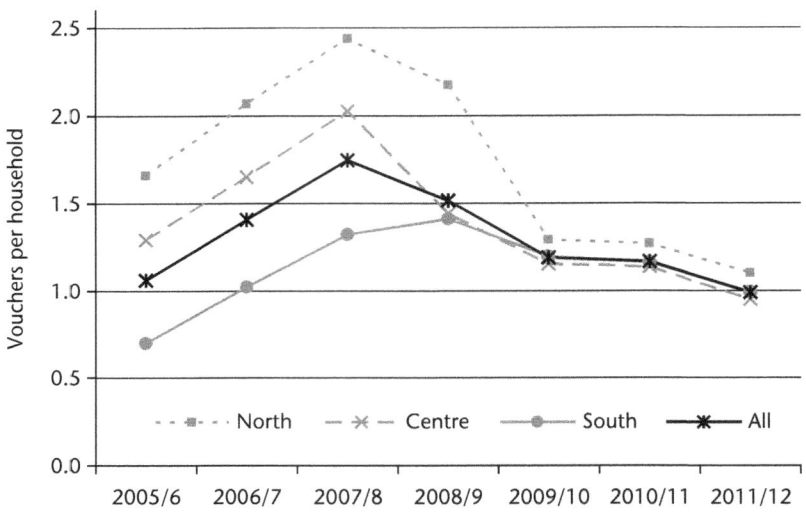

Figure 10.2. Maize fertilizer voucher redemption per household per region, 2005/6–10/11

Source: Dorward and Chirwa (2012c).

southern region reducing regional differences in redemptions per household. Figure 10.2 shows the changing pattern of maize fertilizer redemptions per household by region from 2005/6 to 2010/11.

It also appears that districts with higher potential (roughly categorized by altitude) were generally allocated proportionally more coupons than low potential areas in 2006/7, but differentiation fell between 2006/7 and 2010/11. This normally involved reduced allocations across the board in districts with lower allocations, not the complete exclusion of significant areas. There is no evidence of greater proportionate allocation to districts with more poor households, although this increased substantially from 2006/7 to 2010/11 due to the shift in relative coupon allocations to districts with larger numbers of poor people in the south.

This should have led to increased subsidy access by poor people and in turn reduced displacement, increased incremental production, and increased maize and labour market effects, benefiting poor non-beneficiaries as well as poor beneficiaries (School of Oriental and African Studies et al., 2008). These should, other things being equal, improve programme effectiveness and efficiency in promoting national and household food production, self-sufficiency, food security, social protection, and poverty reduction for both beneficiaries and non-beneficiaries.

These effects may, however, be undermined if incremental production per unit input is lower for new beneficiaries in the south as compared with previous beneficiaries in the centre and north and if targeting of the poor is less effective in the south. Others, such as Mason and Ricker-Gilbert (2012), find that district allocations of the subsidized inputs appear to be politically driven with households in districts that the ruling party won in the general election receiving on average 1.7 kg more subsidized seeds and 11.4 kg more subsidized fertilizers than districts lost by the ruling party.

The targeting outcomes at beneficiary level reveal that a large proportion of households receive less than 2 fertilizer coupons, partly due to the redistribution process that takes place at village level. Survey data show that the proportion of households who lose or gain coupons as a result of redistribution (those household with only one coupon) has increased steadily from 2006/7 to 2010/11 (from 27% to 36% to 41% across 2006/7, 2008/9, and 2010/11) and that this is most common and has increased most in the south (Table 10.3). However, apart from a lower occurrence of redistribution in the north, the changes appear to be largely the result of increases in the numbers of coupons and proportions of households receiving coupons in the south—if we examine the households receiving one coupon as a percentage of households receiving any coupons (i.e. excluding households not receiving any coupons), then this remains relatively constant across the three survey seasons (around 30% in the north, between 52% and 63% in the centre, and around 57% in the south).

Rural people's perceptions of targeting outcomes also do not suggest strong targeting to benefit poorer or more vulnerable households, nor any increases in such targeting. Table 10.4 illustrates the characteristics of rural households by the number of coupons for subsidized fertilizer in 2008/9,

Table 10.3. Fertilizer coupon receipts per household, 2006/7–10/11 (%)

Coupons/hh	Zero			1 coupon/hh			2 coupons/hh			>2 coupons/hh		
Survey year	06/7	08/9	10/11	06/7	08/9	10/11	06/7	08/9	10/11	06/7	08/9	10/11
% all households by number of coupons/hh												
North	38	28	24	18	14	23	37	50	47	7	8	5
Centre	45	35	31	28	39	38	21	20	24	5	3	1
South	49	33	11	28	37	47	19	24	35	4	3	2
National	46	33	21	27	36	41	22	25	31	5	3	2
% recipient households by number of coupons/hh												
North	n/a	n/a	n/a	29	19	31	60	69	63	11	11	7
Centre	n/a	n/a	n/a	52	63	60	39	32	38	9	5	2
South	n/a	n/a	n/a	55	58	56	37	38	42	8	5	2
National	n/a	n/a	n/a	50	56	55	41	39	42	9	5	3

Source: School of Oriental and African Studies et al. (2008), Dorward et al. (2010b), and Chirwa et al. (2011b).

Table 10.4. Mean attributes of households by number of fertilizer subsidy coupons received, 2008/9

Household characteristics	Fertilizer coupon numbers per household					Sig.
	Zero	0.5 to 1	1.5 to 2	> 2	All	
% female-headed households	26	31	24	17	27	*
Owned area in hectares	1.16	1.09	1.48	2.17	1.27	**
Value durable assets (MK)	19,621	15,630	20,340	28,111	18,702	
Value livestock assets (MK)	18,689	22,947	41,807	58,946	28,699	*
Subjective score of HH food consumption over past 12 months (1 = inadequate, ..., 3 = more than adequate)	1.5	1.5	1.6	1.7	1.5	*
Subjective score on welfare (1 = very unsatisfied, ..., 5 = very satisfied)	2.3	2.2	2.5	2.8	2.3	**
Month after harvest that maize ran out	7.2	7.1	7.9	8.6	7.4	*

Notes: * = one or more differences significant at p = 0.05, ** = one or more differences significant at p = 0.01.
Source: Dorward et al. (2010b).

and the pattern is similar to other survey years in 2006/7 and 2010/11 as targeting continues to tend to favour the non-poor. Holden and Lunduka (2012a) find similar evidence, suggesting that the non-poor are more likely to get subsidized fertilizers than the poor. The characteristics of households receiving one coupon show a persistent pattern of poverty across the survey years. Land and other asset holdings and subjective welfare indicators suggest that across different survey years these households are consistently nearly as poor or sometimes poorer than households not receiving any coupons. The relative bias against the poor suggests that when redistribution occurs it is poorer households who share one of their coupons (less-poor households with two coupons tend to hold onto both), and poorer households who receive the redistributed coupons. This involves both exclusion errors (with exclusion of poor and vulnerable households who ought to be included according to the targeting criteria) and inclusion errors (with inclusion of less-poor households who ought to be excluded according to the targeting criteria). Holden and Lunduka (2012a) find that targeting efficiency in 2008/09 was poor and no better than under the targeted input programme in 2000/1 and 2001/2. This poor targeting is attributed to leakages of coupons and fertilizers before they reach the households (as discussed in Chapter 5) and poor targeting criteria. However, the lack of clarity in targeting criteria and the large numbers of relatively less-poor people (who can nevertheless be considered to meet the targeting criteria) make it difficult to identify exclusion and inclusion errors with any precision or confidence.

10.3. Factors determining access to subsidies[4]

The lack of clarity of the targeting criteria implies that they are subject to different interpretations and application at local level. Several studies have used multivariate regression analysis to isolate factors that are important determinants in access to subsidized farm inputs (School of Oriental and African Studies et al., 2008; Chirwa et al., 2011c), whether those that received coupons were more likely to be food insecure (Holden and Lunduka, 2012a), and factors determining the quantity of subsidized fertilizers received by the household (Ricker-Gilbert, 2011). Access to inputs is measured in two ways: receipt of fertilizer coupons and amount of subsidized fertilizers acquired by the households. Chirwa et al. (2011c) use a probit regression approach for estimating the likelihood of accessing subsidized fertilizer coupons and a tobit approach for determining factors that affect access to quantities of subsidized fertilizers. Several factors are used to explain access to subsidized farm inputs and these include household characteristics (composition, headship, and assets); farming characteristics (land size, degree of commercialization, cash crop cultivation, quantity of commercial fertilizers bought in previous season); poverty and vulnerability indicators (own poverty assessment, adequacy in food consumption, participation in safety nets, receipt of subsidy in previous season); and other control variables (labour market participation, remittances, business enterprise, open forum allocation of coupons, and regional fixed effects). Table 10.5 shows results from probit and tobit regression estimates of factors affecting access to subsidized fertilizers.

Several insights emerge from the results on the determinants of access to subsidized fertilizers. First, with respect to the age of the household, the results show that age matters. As the age of household heads increases, such households are more likely to receive coupons and the probability of getting a coupon increases by 0.3%. However, households that are headed by the elderly (those above 64 years) are unlikely to receive fertilizer coupons and the probability falls by 13%. Similarly, with respect to quantity of fertilizers acquired, there is a positive relation between age and quantity acquired but the elderly are disadvantaged. This is contrary to the emphasis on special vulnerable groups that has been placed recently in the targeting criteria for the subsidy programme. It may also be the case that elderly-headed households are labour-constrained for farming activities and are least likely to use the coupons in farming.

Second, households with larger parcels of land under cultivation are more likely to receive subsidized fertilizer coupons and tend to acquire larger

---

[4] This section draws heavily on Chirwa et al. (2011c).

Table 10.5. Estimates for factors affecting access to subsidized fertilizer in 2008/9

Variables	(1) Whether obtained subsidized fertilizer coupons PROBIT		(2) Kilograms of subsidized fertilizer acquired TOBIT	
	dF/dx	z	coeff	z
Age of household head (years)	0.0032	3.11[a]	0.227	1.69[c]
Male headed household (0/1)*	0.0021	0.08	1.698	0.49
Elderly headed household (0/1)*	-0.1304	-2.75[a]	-7.94	-1.49
Household size (adult equivalents)	-0.0113	-2.02[b]	-1.172	-1.62
Value of assets in US dollars in 2008/9	0.00001	-0.67	-0.004	-1.09
Cultivated land in hectares in 2008/9	0.0561	3.03[a]	12.947	4.75[a]
Tobacco cultivation in 2008/9 (0/1)*	0.172	5.29[a]	27.639	7.21[a]
Maize marketing in 2008/9 (0/1)*	0.1126	3.22[a]	15.934	3.32[a]
Quantity of commercial fertilizers bought in 2007/8 (kg)	-0.0002	-2.50[b]	-0.014	-1.28
Own poverty assessment as poor in 2007/8 (0/1)*	-0.0802	-2.19[b]	-15.299	-2.62[a]
Adequate food consumption in 2008/9 (0/1)*	0.0202	0.91	6.501	2.23[b]
Business enterprise in 2007/8 (0/1)*	0.0051	0.23	0.432	0.15
Labour market participation in 2007/8 (0/1)*	-0.0411	-1.83[c]	-8.217	-2.85[a]
Remittance receipts in 2007/8 (0/1)*	0.0747	3.26[a]	5.049	1.63
Access to social safety nets in 2007/8 (0/1)*	0.0704	2.36[b]	4.666	1.4
Access to fertilizer coupons in 2007/8 (0/1)*	0.446	20.21[a]	56.109	15.82[a]
Open forum allocations 2008/9 and poor 2007/8 (0/1)*	0.0981	3.39[a]	13.167	3.36[a]
Central region (0/1)*	-0.0367	-1.11	-24.973	-6.35[a]
Southern region (0/1)*	-0.0321	-0.99	-18.023	-4.51[a]
Constant	-	-	3.257	0.35
Number of observations	1982		1982	
Pseudo R-squared	0.2703		0.0406	

Note: The dependent variable in (1) is a dummy variable for access to subsidized fertilizer coupons received in the 2008/09 agricultural season. (*) dF/dx (marginal effect) is for discrete change of dummy variable from 0 to 1. The dependent variable in (2) is the quantity of subsidized fertilizers acquired in the 2008/9 season. Robust t-statistics with superscripts a, b, and c denote significance at the 1, 5, and 10% levels, respectively.

Source: Chirwa et al. (2011c).

quantities of subsidized fertilizers than those with smaller parcels. The positive relationship is expected since land is one of the main criteria for targeting smallholder farmers. Third, the household's commercial orientation is also an important factor as reflected in the significance of tobacco cultivation and marketing of maize in both models. This implies that fertilizer coupons are likely to go to those smallholder farmers that earn cash incomes from agriculture with the potential to purchase fertilizers at prevailing market prices. This would not seem to support current targeting objectives and criteria, and suggests the existence of inclusion errors. However, households that bought commercial fertilizers in the previous season are less likely to be allocated subsidized fertilizer coupons, and purchase of commercial fertilizers marginally leads to reduction in the probability of accessing coupons. This suggests weak adherence to targeting that should reduce inclusion errors and ineffectiveness and inefficiency from subsidizing farmers who would have bought commercial fertilizer without the subsidy.

Fourth, households that view themselves as poor are less likely to receive coupons. In the first two years of the subsidy, evidence of households having cash for coupon redemption was a precondition in some communities for households to receive fertilizer coupons (Imperial College et al., 2007; School of Oriental and African Studies et al., 2008). With respect to the quantity of fertilizers acquired, the poor acquire 15.4 kg less subsidized fertilizers than the non-poor. School of Oriental and African Studies et al. (2008) find similar results on the effect of own poverty evaluation on the likelihood of receiving fertilizers, with wealthier households receiving disproportionately more coupons than poor households.

Fifth, participation in the labour market either through salaried or *ganyu* employment in the 2007/8 season reduced the household's chances of receiving coupons in the 2008/9 season. Similarly, households that participated in the labour market tended to acquire 8.2 kg less subsidized fertilizers than non-participants in the labour market. This implies that those in salaried employment are excluded as they are capable of purchasing fertilizers at commercial prices and those in *ganyu* employment may be those households that do not have adequate land and use their labour resource in *ganyu* labour. Nonetheless, *ganyu* labour is also the second most important source of cash for redeeming the coupons (School of Oriental and African Studies et al., 2008; Dorward et al., 2010b).

Sixth, receipt of remittances in the previous season increases the probability of receiving coupons, but this does not significantly determine the quantity of subsidized fertilizers acquired by the household. Remittances are, however, an important source of cash for redemption of coupons and for purchase of farm inputs in the rural areas.

Seventh, access to other social safety nets in the previous season is positively associated with receipt of fertilizer coupons in the 2008/09 season, although this does not significantly affect the quantity of subsidized fertilizers acquired by the household. This implies that participants in other social safety nets are not excluded from the fertilizer vouchers, and if these safety nets are well targeted then they can provide additional information about the vulnerable households in the communities. Some of the social safety nets, such as cash-for-work or public works programmes, if well coordinated can ease the cash constraint of vulnerable households and enable them to redeem the fertilizer coupons.

Eighth, households that benefited from the subsidy in the previous season were more likely to receive the coupons in the next season. The probability of receiving fertilizer coupons increases by 45% for households targeted in the previous season who tend to acquire 56.1 kg more subsidized fertilizers than those that did not receive coupons in the previous season. The targeting impacts of this of course depend upon the criteria used in targeting the previous year and on criteria used in excluding previous beneficiaries and including new ones.

Finally, transparency and accountability in allocation of coupons at the local level tends to be beneficial for the poor. Open forums for allocating coupons increase the chance of targeting those that ranked themselves in the poor category. Similarly, the poor tend to acquire 13.2 kg more of subsidized fertilizer when open forums are used than when coupon allocations are discrete. This suggests that community-based targeting may be superior to allocations that involve traditional leaders and committees, as was previously the case in the 2005/6 up to the 2007/8 season.

Overall, the results suggest that although the poor are not excluded from access to subsidized farm inputs, where they receive subsidized inputs they tend to receive fewer coupons and acquire less subsidized fertilizers than the non-poor. Holden and Lunduka (2012a), Ricker-Gilbert (2011), and to a lesser extent Chibwana et al. (2010) reach similar conclusions, with households receiving coupons being better off in terms of their livestock endowments and assets than those that did not receive coupons. The re-distribution of coupons at the village level tends to increase such a bias in which the poor tend to share the coupons and the non-poor tend to retain the two expected fertilizer coupons. The results also suggest that the fortunes of the poor in accessing subsidized farm inputs, and hence improvements in targeting efficiency, can increase with increased use of coupon allocation processes such as open forums. Hence, transparency and accountability of systems are critical in achieving development results and outcomes. School of Oriental and African Studies et al. (2008) and Ricker-Gilbert and Jayne (2011) also found that in 2006/7 and 2008/9 the receipt of subsidized fertilizer was also associated with the presence of a resident MP in the community.

10.4. Gender and use of subsidized inputs[5]

Gender issues in FISP are considered in the targeting criteria, where female-headed households are categorized as part of vulnerable groups requiring particular attention in the targeting of subsidized farm inputs. However,

---

[5] This section draws heavily on Chirwa et al. (2011e).

it is also important to consider how gender relations are affected or affect the use of subsidized inputs at household level.

The analysis of gender issues in the FISP has mostly concentrated on differential access between male-headed and female-headed households. Figure 10.3 shows the proportion of male-headed and female-headed households receiving fertilizer coupons from survey data in the 2006/7, 2008/9, and 2010/11 agricultural seasons. A relatively higher proportion of male-headed households had access to subsidized fertilizer coupons as compared with female-headed households in 2006/7 and 2010/11, while in the 2008/9 season a slightly higher proportion of female-headed households got subsidized fertilizer coupons than male-headed households.

However, School of Oriental and African Studies et al. (2008) also find that male-headed recipient households tended to receive more maize fertilizer coupons than female-headed recipient households, with male-headed households receiving on average 1.55 coupons compared to 1.45 coupons received by female-headed households in 2008/9 (with 1.7 compared to 1.3 coupons received per households in 2006/7). Holden and Lunduka (2012a), in a study of six districts in central and southern Malawi, find that 11% of female-headed households received the full package of 2 bags compared to 29% of male-headed households. With respect to communities' perceptions on who is likely to receive coupons, there were no significant differences between

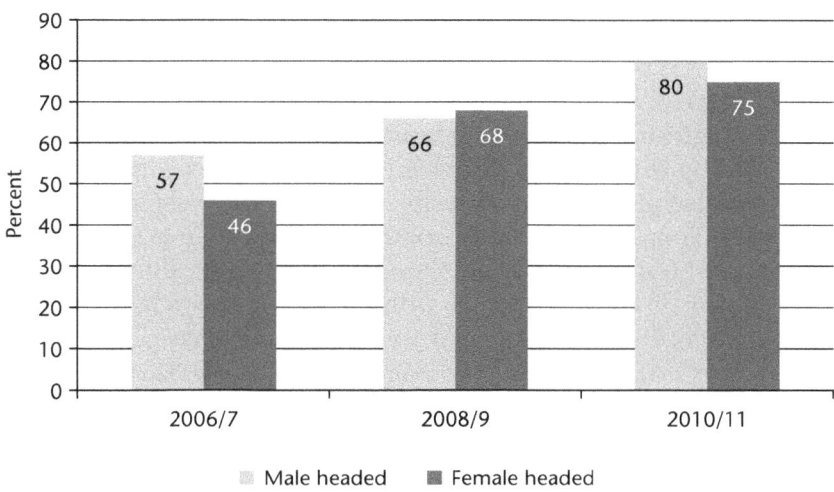

Figure 10.3. Proportion of male- and female-headed households receiving fertilizer coupons, 2006/7–10/11 (%)

Source: Computed from School of Oriental and African Studies et al. (2008), Dorward et al. (2010b), and Dorward and Chirwa (2011a).

male-headed and female-headed households across regions (Dorward et al., 2010b).

Chirwa et al. (2011e) exploit detailed plot level information on decision-making on farming activities by specific members of the household to understand intra-household decision making in allocation of subsidized fertilizers on male- and female-controlled plots. Using probit regression models, the gender of the household member who controls input and farming decisions on the plot is the main variable of interest. The control variables in the model include farmer characteristics and other household characteristics such as plot size, age of household head, headship of household, cultivation of tobacco, sale of maize, access to safely nets, previous access to subsidized fertilizers, and district dummies. Female membership was interacted with household receipt of fertilizer coupons, male-headed membership, and with household with commercial fertilizers. Table 10.6 presents results of probit regressions showing: (1) intra-household use in households with any fertilizers (regardless of the source of the fertilizers); (2) intra-household use in households with subsidized fertilizer (with or without additional unsubsidized fertilizer); and (3) intra-household use in households that only used subsidized fertilizers (with no purchases of unsubsidized fertilizer).

First, the results show that significant gender differentials exist in the allocation of fertilizers to plots within the households, with female-controlled plots less likely to have fertilizer applications compared to male-controlled plots. This is only in the case where we pool the sample of subsidized and unsubsidized households. The probability of applying fertilizer falls by 0.28 points for female-controlled plots, and the marginal effect is statistically significant at the 1% level. These results are similar to the findings in other studies in African agriculture such as Doss and Morris (2001) and Chirwa (2005), although in both those studies the coefficients of female control were statistically insignificant. However, model (1) results also show that female-controlled plots in coupon-recipient households were more likely to be fertilized as compared with male-controlled plots and female-controlled plots in female-headed households. Access to subsidized fertilizers improves the odds for female-controlled plots, with the probability of fertilizer application increasing by 35% compared to female-controlled plots in male-headed and non-coupon recipient households. This implies that for a female household member in a coupon recipient household the mean increase in the probability of applying fertilizer on the plot is 0.07 points compared to a decrease of 0.28 points for a female member in a household without subsidized fertilizers.

Female-controlled plots in male-headed households were less likely to be fertilized than either male-controlled plots or female-controlled plots in female-headed households. This is consistent with observations in focus

Table 10.6. Marginal effects from probit estimates of intra-household fertilizer use

Dependent variable: Plot controlled by member in household was fertilized (0/1)	(1) All households		(2) Use any fertilizer		(3) Only use subsidy fertilizer	
	dF/dx	t-ratio	dF/dx	t-ratio	dF/dx	t-ratio
Female household member*	-0.2844	-3.50[a]	0.078	1.3	0.0401	0.42
Female member in coupon recipient household*	0.3502	13.09[a]	-	-	-	-
Female member in male-headed household*	-0.2848	-3.32[a]	-0.1581	-2.03[b]	-0.073	-0.65
Female in household with commercial fertilizer*	0.2154	7.30[a]	0.0729	2.66[a]	-	-
Plot size in hectares	0.4308	12.59[a]	0.4664	11.99[a]	0.4502	8.42[a]
Male-headed households*	0.1223	1.65[c]	0.0535	0.84	0.012	0.12
Age of household head	-0.0008	-1.45	-0.0003	-0.64	0	-0.07
Number of adult equivalents	-0.0043	-1.12	-0.0085	-2.37[b]	-0.0086	-1.66[c]
Log of household land size in hectares	-0.2389	-15.05[a]	-0.1672	-13.34[a]	-0.2527	-11.52[a]
Household that grew tobacco*	0.1368	6.88[a]	0.1067	6.19[a]	0.0755	2.51[b]
Household that sold maize*	0.1255	4.90[a]	0.0817	3.59[a]	0.0937	2.82[a]
Household had commercial fertilizers in 2007*	0.151	8.59[a]	0.0776	4.58[a]	0.0101	0.31
Household own assessment as poor in 2007*	-0.063	-2.99[a]	-0.0447	-2.29[b]	0.0069	0.22
Household had access to safety nets 2007*	0.0109	0.49	0.0017	0.08	0.0276	0.96
Household had subsidized fertilizers 2007*	0.1698	9.44[a]	0.057	3.05[a]	0.0389	1.43
District fixed effects?	Yes		Yes		Yes	
Number of observations		4727		3551		1944
Pseudo R-squared		0.2281		0.1826		0.2003

Notes: (*) dF/dx is for discrete change of dummy variable from 0 to 1. Superscripts a, b, and c denote statistically significant at 1, 5, and 10% level, respectively.
Source: Chirwa et al. (2011e).

group discussions in Chirwa et al. (2011c) that typically, in male-headed households, resources are likely to be controlled by husbands. However, this is only the case when commercial fertilizers are also available to the household (models (1) and (2)) but it is not the case when households have access to subsidized fertilizers only (model 3). The results show that being a female member controlling a plot in a male-headed household reduces the probability of applying fertilizers by 28% in the model of subsidized and unsubsidized households (model (1)), but this bias reduces to 15% in subsidized households (model (2)). Hence, the bias against female-controlled plots in male-headed households is reduced as compared with the case when commercial fertilizer is also available at the household level. In model (1), the results imply that the mean decrease in the probability of a female-controlled plot being fertilized in a coupon-recipient and male-headed household is 0.21 points. In model (2), the decrease in the mean probability of applying fertilizer on female-controlled plots in male-headed households is only 0.08 compared to a decrease of 0.57 points for the same situation in model (1).

Second, the results also show that access to commercial fertilizers in the 2008/09 season also favoured women-controlled plots in the application of fertilizers and raised the probability of application of fertilizers on the plot by 21% compared to male-controlled or female-controlled plots in households without commercial fertilizers. This is lower than the increase in the probability of 32% with household receipt of subsidized fertilizer. Third, larger plots are more likely to be fertilized than smaller plots. However, plots that belong to households with larger land holdings tend to be less fertilized. This may be due to the fact that most rural households are cash constrained to afford fertilizers and tend to be very selective on the plots that they apply fertilizers to.

Fourth, commercialization of agricultural activities, using indicators such as cultivation of tobacco and sale of maize, and acquisition of commercial fertilizer in the previous season by households is positively related to the probability of the plots being fertilized. This commercialization enables households to invest in fertilizers across all plots. Fifth, self-reported poverty in the 2007/8 season may be one of the constraints to the 2008/9 application of fertilizers by households, with plots that belong to poor households less likely to be fertilized regardless of availability of commercial or subsidized fertilizers. Finally, households' access to subsidized fertilizers in the previous season increases the probability of the plot being fertilized, demonstrating the positive cumulative effects of fertilizer adoption or continued access to subsidized fertilizers. However, this relationship is only statistically significant at the 1% level in models where commercial fertilizers are also available among households but not significant among purely subsidized households.

Overall, although female-headed households are less likely to receive coupons, potentially joint decision making prevails when it comes to use of subsidized fertilizers within the household, hence reducing the bias against female-controlled plots. This may be due to the fact that most of the subsidized fertilizer is meant for the cultivation of maize for subsistence needs, in which case women may have a stronger countervailing power as providers of basic food needs at the household level. It is therefore important that analysis of gender issues in the subsidy programme goes beyond examination of differential access of subsidized fertilizers among male-headed and female-headed households, and also includes examination of intra-household use of subsidized fertilizers. The study implies that social transfers that focus on provision of basic services, such as input subsidy for household food security, are likely to be efficiently used even if they are targeted at the household level instead of at individual household members.

10.5. Challenges of access for the most vulnerable groups[6]

As noted in Section 10.2 above the targeting criteria in the FISP have recently emphasized the need to reach out to the most vulnerable groups, such as resource poor female-headed households, resource poor elderly-headed households, resource poor orphan-headed households, HIV-positive resource poor household heads, resource poor physically-challenged households, and resource poor households looking after elderly and/or physically challenged persons (Farmers Union of Malawi, 2011). These vulnerable groups may experience more challenges in accessing coupons and acquiring subsidized fertilizers due to the processes and problems experienced in the implementation of the programme. Mvula et al. (2011) provide a detailed analysis of some of the challenges that the most vulnerable households experience in accessing subsidized farm inputs, and we highlight some of the major issues in this section. The problems of access to farm inputs relate to access to coupons and access to subsidized fertilizers.

With respect to access to subsidized fertilizer coupons, several problems were documented, which include shortage of coupons earmarked for the villages, missing of beneficiary names that were identified and verified, sharing of coupons, alleged sales of coupons by government agents and traditional leaders, and the process of beneficiary identification and coupon distribution. These findings are consistent with assessment by Farmers Union of Malawi (2011) where they find that among the 30% of respondents reporting problems of coupon distribution, the main problems were: not enough coupons (34% of respondents reporting problems, 10% of all respondents); not receiving coupons though eligible (23% of respondents reporting problems, 7% of all respondents) and being forced to share a coupon with those who did not register (17% of respondents reporting problems, 5% of all respondents). Although these problems tend to be common to all beneficiaries, they tend to be worse for vulnerable groups. For instance, limited numbers of coupons available for villages against the number of resource poor households and vulnerable households tends to result in the most vulnerable households being left out. Similarly, the widespread reported practice of sharing of coupons on average favours less-poor beneficiaries (in that poor beneficiaries share their coupons but less-poor beneficiaries do not) and makes vulnerable groups

---

[6] This section relies heavily on Mvula et al. (2011).

benefit less than the official entitlement. The poor tend to share among the poor or share with the less-poor not in the beneficiary list. Less-poor beneficiaries tend to be less affected by the village level politics of sharing and usually retain their normal share of the coupons. In addition, the requirements for identification documents excluded some of the most vulnerable groups from access to the subsidy.[7]

Even with a coupon there are severe challenges in the process of acquiring subsidized fertilizers, with major implications for the most vulnerable groups. These challenges, discussed in Chapter 5, include long queues at the coupon redemption points, payment of 'tips', stock-outs, presence of thieves at the markets, distances to markets, lack of money to redeem coupons, and rudeness of some input selling clerks. First, long queues at input suppliers (requiring some households to spend days and nights buying inputs) and long distances to selling points are a major challenge for the most vulnerable groups such as female-headed, physically challenged, and elderly-headed households. Second, frequent stock-outs at markets lead to scrambles for farm inputs whenever they are in stock and this disadvantages female-headed households and the elderly, particularly where there is no provision for special queues for vulnerable groups. Third, where 'tips' or bribes are demanded by sellers of subsidized inputs these are not affordable for the most vulnerable groups. Finally, incidents of theft, difficulties in transportation of inputs, and lack of money to buy inputs are problems that particularly affect women and the elderly.

Overall, the problems in accessing coupons for most vulnerable households were not widespread, while the difficulties in redeeming coupons were most severe for most households, particularly the most vulnerable groups. Access to subsidized inputs was more problematic for vulnerable groups due to long queues, frequent stock-outs, long distances to markets, and payment of tips and bribes. These raise the transaction costs and opportunity costs which most vulnerable groups could not afford. The most vulnerable households had particular challenges in finding money to redeem the coupons let alone payment of tips to purchase subsidized inputs.

10.6. Options for targeting[8]

Given the difficulties noted in previous sections with targeting processes, criteria, and outcomes, we now consider three possible alternative targeting

---

[7] As noted in chapter, voter ID cards have been required for beneficiary registration from the 2009/10 season. This proved particularly difficult for child-headed and elderly-headed households that were either under voting age or too old to participate in the general elections.

[8] This section draws on Dorward and Chirwa (2012c).

approaches. We consider first a universal but smaller per household subsidy providing 50 kg of fertilizer to all households (termed the 'universal programme'), second 'tighter pro-poor targeting' where the same total volume of subsidized fertilizer is targeted with a 100 kg ration to the poorest households, and third 'pro-poor mixed targeting' where the same proportion of households get 100 kg and 50 kg of fertilizer as in 2010/11, but these are better targeted with the poorest households getting 100 kg, less poor households getting 50 kg, and the least poor getting none.[9]

The first approach, universal provision of 50 kg fertilizer, is effectively legitimizing and extending the widespread practice of redistribution. It has a number of advantages:

- Elimination of targeting costs and difficulties.
- Increased transparency and accountability, as all households know their entitlement.
- High correspondence between planned targeting outcomes and those achieved.
- Increased effectiveness in targeting the poor as compared with 2010/11, as all the poor would receive some subsidized inputs.
- Despite some increase in the number of less-poor households receiving fertilizers, the total quantity of fertilizer going to less-poor households would be similar to 2010/11 as households would receive only 50 kg per household. This may be seen as offering compensation for lower prices for less poor farmers' surplus maize.
- Reduced demands on coupon allocation and distribution processes may allow earlier coupon distribution and input purchase and use, greater farmer confidence in subsidy receipt, and also release staff time for more extension support to farmers.

There are, however, also difficulties with this approach. First, it may appear to be a reversion to the former 'starter pack' approach, although there are substantial differences with the larger scale of the subsidized 'pack' and in its objectives, and this may make it politically unacceptable. Second, there are concerns that incremental production from a smaller ration of subsidized inputs for each household may not provide poor households with enough productivity gains to 'lift' them over productivity and asset thresholds needed for graduation. Finally, graduation could only be achieved if the whole programme were withdrawn from all beneficiaries in an area at the same time.

---

[9] For simple exposition, and also reflecting the high economic and social value of fertilizer, we frame these options in terms of fertilizer allocations. In practice matching allocations of maize and legume seed should be considered with fertilizer allocations.

Progressive beneficiary graduation and targeting would undermine the core benefits of universal targeting. However graduation might be pursued by progressive lowering of the subsidy with increasing beneficiary redemption payments, with cash transfers to households not able to graduate.

The second approach, tight pro-poor targeting of 100 kg fertilizer, is broadly the approach that is supposed to be used currently. If implemented effectively this would provide the lowest displacement and the highest pro-poor growth potential. There are, however, serious difficulties in applying this method, as discussed in this chapter, and targeting outcomes do not match aspirations. Improving the implementation of this approach must address current difficulties in both setting and applying measurable targeting criteria.

The third approach, mixed pro-poor targeting of 50 and 100 kg fertilizer, is closest to the approach that is actually currently used, where there is redistribution of subsidy coupons. However, whereas in the current system most redistribution seems to involve sharing by poor recipients with poor non-recipients, a more pro-poor approach would prioritize poorer recipients keeping their 100 kg fertilizer allocation, while less-poor recipients would get 50 kg each, and the least poor would get nothing. While this lacks the strong transparency and accountability of the universal approach, it may provide better targeting and have wider community and political support than the tight pro-poor approach. In some ways this might allow easier implementation—but it will still run up against the interests of powerful people who may be excluded from subsidy benefits, and will still face challenges in setting and applying criteria to identify target households. These are likely to make it more difficult to implement. It might also allow a natural beneficiary graduation system with households being shifted from a 100 to 50 kg to zero fertilizer allocation.

Nonetheless, all systems face major practical challenges in determining the number of eligible farm families in each area. Attention is also needed to processes of coupon redemption, as these can be highly exclusionary to poorer and more vulnerable people. Options include distribution centre committees, more private sector involvement in subsidized input sales to promote competition (as discussed in Chapter 8), more effective market monitoring and auditing, and better integration with cash transfers for the productive poor who cannot afford redemption payments. In addition, the development of methods for better identifying beneficiaries is a key requirement for improving targeting, unless it is accepted that difficulties with this (together with power, politics, and problems of lack of accountability and transparency) make the universal approach the best practical approach.

Two main approaches may be considered for improving targeting: proxy wealth/income measures, and community targeting. Both these methods

- require formal identification of targeting criteria and systems that, when implemented, provide improvements that justify their costs;

- pay insufficient attention to difficulties associated with the large number of households clustered around the poverty cut-off point, and hence local concerns about 'fairness'; and

- need to overcome interests of less-poor groups, with enforcement of more transparent and accountable allocation and distribution processes–with open and inclusive processes and/or published recipients lists and allocation criteria.

There is potential merit in the use of proxy poverty indicators, for example, but also major costs and challenges in gathering and using reliable data. Houssou and Zeller (2011) propose an indicator-based system for setting targeting criteria for FISP and argue that this approach would be more target- and cost-effective than the 2006/7 system in improving welfare transfers to the poor.[10] This approach presupposes (a) that the integrated household survey data and its estimation of income poverty (with its various challenges)[11] provide more valid poverty measures than more subjective local definitions which may take account of wider definitions of poverty,[12] (b) that poverty targeting is the most effective way of meeting the range of programme objectives discussed earlier in Section 10.2, (c) does not recognize the complex interactions between area and beneficiary targeting that are important in the practicalities of targeting, and (d) does not pay sufficient attention to difficulties noted earlier with large numbers of households clustered around the poverty cut-off point, and hence local concerns about 'fairness'.[13]

Nevertheless, given the cost implications, it may be useful to consider and develop alternative ways of implementing this (for example, criteria might be developed by a process of participatory consultations with rural people, and a small number of low cost indicators combined into a points system for household prioritization in subsidy allocation). Community targeting with open meetings is the approach supposed to be used for identifying FISP

---

[10] Ten indicators are proposed (household size, radio ownership, cement floor of house, bicycle ownership, use of electricity for lighting, panga ownership, educational qualification in household, use of bed net, rubbish disposal facility, and household head literacy) and also area based factors based on Agricultural Development Divisions.

[11] See, for example, Chirwa et al. (2012) on poverty estimation difficulties as a result of seasonality.

[12] See for example, World Bank (2000) for discussion of issues such as vulnerability, power, voice, assets, wealth, and well-being as poverty concepts alongside income or expenditure measures.

[13] Houssou and Zeller (2011) do consider different patterns of distribution, including a 'fair targeting' approach that does not lift anyone above the poverty line—but this involves reducing subsidy receipts for households just below the poverty line to ensure that it does not lift them over it—a very challenging process, both politically and administratively.

beneficiaries. There is widespread concern that traditional leaders, government officials, and others are appropriating coupons and/or directing them to themselves and/or friends and relatives. This perception is promoted by lack of transparency in allocation, misunderstanding of coupon allocations and targeting processes, and widespread belief that there should be more coupons. It may be difficult for targeting to be perceived to be fair if less than around 80% of households are targeted, and community targeting needs fairly costly training and facilitation with checks and balances to stop elite capture.

10.7. Summary

Targeting is one of the critical elements of the Farm Input Subsidy Programme with implications for displacement, productivity, economy-wide effects, and graduation. It is also important that targeting criteria and processes are consistent with the objectives of the programme in order to maximize the impact. Different programme objectives may entail different targeting objectives with implications for targeting criteria and processes. Hence, there should be a strong link between programme objectives, targeting systems, targeting outcomes, and programme impacts. These links have not been clearly articulated in the Farm Input Subsidy Programme, although targeting occurs at both area and beneficiary levels. While changes have occurred over the life time of the programme, the alignment between programme objectives and targeting objectives and outcomes, and their interaction with political objectives and processes, remains an important issue in the implementation of the programme.

Changes in area targeting have resulted in more equitable distribution of input vouchers per household with per household regional differences narrowing over time. There has been considerable scope for and some evidence of political considerations and processes affecting area distributions, particularly in the earlier years of the programme. Major issues remain on how allocations to areas, villages, and perhaps most importantly to beneficiaries are determined. No major changes have taken place in the targeting criteria and processes of targeting at beneficiary level, apart from increasing emphasis on vulnerable households and the promotion of open forums at community level in the identification of beneficiaries and allocation and distribution of coupons.

The broadness of the beneficiary targeting criteria, covering a large proportion of poor households, has allowed wide variations in the application of the criteria at community level. This has resulted in biases in receipt of subsidized farm input coupons against the poor, with the non-poor more likely to get coupons and then likely to get more coupons than the poor. The wide and increasing practice of redistribution and 'sharing' of coupons reduces the bias where by the poor are less likely to receive coupons. On the other hand, however, it increases the likelihood of poorer recipients receiving fewer coupons than less-poor recipients. However, open forum meetings for allocation of coupons appear to increase the likelihood of the poor receiving fertilizer coupons and acquiring more than the poor in areas where the coupon allocation was not made in an open manner. There are also gender biases in receipt of coupons and access to subsidized fertilizers, with female-headed households receiving fewer coupons than male-headed households. However, this gender bias is not evident in the allocation of subsidized fertilizers on plots controlled by different members of the households. The analysis of intra-household use of inputs shows that female-controlled plots are less likely to have fertilizer applied when commercial fertilizer is available in the household, but this bias vanishes among households that acquire subsidized fertilizer inputs. Overall, however, the extent of elite capture does not appear to be as great as that reported by Pan and Christiaensen (2012) in Tanzania.

Options for targeting have been considered for improving patterns of coupon distribution among poorer and less-poor households, with discussion of alternative targeting criteria and processes to achieve these patterns. Regressive patterns appear to be undesirable due to associated high displacement (leading to low incremental production even if there is higher input productivity) and low linkage effects. Three alternative approaches are considered—'tight pro-poor targeting', 'mixed pro-poor targeting', and universal (but more tightly rationed) access. Although 'tight pro-poor targeting' is the current desired outcome, difficulties in setting criteria and with distribution and redistribution processes lead to outcomes that are very different from those that are desired. In any case, except for the universal approach, targeting requires efficient and cost-effective ways of improving the criteria for identifying beneficiary households.

11

Graduation[1]

11.1. Introduction

Graduation has emerged as an issue in debates about the future of the farm subsidy programme at the interface of a number of issues. The high costs of the programme pose serious questions about its fiscal and macro-economic sustainability and suggest a need for a process that goes beyond simple exits (as discussed in Chapter 2) to allow a phased scaling down that builds on (rather than undermines) the growth, food security, and market development impacts of the programme.

11.2. Conceptualizing graduation

Graduation is a concept that is found in discussions about the impact, dependency, exit, and sustainability of social protection programmes, addressing questions about the extent to which the financial transfers to beneficiaries should and can enable them to exit from the programme of assistance and hence reduce the scope and costs of social protection over time. Governments with tight budgets may be more willing to support social protection if access is time-bound or if there are clear prospects of a higher proportion of the target beneficiaries voluntarily exiting over time. The issue of graduation from social protection is thus closely linked to the developmental or transformative role of social protection, and also to the need to avoid 'dependency syndrome' among beneficiaries (Devereux, 2010).

These issues are highly relevant to the FISP, and Chirwa et al. (2011a) discuss the application to the FISP of the conceptualization of graduation in social protection. A review of this conceptualization leads to the conclusion

[1] Much of this chapter draws heavily on Chirwa et al. (2011a).

that graduation is viewed as the achievement of 'the potential to embark on sustainable, independent livelihoods without social protection' (p. 3). This requires further 'unpacking', leading them to define *potential graduation* as the use of transfers to achieve a shift in livelihood activities with 'stepping up' (intensification and increased productivity in existing activities) and 'stepping out' (into new more productive activities), and reduced emphasis on 'hanging in' (avoidance of 'falling down and out') (Dorward et al., 2006, 2009a). These changes involve investing some of the transfers into productive activities and the building of assets, capabilities, or livelihood changes that allow beneficiaries to embark on sustainable, independent livelihoods without transfers. *Actual graduation* is then the removal of access to a transfer programme that does not leave current beneficiaries supported by the programme unable to pursue sustainable independent livelihoods. The distinction between actual and potential graduation is explored in Figure 11.1, where a movement from left to right (from A or C to B or D) represents the termination either of access to programme benefit or of a programme itself, a movement from A to C downwards represents potential graduation, and a movement from A to D represents actual graduation.

These concepts can be applied at different scales of analysis (individual, household, area, or programme), where they raise questions about the relationships between graduation at different scales. These are particularly important when considering a large-scale programme with both household and economy-wide effects.

The more obvious relationship is dependence of graduation at wider scales on the graduation of its components—for example, the dependence of

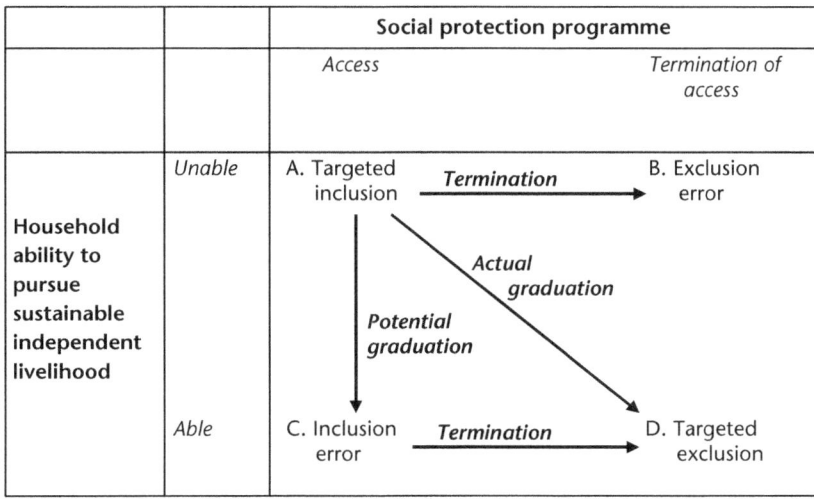

Figure 11.1. Termination, potential graduation, and actual graduation

programme graduation on achievement of some minimum scale of (potential) area graduation, and of area graduation on achievement of some minimum scale of (potential) household graduation). This raises questions about the criteria used at different scales, in both the definition of (potential) household graduation and the required number or percentage of households graduating (or conversely the maximum number or percentage of ungraduated households) for area and/or programme graduation.

However, Chirwa et al. (2011a) also note that lower units' potential graduation may sometimes depend upon the continuation of transfers (rather than graduation or termination) at a wider scale of analysis. The most likely causes of this in a social protection programme will be where there are significant insurance or indirect effects from transfers. The first case may arise when the presence of a programme offering transfers gives households insurance against livelihood shocks and stresses and this allows them to take 'stepping up' and 'stepping out' investment risks even when they are not direct beneficiaries of a programme. Their pursuit of (and hence graduation to) independent sustainable livelihoods may then be dependent on the presence of a transfer programme rather than on their direct receipt of benefits from it. Households that seem to have graduated from the programme may in fact still be dependent on its existence, though not, under normal circumstances, on their direct engagement with it. An example of such indirect effects is where there are significant multiplier effects from households in receipt of transfers, for example where these lead to greater demand by recipient households of particular services whose supply provides income for other households. Where this is the case then withdrawal of transfers from a significant number of households in an area may lead to a reduction in these multipliers and undermine the livelihoods of households who appeared to have achieved independent sustainable livelihoods.

Consideration of these multi-scale relationships allows the definition of an apparently simple core requirement for graduation: that removal of access to a programme (termination) does not leave beneficiaries currently supported by the programme unable to pursue sustainable independent livelihoods.

This requirement is only apparently simple because there are major practical and theoretical challenges in defining and measuring criteria for determining the point at which beneficiaries can be weaned off a transfer with some minimum acceptable standard of welfare or probability of achieving a stable or upward welfare or livelihood trajectory. Devereux (2010) argues that there are difficulties in identifying both indicators or variables and critical attainments of welfare and self-reliance, such as threshold values of incomes and assets that will not result in graduating households reverting back to situations of vulnerability. These thresholds may involve some minimum income line, the accumulation of control and access to assets (physical, social, human, financial, and natural capital) that are necessary for sustainable livelihoods that can cope with shocks and stresses. These however, are likely to vary with household structure (for example, gender composition and dependency ratios), with socio-economic and cultural context, with livelihood strategies and opportunities, and with complex interactions between the different forms of capital listed above. Critically, graduation measures need to be concerned with the achievement of conditions (inputs and processes) necessary for the pursuit of sustainable independent livelihoods rather than the achievement of welfare outcomes which may tell us little about livelihoods, independence, or sustainability.

A further complexity arises with the conceptualization of poverty traps operating at wider scales of analysis in local economies (Rodenstein-Rodan, 1943; Dorward et al., 2005a, b, 2009). This is linked to different scales or units of graduation, as discussed above, and demands consideration of variables and thresholds for determining area and programme graduation. Determination of potential graduation for areas and programmes is likely to involve some threshold number or percentage of beneficiary graduation at the area or programme level, and consideration of volumes of livelihood activities at these wider scales.

A final comment is needed on the importance of social and political influences on processes and decisions in graduation from transfers. Termination decisions are highly political, in terms of local, national, and bureaucratic policies concerned with, respectively, questions about which people and groups of people benefit from transfers; which areas, constituencies, and ethnic groups benefit; and how limited resources are allocated between agencies and sectors.

11.3. Graduation pathways for the Malawi Farm Input Subsidy Programme

We now consider a definition of graduation specific to the FISP in order to identify possible processes, pathways, and criteria for graduation and design and implementation features that could promote graduation within the programme. This brings together insights from more general discussion of graduation processes (in Section 11.2) with particular understanding of the role of FISP in promoting livelihood development and economic growth, as set out in Chapters 2, 4, 6, and 7.

Our discussion of graduation processes in transfer programmes in Section 11.2 emphasized the processes of stepping up and stepping out; multi-scale aspects of interactions between graduation and termination; and alternative income, livelihood activity, and asset variables and thresholds in defining potential graduation. Other issues discussed by Chirwa et al. (2011a) include the importance of a range of different conditions facilitating (or impeding) graduation (including the depth and incidence of poverty among beneficiaries and non-beneficiaries; the value, nature, and duration of benefits; complementary services, and the wider socio-economic environment); and socio-political factors. Graduation was defined as the removal of access to a transfer programme that does not leave current beneficiaries supported by the programme unable to pursue sustainable independent livelihoods.

Discussion of the impacts of FISP throughout this book have raised similar issues regarding stepping up and stepping out processes; multi-scale interactions; changes in livelihood activities as critical elements in economic growth and structural change within local and wider economies; and the importance of complementary services and the wider socio-economic environment. Issues which were implicitly rather than explicitly considered include effects on livelihoods of the depth and incidence of poverty among beneficiaries and non-beneficiaries; and the value, nature, and duration of subsidized benefits. Socio-political considerations in area and household targeting have also been discussed more specifically in Chapters 4, 5, and 10, while input market development is a major issue in Chapter 8.

Our consideration of multi-scale and dynamic subsidy programme contributions to development suggests that the core requirement for graduation from the subsidy programme should be that removal of access to the subsidy programme does not critically reduce land, labour, and capital productivity in maize production in the livelihoods of beneficiaries and in the economy as a whole. This provides a definition of graduation analogous to our earlier general definition of actual graduation from transfer programmes and it also, and importantly, allows the identification of a number of 'potential graduation conditions' which are required in some combination as a result of and during the implementation of the FISP for subsequent actual graduation. These comprise

1. Falls in unsubsidized farm-gate input prices and costs compared to pre-programme prices and costs.
2. Reduced requirements for the purchase of previously subsidized inputs due to increased efficiency in use.
3. Reduced requirements for the purchase of previously subsidized inputs due to substitution by cheaper inputs.
4. Increase in working capital among poor beneficiary households for the purchase of previously subsidized inputs.
5. Poor beneficiary households' diversification out of maize production through either transfer of land to other high value production use

(diversification or stepping out of maize within agriculture) or transfer of land to another user with diversification or stepping out of agriculture into non-farm activities.

6. Access to low-cost credit by poor beneficiary households for the purchase of previously subsidized inputs.

These conditions share a number of features:

• None of these potential and desirable changes can be ruled out as irrelevant or impossible, nor can any be identified as being of paramount importance.

• Thresholds within each of these conditions cannot be determined independently of achievement of other conditions.

• They are all dependent on the multi-scale processes of stepping up and stepping out to create the systemic conditions under which sufficient change can be achieved for them to contribute to graduation by some households.

• They can all benefit from promotion in design and implementation.

We can, however, note that they are likely to vary in the extent to which they will be accessible to different households and in the speed at which necessary changes will happen. These changes also, of course, require different types of promotion in programme design and implementation and in complementary investments.

Table 11.1 summarizes the likely processes and requirements needed for each of the 'potential graduation conditions' listed above. The final two columns of the table classify these by the scale at which changes operate and the speed at which it is reasonable for the changes to become effective in promoting potential graduation. All processes and requirements operate at multiple scales, relying on wider structural, policy, and service changes at national and area level to support and be supported by each other and by changes within businesses or households' livelihood activities. The speed of change then depends upon households' initial structures and resource holdings, their receipt of subsidized inputs over the life of the subsidy programme, events and shocks affecting their welfare and resources, and both policy-induced and other changes in the local and wider socio-economic environment.

Most of the entries in Table 11.1 require little elaboration. For reduced input prices (1), there are a large number of reports on the potential for reducing prices for inorganic fertilizers by improving transport systems and management during importation and distribution, by switching from 23:21:12 to a cheaper but equally effective formulation, and possibly by investing in a

Table 11.1. Graduation processes, requirements, and sequencing of changes

Potential graduation conditions	Likely processes and requirements	Scale	Order
1. Reduced input prices	Efficient & competitive importers, supplier(s), transporters; improved transport infrastructure	Business, area, national	1
2. Increased efficiency in input use	Improved agronomy, complementary seed, inorganic & organic fertilizers, soil management. Investment in agricultural research and extension	Household, area, national	1
3. Substitution by cheaper inputs	Increased legume cultivation with rotational fallows. Good legume seed supply, produce demand & markets. Stable & reliable low maize prices & high maize productivity for transition before subsidy removal	Household, area, national	1
4. Increase working capital for input purchases	Increased incomes, diversified incomes with reduced income seasonality	Household, area, national	1
5. Diversification out of maize production	Stable & reliable low maize prices, strong demand for high value farm products and/or non-farm goods & services, land markets & safety nets	Household, area, national	2
6. Access to low-cost credit for input purchases	Increased & diversified incomes, innovative & low-cost micro-finance systems.	Household, area, national	2

fertilizer blending plant in Malawi (for example, Munthali, 2007). Increasing working capital of beneficiary households (4) is the most commonly considered pathway for potential graduation in social protection programmes (as discussed earlier). Its effectiveness in actually allowing potential graduation, however, is also very dependent upon a household's initial asset status relative to some threshold needed for sustainable independent livelihoods, and upon structural issues (such as household composition) and exposure to adverse shocks. Diversification out of maize production (5) is likely to take some time as it depends upon wider structural change and developing confidence of low and stable maize prices in consumer markets. It is, however, likely to be a condition for the development of access to low-cost credit (6), since this is only likely to be possible with some form of micro-finance system where borrowers engage in different micro-enterprises with different seasonal patterns of income and expenditure and different risks (see, for example, Dorward et al., 2001).

Turning now to consider (3)—'increased efficiency in input use'—there is considerable evidence for the potential of raising returns to fertilizer use by greater use of high yielding seed, more timely planting, more effective soil health management, timely weeding, more effective fertilizer application methods, and greater use of complementary organic fertilizers (Maize Productivity Task Force, 1997; Snapp et al., 2010). Holden and Lunduka (2012b) report encouraging findings of complementary use of organic and inorganic fertilizers in a sample of farmers from six districts in the Southern and Central Regions of Malawi.

Organic fertilizers and legume intercropping and rotation can also substitute for and augment inorganic fertilizers—listed under (4) above, 'substitution by cheaper inputs'. However, major difficulties with the adoption of such systems have been the labour and/or land requirements for fallows, for tree planting and maintenance, and for growing green manures and mulches (for example, Barrett et al., 2002). These labour and land requirements are particularly problematic and high for land- and labour-constrained poor households who suffer most from the Low Maize Productivity Trap outlined in Chapter 4. Such households might be expected to gain significant benefits from an improved maize/semi-perennial legume (pigeon pea and groundnut inter-crop) rotation system which can offer equivalent maize production to unfertilized maize but with added legume grain sales and high protein consumption (Snapp et al., 2010). However, adoption of these systems faces major transition problems as a result of lost maize production when introducing a legume crop in the first year of a rotation. Participation in the subsidy programme, however, offers opportunities to address this problem in three ways:

1. By increasing maize productivity on people's land, the programme should help farmers to get more maize from their land, so that if they allocate say 1/3 of their land to groundnuts/pigeon peas in year 1 and use fertilizer on the other 2/3 of their land, they could still have roughly the same or more maize as they would with all their land under maize production without the subsidy, plus the legume grain. In year 2 they could do the same but because of the benefits from the land rotated under the previous year, they would get more maize, and by year 4 they would have all their land under rotation.

2. By reducing the price of maize and raising wages, the programme should also make farmers less desperate to grow all their own maize, allowing them to buy any shortfall for less. This should reduce the risks of not producing enough maize during the transition.

3. By raising real incomes the programme should increase the demand for legumes within households and in the wider market, raising the value to households of their legume grain production.

11.4. Programme design and implementation to promote graduation

The identification of different and complementary potential graduation pathways has immediate implications for two aspects of programme design and implementation: first the programme should be implemented in ways that actively promote these graduation pathways, and second actual graduation procedures should be built into programme implementation.

The interventions needed to promote graduation pathways vary between pathways and generally align with and strengthen the importance of existing programme or development objectives. Thus, interventions to promote lower input prices and to increase efficiency in input use and substitution by cheaper inputs should all raise the efficiency of the programme—and indeed have substantial contributions to make in their own right, independent of the programme. Similarly, increases in working capital among poor beneficiary households should be aligned with programme objectives. Encouraging diversification out of maize and agriculture and promoting access to low-cost credit are valuable general objectives for rural development, but are not so obviously complementary to the implementation of FISP, and may therefore need special (and specialized) attention alongside FISP.

What is striking, however, about the graduation conditions, processes, requirements, and scales of change detailed in Table 11.1 is the importance of the multi-scale interactions between national, area, and household processes of change. This is supported by the analysis reported in Chapter 7 suggesting that indirect benefits may be larger than direct beneficiaries for poor beneficiaries in poorer areas, with beneficiary graduation therefore critically dependent upon wider processes of change and potential area graduation. This requires a holistic multi-scale approach that coordinates programme design and implementation with complementary policies and investments that operate outside the programme—in infrastructure, research, extension, stable maize markets, and the development of the non-farm economy. Since (as set out in Chapter 2, in the causal pathway in Figure II.1 and in the links between Chapters 6 and 7) this holistic approach is needed to obtain maximum food security and wider development benefits from the programme, there should be strong synergies between an emphasis on graduation and the wider pursuit of greater and lower cost achievement of a wide set of potential programme benefits.

As regards actual graduation (and termination) procedures, three broad approaches may be followed, singly or in any combination: (a) reductions in subsidy per household; (b) a reduction in the number of areas or districts served by the programme with phased withdrawal of the programme from particular areas or districts; and (c) withdrawal of the programme from particular households. Options (b) and (c) require criteria for determining graduation or termination of the subsidy by area or household, and these should be closely linked to targeting criteria and systems— the discussion on targeting in Chapter 10 is therefore critically relevant and consideration of the targeting alternatives discussed there should take account of the graduation options discussed here. One concern raised in focus group discussions and life histories about a smaller universal subsidy was that such subsidies were too small to improve households' livelihoods sufficiently for them make any progress towards graduation (see Section 6.7), although this perhaps would not be such a concern if the subsidy was effectively driving positive economy-wide effects in maize prices, wages and livelihood, and local economy diversification. Where area and household targeting are employed then graduation (and hence targeting) criteria are likely to include consideration, at household and area scales, of budgetary constraints, political factors, efficiency differentials, and potential graduation.

Political issues associated with different approaches to graduation require a special mention. Political difficulties with reducing the scale of the subsidy per household by increasing farmer payments are evident from the determinants of falling nominal payments for subsidized fertilizer as reported earlier in Section 5.5.1. Farmer's concerns expressed in focus group discussions and life histories (summarized in Chapter 6) suggest that there are also political difficulties with reducing household entitlements to one bag of fertilizer and associated seed. Reducing the number of subsidized households rather than the scale of subsidies to all households (by withdrawal of subsidies from particular areas and/or particular households) may face greater political opposition from smaller numbers of people. Political calculations will then consider which interest groups are politically most important or powerful with respect to the aspirations, strengths, and weaknesses of political leaders with responsibility for and/or power over the programme. Such calculations may not give technocratically preferred graduation policies, or any graduation policy at all.

Potential graduation may be measured using variables related to the potential graduation changes identified in Table 11.1. Attention should also be paid to questions about relationships between area graduation/termination and household graduation as touched on earlier in Section 11.2. Just as there are synergies between measures that will promote graduation and those that will promote wider achievement of programme objectives, there should be similar synergies between the development and use of graduation criteria and wider monitoring and evaluation of programme achievements. It is, however, also important to note that the use of poor criteria or procedures in trying to promote graduation is also likely to damage the effectiveness of the wider programme (if, for example, termination rather than graduation were to be an important target in programme implementation, either explicitly or as a result of poor setting or application of graduation criteria).

11.5. Summary

In this chapter we have considered ways in which the concept of graduation may be usefully applied to the FISP. The conceptualization of graduation as the removal of access to transfers that does not leave current beneficiaries unable to pursue sustainable independent livelihoods allows a distinction to be made between potential graduation, actual graduation, and termination of access. It also helps in consideration of the differences and inter-relationships between graduation and termination at different scales, such as household, area, and programme. These conceptual issues suggest that measures of graduation should use variables and thresholds that measure assets and activities supporting sustainable independent livelihoods rather than income measures, and such measures need to take account of the different opportunities, threats, and difficulties facing different people in different contexts.

This conceptualization provides an explicit focus on graduation which, as shown in Chapter 3, appears to be lacking from most programmes, and indeed, as is evident in Chapter 2, is also lacking from most wider discussion of programme exits, despite the widespread consideration of time-bound exits as a key feature of 'smart subsidies' (for example, Minde et al., 2008; Morris et al., 2007). This conceptualization has important implications for core political and technical issues in programme design and implementation.

Application of these lessons to graduation in agricultural input subsidy programmes like the Malawi FISP requires some understanding of the processes by which these programme promote sustainable independent livelihoods. In the Malawi FISP this allows a specific definition of graduation as a removal of access to the subsidy programme that does not reduce land, labour, and capital productivity in maize production. 'Potential graduation conditions' that promote this include reduced input prices, increased efficiency in input use, substitution by cheaper inputs, increased working capital for input purchases, diversification out of maize production, and access to low-cost credit for input purchases. Identification of these potential graduation conditions is valuable for suggesting types of change that programme designers and implementers should seek to promote, as well as variables that may be used in making decisions about graduation criteria and processes. Further work is needed to determine what criteria (variables and thresholds) may be best for judging potential graduation at different scales. However, graduation, the withdrawal of access to subsidies, is an intensely political issue, and both political and technical considerations will be important determinants of graduation policies and their implementation. The importance of wider indirect impacts of the programme for potential household and area graduation also suggests that there should be strong synergies between on the one hand a greater emphasis on graduation within the programme and on the other a more effective and efficient achievement of a food security and wider development objectives.

12

Conclusions

12.1. Introduction

This book attempts to contribute to greater understanding of agricultural input subsidies' potential contributions and pitfalls as instruments promoting food security, poverty reduction, social protection, and wider economic growth in poor agrarian economies. This has been approached through a theoretical and practical discussion of agricultural input subsidies and their impacts (in Chapters 2 and 3), through detailed examination of Malawi's experience in implementing a large-scale agricultural input subsidy programme (in Chapters 4 to 9), and (in Chapters 10 and 11) through consideration of targeting and graduation as two specific issues needing more strategic attention in the design and implementation of large-scale agricultural input subsidies in contemporary low-income agrarian economies. This concluding chapter draws these three topics together, and links them to a discussion of a major concern for agricultural input subsidies: their sustainability. We consider each of these topics (subsidies' changing theory and practice, Malawi's experience, targeting and graduation, and sustainability) in turn. We conclude by considering possible lessons and ways forward from this for the wider application of agricultural input subsidies in Africa.

12.2. Subsidies' changing theory and practice

Consideration of conventional and more recent theoretical and empirical analysis of agricultural input subsidies in Chapter 2 suggests a number of potential contributions that input subsidies can make to economic development in poor agrarian economies. In addition to reducing food insecurity, ameliorating soil fertility problems, and increasing land and agricultural labour productivity, they can also drive wider, dynamic processes of pro-poor growth, structural change, economic diversification, and market thickening and development.

There are, however, a number of necessary conditions in order for subsidy programmes to make these contributions. The principle conditions are targeting of subsidies to address market failures (in, for example, access to knowledge or to input or capital markets) with significant and normally labour-demanding productivity increases for crops produced by large numbers of smallholders. Such crops will generally be staple crops, with a 'double benefit' if staple food markets are relatively isolated from international markets, in which case the provision of inputs may also promote possible market or pecuniary externalities from staple crop cultivation. Programme design and implementation should then pay attention to, or at least be integrated with, policies promoting wider processes of growth and, where double benefits can be achieved, to net buyer's interests in programme impacts.

Large per unit price subsidies may be needed to address 'affordability' constraints on input purchases and use, and these lead to a particular need for good targeting and rationing systems. Poor systems may reduce programme effectiveness and efficiency as problems of 'exclusion' limit receipt of subsidized inputs by farmers facing market failures and able to make the most productive use of these inputs. Problems of 'inclusion', on the other hand, raise costs of supply to farmers whose productive input use is not otherwise constrained by the market failures addressed by the subsidy, and whose receipt of subsidies therefore does not yield benefits from incremental production. Inclusion of such farmers may also inhibit the development of unsubsidized input supply markets, and these may also be damaged by subsidy systems that undermine private sector investment incentives. Poor design and/or implementation of graduation policies may lead to increasing problems of exclusion, together with rising and unsustainable subsidy costs, falling benefits, and increasing opportunity costs from crowding out of more productive investment of scarce government resources. Effective input subsidies may also need attention to complementary policies and investments—needed to improve direct input uptake and production impacts, or to facilitate wider, dynamic benefits.

Finally, political commitment is critically important for major resource investments in large-scale input subsidies. However this itself raises major difficulties where such commitment is driven by short-term patronage interests rather than longer term developmental interests.

The examination in Chapter 3 of recent subsidy programmes in sub-Saharan Africa suggests that recognition of and attention to these issues is mixed—across countries and issues. Thus, almost all the national programmes reviewed involved large-scale subsidies for inputs for staple food production by large numbers of smallholders, with substantial price reductions, generally addressing (implicitly at least) affordability constraints on farmers' input purchases. This is associated with a general focus on producer benefits, including producers' food security (though in Mali and Senegal it was also intended to reduce urban rice prices). Late delivery of inputs, and hence reduced returns to farmers, were common. In no programme was there any reported recognition of potential wider dynamic growth benefits, nor any consideration of graduation processes and criteria. With regard to graduation, aspirations of time limits and scaling down were expressed in some cases, but there was no apparent in-depth consideration of processes by which the need for subsidies would be reduced (apart from some explicit support to input supplier development).

Support to input suppliers was therefore one issue where intentions and practice varied across programmes—with some programmes giving it little or no attention, others recognizing its importance without effective action (and perhaps in practice undermining it), and others seriously pursuing it. Attention to targeting was similarly varied as regards stated intentions, but there were few if any cases of the achievement of effective targeting. Voucher-based entitlement systems were common but not universal. Integrated attention to complementary policies and investments was relatively rare and where present appeared to be restricted to direct promotion of programme effectiveness in raising on-farm input productivity or supporting input supplier development. Political factors around programme initiation and implementation are not widely discussed, but are specifically reported in some programmes and their general importance and influence may be inferred for most.

12.3. The Malawi experience

The introduction of the large-scale Farm Input Subsidy Programme in 2005/6 in Malawi and its subsequent continuation have to be understood in the context of Malawi's specific political, social, economic, food security, and agricultural policy history and conditions as set out in Chapter 4. These led to the emergence of 'fertilizer politics', with popular demands for fertilizer subsidies providing political opportunities that also had a technical rationale in addressing food insecurity and, with the 'low maize productivity trap', potential wider dynamic benefits for peoples' livelihoods and wider economic growth. The first four years of the programme were, however, also shaped by very specific political challenges facing the minority government of President Bingu wa Mutharika.

The detailed description of the FISP in Chapter 5 shows that the FISP focused largely (but not exclusively at first) on staple crop production, operated on a very large scale (reaching an impressively large number of dispersed smallholders), provided large (and generally growing) price reductions explicitly addressing affordability constraints on input purchases, and focused on producers' (as opposed to buyers') welfare and food security. The programme did not explicitly articulate any longer term dynamic growth objectives, and consideration of graduation processes was initially absent, but has become more of an issue over time. However, the issue of graduation has not found its way into policy articulation and programme design. Engagement with input suppliers has varied—with fairly consistent engagement with private sector seed suppliers and fertilizer importers and transporters, but policy reversals on the involvement of private sector fertilizer retailers. Targeting objectives, criteria, and methods have evolved, but without dramatic changes in outcomes. Complementary policies and investments have focused on direct promotion of complementary inputs (seeds and maize storage chemicals), with some attention to extension messages and some complementary research on integrated soil fertility technologies.

There have been substantial changes in various aspects of programme design and implementation over the life of the programme. These have incorporated growing experience, responded to emerging problems and different stakeholder interests, and recognized local solutions and good practice. Changes have involved removal of cash crop subsidies and modifications to targeting and allocation systems, to tender award and importation processes, and to coupon design and printing. These have led to improvements in timing of input purchase and distribution and in control of some aspects of fraud. There is also greater emphasis on the need for transparency in allocation and distribution of coupons, although in practice this has proved difficult to implement. However there are, inevitably, continuing challenges on these issues, and little evidence of improved targeting. Political considerations have appeared to dominate others, certainly up to the 2008/9 elections, and these appear to have been a major influence on the growing programme scale and costs from 2005/6 to 2007/8 (exceptionally high fertilizer prices led to a spike in costs in 2008/9, with subsequent costs being more tightly controlled).

The discussion of direct programme impacts in Chapter 6 is constrained by weaknesses in critical data on crop production and the number of farm families. However it suggests that production impacts have been smaller than might be suggested by increases in official production estimates following the introduction of the subsidy, with very high maize prices in some years. Nevertheless, it still appears that there were substantial production impacts. Study of specific impacts on beneficiary households shows immediate benefits in maize production, net crop income, household income, and to a lesser extent food consumption, with continued (lagged) benefits on beneficiaries' maize production, and to a lesser extent food consumption. School enrolment and child health also appear to have benefited from subsidy receipt. No significant impacts of subsidy receipt were detected on subjective well-being and investment in physical assets, but this may be affected by investment of gains from increased maize production in food consumption, school

263

enrolment, and health. The widespread practice of sharing subsidized fertilizers and more general increases in subjective well-being and asset ownership may also mask direct benefits. However, as discussed in Chapter 10, use of fertilizer on female controlled plots is increased by subsidy receipt.

As argued in Chapter 2, large-scale subsidy programmes like the Malawi FISP should have beneficial economy-wide impacts affecting both subsidy recipients and non-recipients. Chapter 7 reports difficulties with attribution of macro-economic changes to the FISP and with possible unreliability in GDP estimates. However, implementation of the FISP appears to be associated with good agricultural GDP growth, although high costs of the FISP in 2008/9 were also a contributor to an increased budget deficit—along with other expenditures related to the 2009 elections. There has also been some improvement in maize trade balances (except in 2008/9). There is stronger evidence of increases in real wage rates as a result of the FISP (despite more mixed evidence on maize price impacts), some evidence of increased national food availability and improved child nutrition, and mixed evidence on national changes in income and poverty incidence. Chapter 6 also reports wider positive changes in maize production, net crop income, subjective well-being, physical assets, school enrolment, and child health. Overall there is evidence of economy-wide changes, but it is not as strong as one would expect and hope for from a programme as large as the Malawi FISP.

FISP's engagement with and impacts on suppliers, fertilizer importers and retailers, and seed growers and retailers is reported in Chapter 8.

The increasing use of private fertilizer importers has been associated with an increase in the number of firms tendering and being awarded tenders, but some of these have not been able to deliver timely supplies. Tenders have also been affected by late awards and payments, which increase supplier costs and risks and hence prices, although there have been some improvements in tender procedures during the life of the programme. Engagement with fertilizer retailers has been limited, with six retail firms contracted to sell subsidized fertilizers in 2006/7 and 2008/9, and sudden termination of these arrangements at the start of the 2008/9 season. There is potential for re-engagement with private retailing of subsidized fertilizers, but this requires increased mutual trust and would be more effective if it was open to a wider range of retail outlets, including agro-dealers (and applying lessons from experience with seed retail systems). Potential benefits from private sector involvement with retailing of subsidized fertilizers include greater efficiency with lower costs, freeing and adding to government resources (including staff, transport logistics, and storage facilities), potential promotion of input outlets in remote areas, broadening of farmer choice with competition between outlets, and reduced farmer transaction costs and queuing. Impacts of the programme on private retail sales of fertilizer have been mixed, with some displacement of unsubsidized purchases by subsidized purchases, but also more recent evidence of some 'crowding in' and increases in unsubsidized purchases.

Seed procurement has been exclusively from private organizations, with the number of suppliers growing from 6 to 12. These suppliers are responsible for seed distribution to both parastatal and private retailers including agro-dealers, removing from government all responsibilities for managing and coordinating supply and also removing the risk of unsold stock holdings. Despite the increase in the number of seed suppliers, the market remains oligopolistic with collective negotiation of prices charged to the government for subsidized seed supply. Large increases in the number of agro-dealers selling subsidized seeds have, however, contributed to increased competition and farmer choice among retail outlets. There is limited industry information available on unsubsidized seed sales. Farmers reported purchases suggest substantial rates of displacement of unsubsidized by subsidized maize seed purchases, but large increases in total purchases due to the large increases in subsidized maize seed supply.

Chapter 9 identifies a number of challenges in estimating the benefits and costs of the FISP, and of input subsidy programmes in general. These include problems with data availability, with practicable methodologies that capture both indirect and direct impacts, and with consistency and comparability across estimates of costs and returns for different investments. Extension of standard partial equilibrium methods to include estimates of economy-wide impacts increases estimated benefit–cost ratios for the programme. This suggests that the programme has yielded an average BCR of around 1.35 after allowing for the effects of multipliers but ignoring potential long-term benefits from improved food consumption on children's physical and mental development and long-term development of human capital. The most valuable use of these methods, however, is in identification of design and implementation parameters with critical impacts on programme efficiency and effectiveness. Returns would be improved by measures that increase yield responses to fertilizer (for example, earlier input delivery, greater emphasis on integrated soil fertility management, improved application, more cost effective formulations, more targeting to the poor) and that reduce displacement and costs (for example, better regional and household targeting, better control of diversion and fraud, earlier registration and input delivery). The inclusion of multipliers in the BCA strengthens the importance of all of these issues and also adds further weight to the importance of targeting, of ensuring that maize marketing policies allow increased maize production to lower maize prices, and of complementary investments in measures facilitating the growth of the non-farm economy and of non-staple agriculture in response to subsidy-led growth in real incomes. Difficulties with the availability of data needed for benefit–cost analysis highlight the need for critical agricultural production statistics.

This summary of FISP's features shows that it shares many of the features of the other African programmes reviewed in Chapter 3: indeed many of these programmes were influenced by reports of dramatic success with the Malawi programme. These features include its emphasis on staple crop production, its scale, its large price reductions, its focus on producers' welfare and food security, its lack of dynamic growth objectives or consideration of graduation, its variable engagement with inputs suppliers, the challenges it has faced with targeting, and limited complementary policies and investments, focusing on complementary inputs and to a lesser extent research and extension.

The very limited information on the impacts of the programmes discussed in Chapter 3 makes comparison with FISP's impacts difficult. Reports of late delivery of inputs are common, as are reports of impacts on private sector input suppliers—though these are sometimes positive and sometimes negative. Incremental input use and increased production and productivity are reported for some. There is only one programme where an *ex post* estimated benefit–cost ratio is reported, and the benefits considered are restricted to the direct value of incremental production. There is virtually no consideration of macro-economic impacts, and no discussion of wage rate or wider growth impacts. Most of the estimates in Chapters 6 and 7 of the direct and indirect impacts of the Malawi FISP are unique. Detailed consideration of the political, livelihood, and economic background and context of the FISP is also unique, though less detailed examination of the policy and rural livelihood context is not uncommon. This raises critical questions as regards the uniqueness and importance for the Malawian programme of the emergence of 'fertilizer politics', of the particular challenges facing President Bingu wa Mutharika's minority government in the first four years of the programme, and of the nature and extent of the 'low maize productivity trap' in Malawi.

12.4. Targeting and graduation

Targeting is an issue that was given a considerable amount of attention in Chapter 2 as a critical element in input subsidy programmes, with implications for displacement, productivity, economy-wide effects, graduation, programme costs, and distribution of direct beneficiary benefits. It is an important issue across the Malawi FISP and a number of the programmes reviewed in Chapter 3—either because it is being attempted but not very successfully, or because it does not appear to be considered an important issue.

Chapter 10 develops ideas introduced in Chapter 2 with a conceptual framework looking at the links between targeting and programme objectives and distinguishing between area and beneficiary targeting. Both of these face political difficulties, of different kinds, while there are also common practical information and methodological difficulties with beneficiary targeting. It is suggested in the Malawian context that these difficulties are sufficiently serious for there to be a strong case for providing a universal but smaller subsidy to all households. This would also reduce opportunities for diversion and fraud that arise from lack of transparency and accountability in targeting processes.

Discussion of such targeting options, however, also raises complex questions about graduation thresholds and processes. As outlined in Chapter 2, a major criticism of agricultural subsidies has been their tendency to continue long after they have outlived their usefulness in overcoming specific market failures. As a result 'exits' are a core feature of 'smart subsidies'. These tend to focus on subsidies' roles in farmers' learning about input benefits and use, and on development of private sector input suppliers. There is, however, relatively little explicit consideration of other processes by which access to subsidies may lead to recipient households no longer needing them. Chapter 11 therefore extends the concept of 'graduation' from social protection programmes to the multi-scale dynamic processes of structural change promoted by large-scale agricultural input subsidy programmes in poor agrarian economies. A definition of graduation as the removal of access to subsidies without critical livelihood or wider reductions in land, labour, and capital productivity in staple crop production allows, in the Malawi case, the identification of a set of 'graduation conditions'. These in turn allow identification of processes and requirements needed to achieve potential graduation conditions, and design and implementation focus on these processes and requirements. Adopting this approach in programme design and implementation could offer major benefits, not only by its promotion of graduation but through its focus on the core processes by which agricultural input subsidy programmes can stimulate and facilitate core developmental processes of productivity growth, market development, and structural change. Success here could in turn reduce the political pressures that militate against graduation and the withdrawal of subsidies from particular groups of people or areas.

12.5. Sustainability

An important issue that has not been addressed in previous chapters is sustainability. Short-term programmes that have strict time-bounds and exits do not need to be sustainable, although they should promote sustainable change. However, international experience suggests that quick exits from large input subsidy programmes are difficult and rarely achieved. It has been argued in Chapters 2 and 4 and in various parts of our analysis of the Malawi FISP that longer term subsidy implementation is often needed to achieve and embed wider structural changes. In such circumstances a range of different aspects of programme sustainability become important—we consider fiscal, political, and agro-ecological sustainability.

Fiscal sustainability basically means that programmes must be fiscally affordable. Problems of high costs and crowding out of competing and complementary investments are a common concern. Fiscal sustainability therefore requires constant striving for reductions in programme cost without compromising programme outputs and impacts. This may be promoted by a range of measures promoting programme effectiveness and efficiency—for example, better use of private suppliers, control of fraud, improvements in input purchasing and distribution systems, more effective agronomic practices, budgeting and cost control, improved timing of input distribution, better targeting, increased farmer contributions, and judicious complementary investments, with constant adjustments to match changing circumstances. What is affordable depends, of course, upon available funds and competing claims on those funds. Ellis and Maliro (in press), for example, suggest that, based on Malawi's expenditures on subsidies and cash transfers, a mix of subsidy and social transfer programmes could be affordable, with space for strategic choices on combinations of policies providing both safety nets and livelihood opportunities. However, high international fertilizer prices can pose particular problems, as experienced by Malawi in 2008/9. If these costs are not passed on to farmers in higher contributions then this can lead to dramatic increases in programme costs. However, passing such costs onto farmers may make inputs unaffordable, and hence defeat the purpose of the subsidy and undermine farmer confidence in the processes of change that are being promoted.

Continued *political commitment* to programme investment is essential for the resource allocations needed to sustain large-scale agricultural input programmes. Such programmes are politically attractive as fast and highly visible responses to food security problems, with potential opportunities for directing patronage to garner political support. Challenges are faced here in combining often short-term political interests with the longer term technical requirements of effective targeting and cost control to make the most developmental use of invested resources. The analysis of Poulton (2012) may be helpful here, where he suggests that effective agricultural policies result from convergence between technocratic and political interests, but effectiveness may weaken over time with divergence in interests. Such divergence is likely unless governments face quite substantial threats that are best countered by sustained government support from rural electorates.

Finally, we consider the *agro-ecological sustainability* of input subsidy programmes. In the programmes reviewed in Chapter 3 and in the case of Malawi there is a strong emphasis on inorganic fertilizer subsidies. Very low fertilizer use in many African countries, as discussed in Chapter 1, is not sustainable, neither socially in supporting rural populations nor agro-ecologically, as continual cultivation without fertilization leads to soils losing their structure and becoming prone to erosion, while falling yields and growing populations encourage farmers to expand or shift cultivation to forests and steeper slopes—with consequent erosion and loss of trees. Over- or poor application of fertilizers can also have damaging impacts on water courses and on soil health and fauna, while inorganic nitrogenous fertilizer use encourages greenhouse gas emissions from the release of nitrous oxide (N_2O) and from CO_2 emissions from large energy use in its manufacture.

Judicious combinations of organic and inorganic fertilizers in integrated soil fertility management (ISFM) offer the potential for lower cost, economically and ecologically efficient processes for increasing land and labour productivity. Input subsidy programmes that promote this could, in principle, be designed and implemented. Section 11.3 discusses ways that subsidized inorganic fertilization of maize could be combined with legume cultivation to reduce the need for and cost of inorganic fertilizers, increase the efficiency of their use, and promote agricultural and livelihood diversification. Developing and implementing such subsidy approaches presents a great opportunity and challenge.

12.6. Conclusions

We conclude by returning to the fundamental problems with which this book opened: low cereal yields and input use, particularly of fertilizers, as a major cause of continuing poverty in many countries in sub-Saharan Africa. Can large-scale agricultural input subsidies help overcome these problems?

Druilhe and Barreiro-Hurlé (2012) consider that large-scale agricultural input subsidies have become a *de facto* part of agricultural policies in many countries in sub-Saharan Africa. They conclude that most of the programmes they reviewed had been successful in raising agricultural production, but that they were generally poorly designed, poorly implemented, 'highly politicised, very costly, lack any strategy for phasing out, and are unsustainable in the long term'. Despite some smart subsidy innovations in targeting and in support to private sector distribution, 'the new subsidies carry many of the problems of the past' (p. 36). They then discuss possible disadvantages of subsidies (for example, over-reliance on fertilizer subsidies as a 'magic bullet'), but conclude that 'their quick and visible results and direct political payoff' means that they continue to be very attractive to governments. They go on to recommend means for improving implementation, which may be summarized as integrating subsidy programmes with complementary measures promoting wider rural development and social protection, clear and complementary (not multiple and conflicting) objectives, simultaneous measures addressing supply and demand constraints on fertilizer use, and greater use of 'smart' design and implementation features, including appropriate targeting and entitlement systems, market friendliness, exit strategies, and monitoring and evaluation. They recognize, however, that these 'smart design' features make implementation more challenging.

These are in many ways admirable conclusions and recommendations. They may, however, be considered to be both too narrow and unambitious on the one hand and unrealistically over-ambitious on the other. They are too narrow and unambitious because they do not recognize the potential of such programmes to drive and support broad-based economic growth and economic structural change if they are able to fulfil their potential. On the other hand they are unrealistically over-ambitious because they do not address the fundamental paradox of political interests and processes both driving the introduction of large-scale agricultural input subsidies and undermining their better implementation.

Identifying mechanisms and processes which avoid this political paradox is very difficult. One approach that might help, however, could involve raising ambition with greater recognition of the role of agricultural input subsidies and their inclusion in national, rather than sectoral, economic policy. This could carry its own risks and difficulties, diluting responsibility outside the Ministry of Agriculture (normally responsible for such programmes) and reducing commitment to its success. However it could also lead to greater commitment by the Ministries of Finance and of Economic Development to ensuring timely availability of financial resources and to sharper monitoring of implementation, resource use, and outputs that extended beyond the agricultural sector to encompass much wider impacts (as, for example, set out earlier in Figure II.1). Reduced responsibilities for the Ministry of Agriculture would no doubt risk bureaucratic and power difficulties, but if handled well could be used to increase local government and private sector involvement in programme implementation—one means of reducing implementation challenges with 'smart subsidies'. This could free up Ministry of Agriculture staff and other resources for greater involvement in the promotion of efficient input use with, for example, complementary use of organic fertilizers in integrated soil fertility management. Politically, spreading interest in and visibility of the longer term and wider objectives of such programmes across what are often the more powerful government ministries could provide more political and technical interest in improved design and implementation. This might fit well with urban middle-class demands for accountability in the use of likely increasing earnings from hydrocarbons and minerals in many countries in sub-Saharan Africa.

These ideas may or may not work. They would face many challenges: in their genesis and adoption and in their execution. A particular initial challenge is in identifying the circumstances where agricultural input subsidies do and do not have the potential to drive wider economic growth—the necessary conditions summarized in Section 12.2 above. The wider impacts of the Malawi programme, though smaller than one would have hoped, suggest that this potential does exist in Malawi and much stronger wider impacts could be realized with greater programme effectiveness and efficiency and with better integration with complementary policies and investments. This is a prize worth pursuing in Malawi and, though Malawi's situation is in some ways unique, it is likely to be a prize worth pursuing in other sub-Saharan African countries too.

Bibliography

Abdulai, A. 2007. Spatial and vertical price transmission in food staples market chains in Eastern and Southern Africa: What is the evidence? Paper presented at the FAO Trade and Markets Division Workshop on Staple Food Trade and Market Policy Options for Promoting Development in Eastern and Southern Africa, Rome, 1–2 March 2007. Rome: FAO.

Adams, D. W. & Vogel, R. C. 1986. Rural financial markets in low-income countries: Recent controversies and lessons. *World Development*, 14, 477–87.

Africa Progress Panel. 2012. *Africa Progress Report 2012: Jobs, justice and equity: Seizing opportunities in times of global change*. Geneva: Africa Progress Panel.

AGRA. 2008. *Policies for Achieving the African Green Revolution*. Nairobi: AGRA.

Akande, T., Andersson, A., Djurfeldt, G. & Ogundele, F. 2011. Has the Nigerian green revolution veered off track? In: Djurfeldt, G., Aryeetey, E. & Isinika, A. C. (eds) *African Smallholders: Food Crops, Markets and Policy*. Wallingford: CAB International.

Alassan, I. 2012. Supply of subsidised fertiliser delays … Ashanti farmers worried over development. *The Chronicle*. <http://ghanaian-chronicle.com/?p=44142> [accessed 1 December 2012], 1093–112.

Alston, J. M., Chan-Kang, C., Marra, M. C., Pardey, P. G. & Wyatt, T. J. 2000. A meta-analysis of rates of return to agricultural R&D: Ex Pede Herculem? Research Report 113. Washington DC: IFPRI.

Ariga, J. & Jayne, T. S. 2011. Fertilizer in Kenya: Factors driving the increased usage by smallholder farmers. In: Chuhan-Pole, P. & Abngwafo, M. (eds) *Yes Africa Can: Success Stories from a Dynamic Continent*. Washington DC: World Bank.

Ariga, J., Jayne, T. & Nyoro, J. 2008. Trends and patterns in fertilizer use in Kenya, 1997–2007. Working Paper. Nairobi: Egerton University, Tegemeo Institute.

Banful, A. B. 2009. Operational details of the 2008 fertilizer subsidy in Ghana. Preliminary report, draft. Washington DC: IFPRI.

Banful, A. B. 2011. Old problems in the new solutions? Politically motivated allocation of program benefits and the 'new' fertilizer subsidies. *World Development*, 39, 1166–76.

Banful, A. B. & Olayide, O. 2010. Perspectives of selected stakeholder groups in Nigeria on the federal and state fertilizer subsidy programs. Nigeria Strategy Support Program (NSSP) Report 08. Washington DC: IFPRI.

Banful, A. B., Nkonya, E. & Oboh, V. 2010. Constraints to fertilizer use in Nigeria: insights from the agricultural extension service. IFPRI Discussion Paper 01010. Washington DC: IFPRI.

Barrett, C. B. 2008. Smallholder market participation: concepts and evidence from eastern and southern Africa. *Food Policy, 33*, 299–317.

Benin, S., Thurlow, J., Diao, X., McCool, C. & Simtowe, F. 2008. Agricultural growth and investment options for poverty reduction in Malawi. IFPRI Discussion Paper 00794. Washington DC: IFPRI.

Bigsten, A. & Tengstam, S. 2008. Smallholder income diversification in Zambia: the way out of poverty? *Policy Synthesis 30.* Food Security Research Project—Zambia, Ministry of Agriculture & Cooperatives, Agricultural Consultative Forum, Michigan State University.

Binswanger, H. P. & McIntire, J. 1987. Behavioral and material determinants of production relations in land-abundant tropical agriculture. *Economic Development and Cultural Change, 36,* 73–99.

Binswanger, H. P. & Rosenzweig, M. 1986. Behavioural and material determinants of production relations in agriculture. *Journal of Development Studies, 22,* 503–39.

Booth, D., Cammack, D., Harrigan, J., Kanyongolo, E., Mataure, M. & Ngwira, N. 2006. Drivers of change and development in Malawi. Working Paper 261. London: Overseas Development Institute, London; Insititute for Policy Research, Analysis and Dialogue, Blantyre.

Bryceson, D. 1999. Sub-Saharan Africa betwixt and between. Working Paper. Leiden: African Studies Centre, University of Leiden, Netherlands.

Buffie, E. F. & Atolia, M. 2009. Agricultural input subsidies in Malawi: Good, bad, or hard to tell? Working Paper. Rome: FAO.

Bumb, B. L., Johnson, M. E. & Fuentes, P. A. 2011. Policy options for improving regional fertilizer markets in west Africa. IFPRI Discussion Paper 01084. Washington DC: IFPRI.

Burke, W. J., Black, J. R. & Jayne, T. S. 2012. Getting more 'bang for the buck': Diversifying subsidies beyond fertilizer and policy beyond subsidies. FRSP Policy Synthesis 52. Lusaka: FRSP.

Cammack, D., Kelsall, T. & Booth, D. 2010. Developmental patrimonialism? The case of Malawi. Africa Power and Politics Programme, Working Paper 12. London: Overseas Development Institute.

Chibwana, C., Fisher, M., Jumbe, C., Masters, W. & Shively, G. 2010. Measuring the impacts of Malawi's farm input subsidy program. Paper for discussion at BASIS AMA CRSP TC meeting.

Chibwana, C., Fisher, M. & Shively, G. 2012. Cropland allocation effects of agricultural input subsidies in Malawi. *World Development, 40,* 124–33.

Chinsinga, B. 2006. Reclaiming policy space: lessons from Malawi's 2005/2006 fertilizer subsidy programme. Working Paper. Brighton: Future Agricultures Consortium.

Chinsinga, B. 2007. Social protection policy in Malawi: Processes, politics and challenges. Working Paper. Brighton: Future Agricultures Consortium.

Chinsinga, B. 2009. *Participation of Civil Society in the Monitoring of the Agricultural Input Subsidy Programme (AISP). A Monitoring Exercise Carried out for the Consortium of FUM, CISANET and MEJN.* Zomba: Chancellor College, University of Malawi.

Chinsinga, B. 2011. Agro-dealers, subsidies and rural market development in Malawi: A political economy enquiry. FAC Working Paper 031. Brighton: Future Agricultures Consortium.

Chinsinga, B. 2012a. The future of the Farm Input Subsidy Programme (FISP): A political economy investigation. A discussion paper prepared for the Civil Society Network on Agriculture (CISANET). Zomba.

Chinsinga, B. 2012b. The political economy of agricultural policy processes in Malawi: a case study of the fertilizer subsidy programme. Working Paper 39. Brighton: Future Agricultures Consortium.

Chirwa, E. W. 2005. Adoption of fertilizer and hybrid seeds by smallholder maize farmers in southern Malawi. *Development Southern Africa, 22,* 1–12.

Chirwa, E. W. 2009. Sustained increases in food prices: effect and policies in Malawi. Paper presented at the FAO Regional Workshop on Policies for the Effective Management of Food Price Swings in African Countries held on 2–3 April. Kunduchi Hotel, Dar-es-Salaam, Tanzania.

Chirwa, E. W. 2011. Fiscal and monetary policy reforms and growth performance for poverty reduction in Malawi. Paper prepared for UNCEA Economic Development and NEPAD Division. Addis Ababa, Ethiopia.

Chirwa, E. W. & Zakeyo, C. 2006. Malawi. In: Thomas, H. (ed.) *Trade Reforms and Food Security: Country Case Studies and Synthesis.* Rome: FAO.

Chirwa, E. W. & Dorward, A. R. 2012. Private sector participation in the farm input subsidy programme in Malawi, 2006/07–2011/12. Working Paper. London: School of Oriental and African Studies, University of London.

Chirwa, E. W., Kydd, J. G. & Dorward, A. R. 2006. Future scenarios for agriculture in Malawi: Challenges and dilemmas. Paper presented at Future Agricultures Review Workshop, 20–22 March 2006, Institute of Development Studies, University of Sussex, Brighton, UK.

Chirwa, E. W., Kumwenda, I., Jumbe, C., Chilonda, P. & Minde, I. 2008. Agricultural growth and poverty reduction in Malawi: Past performance and recent trends. ReSAKSS-SA Working Paper No. 8. Johanesburg, South Africa: ReSAKSS-SA.

Chirwa, E. W., Dorward, A. & Matita, M. M. 2011a. Conceptualising graduation from agricultural input subsidies in Malawi. FAC Working Paper 029. Brighton: Future Agricultures Consortium.

Chirwa, E. W., Dorward, A. R. & Matita, M. M. 2011b. Initial conditions and changes in commercial fertilizers under the farm input subsidy programme in Malawi: Implications for graduation. FAC Working Paper 030. Brighton: Future Agricultures Consortium.

Chirwa, E. W., Matita, M. M. & Dorward, A. 2011c. Factors influencing access to agricultural input subsidy coupons in Malawi. FAC Working Paper 027. Brighton: Future Agricultures Consortium.

Chirwa, E. W., Matita, M. M., Mvula, P. M. & Dorward, A. R. 2011d. Impacts of the Farm Input Subsidy Programme in Malawi. Paper prepared for Malawi Government/DFID Evaluation of Malawi Farm Input Subsidy Programme. School of Oriental and African Studies, University of London.

Chirwa, E. W., Mvula, P. M., Dorward, A. R. & Matita, M. M. 2011e. Gender and intra-household use of fertilizers in the Malawi Farm Input Subsidy Programme. FAC Working Paper 028. Brighton: Future Agricultures Consortium.

Chirwa, E. W., Dorward, A. R. & Vigneri, M. 2012. Seasonality and poverty: The 2004/05 Malawi Integrated Household Survey. In: Sabates-Wheeler, R. & Devereux, S. (eds) *Seasonality, Rural Livelihoods and Development.* London: Earthscan.

Christiaensen, L., Demery, L. & Kuhl, J. 2011. The (evolving) role of agriculture in poverty reduction—An empirical perspective. *Journal of Development Economics, 96,* 239–54.

Civil Society for Poverty Reduction 2005. *Targeting Small Scale Farmers in the Implementation of Zambia's Poverty Reduction Strategy Paper (PRSP): An Assessment of the Implementation and Effectiveness of the Fertilizer Support Programme.* Lusaka: Civil Society for Poverty Reduction (CSPR).

Collier, P. & Dercon, S. 2009. African agriculture in 50 years: smallholders in a rapidly changing world? Expert Meeting on How to Feed the World in 2050. Rome: FAO.

Covarrubias, K., Davis, B. & Winters, P. 2012. From protection to production: productive impacts of the Malawi Social Cash Transfer scheme. *Journal of Development Effectiveness, 4,* 50–77.

Crawford, E. W., Jayne, T. S. & Kelly, V. A. 2006. Alternative approaches for promoting fertilizer use in Africa. Agriculture and Rural Development Discussion Paper 22. Washington, DC: World Bank.

Datt, G. & Ravallion, M. 1996. Why have some Indian states done better than others at reducing rural poverty? Policy Research Working Paper Series 1594.

Davies, S. & Davey, J. 2008. A regional multiplier approach to estimating the impact of cash transfers on the market: The case of cash transfers in rural Malawi. *Development Policy Review, 26,* 91–111.

de Janvry, A. & Sadoulet, E. 2010. Agricultural growth and poverty reduction: Additional evidence. *The World Bank Research Observer, 25,* 1–20.

de Onis, M., Onyango, A.W., Borghi, E., Garza, C., Yang, H. & WHO Multicentre Growth Reference Study Group. 2006. Comparison of the World Health Organization (WHO) Child Growth Standards and the National Center for Health Statistics/WHO international growth reference: implications for child health programmes. *Public Health and Nutrition, 9,* 942–47.

Delgado, L. C., Hopkins, J. & Kelly, V.A. 1998. Agricultural growth linkages in Sub-Saharan Africa. IFPRI Research Report. Washington DC: IFPRI.

Denning, G., Kabambe, P., Sanchez, P., Malik, A., Flor, R., Harawa, R., Nkhoma, P., Zamba, C., Banda, C., Magombo, C., Keating, K., Wangila, J. & Sachs, J. 2009. Input subsidies to improve smallholdermaize productivity in Malawi: Toward an African green revolution. *PLoS Biology, 7,* 2–10.

Department for Work and Pensions. 2012. *Fraud and Error in the Benefit System: Preliminary 2011/12 Estimates (Great Britain) Revised Edition.* London: Department for Work and Pensions.

Devereux, S. 2006. Cash transfers and social protection. Paper prepared for the regional workshop on 'Cash transfer activities in southern Africa', co-hosted by the Southern African Regional Poverty Network (SARPN), Regional Hunger and Vulnerability Programme (RHVP) and Oxfam, GB, Johannesburg, South Africa, 9–10 October 2006.

Devereux, S. 2010. Dependency and graduation. Frontiers of Social Protection Brief No. 5, February, 2010. Johannesburg: Regional Hunger and Vulnerability Programme.

Diao, X., Dorosh, P. & Rahman, S. M. 2003. *Market Opportunities for African Agriculture: An Examination of Demand-side Constraints on Agricultural Growth.* Washington DC: IFPRI.

Djurfeldt, G., Holmen, H., Jirstrom, M. & Larsson, R. (eds) 2005. *The African Food Crisis: Lessons from the Asian Green Revolution*. Wallingford: CAB International Publishing.

Dorward, A. R. 1996. Modelling diversity, change and uncertainty in peasant agriculture in northern Malawi. *Agricultural Systems, 51*, 469–86.

Dorward, A. R. 2006. Markets and pro-poor agricultural growth: insights from livelihood and informal rural economy models in Malawi. *Agricultural Economics, 35*, 157–69.

Dorward, A. R. 2007. Impacts of the Agricultural Input Subsidy Programme in Malawi: Insights from rural livelihood modeling. Draft Working Paper. London: SOAS, University of London.

Dorward, A. R. 2009a. Integrating contested aspirations, processes and policy: development as hanging in, stepping up and stepping out. *Development Policy Review, 27*, 131–46.

Dorward, A. R. 2009b. Rethinking agricultural input subsidy programmes in developing countries. In: Elbehri, A. & Sarris, A. (eds) *Non-Distorting Farm Support To Enhance Global Food Production*. Rome: FAO.

Dorward, A. R. 2011. Getting real about food prices. *Development Policy Review, 29*, 647–64.

Dorward, A. R. 2013. Agricultural labour productivity and food prices: sustainable development impacts and indicators. *Food Policy, 39*, 40–50.

Dorward, A. R. 2012a. Conceptualising the effects of seasonal financial market failures and credit rationing in applied rural household models. *Quarterly Journal of International Agriculture, 51*, 113–33.

Dorward, A. R. 2012b. The short and medium term impacts of rises in staple food prices. *Food Security, 4*, 633–45.

Dorward, A. R. & Kydd, J. G. 2004. The Malawi 2002 food crisis: The rural development challenge. *Journal of Modern Africa Studies, 42*, 343–61.

Dorward, A. R. & Kydd, J. G. 2005. Starter pack in rural development strategies. In: Levy, S. (ed.) *Starter Packs: A Strategy to Fight Hunger in Developing and Transition Countries? Lessons from the Malawi Experience, 1998–2003*. Wallingford: CAB International.

Dorward, A. R. & Chirwa, E. W. 2009. *The Agricultural Input Subsidy Programme 2005 to 2008: Achievements and Challenges*. London: SOAS, University of London.

Dorward, A. R. & Chirwa, E. W. 2010a. *Evaluation of the 2008/9 Agricultural Input Subsidy Programme, Malawi: Maize Production and Market Impacts*. London: SOAS, University of London.

Dorward, A. R. & Chirwa, E. W. 2010b. A review of methods for estimating yield and production impacts. Paper prepared for Malawi Government/DFID Evaluation of Malawi Farm Input Subsidy Programme. SOAS, University of London.

Dorward, A. R. & Chirwa, E. W. 2011a. *Evaluation of the 2010/11 Farm Input Subsidy Programme, Malawi: Report on Programme Implementation*. London: SOAS, University of London.

Dorward, A. R. & Chirwa, E. W. 2011b. Improving benefit cost analysis for Malawi's Farm Input Subsidy Programme, 2006/7 to 2010/11. Paper prepared for Malawi

Government/DFID Evaluation of Malawi Farm Input Subsidy Programme. London: SOAS, University of London.

Dorward, A. R. & Chirwa, E. W. 2011c. The Malawi Agricultural Input Subsidy Programme: 2005–6 to 2008–9. *International Journal of Agricultural Sustainability, 9*, 232–47.

Dorward, A. R. & Chirwa, E. W. 2012a. *Evaluation of the 2011/12 Farm Input Subsidy Programme, Malawi: Report on Programme Implementation and Benefit Cost Analysis.* London: SOAS, University of London.

Dorward, A. R. & Chirwa, E. W. 2012b. Informal rural economy modelling of programme impacts, 2005/6 to 2010/11. Discussion Paper. Evaluation of the 2010/11 Farm Input Subsidy Programme, Malawi. London: SOAS, University of London.

Dorward, A. R. & Chirwa, E. W. 2012c. Targeting. Discussion Paper Prepared for Malawi Government/DFID Evaluation of the 2011/12 Malawi Farm Input Subsidy Programme. London: SOAS, University of London.

Dorward, A. R., Kydd, J. G. & Poulton, C. D. 1998. Conclusions: NIE, policy debates and the research agenda. In: Dorward, A. R., Kydd, J. G. & Poulton, C. D. (eds) *Smallholder Cash Crop Production under Market Liberalisation: A New Institutional Economics Perspective.* Wallingford: CAB International.

Dorward, A. R., Moyo, S., Coetzee, G., Kydd, J. & Poulton, C. 2001. Seasonal finance for staple crop production: problems and potential for rural livelihoods in sub-Saharan Africa. Working Paper. DFID Policy Research Programme project 'Diverse income sources and seasonal finance for smallholder agriculture: applying a livelihoods approach in South Africa'. Wye, UK: Imperial College London.

Dorward, A. R., Poole, N. D., Morrison, J. A., Kydd, J. G. & Urey, I. 2002. Critical linkages: Livelihoods, markets and institutions. Paper presented at the seminar on 'Supporting Institutions, Evolving Livelihoods', Bradford Centre for International Development, University of Bradford 29–30 May 2002.

Dorward, A. R., Poole, N. D., Morrison, J. A., Kydd, J. G. & Urey, I. 2003. Markets, institutions and technology: missing links in livelihoods analysis. *Development Policy Review, 21,* 319–32.

Dorward, A. R., Kydd, J. G., Morrison, J. A. & Urey, I. 2004a. A policy agenda for pro-poor agricultural growth. *World Development, 32,* 73–89.

Dorward, A. R., Wobst, P., Lofgren, H., Tchale, H. & Morrison, J. A. 2004b. *Modelling Pro-Poor Agricultural Growth Strategies in Malawi: Lessons for Policy and Analysis.* Wye, UK: Centre for Development and Poverty Reduction, Department of Agricultural Sciences, Imperial College London.

Dorward, A. R., Kydd, J. G., Morrison, J. A. & Poulton, C. D. 2005a. Institutions, markets and economic coordination: Linking development policy to theory and praxis. *Development and Change, 36,* 1–25.

Dorward, A. R., Kydd, J. G. & Poulton, C. D. 2005b. Beyond liberalisation: 'Developmental coordination' policies for African smallholder agriculture. *IDS Bulletin, 36,* 80–5.

Dorward, A. R., Sabates Wheeler, R., MacAuslan, I., Penrose Buckley, C., Kydd, J. G. & Chirwa, E. W. 2006. Promoting agriculture for social protection or social protection for agriculture: Policy and research issues. Future Agricultures Consortium Workshop, Brighton, March 2006.

Dorward, A. R., Chirwa, E. W. & Poulton, C. 2008. Improving access to input and output markets. Paper presented at Southern Africa Regional Conference on Agriculture: 'Agriculture-led Development for Southern Africa: Strategic Investment Priorities for Halving Hunger and Poverty by 2015', Gaborone, Botswana, 8–9 December 2008.

Dorward, A. R., Kydd, J. G., Poulton, C. D. & Bezemer, D. 2009. Coordination risk and cost impacts on economic development in poor rural areas. *Journal of Development Studies, 45*, 1–20.

Dorward, A. R., Chirwa, E. W. & Slater, R. 2010a. *Evaluation of the 2008/9 Agricultural Input Subsidy Programme, Malawi: Report on Programme Impact.* London: SOAS, University of London.

Dorward, A. R., Chirwa, E. W. & Slater, R. 2010b. *Evaluation of the 2008/9 Agricultural Input Subsidy Programme, Malawi: Report on Programme Implementation.* London: SOAS, University of London.

Doss, C. R. & Morris, M. L. 2001. How does gender affect the adoption of agricultural innovations? The case of improved maize technology in Ghana. *Agricultural Economics, 25*, 27–39.

Douilleta, M., Pauw, K. & Thurlow, J. 2012. *A 2007 Social Accounting Matrix for Malawi.* Washington DC: IFPRI.

Druilhe, Z. & Barreiro-Hurlé, J. 2012. Fertilizer subsidies in sub-Saharan Africa. ESA Working Paper No. 12-04. Rome: FAO.

Duflo, E., Kremer, M. & Robinson, J. 2011. Nudging farmers to use fertilizer: Theory and experimental evidence from Kenya. *American Economic Review, 101*, 2350–90.

Dugger, C. W. 2007. Ending famine, simply by ignoring the experts. *New York Times,* December 2, p. 1.

Economist. 2008. Malawi: Can it feed itself? An expensive fertiliser subsidy delivers a bumper harvest—but at what cost? 1 May.

Economist Intelligence Unit. 2008. *Lifting African and Asian Farmers out of Poverty: Assessing the Investment Needs. A Custom Research Project for the Bill and Melinda Gates Foundation.* New York: The Economist Intelligence Unit.

Ellis, F. 1992. *Agricultural Policies in Developing Countries.* Cambridge: Cambridge University Press.

Ellis, F. 1998. Livelihood diversification and sustainable rural livelihoods. In: Carney, D. (ed.) *Sustainable Livelihoods: What Contribution Can we Make?* London: Department for International Development (DFID).

Ellis, F. 2000. *Rural Livelihoods and Diversity in Developing Countries.* Oxford: Oxford University Press.

Ellis, F. 2007. Food Security Pack, Zambia. REBA Case Study Brief No 10. Johannesburg: RVHP.

Ellis, F. & Maliro, D. in press. Fertilizer subsidies and social cash transfers as complementary or competing instruments for reducing vulnerability to hunger: Illustrated by Malawi. *Development Policy Review.*

Fan, S., Thorat, S. & Rao, N. 2003. Investment, subsidies, and pro-poor growth in rural India. Draft report, Institutions and Economic Policies for Pro-Poor Agricultural Growth. Washington DC: IFPRI.

Fan, S., Gulati, A. & Thorat, S. 2007. Investment, subsidies, and pro-poor growth in rural India. IFPRI Discussion Paper 716. Washington DC: IFPRI.

FAO 2012. FAOSTAT (production, resources). Rome: FAO.

Farmers Union of Malawi 2011. *Promoting the Participation of Civil Society in the Management of the Farm Input Subsidy Programme (FISP)*. Lilongwe: Farmers Union of Malawi.

Feder, G., Just, R. & Zilberman, D. 1985. Adoption of agricultural innovations in developing countries: A survey. *Economic Development and Cultural Change, 33,* 255–98.

FEWS NET. 2007. *Malawi Food Security Update November 2007*. Lilongwe: FEWS NET.

FEWS NET. 2008. *Malawi Food Security Outlook April to September 2008*. Lilongwe: FEWS NET.

FEWS NET. 2011. *Malawi Food Security Outlook Update September 2011*. Lilongwe: FEWS NET.

FEWS NET. 2012. *Malawi Food Security Outlook August 2012 to January 2013*. Lilongwe: FEWS NET.

Filipski, M. & Taylor, J. E. 2011. *A Simulation Impact Evaluation of Rural Income Transfers in Malawi and Ghana*. University of California, Davis.

Gale, F., Lohmar, B. & Tuan, F. 2005. China's new farm subsidies. *Electronic Outlook Report from the Economic Research Service*. Washington, DC.

Ghana News Agency 2012. Farmers sensitised on new fertilizer subsidy programme. 21 July.

Govereh, J., Malawo, E., Lungu, T., Jayne, T., Chinyama, K. & Chilonda, P. 2009. Trends and spatial distribution of public agricultural spending in Zambia: Implications for agricultural productivity growth. ReSAKSS Working Paper No. 26. Pretoria: Regional Strategic Analysis and Knowledge Support System (ReSAKSS).

Government of Malawi. 2011. A *Medium Term Plan for the Farm Inputs Subsidy Programme (2011–2016)*. Lilongwe: Ministry of Agriculture and Food Security.

Government of Malawi & World Bank. 2006. *Malawi Poverty and Vulnerability Assessment. Investing in Our Future*. Lilongwe: Ministry of Economic Planning and Development.

Gregory, I. 2006. The role of input vouchers in pro-poor growth. Background Paper Prepared for the African Fertilizer Summit, Abuja, Nigeria, 9–13 June. Muscle Shoals, Alabama: IFDC.

Gulati, A. & Pursell, G. 2008. Distortions to agricultural incentives in India and other South Asia. Agricultural Distortions Working Paper—World Bank. Washington, DC: World Bank.

Haantuba, H., Wamalume, M. & Bwalya, R. 2011. The fertilizer support programme and the Millennium development challenge in Zambia: Is government a problem solution? In: Djurfeldt, G., Aryeetey, E. & Isinika, A. C. (eds) *African Smallholders: Food Crops, Markets and Policy*. Wallingford: CAB International.

Haggblade, S., Hazell, P. & Brown, J. 1989. Farm non-farm linkages in rural sub-Saharan Africa. *World Development, 17,* 1173–1201.

Haggblade, S., Hazell, P. & Dorosh, P. 2007a. Sectoral growth linkages between agriculture and the rural non-farm economy. In: Haggblade, S., Hazell, P. & Reardon, T. (eds) *Transforming the Rural Non-Farm Economy*. Baltimore: Johns Hopkins University Press.

Haggblade, S., Hazell, P. B. R. & Reardon, T. (eds) 2007b. *Transforming the Rural Nonfarm Economy: Opportunities and Threats in the Developing World*. Baltimore: Johns Hopkins University Press.

Harrigan, J. 2003. U-turns and full circles: Two decades of agricultural reform in Malawi 1981–2000. *World Development, 31*, 847–63.

Hazell, P. 2012. Options for African agriculture in an era of high food and energy prices. Elmhirst Lecture, 27th International Conference of Agricultural Economists, Foz do Iguaçu, Brazil, August.

Hazell, P. & Rosegrant, M. 2000. *Rural Asia: Beyond the Green Revolution*. Hong Kong: OUP/ADB.

Hazell, P., Poulton, C., Wiggins, S. & Dorward, A. R. 2010. The future of small farms: Trajectories and policy priorities. *World Development, 38*, 1349–61.

Headey, D. 2011a. Turning economic growth into nutrition-sensitive growth. Background paper for the conference 'Leveraging agriculture for improving nutrition and health', New Delhi. Washington DC: IFPRI.

Headey, D. 2011b. Was the global food crisis really a crisis? Simulations versus self-reporting. IFPRI Discussion Paper 01087. Washington DC: IFPRI.

Hoff, K. 2001. Beyond Rosenstein-Rodan: The modern theory of underdevelopment traps. In: Pleskovic, B. & Stern, N. (eds) *World Bank Economic Conference 2000*. Washington DC: World Bank.

Holden, S. & Lunduka, R. 2010a. Impacts of the fertilizer subsidy programme in Malawi: targeting, household perceptions and preferences. Noragric Report. Ås, Norway.

Holden, S. & Lunduka, R. 2010b. The political economy of input subsidies in Malawi: Targeting efficiency and household perceptions. Draft for comment. Ås, Norway: School of Economics and Business, Norwegian University of Life Sciences.

Holden, S. & Lunduka, R. 2010c. Too poor to be efficient? Impacts of the targeted fertilizer subsidy programme in Malawi on farm plot level input use, crop choice and land productivity. Noragric Report. Ås, Norway.

Holden, S. & Tostensen, A. 2011. *Appraisal of the Malawi Medium Term Plan for the Farm Inputs Subsidy Programme (FISP-MTP) (2011–2016)*. Lilongwe: FISP-MTP.

Holden, S. & Lunduka, H. 2012a. Who benefits from Malawi's Targeted Farm Input Subsidy Program? Forum for Development Studies, DOI:10.1080/08039410.2012.6 88858, 1–25.

Holden, S. & Lunduka, R. 2012b. Do fertilizer subsidies crowd out organic manures? The case of Malawi. *Agricultural Economics, 43*, 303–14.

Houssou, N. & Zeller, M. 2011. To target or not to target? The costs, benefits, and impacts of indicator-based targeting. *Food Policy, 36*, 626–36.

Imperial College, Wadonda Consult, Overseas Development Institute & Michigan State University 2007. Evaluation of the 2006/7 Agricultural Input Supply Programme, Malawi: Interim Report. Imperial College London, March.

Jayne, T. S., Yamano, T., Weber, M., Tschirley, D., Benfica, R., Neve, D., Chapoto, A. & Zulu, B. 2001. Smallholder income and land distribution in Africa: Implications for poverty reduction strategies. MSU International Development Paper 24.

Jayne, T. S., Govereh, J., Xu, Z., Ariga, J. & Mghenyi, E. 2006. Factors affecting small farmers' use of improved maize technologies: evidence from Kenya and Zambia. Paper presented at the Symposium on Seed-Fertilizer Technology, Cereal Productivity and Pro-Poor Growth in Africa: Time for New Thinking? International Association of Agricultural Economics Tri-Annual Meetings, Gold Coast, Australia, 12–18 August.

Jayne, T. S., Govereh, J., Zu, X. 2007. Fertilizer promotion in Zambia: Implications for strategies to raise smallholder productivity. Seminar at World Bank, Washington DC, 7 November 2007.

Jayne, T. S., Minot, N. & Rashid, S. 2009. Fertilizer marketing in eastern and southern Africa. Background document for Seminar: 'Fertilizer Policy Symposium', Livingstone, 15–19 June.

Jayne, T. S., Sitko, N., Ricker-Gilbert, J. & Mangisoni, J. 2010. *Malawi's Maize Marketing System*. Michigan State University.

Jayne, T. S., Mason, N. M., Burke, W. J., Shipekesa, A., Chapoto, A. & Kabaghe, C. 2011. Mountains of maize, persistent poverty. Food Security Research Project— Zambia Policy Brief 48. Lusaka: Ministry of Agriculture & Cooperatives, Agricultural Consultative Forum, Michigan State University.

JiKun, H., XiaoBing, W., HuaYong, Z., ZhuRong, H. & Rozelle, S. 2011. Subsidies and distortions in China's agriculture: evidence from producer-level data. *Australian Journal of Agricultural and Resource Economics*, 55, 53–71.

Jorgensen, S. L. & Loudjeva, Z. 2005. A poverty and social impact analysis of three reforms in Zambia: land, fertilizer, and infrastructure. Poverty and Social Impact Analysis (PSIA), Social Development Papers 49. Washington DC: World Bank.

Kelly, V., Boughton, D. & Lenski, N. 2010. Malawi Agricultural Inputs Subsidy Program evaluation of the 2007/08 and 2008/09: Input supply sector analysis. Report prepared for the Ministry of Agriculture and Food Security and DFID. Lilongwe.

Kelly, V., Crawford, E. & Ricker-Gilbert, J. 2011. The new generation of African fertiliser subsidies: panacea or Pandora's box? Policy Synthesis 87. East Lansing, Michigan: Michigan State University/United States Agency for International Development Food Security III Cooperative Agreement (GDGA-00- 000021-00).

Kiger, B. & Adodo, K. 2010. Getting fertiliser into farmers' hands. Inter-Reseaux Development Rural. *Grain de Sel*, 51, July–September.

Kodamaya, S. 2011. *Agricultural Policies and Food Security of Smallholder Farmers in Zambia*. *African Study Monographs*, Suppl 42, 19–39. Kyoto: The Research Committee for African Area Studies, Kyoto University.

Krausova, M. & Banful, A. B. 2010. Overview of the agricultural input sector in Ghana. IFPRI Discussion Paper 01024. Washington DC: IFPR.

Kydd, J. G. & Christiansen, R. 1982. Structural change in Malawi since independence: consequences of a development strategy based on large scale agriculture. *World Development*, 10, 355–75.

Kydd, J. G. & Dorward, A. R. 2004. Implications of market and coordination failures for rural development in least developed countries. *Journal of International Development*, 16, 951–70.

Levy, S. (ed.) 2005. *Starter Packs: A Strategy to Fight Hunger in Developing and Transition Countries? Lessons from the Malawi Experience, 1998–2003*. Wallingford: CAB International.

Liverpool-Tasie, S. 2012. Targeted subsidies and private market participation: An assessment of fertilizer demand in Nigeria. IFPRI Discussion Paper 01194. Washington DC: IFPRI.

Liverpool-Tasie, S., Banful, A. B. & Olaniyan, B. 2010a. Assessment of the 2009 fertilizer voucher program in Kano and Taraba, Nigeria. Nigeria Strategy Support Program (NSSP) Working Paper No. 0017. Washington DC: IFPRI.

Liverpool-Tasie, S., Olaniyan, B., Salau, S. & Sackey, J. 2010b. A review of fertilizer policy issues in Nigeria. NSSP Working Paper No. 0019. Abuja: Nigeria Strategy Support Program (NSSP), IFPRI.

Logistics Unit. 2008. *Final Report: Implementation of Agricultural Inputs Subsidy Programme 2007/08*. Lilongwe: Logistics Unit.

Logistics Unit. 2009. *Final Report: Implementation of Agricultural Inputs Subsidy Programme 2008/09*. Lilongwe: Logistics Unit.

Logistics Unit. 2010. *Final Report: Implementation of Agricultural Inputs Subsidy Programme 2009/10*. Lilongwe: Logistics Unit

Logistics Unit. 2011. *Final Report: Implementation of Agricultural Inputs Subsidy Programme 2010/11*. Lilongwe: Logistics Unit.

Logistics Unit. 2012. *Final Report: Implementation of Agricultural Inputs Subsidy Programme 2011/12*. Lilongwe: Logistics Unit.

Lunduka, H., Fischer, M. & Snapp, S. 2012. Could farmer interest in a diversity of seed attributes explain adoption plateaus for modern maize varieties in Malawi? *Food Policy*, 37, 504–10.

Maize Productivity Task Force. 1997. The 1995/6 fertiliser verificiation trial—Malawi: Economic analysis of results for policy discussion. Unpublished mimeo, report by Action Group 1. Lilongwe: Ministry of Agriculture and Livestock Development, Government of Malawi.

Makumba, W. I., Matumba, L., Liwimbi, L. & Chisama, B. 2012. Improved nutrient management for maize production in Malawi in smallholder farms (mimeo). Chitedze: Department of Agricultural Research, Ministry of Agriculture and Food Security.

Malawi National Vulnerability Assessment Committee. 2005. Malawi baseline livelihood profiles Version 1. Lilongwe: MVAC.

Mason, N. M. 2011. Marketing boards, fertilizer subsidies, prices, and smallholder behavior: Modeling and policy implications for Zambia. PhD, Michigan State University.

Mason, N. M. & Ricker-Gilbert, J. 2012. Disrupting demand for commercial seed: Input subsidies in Malawi and Zambia. Working Paper No. 63. Lusaka: Indaba Agricultural Policy Research Institute (IAPRI).

Mason, N. M., Burke, W. J., Shipekesa, A. & Jayne, T. S. 2011. The 2011 surplus in smallholder maize production in Zambia: Drivers, beneficiaries, and implications for agricultural and poverty reduction policies. Food Security Research Project Working Paper No. 58. Lusaka: FSRP.

Mathiassen, A. 2006. A statistical model for simple, fast and reliable measurement of poverty. A revised version of DP 415. Research Department of Statistics Norway.

Mellor, J. W. 2000. *Faster More Equitable Growth: The Relation Between Growth in Agriculture and Poverty Reduction*. Boston, MA: Harvard University CAER.

Meyer, R. L. 2008. Evaluating the efficiency of inter-regional trade and storage in Malawi maize markets. Report for the World Bank. East Lansing, MI: Michigan State University.

Minde, I., Jayne, T. S., Ariga, J., Govereh, J. & Crawford, E. 2008. Fertilizer subsidies and sustainable agricultural growth in Africa: Current issues and empirical evidence from Malawi, Zambia, and Kenya. Paper prepared for the Regional Strategic Agricultural

Knowledge Support System (Re-SAKSS) for Southern Africa, draft June 2008. Food Security Group, Michigan State University.

Ministry of Agriculture and Cooperatives. 2011. *Farmer Input Support Programme (FISP): Implementation Manual, 2011/2012 Agricultural Season.* Lusaka: Ministry of Agriculture and Cooperatives.

Ministry of Agriculture and Food Security. 2007. *National Crop Estimates 2006/7.* Lilongwe: Ministry of Agriculture and Food Security.

Ministry of Agriculture and Food Security. 2008. *The 2008/2009 Farm Input Subsidy Programme: Implementation Guidelines.* Lilongwe: Ministry of Agriculture and Food Security.

Ministry of Agriculture and Food Security. 2010. *National Crop Estimates 2009/10.* Lilongwe: Ministry of Agriculture and Food Security.

Ministry of Agriculture Food Security and Cooperatives. 2012. Accelerated Food Security Project (Credit 4619-TA): Progress Report August 2009–June 2012. Dar es Salaam: Government of Tanzania.

Minot, N. 2009. Fertilizer policy and use in Tanzania (presentation). Fertilizer Policy Symposium of the COMESA African Agricultural Markets Programme (AAMP). Livingstone, Zambia.

Minot, N. & Benson, T. 2009. Fertilizer subsidies in Africa. IFPRI—Issue Brief. Washington DC.

Mogues, T., Morris, M., Freinkman, L., Adubi, A. & Ehui, S. 2008. *Nigeria Agriculture Public Expenditure Review.* Abuja: IFPRI.

Morris, M., Kelly, V. A., Kopicki, R. & Byerlee, D. 2007. *Fertilizer Use in African Agriculture.* Washington DC: World Bank.

Morris, M., Ronchi, L. & Rohrbach, D. 2009. Building sustainable fertilizer markets in Africa. In: International Livestock Research Institute (ILRI) (ed.) *Towards Priority Actions for Market Development for African Farmers.* Nairobi: ILRI.

Muleba, M. 2008. Fertilizer support is a subsidy disaster. MS ActionAid Denmark. *MS Zambia Newsletter*, October.

Munthali, M. W. 2007. Integrated soil fertility management technologies: A counteract to existing milestone in obtaining achievable economical crop yields in cultivated lands of poor smallholder farmers in Malawi. In: Bationo, A., Waswa, B., Kihara, J. & Kimetu, J. (eds) *Advances in Integrated Soil Fertility Management in sub-Saharan Africa: Challenges and Opportunities.* Netherlands: Springer.

Mvula, P. M., Chirwa, E. W., Matita, M. M. & Dorward, A. R. 2011. Challenges of access to farm input subsidy by vulnerable groups in Malawi. Paper prepared for Malawi Government/DFID Evaluation of Malawi Farm Input Subsidy Programme. School of Oriental and African Studies, University of London.

Nagy, J. G. & Edun, O. 2002. Assessment of Nigerian Government Fertilizer Policy and Suggested Alternative Market-Friendly Policies. Cited by Liverpool-Tasie et al. (2010).

Nakhumwa. T. O. 2006. Rapid evaluation of the 2005 fertiliser subsidy programme in Malawi. CISANET Policy Paper No 10. Lilongwe: CISANET.

National Statistical Office. 2005a. *Integrated Household Survey 2004–2005.* Zomba: National Statistical Office.

National Statistical Office. 2005b. *Welfare Monitoring Survey 2005.* Zomba: National Statistical Office.

National Statistical Office. 2007. *Welfare Monitoring Survey 2006*. Zomba: National Statistical Office.

National Statistical Office. 2008a. *2008 Population and Housing Census Main Report*. Zomba: National Statistical Office.

National Statistical Office. 2008b. *Welfare Monitoring Survey 2007*. Zomba: National Statistical Office.

National Statistical Office. 2009. *Welfare Monitoring Survey 2008*. Zomba: National Statistical Office.

National Statistical Office. 2010a. National Census of Agriculture and Livestock (NACAL).

National Statistical Office. 2010b. *Welfare Monitoring Survey 2009*. Zomba: National Statistical Office.

National Statistical Office. 2011. *Statistical Yearbook 2010*. Zomba, Malawi: National Statistical Office.

National Statistical Office. 2012. *Integrated Household Surevy 2010–11: Household Socio Economic Characteristics Report*. Zomba: National Statistical Office.

National Statistical Office & ICF Macro. 2011. *Malawi: Demographic and Health Survey 2010*. Zomba, Malawi and Calverton, Maryland, USA: National Statistical Office and ICF Macro.

National Statistical Office & ORC Macro. 2001. *Malawi: Demographic and Health Survey 2000*. Zomba, Malawi and Calverton, Maryland, USA: National Statistical Office and ORC Macro.

Newberry, D. & Stiglitz, J. E. 1981. *The Theory of Commodity Price Stabilization: A Study in the Economics of Risk*. Oxford: Clarendon Press.

Olson, M. 1993. Dictatorship, democracy, and development. *The American Political Science Review, 87*, 567–76.

Pan, L. & Christiaensen, L. 2012. Who is vouching for the input voucher? Decentralized targeting and elite capture in Tanzania. *World Development, 40*, 1619–33.

Patel, S. 2011. *Tanzania National Agricultural Input Voucher Scheme (NAIVS) Impact Evaluation: Baseline Report*. Washington DC: World Bank, Development Impact Evaluation Initiative (DIME), Development Economics—Operations and Strategy (DECOS).

Pohl, G. & Mihaljek, D. 1992. Project evaluation and uncertainty in practice: A statistical analysis of rate-of-return divergences of 1,015 World Bank projects. *World Bank Economic Review, 6*, 255–77.

Poulton, C. D. 2012. Democratisation and the political economy of agricultural policy in Africa. Working Paper 43. Brighton: Future Agricultures Consortium.

Poulton, C. D. & Dorward, A. R. 2008. Getting agricultural moving: Role of the state in increasing staple food crop productivity with special reference to coordination, input subsidies, credit and price stabilisation. Paper prepared for AGRA Policy Workshop, Nairobi, Kenya, 23–25 June 2008.

Poulton, C. D., Dorward, A. R. & Kydd, J. G. 2010. The future of small farms: New directions for services, institutions and intermediation. *World Development, 38*, 1413–28.

Prowse, M. 2007. Burley tobacco, food security and vulnerability: The changing nature of rural livelihoods in the central region of Malawi. PhD, University of Manchester, UK.

Reardon, T. 1998. Rural non-farm income in developing countries. In: FAO (ed.) *The State of Food and Agriculture 1998*. Rome: FAO.

Reserve Bank of Malawi 2012. *Financial and Economic Review, April–June 2012*. Lilongwe: Reserve Bank of Malawi.

Ricker-Gilbert, J. 2011. Household-level impacts of fertilizer subsidies in Malawi. PhD, Michigan State University.

Ricker-Gilbert, J. & Jayne, T. 2010a. The impact of fertilizer subsidies on displacement and total fertilizer use. Powerpoint presentation. Lilongwe.

Ricker-Gilbert, J. & Jayne, T. S. 2010b. What are the enduring effects of fertilizer subsidy programs on recipient farm households? Evidence from Malawi. Paper presented at the African Association of Agricultural Economists Meeting. 19–23 September 2010; Cape Town, South Africa (powerpoint).

Ricker-Gilbert, J. & Jayne, T. S. 2011. What are the enduring effects of fertilizer subsidy programs on recipient farm households? Evidence from Malawi. Staff Paper—Department of Agricultural, Food and Resource Economics, Michigan State University.

Ricker-Gilbert, J. & Jayne, T. S. 2012. Addressing the 'wicked problem' of input subsidy programs in Africa: A review. Paper presented at the American Agricutural Economists Association, Seattle, August 2012.

Ricker-Gilbert, J., Jayne, T. S. & Black J.R. 2009. Does subsidizing fertilizer increase yields? Evidence from Malawi. Paper presented at the Agricultural & Applied Economics Association 2009 AAEA & ACCI Joint Annual Meeting, Milwaukee, Wisconsin, 26–29 July.

Ricker-Gilbert, J., Jayne, T. S. & Chirwa, E. 2010. Subsidies and crowding out: A double hurdle model of fertilizer demand in Malawi. *American Journal of Agricultural Economics, 93*, 26–42.

Rodenstein-Rodan, P. 1943. Problems of iIndustrialisation of Eastern and Southeastern Europe. *Economic Journal, 53*, 202–11.

Sadoulet, E. & de Janvry, A. 1995. *Quantitative Development Policy Analysis*. Baltimore: Johns Hopkins University Press.

Sahley, C., Groelsma, R., Marchione, T. & Nelson, D. 2005. *The Governance Dimension of Food Security in Malawi*. Lilongwe: USAID, Malawi.

Sánchez, P., Izac, A. M., Buresh, R., Shepherd, K., Soule, M., Mokwunye, U., Palm, C., Woomer, P. & Nderitu, C. 1997. Soil fertility replenishment in Africa as an investment in natural resource capital. In: Buresh, R. J., Sánchez, P. A. & Calhoun, F. (eds) *Replenishing Soil Fertility in Africa*. Madison, WI: Soil Science Society of America.

School of Oriental and African Studies, Wadonda Consult, Overseas Development Institute & Michigan State University. 2008. Evaluation of the 2006/7 Agricultural Input Supply Programme, Malawi: Final Report. London: School of Oriental and African Studies; March 2008.

Siamwalla, A. & Valdes, A. 1986. Should crop insurance be subsidized? In: Hazell, P., Pomareda, C. & Valdes, A. (eds) *Crop Insurance for Agricultural Development: Issues and Experience*. Baltimore: IFPRI/Johns Hopkins University Press.

Slater, R. & Tsoka, M. 2007. Malawi Social Protection Status Report. Report No. 40027 - MW. Washington DC: World Bank.

Snapp, S. S., Blackie, M. J., Gilbert, R. A., Bezner-Kerr, R. & Kanyama-Phiri, G. Y. 2010. Biodiversity can support a greener revolution in Africa. *Proceedings of the National Academy of Sciences, 107*, pp. 20840–5. DOI: 10.1073/pnas.1007199107.

Tambulasi, R. I. C. 2009. The public sector corruption and organised crime nexus: The case of the fertiliser subsidy programme in Malawi. *African Security Review, 18,* 19–31.

Taylor, J. E. 2012. A methodology for local economy-wide impact evaluation (LEWIE) of cash transfers. United Nations Food and Agricultural Organization and UNICEF-ESARO, May.

Thirtle, C., Lin, L. & Piesse, J. 2003. The impact of research-led agricultural productivity growth on poverty reduction in Africa, Asia and Latin America. *World Development, 31,* 1959–75.

Timmer, C. P. 1989. Indonesia: transition from food importer to food exporter. In: Sicular, T. (ed.) *Food Price Policy in Asia.* Ithaca: Cornell University Press.

Timmer, C. P. 2004. Food security and economic growth: An Asian perspective. Center for Global Development: Working Paper Number 51.

Tschirley, D. L. & Jayne, T. S. 2010. Exploring the logic behind southern Africa's food crises. *World Development, 38,* 76–87.

United Nations Economic Commission for Africa (UNECA) & African Union. 2012. *Economic Report on Africa: Unleashing Africa's Potential as a Pole of Global Growth.* Addis Ababa: United Nations Economic Commission for Africa and African Union.

Van de Walle, N. 1999. *African Economics and the Politics of Permanent Crisis, 1979–1991.* Cambridge: Cambridge University Press.

Verpoorten, M., Arora, A. & Swinnen, J. 2012. Self-reported food insecurity in Africa during the food price crisis. LICO Discussion Paper 303/2012. Leuven: KUL LICOS Centre for Institutions and Economic Performance.

Vondolia, G. K., Eggert, H. & Stage, J. 2012. Nudging Boserup? The impact of fertilizer subsidies on investment in soil and water conservation. Environment for Development Discussion Paper 12-08. Gothenburg and Washington DC: University of Gothenburg and Resources for the Future.

Ward, M. & Santos, P. 2010. Looking beyond the plot: The nutritional impact of fertilizer policy. Selected Paper prepared for presentation at the Agricultural & Applied Economics Association 2010 AAEA, CAES & WAEA Joint Annual Meeting Denver, Colorado, 25–27 July.

Webb, P. & Block, S. 2012. Support for agriculture during economic transformation: Impacts on poverty and undernutrition. *Proceedings of the National Academy of Sciences, 109,* 12309–14.

Wiggins, S. & Leturque, H. 2010. Helping Africa to feed itself: Promoting agriculture to reduce poverty and hunger. Occasional Paper 002. Brighton: Future Agricultures Consortium.

Wiggins, S. & Brooks, J. 2012. The use of input subsidies in developing countries. In: Brooks, J. (ed.) *Agricultural Policies for Poverty Reduction.* Paris: OECD.

World Bank. 1981. *Accelerated Development in Sub-Saharan Africa: An Agenda for Action.* Washington DC: World Bank.

World Bank. 2000. *World Development Report, 2000.* Washington DC, World Bank.

World Bank. 2007a. *World Development Indicators.* Washington DC, World Bank.

World Bank 2007b. *World Development Report 2008: Agriculture for Development.* Washington DC: World Bank.

World Bank. 2009. Accelerated food security programme: Emergency program paper Report No: 48549-TZ. Washington DC: World Bank.

World Bank. 2010a. Malawi country economic memorandum: seizing opportunities for growth through regional integration and trade Volume I: Summary of main finding and recommendations. Report No. 47969-MW. Poverty Reduction and Economic Management. Africa Region.

World Bank. 2010b. Zambia Impact Assessment of the Fertilizer Support Program, Analysis of Effectiveness and Efficiency. Report No. 54864-ZM. Washington DC.

World Bank. 2011. *World Development Indicators* (Edition: April 2011). ESDS International, University of Manchester.

World Bank. 2012. Monthly world prices of commodities and indices (pink sheets).

Xu, Z. Y., Burke, W. J., Jayne, T. S. & Govereh, J. 2009a. Do input subsidy programs 'crowd in' or 'crowd out' commercial market development? Modeling fertilizer demand in a two-channel marketing system. *Agricultural Economics, 40,* 79–94.

Xu, Z. Y., Guan, Z., Jayne, T. S. & Black, J. R. 2009b. Factors influencing the profitability of fertilizer use on maize in Zambia. *Agricultural Economics, 40,* 437–46.

Yaron, J. 1992. Rural finance in developing countries. Policy Research Working Papers. Washington DC: World Bank.

Yawson, D. O., Armah, F. A. & Afrifa, E. K. A. 2010. Ghana's fertilizer subsidy policy: Early field lessons from farmers in the central region. *Journal of Sustainable Development in Africa,* 12, 191–203.

Zambia Agricultural Consultative Forum. 2009. Report on proposed reform for the Zambian fertilizer support programme.

Author index

Subject index